JACKA VC

RETURN OF THE GALLIPOLI LEGEND:

JACKA VC

MICHAEL LAWRIWSKY

First published 2010
First Australian Paperback Edition 2010

RETURN OF THE GALLIPOLI LEGEND: Jacka VC © 2010 Michael Lawriwksy

ISBN 978 1 92168 564 4

Australian Copyright 2010
New Zealand Copyright 2010

Published by
Mira Books
Level 5, 15 Help Street
CHATSWOOD NSW 2067 AUSTRALIA

MIRA and the Star Colophon are trademarks used under license and registered in Australia, New Zealand, the United States Patent & Trademark Office and in other countries.

Typeset by Midland Typesetters, Australia
Printed by McPhersons Printing Group

Every effort has been made to trace and acknowledge copyright. The publisher apologises for any accidental infringement, and welcomes information that would rectify this situation.

"RETURN OF THE GALLIPOLI LEGEND"

A foreword by General Peter Cosgrove (Retd)

This new book by Michael Lawriwsky is another cracker!

In Michael's first book, *Hard Jacka* we read about the paladin of the 1ˢᵗ Australian Imperial Force, Captain Albert Jacka, VC, MC and bar. An astonishing courage under continuous circumstances of mortal danger was the quality at the core of this famous man, so naturally the first book told the story of how Jacka became Australia's first VC winner of World War I and how he soldiered on in the most gallant way throughout the rest of that vicious and bloody conflict. *Hard Jacka* was a thrilling read with Michael's device of ascribing dialogue to emotions and events working particularly well because it put the living flesh of realism on the dry bones of history. We felt we were in the trenches with Bert Jacka and his comrades-in-arms. But we needed to know more about this Australian, lionised and cherished not only by the men with whom he served but also by the nation in whose service he excelled.

In the sequel, *Return of the Gallipoli Legend*, Michael has again brought his forensic microscope of accuracy and his empathetic and persuasive ear for the human interaction involved in this, the wider story of Albert Jacka, a hero returned home, a returned man trying to make a home. We reflect and read about a man who can never escape his public prominence but who is subject to the same doubts, inadequacies and failures of many of his comrades in the peace which followed war. Before I started the *Return*,

I wondered if my feelings towards Jacka would change for the worse after reading of his life out of uniform, all too soon cut short. Of course, the opposite is true – the ordinariness of Bert Jacka, his anxiety, his setbacks, his estrangements all just underscore his courage, stamina and iron will in his years on the battlefield.

At the time of writing I am the chairman of the Council of the Australian War Memorial, and as such, as a rule I refrain from writing forewords or otherwise endorsing publications not authored within the War Memorial staff. However I recall saying to Michael after reading *Hard Jacka* and writing a foreword for it that there ought to be a sequel and I would be honoured to write the foreword. I am thus honoured; this is a great story of a great man which gives a context to some of the most gallant deeds ever performed by an Australian. Well done, Michael!

Peter Cosgrove
General (Retd)

TABLE OF CONTENTS

GLOSSARY

AIF	Australian Imperial Force
Amsterdam end	The western end of Collins Street was known as the "Amsterdam end" with ornate office buildings such as The Olderfleet and The Rialto
AWL	Absent Without Leave
Brig.-Gen.	Brigadier-General
Capt.	Captain
CMG	Companion of the Order of St Michael and St George
CO	Commanding Officer
DCM	Distinguished Conduct Medal
DSO	Distinguished Service Order
Duntrooner	Graduate of the Royal Military College, Duntroon
Heliographs	A mirror device used to signal by reflecting the sun's rays
HQ	Headquarters
MC	Military Cross
MLA	Member of the Legislative Assembly
MM	Military Medal
MO	Medical Officer
Nicker	Colloquial expression for "money"
Pannikin	A tinplate cup with handle for drinking
Pinnace	A small steam powered boat
RACV	Royal Automobile Club of Victoria
Ratted	Colloquial expression for "stolen"

RSSILA	Returned Sailors' and Soldiers' Imperial League of Australia – predecessor of the RSL (Returned Services League of Australia)
Sap	A narrow trench, normally used for communication
Strangers' Room	A room in a club where non-members waited for their host.
Ten bob	Ten shillings, or half a pound
Traverse	Protrusions of earth or sandbags in a trench to reduce the effect of shells landing in the trench.
UAP	United Australia Party
VAD	Voluntary Aid Detachment
VC	Victoria Cross
Zac	Colloquial expression for a "sixpenny coin"

For my father-in-law who was a good man.

JACKA FAMILY TREE

Sophia Jacka
b. 1855 – d. 1899

Josiah Jacka
b. 1859 – d. 1954

William Henry Jacka
b. 1863

Samuel Everitt Jacka
b. 1864

William Jacka
b. 1794
Cornwall, Eng.

Josiah Jacka
b. 1832
Cornwall, Eng.

Charles Hamilton Jacka ——— Irene Jacka
b. 1876

Grace Hollow

Thomas Jacka
b. 1866

Nicholas Tremewan Bottrell
b. 1796
Cornwall, Eng.

Elizabeth Jane
Tremewan Bottrell
b. 1836
Cornwall, Eng.
d. 1928
Geelong

Mercy Jane Jacka
b. 1869

Fanny Jacka
b. 1887 – d. 1931
m. Isaiah Olive

Esther Jacka
b. 1871 – d. 1914

Samuel Jacka
b. 1886 – d. 1942
m. Elizabeth Hanson

Mary Ann Vingo
d. 1857
Geelong

Eliza Grace Jacka
b. 1872 – d. 1941

Elsie Jacka
b. 1891
m. Alfred Ernest Saunders

Archie Jacka
b. 1876 – d. 1879

Albert Jacka
b. 1893 – d. 1932
m. Veronica Carey
b. 1900 – d. 1966

Nathaniel Jacka
b. 1861 – d. 1943

Sidney Jacka
b. 1894 – d. 1950s
m. Veronica May Stevens
b. 1901

William Kettle
b. 1840
Leicester, Eng.

Elizabeth Kettle
b. 1864
Oakham, Eng.
d. 1940
Melbourne

William Jacka
b. 1897 – d. 1978
m. Joan Jacka

Elizabeth Horsepool
b. 1836
Oakham, Eng.
d. 1929
Wedderburn

Bessie Jacka
b. 1899
m. Harold Stanley Dowrick
b. 1899

RETURN OF THE LEGEND

11 am, St Kilda Road, Melbourne, Monday, 20 October 1919

A convoy of eighty-five private cars made its way along Melbourne's grandest boulevard, which was lined with elms, and flanked by magnificent mansions. The latest quota of Australian soldiers had returned, and the lead car carried the young man being described as, "Australia's finest front line soldier", Captain Albert Jacka, VC, MC and Bar – "Bert" to his friends.

Makeshift banners hung from modest terraces in Port Melbourne had screamed, "Jacka will do us!" Now the column motored past the sedate and elegant Italianate verandahs and tall towers of stately homes. They passed "Airlie", the boyhood residence of Stanley Melbourne Bruce, MC, the returned soldier, business tycoon and aspiring Nationalist Party politician. A few doors down, they passed the home of the Honourable Isaac Isaacs, noted barrister, judge, and future Governor-General of Australia.

Far from these shores the Great War had been fought and won, but at a huge cost. Then the worldwide influenza epidemic struck. Finally, spring had arrived, and a new optimism was taking root in people's minds. The future certainly looked bright for the young man of the moment. Over the previous five years his name had been etched into the psyche of almost every Australian. His face had been featured on recruitment posters, war bond advertisements and newspapers – even matchboxes. He was the country's first Victoria Cross winner during the Great War, who had come to symbolise the "man" in "Australian manhood".

He had returned from England on the *Euripides*, a ship named after the ancient Greek writer of tragedies. Was it an omen? At Port Melbourne, at 9 am that morning he had been met by a distinguished party that included the Governor-General, the Acting Minister for Defence and the Secretary for Defence.

Bert sat next to the driver, Dr R.E. Weigall, president of Royal Automobile Club. In the car behind him rode the Commandant of the 3rd Military District (Victoria), Brigadier-General Charles Brand. In France the relationship between Bert and his brigadier had been a stormy one, as Brand had carried out some unfortunate orders at the Battle of Bullecourt. Bert's opposition had only been possible because he was a VC.

The Brigadier was used to being the centre of attention. It came with the job, and he was comfortable with it. Today Bert was out in front – his face was flushed, and he wore an uncertain expression. As the car drove past the waving crowds, women's hands reached out to touch his arm. He couldn't understand why they were making such a fuss. Seeing his family was what occupied his thoughts right now.

Thousands of people blocked the intersection of Collins and Swanston Streets, forcing the car to a standstill. In the street, a young woman jumped onto the sideboard of the car and, mistaking a soldier in the back seat for Bert, gave him a big kiss on the cheek.

"That's from sister Susie!"

The crowd cheered her on, and she melted back into it. Yet that simple kiss was to echo in posterity, as reporters recorded her demonstration for the afternoon paper. The car edged forward, but came to a halt again when a group of men, veterans of the 14th Battalion, jumped on the car, and pelted it with roses to thank Bert for the inspiration he gave them. But too many jumped on board, and the hood was dented. Dr Weigall thumped the horn of his car in vain, as the weight of the lads grounded the mudguards to the tyres. He could hardly be heard above the roar of the crowd and the strains of *Over There* being played by a military band.

The Lord Mayor of Melbourne, Alderman William Whyte Cabena, and other dignitaries waited under the portico. Dr Weigall braked, giving a sigh of relief as the car lurched to a stop. A cordon of ex-14th Battalion men and police protected Bert's passage to the waiting delegation, and every one of them shook his hand.

"Good on yer, Bert!"

One journalist with pen and pad in hand broke through. "Congratulations on your remarkable record of achievement during the war…"

"I have nothing to say…"

Bert was now under the arch of the portico, where the Mayor was waiting to greet him. Brand was just behind him.

"Captain Jacka, it is a great honour to greet you on behalf of the people of Melbourne…" Mercifully, the Mayor's speech was not too long, and it disappointed the crowd to see Bert making for the car so quickly.

"Stand him up!" someone called out. "Let's have a look at him!" Bert heard it, and briefly stood up in full view of the crowd. A huge cheer went up, as the citizens of Melbourne welcomed their reluctant hero. Dr Weigall swung the car around and slowly drove back towards the Army Depot in Sturt Street, South Melbourne.

* * *

They crossed the arched Princes' Bridge, built three decades earlier from an ancient Roman design. The drafting and supervision of the stonework had been the first real job of an ambitious twenty-one year old engineer called John Monash, who later commanded the 4th Brigade at Gallipoli when Bert won his VC. At the depot they found another huge crowd was being held back by police. As Bert came into the hall he smiled for the first time.

"Millis you old Dig!" he said.

"By Jingo I thought I'd never see you again," admitted the bushy browed Lieutenant Millis, "but, you've made it, son!" It was the same man who, in the Third London Hospital at Wandsworth, had helped Bert come through the shellshock he had suffered on the Somme. Millis limped forward as fast as his stiff knee allowed him, and gave Bert an almighty handshake.

"Great to see you out and about. What are you up to?"

"I've been helping with the arrangements for the reception."

Brand was almost upon them, with a number of newspaper reporters trailing after him.

"Is everything in order, Millis?" asked Brand.

"Yes, sir."

Brand whispered to Bert out of the corner of his mouth. "You've got Melbourne, and the whole of Australia clamouring at your feet."

Bert said nothing, he couldn't have cared less.

"Have you thought of the possibilities?" Brand continued. Bert couldn't even hear him now. The clapping started as he walked into the hall.

"Allow me to introduce Captain Ferdinand Wright," said Millis. "He's in charge of this function."

"Pleased to meet you, Captain Jacka," Wright said, raising his voice above the crowd, saluting and then shaking his hand. Bert remembered Captain Wright – he had been second in command of the 14th Battalion's A Company at the Gallipoli landing. The din of chattering increased as more people began to enter. Bert's nausea began to well up again.

"You're going to have to tell me everything when you get a chance..." Millis continued.

"What is your view on conscription?" a reporter asked. Bert suddenly swung away from Millis and Wright to answer the reporter.

"I supported conscription."

"Is that all?"

"Yes."

There was a lot of emotion in that one. Millis tapped Bert on the shoulder. "Look who's here," he said with that old sparkle in his dark eyes. When Bert swung around again he saw his brother standing in his AIF uniform.

"Welcome home Bert," his brother said, extending a firm hand.

"Hullo bro… It's been a long time. Where's Mum?" He knew she couldn't be far.

"Just behind me," Sid assured him, as he stepped aside.

"Mother…" he sighed as she hugged him with all her strength. He was bigger than she had remembered him, and heavier. She felt so soft to him, and comfortable.

"Oh Albert…" she cried through teary eyes, "I've missed you so." When she came away she kissed him again on the cheek. "I'm ever so proud of you."

She cried at the physical effect the war had taken on him. Bert was much more mature now; almost like a different person. His face had thickened, and he gave the impression of a man at least ten years older. The lost years made her cry too, because she had missed them. "His youth has been stolen from him," she thought. Still, he was home. She thanked God that all three of her boys who had volunteered, and fought, had come through safely.

Not far away tea was being served to the guests, and Captain Wright called over to the young VADs who were serving it.

"Captain Jacka will have a cup of tea, Miss Edmonson…" Wright began.

"I don't want any tea!" Bert said in an agitated tone. Miss Edmonson stopped. Bert closed his eyes momentarily.

"Bert?" his mother said.

"Are you right, Bert?" asked Millis.

Just then a photographer tapped Bert on the shoulder and asked for a photograph, but he refused. He walked over to Captain Wright, and pulled him by the arm.

"Listen," he asked Wright. "Could you organise a motorcar for me?"

"When do you need it?"

"Now."

"Right *now*?" Wright asked in disbelief.

"That's right."

Wright walked off, and a few minutes later popped his head through the door and motioned to Bert.

"Come on, let's go," Bert said, locking arms with his mother. He had arranged for leave to visit his family.

"Everyone is waiting for us at Aunt Margaret's place," Sid assured him.

Naturally the people in the room were disappointed that Bert had disappeared so soon. The reporters turned back to Brand, who was happy to accommodate them.

"He was one of the Fourth Brigade," Brand said proudly. "They were doers, not talkers..."

Brand was good at those one-liners – a sure sign of a politician in the making – and the reporters jotted it down, their ears pinned back. Ironically, Brand *led* the Fourth Brigade, and he was a talker, but the inconsistency didn't appear to bother him.

"...I can recall that a company under the command of Captain Jacka could accomplish the work of a battalion. Simply extraordinary..."

One reporter broke off from the pack and followed Bert out of the hall.

"Captain Jacka!" he called out. "Do you have a final statement?"

"Yes...I've got nothing to say." But then he stopped, and swung around. "There is one thing...I would like to ask *you*. Where do you fellows get your information from? I've read some misrepresentations of the facts in the press. At one point I read that I'd been recovering from wounds in Malta...I've never *been* to Malta. Would you care to print *that*?"

* * *

Aunt Margaret lived at 35 Rowe Street, North Fitzroy, and the chauffeur took the round about route via Hoddle Street and Collingwood to get there. In the back seat of the car Bert whispered into his mother's ear.

"Mum…where's Dad?"

She quietly explained that he had a lot of work on and couldn't come to Melbourne at such short notice. Bert nodded, with disappointment.

"There's the Collingwood Town Hall," Sid explained some minutes later. "Your mate John Wren recently threw a huge party there for returning diggers."

"He's not my mate, Sid," Bert replied, setting the record straight.

"But he's been very kind to you, Bert," his mother added. The millionaire had honoured his promise to Australia's first VC, and had deposited five hundred pounds into Bert's bank account.

Moments later the car crossed Johnston Street, where it had all started for Wren. Thirty something years earlier, Wren was a working class lad in a Collingwood tannery. The next minute he was running an illegal off-track betting house in Johnston Street, protected by an elaborate security system of complicit police officers, "neighbourhood watchers" and secret trapdoors. Eventually he was forced to close "the Tote", and used its profits to finance legitimate businesses, mostly in sports and entertainment.

"How *is* Wedderburn, Mum?" Bert asked.

"It's the same old place, I suppose…But you won't see the old Korong Flour Mill anymore. It burnt down back in March…"

"Bessie wrote to me about that. She's been wonderful with her letter writing."

"And she's a wonderful dressmaker now, too. All self-taught. You'll soon see the lovely new suit she's made for herself, especially for your homecoming."

He also asked about his older sisters, Fanny and Elsie.

"Remember that big fire at Dockley's Hotel?" Sid said, the mention of the mill fire reminded him of it.

"Ohhh…yes," Bert said, recalling an adventure from his youth.

"We were all over at Grandma Kettle's place that night," Sid explained. "The three of us were knocking about in the street when Bert saw the flames. 'Oh! There's a fire! Come on boys, let's go and have a look!' he said, and we started running up the hill, all excited. The flames were shooting hundreds of feet into the sky. Poor young Bill couldn't keep up with us, so he started to bawl his eyes out, and some kind woman took him back to the house."

"Well, he isn't 'poor young Bill' any longer," his mother said. "He's managed to get himself married ahead of you two. He's a faster worker than the both of you put together," Bert's mother emphasised her point with a finger. She wanted to know all about the wedding from Bert, who promised to tell her everything once they got to Aunt Margaret's. "You're going to love Joan, Mum," he said. "She's a charming girl."

* * *

North Fitzroy's Rowe Street was big and wide — more like a boulevard than a street. It was difficult to miss the house. A large Union Jack hung from its tower, a "Welcome Home" sign was strung above the front door, and there were various other flags and decorations in the front yard. Almost as soon as the car pulled up at the gate, the door of the house opened, and Bert's younger sister Bessie came rushing out looking beautiful in her brand new white suit. Beaming with smiles she flung the front gate open and smothered Bert in hugs and kisses as he stood on the footpath.

"Bert! Bert! I've waited so long for this," she said through tears. Time marches slowly for the young, and as the youngest member of the family, for her it had been the longest wait. Bert was amazed at how much she had grown up.

"Just *look* at you, Bessie," Bert said as a stream of cousins, including the Waldron's daughters emerged from the house. He hugged Aunt

Margaret and shook hands with Uncle Ted and the family. The Waldrons invited everyone inside for the tea and sandwiches that had been prepared for lunch.

The discussion ranged far and wide. Bert gave a full description of the marriage of his youngest brother, Bill, to Joan Jacka in Wales, which was an extraordinary coincidence. Bert's name had appeared in the English press and was noticed by the Jacka family of Taff's Well, situated just north of Cardiff. Mrs Elizabeth Jacka, bearing the same name as his own mother, wrote to Bert asking whether they were related. He had taken the trouble to visit Taff's Well, and concluded that they were not, as their family had originated from west Cornwall, in England. On a later visit Bill had fallen for Miss Joan Jacka and they were soon married, with Bert as best man.

"Have you given much thought to what you might be doing now that you've returned?" asked Uncle Ted.

"I'm establishing an import-export business with some of my army mates," Bert replied. It was a matter of some pride to his mother, Elizabeth, that he would be moving up in the world. "Why shouldn't he," she thought.

"What kinds of things will you be importing?" she asked.

"We will start by importing a non-alcoholic beverage called 'Newman's Fort-Reviver'." Everyone stared at him blankly as they had not heard of it.

"It's a famous British tonic stimulant."

"What is the source of the stimulant then?" asked Aunt Margaret.

"It's a formula of fruit essences, which when combined with aerated water, *tingles* the *taste*buds with a refreshing *tang*," Bert alliterated with all the sincerity of a salesman.

Sid thought he was already starting to sound like a businessman, and it was true. Bert had not been idle all those months in England after the war. He had been laying the groundwork for various business ideas.

* * *

Later in the afternoon, Uncle Ted came back from the corner store carrying a fresh copy of *The Herald* newspaper. There was excitement as it was passed around the room. Three quarters of the front page were devoted to Bert's homecoming, with headlines that read "Welcome of Welcomes for Jacka VC – Roman Triumph Through Thronged City Streets." After a quick scan Sid announced he was going outside for a smoko, and motioned for Bert to join him. Sid thought his brother needed a break from the persistent questioning, and as his closest brother in age, he wanted a bit of private time with him. Stepping into the front yard Sid unclipped his cigarette case and offered one to Bert, who raised his hand to decline.

"Not smoking?"

"I shouldn't."

Sid shrugged his shoulders nonchalantly, pulled out a tailor-made, lit it up and took a drag. Then Bert motioned that he would like a cigarette after all.

"He'll be hopping mad when he reads that *Herald*," Sid said, after Bert had lit up.

"Who?" Bert asked.

"*Dad*…who did you think?"

Bert was about to answer as Uncle Ted opened the door, asking if they could all pose for a photograph in front of the house. He had to record this moment for posterity, and, as he thought about it, felt some pain for his next-door neighbours, the Perrottets, whose son Stephen had been mortally wounded on the first day at Gallipoli when he landed with the First Division. They would have no opportunity for such a cheerful photograph. Everyone went out in front of the fence, which had a hedge behind it. On the way through Bessie slung her arm around Bert's, and Sid's cousin Elsie Waldron tucked her arm under his. Like Bessie, she was a "tailoress" too. Aunt Margaret and Uncle Ted stood behind the gate, with Bert on one side of the gate, and his mother on the other side. While everyone else looked at the camera, Elizabeth Jacka had eyes only for her son Albert, standing almost side-on to the photographer.

* * *

Bert boarded the *Euripides* the following afternoon feeling good after the time spent with members of his family. The *Euripides* was steaming on to Sydney later that day to drop off the rest of the men, and Bert had to go with her because he was the ship's adjutant. As with everything, he would see it through to the end honourably, in spite of the fact that he was overshooting his destination by 500 miles, and would have to return by train. He arrived in Sydney virtually incognito, as the press had not been expecting it. Then he quietly slipped aboard an overnight train bound for Melbourne. He had 60 days leave with pay, which would help him get a start.

* * *

11.30 am, Bendigo to Wedderburn rail line, 28 October 1919

Bert stared out of the window of the train as the tattered trunks of stringy bark eucalypts merged into a grey blur. Gazing through them he could see, in staccato, almost like the flickering scenes of some silent motion picture, the flat fields beyond the dusty road that ran beside the tracks. There was a little moisture in the ground now, as it was spring, but he remembered the day he had departed for the war with his Wedderburn mates. Drought had scorched the land in 1914, and the once mighty Murray River became a series of mud pools that could be crossed on a camel's back. The drought was still going. It was the same parched land he left five years ago.

The previous night he had been to a boxing match in Melbourne. Victoria's champion Chris Jordan fought Tommy Ryan from New

South Wales for the Australian Lightweight Championship, and finished him in the seventeenth round, when the referee stopped the fight. Bert was annoyed by the fact that again he had been made a spectacle of, with a standing ovation from the crowd when it was announced that "Captain Jacka, the famous Victoria Cross winner" was present at the *Pavilion* stadium. He did like the boxing though. Bert's interest in boxing had begun well before the war, and the skills had come in handy during the course of it.

For the last twelve months he'd been sports officer at the Sutton Veny army camp in England, and boxing was the main sport that he had promoted there. What he liked about it was the solitary contest between two men, where one would emerge victorious. It was fair, because there were no other influences, and almost no chance that luck might bring you victory, as in cards, or "two-up". If you walked into a right hook, you deserved it.

At the Sutton Veny camp Bert was walking in the street one day when a couple of burly British blokes stopped him and demanded a cigarette. He told them where to jump, which got up the nose of the big one, who noticed Bert's VC ribbon on his chest. "Bloody war hero!" he screamed as he pushed him in the chest and started swinging punches. Obviously the man hadn't had enough fighting during the war. Bert ducked and pulled out some of the skills he'd applied against the Germans recently, taking them both down in the first round. He was pleased as punch when he found out later that the big one was some kind of noted boxing champion. No wonder he thought he could take on a VC!

His thoughts turned to his father, Nathaniel. It was not like it was supposed to be. The day he left for the war his father had squeezed him tightly with his large, rough hands, and had looked lovingly onto his eyes. But the war had progressively divided them, as it had the nation, and the Labor Party. The issue of conscription had done it, and it was conscription that occupied him now. He knew that the moment of reckoning he had been avoiding was drawing closer.

Wedderburn was coming up soon. It wasn't always called Wedderburn. Up to the 1860s it was known as Korong, an Aboriginal word meaning "canoe" or "boat" according to the language of the Yarra River tribes, or "plenty of water" according to the Murray River tribes. It certainly wasn't the latter lately, as a lack of water had stalled the gold rush in Wedderburn that began in 1852 and swelled the population to 6000 souls for a time. No one knew exactly why the name had been changed to Wedderburn, but the current version reckoned it was suggested by Mr Wills, of the later, famous but ill-fated Bourke and Wills expedition. The story goes that he came up to the town to do some surveying, and upon being asked for an opinion, proposed it be named after a stream that flowed near his hometown.

Bert thought about his early childhood, when his family used to rent a house near the railway line. He remembered the old peach tree that grew down by the old railway workers' houses, and was inconveniently situated next to Sergeant O'Brien's place. Sergeant O'Brien was in charge of Wedderburn's police force – all four of them. How we used to keep a good eye out for those peaches, he thought, and when they were nice and ripe we'd be over there to pinch a few. The trouble was that Sergeant O'Brien liked peaches too, and he'd come out of the house and call out: "My word I'll be after you!" as the boys ran like mad.

He was still lost in thought as the intermittent rooftops of Wedderburn sailed by, and the movement of the treetops slowed to walking pace. The peach tree is still there, he thought with some satisfaction. Clouds of white steam floated past the window as the train glided to a stop – then a final, sudden brake. He was home. He put on his officer's cap, pulled his tan leather valise down from the wire rack above the bench seat, and made his way to the door. It was the completion of a long and dangerous journey that had taken him to the far side of the world, and back.

As he appeared at the door a huge cry went up from the crowd, and the band started to play. "Welcome home!" rang out, as his

1. Mechanic's Institute Hall
2. Korong Flour Mill (now Jacka Park)
3. Wedderburn Primary School
4. Anglican Church
5. Kerr Street (Isaiah and Fanny Olive)
6. Godfrey Street (Kettle family home)
7. St Arnaud Rd (rented by N. Jacka)
8. Ridge Street (Nathaniel and Elizabeth Jacka)
9. Wedderburn railway station
10. Korong Shire Office (now Historical Society)
11. Sam and Elizabeth Jacka's butcher shop

Map of Wedderburn circa 1919–1924

eyes instantly scanned the faces for those who mattered most: his mother, his sisters, his brother, and his father. Nathaniel, now wearing a full grey moustache, was standing next to Elizabeth.

"Welcome home, son," Nathaniel said softly. "We've missed you." His thick calloused hand was still much larger than Bert's, and he noticed the softness in his son's hand that had not been there five years earlier. Young Bessie was there again to greet him, as were his older sisters, Fanny and Elsie.

"Welcome home, my hero brother," Fanny whispered in his ear as she hugged him tightly. Her husband, Isaiah Olive had been wounded in the war but had returned in one piece.

"Dear old Albert, we are so proud of you!" said Elsie, who had married a farmer, Alf Saunders. Then he was greeted by his older brother, Sam, his wife Elizabeth, and their children.

"How do you feel now that you are home at last?" asked the editor of *The Wedderburn Express*.

"Tired of being stared at through train windows," was his honest answer. He felt like a prize bull, and was amazed at how the news of his homecoming seemed to travel ahead of the train. To the Wedderburn crowd's disappointment he was whisked away to Ridge Street in a car. In the disjointed discussions and welcomes that followed later that afternoon, Nathaniel felt a distance between him and his son, and it wasn't just conscription. Later on, when he was alone with Elizabeth, he expressed his unease.

"You know what I think? I think he's toffed up, our Albert," he said.

"What do you mean?" Elizabeth said. She could see no possible fault in *her* Albert.

"His hands are too soft."

"Ohh... it's just because he's become an officer, isn't it? Don't be daft."

* * *

It was like old times that evening, like a time well before the war. Elizabeth was preparing dinner in the kitchen, while Bert and Bessie sat at the table shelling peas into a bowl. Elizabeth loved having him home at last, and Bessie couldn't get over his worldliness. He seemed to know so much and she felt she could listen to him all day.

In the lounge room Bert found that a new picture had taken pride of place – a montage of three separate photographs of him and his brothers in uniform that Elizabeth commissioned from the Mendelssohn Studios in Swanston Street. Bert was in the middle of the photograph, flanked by Bill on the left and Sid on the right. His mother had shown him a few things from the chest where she had saved all the letters he wrote during the war and other memorabilia. They all thumbed through Bert's autograph book that had been started by the Anzac Club of Williamstown and then passed around Melbourne and the countryside. It was filled with poems and notes and little paintings, all wishing that Bert would return safely "like the boomerang". Elizabeth had written a dedication to all three of her boys at the war.

Though far from home and loved ones
And Austral's sunny shores,
Our thoughts are ever with thee,
Our brave and noble boys.

Elizabeth Jacka (mother)
30 December 1916, Wedderburn

Now that they were together at last, Bert could tell them of all the marvellous things he saw in his travels. He concentrated on those times, rather than the brutal reality and horrors of the war.

"We had plenty of fun in between times," he assured them, "and I've met half the Royal Family, Mum," he said with a smile. "The luncheon they served us was superb. The cutlery had gold handles, and there was so much of it…"

The sound of the door handle turning made him stop, and Nathaniel entered looking rather weary. He wasn't getting any younger, and was still operating as a haulage contractor, taking logs to the mills with his dray.

"Don't stop on account of me, son," he announced. Bert looked over at his mother and smiled.

"… the boys didn't know where to start. Then one of the boys, who was brave but not very polished, puts his finger up for a beer, when the whole palace is dry for the duration of the war!"

"I'll bet they had a few swigs when no one was looking," Nathaniel interjected with a dose of cynicism about the royal family. "How far off is dinner, dear?"

"Almost ready," Elizabeth answered. "You wash your hands first." Elizabeth sensed that this was a good time for her and Bessie to leave the room, and give Nathaniel and Bert their first moments alone together.

"Bessie, come along with me will you?" she said. "I want you to help me gather up a few things from the shed."

Elizabeth and Bessie left the kitchen. Nathaniel went away to wash his hands, and when the door snapped shut a silence came over the room. "We're about to have it out," Bert thought. A few long minutes later Nathaniel was back.

"I notice you made a point of telling *The Herald* that you were *for* conscription," Nathaniel said after returning to the kitchen. Bert didn't respond at first, so Nathaniel continued. "Have you got any idea of what's been going on here? We've almost had a civil war, and our family copped it in every imaginable way. Your mother was receiving a stream of threatening letters. Never signed of course… Bloody cowards. After you won the VC it turned the attention of the whole country on all of us. We couldn't sneeze without a newspaper article being written about us."

"Mum wrote…"

Nathaniel cut in: "After one of the articles Sam rode 45 miles from St Arnaud on his bike. That's how worried he was –

wracked by guilt, because he was the *only* Jacka boy who hadn't signed up! But I told him he couldn't go. I forbade it. He had a wife and four children to support, and it wouldn't have been right."

"I know," Bert said softly. He hated that Sam had suffered because of him. "No one in his right mind could have blamed him," he said. "That reporter asked me a direct question, and I couldn't avoid it. It was the only question I answered."

"Do you know how that makes me look?" Nathaniel snapped.

"Do you know how you made me look?" Bert snapped back.

"Not all of them wanted conscription…"

"Agreed, but…"

"And that's why forcing them to go against their own free will was wrong!"

"The job had to be done, Dad."

"Look… Bert. Listen to me. When you, and Bill and Sid volunteered and left our shores, it was as free men leaving a free country. I wanted you to return to a free country, where your mother and sisters would remain free from bondage. That's why I fought conscription so hard."

"And used my name."

"*Everyone* was using your name."

"And I hated it," Bert shot back. "You say you wanted Australia to be free. Why do you think we went at all if it wasn't to keep Australia free?"

"That's what Hughes wanted everyone to think. But there was never any danger of Britain falling, let alone Australia… Come… on?"

"You 'come on'. Someone had to stop the Hun."

"Conscription would have made us just as bad as the Hun… driving the workers till they dropped dead under the mailed fist of capitalism… Australia did do her duty to the extent that she could afford."

"The Bolsheviks would say that…"

"Rubbish. It's the best traditions of democracy that I've sought to uphold," his father fumed. "Freedom…is what *I* fought for, right here… in Australia."

Bert cut in. "Well we fought for it with Australian blood at Gallipoli, Palestine and France. We put Australia on the map."

"Don't you misunderstand me, son," Nathaniel said sincerely. "I'm prouder than anyone of what you and your brothers did… and over the moon that you've all come home safely. But you're not going to tell me that the Turks or the Germans were about to invade Australia, are you? I hope not…Do you know *who* you were fighting for at Gallipoli? It was for the bloody Russian Tsar! And if you'd have succeeded he might still be alive, with his bloody Empire now extending to Constantinople!"

"Your public stand on conscription made things difficult for me, Dad."

"I thought that you were *against* conscription, like Bill," Nathaniel rejoined, and Bert reflected on it for a few seconds.

"Bill was always against it. That's right. Most of the boys were against it in 1916. But we'd lost too many by 1917, and the attitude changed – most wanted it then. We wanted to finish the job, and more men were needed…"

"But it didn't need *Australian* men," Nathaniel interjected. "We'd already made a big contribution to a fight that wasn't even ours. It was all about the political ambitions of bloody Billy Hughes, so he could hobnob his way among the rich people who started the thing."

"Is that what you think about me? Because I've done a bit of 'hobnobbing' as you call it."

"Of course not! But you must understand how close we came to servitude. *The Argus* has been in on it right up to its neck. Do you have any idea of the skulduggery Hughes's cronies got up to?"

"Only generally," Bert admitted. "I didn't agree with it."

"I've got it right here. I've been saving it for this moment. You just wait on a few minutes." Nathaniel left the room to search the trunk that he kept all his documents and letters in. While he was gone Elizabeth and Bessie came back to the kitchen thinking the silence meant it was over. They had been standing outside at a safe distance, waiting for the smoke to clear. Bessie clicked the door shut behind them.

"I was afraid that would be going on forever," Elizabeth said taking a deep breath. She could see that Bert was still flushed.

"Is it over?" Bessie asked timidly.

"Here it is," announced Nathaniel, coming back to the kitchen. "You're back… Good." He spread two sheets of *The Argus* out on the kitchen table. "Here's the one from the 1916 referendum," he said tapping the table. "A letter from a 'Reg W. Turnbull' of Wedderburn, who reckoned that you were his 'old pal', who wrote to him saying: 'By the time you get this letter Australia will be on trial. Do what you can Reg to urge all your friends to vote "Yes"'." Nathaniel looked up at Bert. "Was Reg really your 'pal'?"

"I've never heard of him."

"I've lived in this town for more than twenty years and I've never heard of him either!" Nathaniel impressed. "In the 1917 campaign they went further. On the day of the vote, *The Argus* published a letter written by you to Mrs Macarthur at Heathcote. They photographed the letter and put the whole thing into the paper. It reads: 'France, 13-12-16. Dear Mrs Macarthur, I have been here a fortnight now and am settling down a little…' Sound familiar?"

"Read on."

"'After the way Australian troops have fought to uphold the honour of our little Island, Australia by her vote on conscription has dragged that same honour in the mud. I only wish I had been back, I would have given them some home truths. I am sure it is out of pure ignorance that people voted "No".' So… you think your father's ignorant do you?"

"No!"

"But you don't stop there. Here's the best bit, 'No words of mine can express my admiration for W.H. Hughes. I only wish we could have more statesmen like...*him!*'" Nathaniel trembled with rage. He thrust the paper down on the kitchen table and looked at Bert. Bert had no idea that his letter to Mrs Macarthur would end up being reproduced in one of the country's leading papers.

"That's enough Nathaniel..." Elizabeth said firmly.

"The prime minister used him as a tool to try to put me down!"

"I wasn't his tool! That was done *without* my knowledge."

"A hammer doesn't give its consent either. It's still a tool. If you agreed with conscription why didn't you come back then? You would have found some very interesting things going on," Nathaniel said, snatching the paper back. "Now, Mother, *you* tell him about how they stopped my cable messages getting through to you when I was campaigning for the 'No' vote."

"Is that right?" Bert asked, incredulous.

"Yes, it is, dear," Elizabeth said.

"There was no dirty trick that Hughes wouldn't stoop to," Nathaniel said walking right up to his son. "There's your 'statesman' for you!"

* * *

6.30 pm, Ridge Street, Wedderburn, 29 October 1919

There was a sharp knock at the door, and Elizabeth opened it. Standing outside was Lieutenant Ephraim Edward McHugh, DCM, commanding a contingent of seventy returned diggers, who had lined up on both sides of the path from the front gate to the porch. McHugh had gone off to the Great War with his boyhood chum, Robert William Gregson, together with their horses, to enlist in the Australian Light Horse. He had won his Distinguished Conduct Medal for conspicuous gallantry under machinegun fire from the Turks at Jisr Ed Damie and Black Hill during April–May 1918. Once it had finished "Uncle Eef" came back from the

Middle East, hung up his uniform, put his old grocer's apron on and went quietly back to work at Craig's Grocery, just like nothing had happened. He had dusted his lieutenant's uniform down and put it back on that day, and Elizabeth was impressed.

"Good afternoon Mrs Jacka," said McHugh.

"Albert!" she called. "It's for you." Then, "Hello Eef, you're looking very handsome today!"

Bert was dressed and ready. As soon as he appeared at the doorway the guardsmen snapped to attention. At least he knew these people.

"Sir, your honour guard is here to escort you to the hall!" Lieutenant McHugh said.

"Good evening, Lieutenant," answered Bert, "shall we proceed?" He looked back at his parents.

"You go on," said Nathaniel. "We'll be along shortly."

"Honour Guard!…Atten…shun!" ordered McHugh. The two officers walked down the path and into the middle of the street, where the lieutenant ordered the guardsmen to "quick march" after them. They soon passed the Wedderburn railway line and wheeled around to the main street of the town, which was lined with people as never before. The main double doors of the Mechanics Institute were open, allowing the guest of honour and Lieutenant McHugh to enter, while the guard stayed outside. As Bert came through the doors everyone in the hall instinctively stood by their tables.

Among the distinguished guests present in the hall were Councillor R. Kiniri, President of the Shire, Mr Edmund Jowett, MP, Federal Member for the Grampians and Mr Job Weaver, MP, Local "Farmer's Union" Party Member for Korong in the Victorian Parliament. Bert was introduced and seated among them at the head table. He shook the hands of the smiling politicians and was continuously patted on the back. Out of the corner of his eye he could see that his mother and father had now arrived and were being shown to a table of high honour, where his brother Sam, his sisters and other family members were already sitting.

Bert was greeted by his old classmate, Miss Ida Mortcroft, who was now the President of the Wedderburn Women's Welcome Home Committee. She asked them all to take their seats and the meeting was brought to order. After waiting for half a minute for people to charge their glasses she raised a toast for the fallen, and then a second toast to the King. Over two hundred guests had now been seated for dinner. Then the woman on the piano struck up the chords to *God Save the King*, and they stood up.

At the conclusion of the national anthem, Miss Mortcroft remained standing. "Ladies and gentlemen," she said, "a great honour has been bestowed upon me… that of proposing a toast to our guest, our hero, and our friend. I have been privileged to know Albert Jacka a long time, as we had grown up together and attended school together. We all know Captain Jacka's good points, so I won't dwell upon them, as I know he hates to be reminded of them. So I'll ask you to charge your glasses once more and drink to our guest, to his health and prosperity!"

"To Albert Jacka!"

Mr Edmund Jowett, the Federal Member rose to speak. A grey-haired, wiry man, born in Bradford, Yorkshire, he now controlled more than six million acres across three states.

"I rise today with a greater sense of honour and respect than ever in my life," he said, "to welcome home to his native town, to the town where he spent the whole of his life, Captain Albert Jacka – the man who has played such a heroic part in the Great War. While we have had the honour of taking part in other welcome homes to returned men, I hardly need to say that today there is a deeper significance than ever before. We are welcoming home not only the first winner of the VC in Australia, but one who has proved himself subsequently to be one of the bravest men the world has ever known!"

Mr Jowett could never be accused of understatement.

As spontaneous applause broke out in the hall, Bert looked over to his mother, who was smiling at him with glittering eyes.

"Wedderburn is far removed from the great centres of Australia and the world," Jowett continued, "but by the deeds of Albert Jacka it is now a town that is known well, not only in Australia, but by the whole Empire!" Again, he was interrupted by spontaneous applause, causing Bert's ears to turn red with embarrassment.

"I have had the pleasure of being introduced to Captain Jacka, and I know him to be not only one of the bravest of men, but also one of the most modest and unassuming of men. He brings to my mind a few words ascribed to William Shakespeare: 'No finer thing becomes a man as modesty, stillness and divinity.'"

"Divinity!" Bert thought. "Now *this* is all going too far!"

"Captain Jacka does not like to hear of his achievements, but I ask him to accept as part of his duty as a soldier the words of praise that flow from my lips and put up with me a little longer. Captain Jacka, I feel that we are doing more than welcoming you as an individual. You are the embodiment of all that is best in Australia — all that is bravest of the brave — the Anzacs and the soldiers who fought in France. The embodiment of the spirit of liberty and valour and chivalry, which in this war distinguished the soldiers of Australia and enabled them to stand out as men among men, gentlemen among gentlemen, soldiers among soldiers — the bravest men in the world!"

This time the applause was so thunderous that the floor almost gave way. "Golly, can this man talk. What can I say to match that?" Bert thought. After the applause had died down and Mr Jowett had resumed his seat, the local member, Mr Weaver rose to support the toast.

"This town must feel proud of its record in the war, and as your representative in parliament, I am proud of the part you have played. I believe that Wedderburn held a record for enlistment in the first two years of the war. Then there were the great deeds of our guest. He has made a fine reputation. It is one thing to make a reputation, and quite another thing to live up to it, and I am sure that Albert Jacka will live up to the reputation he has made. He has not only won the greatest of all distinctions, he has also won the Military Cross and added a bar to it."

Again the hall resonated with applause, and Mr Weaver paused momentarily to take a breath and gather his thoughts, and so did Bert. He thought about the great responsibility that had been thrust upon him by winning the first VC of the war. He had a responsibility also to those who had not returned.

"Many brave deeds have been carried out in this war, and many men have fallen in the doing of them, and many are not here. These facts however, do not detract anything from the men who have been fortunate enough to come back. But it is first necessary to find the man in one's self before one can hope to lead others, and Albert Jacka has done that. I am one who believes, without wishing to detract from the merit of other soldiers, that the Australians were the greatest men in the war. Australians, it was a well known fact, were placed in the most dangerous positions. We must all feel deeply thankful to the soldiers for the glorious peace which they have brought about – for the great part they have played in the war. It is our duty to see that the men get a fair deal now that they are back."

Bert had heard these promises before. Senior officers had made promises during the war, and they had been broken. The men had not been fairly treated there. There was a break in the speeches while people completed their meal, and Bert was not very talkative throughout it. He was still thinking about what had been said, and about what he would say when his turn came. He was still lost in thought as Councillor P. Kiairy began speaking on behalf of the Korong Shire Council.

"This is a unique day in the history of Wedderburn," he began without preamble. "We are welcoming a man who has brought Wedderburn into prominence. No man has ever shed so much lustre upon the town and Australia. We at the Korong Shire Council have followed his career with great interest, and I would like to take this opportunity to formally invite you, Captain Jacka, to be present at the next council dinner on the 11th of November. The councillors would deem it an honour.

"At this stage I would like to congratulate the ladies of Wedderburn on their work in arranging for the homecoming of their boys. I feel it is an event that they have been looking forward to in extending a welcome to Captain Jacka." Mr Kiairy turned to Bert as he finished his speech: "Albert Jacka has upheld the very highest traditions of the British race. I wish him long life and prosperity!"

The applause that followed was tumultuous and didn't subside until Bert had been standing ready to speak for some time. Everyone was smiling as they clapped, and cheers rang out above it all. It was so infectious that even Bert permitted himself a half smile after a while. By now the cramped conditions, vigorous clapping and multiple toasts had raised the temperature inside the hall. The anticipation that gripped the hearts and minds of those present rose higher still, until the very sight of their hero waiting patiently for them to stop brought the noise level right down. Suddenly, you could hear a pin drop.

"I am about to start the greatest affair of my life… to respond to the good wishes of my friends," Bert said. "No words of mine could express my feelings on the present occasion. I remember five years ago, when I and three others were farewelled from Wedderburn. One of those has returned badly wounded, while the other two have their last resting place on the other side… They were all soldiers of the first water." Bert's mother and several others in the hall wiped away a tear at this reminder of the human cost of that faraway war to the town of Wedderburn, and what it had done to her son.

Bert continued: "Although I have won the Victoria Cross and other things, I am no different from any other 'digger' who went to fight for the common cause. It has been my luck to have had the opportunity…" He stopped a moment to reflect. "I am naturally pleased to be home, although I've been 'put through the mill' since arriving, and I think that I am now on the verge of a nervous breakdown.

"I do not intend to settle in Wedderburn, as I have entered as a partner into an importing and exporting business in Melbourne... but I will find ample time to visit my native town from time to time... In conclusion, I would like to thank all of you once again for the kind sentiments that have been expressed, and for this reception, and to Lieutenant McHugh for the Guard of Honour."

They might have been disappointed that this was all they got, but it was much more than anyone else had been able to extract from him in the past week, and he had only given it to them because he had grown up there. Once more the hall erupted into applause and after it subsided a toast was called for the returned men and responded to by Mr Gourlay on behalf of the local Returned Soldiers' Association.

Then a toast was raised for Bert's parents. "It is they," said Mr John Craig enthusiastically, "that we have to thank for sending three fine sons to fight for us. It is them that we have to thank for Albert Jacka VC, MC and Bar!"

This time the audience raised their glasses with a good deal of laughter: "To the parents!" they cheered. Everyone looked over to the table where the Jacka family was sitting. There was Nathaniel and Elizabeth, Bessie, Fanny with her husband Isaiah Olive, Elsie and her husband Alf Saunders, and their eldest son Sam and his wife Elizabeth.

Everyone's applause was directed at the parents, but Nathaniel Jacka would not get up, and after some prompting Sam Jacka stood up to respond on behalf of the parents. After that, Sergeant-Major Peter Hansen raised a toast to the Ladies Welcome Home Committee, and the dinner function broke up following the singing of *Auld Lang Syne*.

* * *

The tables were removed from the hall following the dinner, and the chairs were arranged in rows for a concert, which began sharply at 8 pm. As the band struck up *See the Conquering Hero Comes*, Bert made his way up the stairs to the stage and took a seat there. He was followed by twenty more returned diggers who took up seats around him, while the cheering of the crowd shook the building to its foundations. The National Anthem was played, and at its conclusion the chairman, Mrs W.B. Smith, made some opening remarks.

"It is my great pleasure," she said, "and a great pleasure for all those present here tonight, to be extending a welcome to Captain Jacka, VC, MC and Bar, Lieutenant O. Flight, Sergeant-Major A. Morecroft, Trooper Sid Jacka, Private Tom McHugh, and Private Tom Edwards, although I will note that the latter soldier, Sid Jacka and Lieutenant Flight are unable to be with us tonight, and I have asked a relative to receive the medal that will subsequently be presented. But before we move on to the medals ceremony, we have the good fortune of having present this evening the district school inspector, Captain Akeroyd, who will now address us."

The school inspector had a ramrod back and stiff demeanour. "Thank you Mrs Smith," said Captain Akeroyd as he bowed his head sharply to her. "Ladies and gentlemen, boys and girls," he began, as was his custom. "I have come to Wedderburn with a more peaceful errand than that of addressing a gathering. I have come to see how the children are getting on. But as the work of the boys in the past war bears directly on the future citizens of Australia, I will take the opportunity to say a few words.

"The actions of the men who went to this war and the glorious deeds they performed will be recorded in history and instilled into the minds of the children. Those deeds will become an incentive to the children to do their best for the country. The sacrifices of Australia and New Zealand in this war, who rallied to the side of the Mother Country, is something we can all be proud of. And we should also be proud of the wonderful work of the women and their contribution to the winning of this war..."

The applause that followed his speech was interrupted by Mrs Smith, who introduced Mr Jowett, whose task this time would be to present the medals.

"Ladies and gentlemen," Mr Jowett announced as he held up a miniature medal for the audience to see. "I am about to present this medal to the bravest man on Earth!" Then he turned to Bert and continued: "I present this medal as a token of the grateful citizens of this town for what you have done for Wedderburn, Australia and the Empire. The medal is made of pure Bendigo gold, and I trust it will be treasured by you as long as you shall live, and by generations of your descendants. It is a symbol of the people of Wedderburn... who have hearts of gold."

As the cheering went on, Mr Jowett continued to present the remaining medals and at the conclusion, once all the medals had been presented, Bert stood to say a few words of thanks. As he stepped forward to speak a deep silence descended in the hall, so thrilled were they in anticipation.

"I would like to thank all of you on behalf of the recipients of these medals, and the lads for what you have done while we were away... Soldiers like me, who were never speakers before we went away, are rather at a loss when put amongst so many orators... We have always connected speeches with weddings, and have looked upon them with horror. Perhaps that is why so many bashful men have remained single!"

The audience laughed, and the warm response from the town's people encouraged him further. "I have travelled nearly the whole world, but have never yet seen the women who could beat our Australian girls! That is one reason that so many have come back single."

"I second the motion!" shouted Sergeant-Major Peter Hansen, and the audience laughed again.

Every single girl in that audience would have given her right arm then and there for the chance to be Mrs Bert Jacka VC. But they couldn't all marry Bert, and they hadn't at that point fully grasped the sacrifice that many of them would be making for the war effort. Sixty thousand of their young men, their future husbands, now lay in the graves that dotted the shores of Gallipoli, Flanders fields and the Holy Lands. To make matters worse, while as Bert said, many bashful young men like him had returned home single, many had not been bashful. They had either married and stayed on in the United Kingdom, or had married a girl overseas and brought her home with him. These boys were as good as dead too, as far as the Aussie girls were concerned. The race was on if a girl was going to get herself a man.

* * *

At the conclusion of a long night the doors of the hall opened, casting a stream of light across the dark road. As the townspeople began to move off "Eef" assured Bert that as the guest of honour, he need not stay on to help clean up. Then Sergeant-Major Peter Hansen cornered him for a couple of minutes, and told him of his ambitions to go into politics. He was going to take on Job Weaver, running on a Nationalist Party ticket. Bert told Peter he could rely on him for support when the time came. Among the smiling faces he noticed a sad-looking old woman.

"Captain Jacka?" she said.

"It's Mrs Dupuy, isn't it?" he said, shaking her hand. She held on to it and wouldn't let go. Her son Jim was in the 14th Battalion and had disappeared at Gallipoli. All she got back was his hairbrush, pipe bowl, clothes brush, postcards, cigarette cards, a sweater and his copy of the New Testament.

"I'm sorry about Jim," he said. He could only imagine what the ceremony must have been like for this woman. "He was a very fine soldier."

"Can you remember when you last saw him?" she asked through tear-filled eyes. "The Army told us he was killed on the eighth of August, but I had a letter from him where he mentions the death of Corporal Hewitt on the tenth of August, so he couldn't have been killed on the eighth, could he?" It was as if she was hoping against hope that there was some kind of dreadful mistake. Either way, she wanted to know what happened to her son. Bert could never forget the "Bloody Eighth of August" 1915, which was one of the 14th Battalion's worst days of the whole war.

"I think you are right, Mrs Dupuy," Bert replied. "I can remember him after the eighth. I'm fairly certain though that he was killed at Hill 60 sometime between the twentieth and twenty-eighth. I'm sorry, Mrs Dupuy, it was the worst month of fighting we ever had at Gallipoli."

"Thank you," she said with a teary glint in her eyes. "I just wanted to know, that's all." She released his hand.

"Good night, Mrs Dupuy," he said as she silently slipped away.

* * *

There was no electricity anywhere in Wedderburn. Bert began the walk home from the Mechanics Institute with Bessie, Isaiah and his parents. Bert glanced up and saw the great Southern Cross hanging over them, blazing brightly against the soft sky. It reminded him of those nights aboard the *Euripides* after they crossed the equator, when he used to stroll out onto the deck and watch that star-studded cross rise into the sky. It seemed so close sometimes, he felt he could reach up and touch it. Each night it would rise further than the night before, and point south, towards home.

They walked down the centre of the road, and Bert had his arm around Bessie's waist. For a while there was no talking as their ears still hummed in the silence from the loud voices, and music that had resonated throughout the hall. At Kerr Street, Isaiah bade them goodnight. His wife Fanny had taken their three-year-old son Billy home earlier that evening.

"It's a pity that Sid could not be here to receive his medal," Elizabeth remarked firmly, breaking the silence.

"And Bill," Nathaniel added. "He deserved one too."

"If he'd have been here, he would have received a medal," Bert said.

"He's found himself a wife," Nathaniel said. "What about you?"

"I was better at winning medals."

"You were saying that Aussie girls are your type…" Nathaniel began.

"What about Ida?" Elizabeth suggested.

"What about her, Mum?" Bert asked.

"*She's* an Aussie girl."

"Bert doesn't want our suggestions, Mum," Bessie interjected.

"Well, now that you're home you can have the pick of the bunch," Elizabeth added proudly. "I'm sure there are thousands of nice girls who would give anything to be married to you."

Despite a liaison and a brief engagement to a girl in England, Bert still found girls somewhat daunting. Over the years of army life he'd grown ever more comfortable in the presence and company of men. For years he had lived through hell with them. He had eaten, bathed and slept with them. During those freezing cold nights at Gallipoli as winter approached there was no practical choice but to sleep together. Each man was issued with two blankets. If you slept alone it meant one blanket beneath you and one on top. If you shared your blanket with another, it meant three blankets on top of you and a warm body next to you. Bert longed for the warmth of a woman's touch, but was only slowly developing the confidence to initiate a relationship.

* * *

Nathaniel opened the door of their house, which had remained unlocked for the whole time they had been at the hall. He struck a match and lit a kerosene lamp, which bathed all their faces in a dull yellow glow and cast shadows on the walls. He went straight to bed in the master bedroom, Bessie had her own bedroom to go to. Elizabeth lit up another lamp and went into the kitchen for a time, while Bert retired to the third bedroom that used to be his, though not completely. He used to share it with his younger brothers, Sid and Bill. As he pulled back the blanket he recalled the epic pillow fights, when the three boys would slug it out in that room. So long as they kept the giggling down to a minimum they used to get away with it for ages, until they could hardly move and the laughter could be heard. Then their mother would burst in and put a stop to the delirious boyish lunacy.

Thinking of pillow fights reminded Bert of a story that was told to him by one of the Australian soldiers who had returned home on the *Euripides*. At the conclusion of the war Aussie soldiers in Cairo descended on the swankiest hotel in town, *Shepheards*, and engaged in an almighty pillow fight that would not be forgotten for a long time. Such was the intensity of that fight that flurries of feathers came down on the great central staircase like a blizzard in the Antarctic. The white pall covered everything in sight, including the two famous bare-breasted bronze nymphs that guarded the entrance to the staircase. So adored were those nymphs by the lonely men in uniform, that certain parts had become highly polished from constant contact with numerous hands. One officer had even taken the extreme measure of removing one of them, and taking her to bed with him!

"No nymphs here," Bert thought as he slipped between the sheets. He knew that an Australian girl would suit him best, but none of the girls at the hall had caught his eye. He had seen a fair bit of the world now – more than he'd ever imagined before – and through that prism, Wedderburn now looked tiny. There was a knock on the door and his mother popped her head in, carrying a candle that cast shadows on the wall.

"Sweet dreams, Bert," she said. "It's been lovely to have you home, even for this short time."

"Good night, Mummy," he replied, as he always had in the days of his youth. The bed felt so soft. As a boy he thought it was hard, but that was before he had known real hardship of the kind he experienced during the war. Bert was effectively out of the army now, but as the night wore on, and he dreamed of Gallipoli, it was obvious that the army was not out of Bert, not by a country mile.

ADVANCE AUSTRALIA!

12.24 am, Mudros Harbour at Lemnos, 60 miles from Gallipoli, 25 April 1915

Bert woke suddenly with a gasp, propped himself up on his elbows, and looked straight ahead into the night. There was a lot of snoring going on around him, but not everyone was sleeping. Many were too excited. Owing to the heat of the night, most of the thousand men of the 14th Battalion were up on the deck of the *Seeang Choon*. She was a tramp steamer out of China, and sleeping on deck was a way of avoiding the rats, cockroaches and putrid smells below decks. It seemed almost odd that the Commanding Officer of the 4th Brigade, Colonel John Monash, should choose this boat for his headquarters, but he had sailed all the way from Australia with the 14th, and they were now known as "Monash's bodyguard".

Bert began to make out the shape of a soldier wearing a cap, who was sitting perfectly still in a chair on the deck. "Who in blazes is that?" he thought. "And why is he sitting there staring at me? I'll knock his bloody block off if he keeps this up!" Bert rested on his elbows for some time, determined to stare down whoever it was. It was only after what seemed like a long time that Bert's eyes fully focused, and the realisation began to dawn on him that the "friend" was just a pile of clothes with a cap that had been left on top of some kits and haversacks. He smiled to himself once that mystery had been solved. "How could I have been so dopey?"

he thought. "There aren't any chairs on deck – and this is no cruise ship… She's no war ship either." He lay back in his spot and looked up at the black sky as the boat gently rocked to and fro.

"I'm going to be in the war very soon now," he thought. Like the others he was keen to fight. They had trained hard and travelled thousands of miles for this. They had crossed an ocean and three seas, and now they were almost there. Sleeping was not easy that night. Things had just settled down again after one of the boys had fallen overboard at midnight, and caused a great commotion. Captain Wright from A Company heard him go over and called out "Man overboard!" to the Third Officer who was on watch on the bridge. A boat was lowered down in a twinkling, and he was brought up dripping wet. "Sleep-walking," he reckoned.

"Silly blighter," someone said, "he might just as well have waited until tomorrow and chanced earning a VC if he wants to lose his bloody life!"

* * *

12.45 am, 10 miles off the coast of Gallipoli, 25 April 1915

Miles away from Mudros Harbour, a powerful battle fleet steamed towards the Gallipoli Peninsula to deal a death blow to the Ottoman Empire. Led by its flagship, HMS *Queen Elizabeth*, the fleet of eighteen British and French battleships, twelve cruisers and a large number of destroyers and other craft carried the largest amphibious force in history. The Second Division of the Fleet consisted of the battleships *Queen*, *Prince of Wales*, *London* and *Majestic*. On board the *London* the mess halls were buzzing behind blackened portholes as the men of the 1st Division AIF downed a wholesome meal.

"Eat up hearty lads, because there's business doing today!" roared a Regimental Sergeant-Major. Eat up they did. The mood was merry – strangely merry. They brimmed with confidence, as they had the power of the mighty British Navy behind them and glory lay ahead of them. No power on Earth could stop them. They sang and joked with unnatural energy as if they had not a care in the world.

Up on deck, the British war correspondent, Ellis Ashmead-Bartlett, stood alone, staring into the darkness. Now in his mid-thirties, he was the namesake of his American father, Sir Ellis Ashmead-Bartlett, and had been raised with impeccable manners. He often wore a yellow silk morning coat at breakfast, but he was no pansy. His stint of action as a lieutenant in the 2nd Bedfordshire Regiment in South Africa was only the beginning. Since then, as a war correspondent, he had seen the Russo-Japanese War, the French and Spanish armies in Morocco, the Italians in Tripoli, and both the Turks and the Serbs in the Balkans. Another half hour passed and many men had filed up onto the deck.

They had stopped, and it was quiet now – only the occasional whisper. The kind of reverence one would see as a congregation filed into church; and it was beginning to go cold. He had seen many hardened and professional soldiers in his career, but even he was struck by the spirit that resonated among the khaki clad Antipodeans of the 3rd Brigade AIF, arranged in their companies as he moved among them on this battleship. There was something about their mood that he hadn't seen before. "Is it just inexperience?" he asked himself. "Do they know what they are in for?"

The evening was clear, but there was no sign yet of the mysterious shore that lay beyond the cold sea. Rope ladders had been suspended over the side, and at 2.30 am, a number of steam-powered pinnaces each towed four lifeboats in under the bow of the *London*. The signal was given, and the men began climbing over the bow with their heavy packs and rifles slung across their backs. Ellis was dressed in khaki too, not his usual flamboyant attire, but without weapons or military insignia. He wore his old baggy green hat though, which immediately set him apart from the determined felt capped warriors around him.

* * *

It was ten minutes past three in the morning. The moon had just sunk and things became intensely dark on the deck of the *Seeang Choon*, back in Mudros Harbour.

"Bert… Bert…" whispered Rob Earl. "Are you awake?"

"Am now."

"What do yer reckon'll happen tomorrow?"

Rob was only eighteen. He came from Wedderburn, like Bert, and they had left for the war together on the same train. Now they were halfway across the world, and within miles of their final destination, where they would meet their destiny. But they had no idea what that destiny was yet, and only felt anxiety.

"I don't know," whispered Bert. "We'll find out tomorrow."

After a long pause Rob asked: "Do yer reckon they know we're coming?"

"It doesn't matter." Bert assured him. "If they don't know it by now, they'll know about it pretty soon."

"Shhh quiet," an agitated digger whispered. Then Gunner started to bark and run around the deck, jumping over the men's legs and bodies as if they were logs in some forest. Gunner was the 14th Battalion's mascot, a fox terrier that had been smuggled aboard the troopship *Ulysses* at Port Melbourne prior to their embarkation.

"Why doesn't that bloody mongrel ever sleep!" someone yelled. They were still under the impression that they would be going in later that afternoon. Even that was a disappointment, since they had been made the reserve rather than the spearhead of the attack.

* * *

4.30 am, 3 miles off the coast of Gallipoli, 25 April 1915

Slowly the faint outline of the shore came into view. The major battleships were standing in line parallel to that shore. As the motors of the pinnaces chugged away ahead of them those on board the *London* had no sense of them getting closer. It was as if something was holding them back. The shore seemed to keep getting further away, but the pull of each pinnace was relentless, and the white-foamed crests of their wakes lapped above the bows of the boats as they bobbed up and down. To Asmead-Bartlett they looked like snakes, each dragging four fully laden lifeboats in its wake, forty men per boat. Still no sound was heard. The line of boats approached the shore, and at 4.50 am an alarm signal issued from the enemy.

"There's a light," someone said excitedly. But it was just a star, and all went deathly quiet again. The quiet seemed somehow false.

Suddenly there was rapid fire on the beach, and Ashmead-Bartlett looked down at the luminous hands on his wristwatch. It was 4.53 am. As the sound of it wafted across the water to the *London*, Ashmead-Bartlett's pulse quickened. Then silence and the faint sound of a cheer. "That was an Australian cheer!" he thought, which relieved him, for he now knew that the beach had been taken. The first waves were now charging up the steep slopes of what would come to be known as Walker's Ridge and Plugge's Plateau.

* * *

Major Edmund Drake-Brockman, commander of the 11th Battalion, was in one of the boats crammed with his men. *Stroke, stroke, stroke*, the oarsmen worked feverishly to take them to shore. In training they had been told that the sounds of bullets coming at them would appear like little birds flying past. When a machinegun bullet smashed into and splintered the oar being rowed by "Combo" Smithy, a Boer War veteran, they all leaned forward as if to duck the oncoming torrent. A bushman among them, Sergeant Ayling then nudged his mate "Snowy" Howe in the ribs.

"Just like little birds, ain't they Snow," he said in a low drawl, which fairly cracked up the whole boat with laughter, even the Major. On the ground the landing parties were already hauling themselves up through the prickly scrub by grabbing hold of arbutus roots. Taking the first couple of lines from Turkish defenders had been easy. It was almost like a kangaroo shoot.

"Advance Australia!" screamed an officer.

"Cooo-eeee!" yelled one of the bushmen, thinking it *was* a kangaroo shoot.

"Come on men, they can't hit you!" roared Lieutenant Talbot Smith of the 10th Battalion scouts as he led the charge up Plugge's Plateau. "Come on Australians, give them the bayonet – that's all they want!"

The chase was on in earnest. The boys had dropped their packs in their boats or on the beach. They had gone in with cold steel, and were now fighting their way inland. Near the top of Plugge's Plateau "Snowy" Howe and a digger from the 9th caught a Turk who was trying to get away. Snowy tried to shoot him but his rifle jammed, it was so full of sand. So he bayoneted the Turk's haversack and brought him down, while his mate clobbered him with the butt of his rifle.

"Prisoner here!" they yelled.

"Bayonet the bastard!" was the reply, but they just "immobilised" him by cutting off his trouser buttons and sent him back down to the beach with a wounded man. As Major Drake-Brockman reached the top of Plugge's Plateau three Turks jumped out of a trench and came at him with fixed bayonets. That's when "Paddy" Reid got out in front of him and smacked the first Turk's head with the butt of his rifle as if making a cover drive on the hop, swung his rifle around, ducked and went under the next Turk's guard, skewering him. The bayonet blade must have gone through a bone, because he couldn't get it out in time to take the oncoming third man. So he left it impaled there, deflected the next Turk's rifle with his hands, pushed him to the ground, and kept kicking him until he lay still. It was brutal stuff this business, but so lucky for the Major that "Paddy" was there at that precise moment. Ironic too, because the Major was a lawyer in civilian life, and "Paddy" had just had his sentence shortened so he could be at the landing.

Later on, when things had quietened down on Plugge's Plateau, Major Drake-Brockman tried to administer morphine in the mouth of a wounded Turk, who spat it back out at him. Brutality and benevolence were hopelessly mixed up. Most of the boys had never been to war before.

The breaking dawn was much more peaceful back in Mudros Harbour. As the 14th Battalion men on the deck of the *Seeang Choon* woke up or just watched the sun coming up, a ferocious battle was raging 60 miles away at the Gallipoli peninsula.

* * *

7.30 am, Mudros Harbour, 25 April 1915

A little later Bert stood on the deck looking around at the bowed, hatless heads that stood before him. It was already hot, but there was relief from the gentle breeze coming off the sea. He saw that many of the lads were lost in thought, or staring with forlorn expressions, probably thinking of home, their mother, or their sweetheart. The breeze ruffled their hair, especially the salt-and-pepper mop of their beloved chaplain, Captain Andrew Gillison, MA. He stood right at the bow of the *Seeang Choon*, leading the 14th Battalion in prayer. A father of four, he was forty-seven years old, and until recently the Presbyterian Minister at St Georges on Chapel Street in East St Kilda.

Padre Gillison was originally from Scotland, where he graduated from Edinburgh University, and had ministered in South Shields, England, and in the United States before coming to Australia. Ironically, this non-combatant could out-shoot everyone in his current congregation. He was the champion marksman of the Melbourne Rifle Club, setting new "possibles" at a number of rifle ranges in his time. If anyone could challenge him with a rifle it was Captain W.R. Hoggart, of B Company. A Master at Melbourne Grammar, he was born at Buangor, western Victoria, and had won Colonel Monash's shield at Williamstown. The Colonel's wife, Victoria, presented it to him. But the gentle padre was going to war carrying a bible in his hand, rather than a rifle. His duty was to spread the word.

"Almighty God, Father and our Lord Jesus Christ, maker of all things, Judge of all men; we acknowledge and bewail our manifold sins and wickedness, which we, from time to time, most grievously have committed," the Padre intoned as he raised the presentation cups of the 14th Battalion for the communion service.

Earlier that morning he had felt somewhat nervous, as a Presbyterian Minister, to be conducting a Church of England communion service, and had expressed some reservations to his friend Captain Wright, who had assured him: "tut-tut, this is no time for technicalities." They were about to engage the enemy, and this service was of vital importance to bolster the morale of the men.

"Almighty God, our heavenly Father, who of his great mercy hath promised forgiveness of sins to all them that with hearty repentance and true faith turn unto Him. Have mercy upon you, pardon and deliver you from your sins, confirm and strengthen you in all goodness and bring you to everlasting life, through Jesus Christ our Lord Amen."

Bert stood there listening to the priest, and thought about his family: his mother and his father; his grandmothers; and his brothers and sisters. His youngest brother Bill was itching to join up but was too young when Bert went. "He'll need Mum's signature," Bert thought.

He stood close to a couple of mates from Bendigo, Bill Howard and Steve DeAraugo – both of them Catholics. Steve's father had migrated to Australia from Portugal, where everyone was Catholic. At six-foot-one, he was the tallest in the Battalion, and he and Bill used to sing in the choir of the Sacred Heart Cathedral in Bendigo. They'd gotten into some light-hearted mischief in Egypt, but had only been spectators rather than participants at the infamous Battle of the Wazzir, when a small group of AIF and New Zealand men had gone berserk and set fire to a section of Cairo.

"The Mohamads wash themselves before they pray," Bill Howard thought. It made him think of the 250-foot deep well that stood in the yard of the Mohamed Ali Mosque in the Citadel above Cairo. "It's a glorious building," he thought. "Inside there are thousands upon thousands of electric globes. But they're only lit five times a year when the Sultan and his family arrive. My oath we've seen some sights. To think that we've actually stood in the cave where the Blessed Mary took shelter."

"Lift up your hearts," said the Padre.

"We lift them up to the Lord," was the response of the many voices of varying tone on the deck, but it sounded as if it came from one.

"Let us give thanks unto our Lord God."

"It is meet and right so to do," answered the men.

On Bert's left was Fred Anderson, who hailed from Horsham. Like Bert, Fred had been employed by the Victorian Department of Forests when the war broke out. They had cut and planted forests together and had enlisted together, as had Bob Earll, who used to play Australian Rules football in the same team with Fred, and stood on the other side of him. Bob was from Woohlpooer, a small town south of Horsham. They were from different backgrounds, religiously and ethnically, but they all grew up in the western districts of country Victoria and knew the ground.

Padre Gillison turned around and faced the men while holding up the cup and announced: "The Blood of our Lord Jesus Christ, which was shed for thee, preserve thy body and soul unto everlasting life. Drink this in remembrance that Christ's Blood was shed for thee, and be thankful."

The young men of the 14th Battalion formed a long and irregular line on the confined deck of the *Seeang Choon*, and the communion took quite some time for them to pass through. All was silent, except for the gentle breeze. When the last man had participated, Padre Gillison returned to the Lord's Table with the cup, reverently placed it on the table, and covered it with linen cloth. It was especially moving for Padre Gillison, as he knew that in the next few days and weeks he would be saying the funeral rite over the bodies of the young men who had just received their communion from him as living beings. He sighed to himself as he thought about these promising young lives that would soon be cut short by the tragedy of war.

At the conclusion of the service Bert came out of his thoughts as Padre Gillison led them in song. It was his favourite hymn, *Fight the good fight*, which they would sing many times during the long war that was coming. For Captain Wright it was the most moving service he had ever attended, which he told Padre Gillison afterwards.

* * *

The *Seeang Choon* arrived off Gaba Tebe, Gallipoli, at around noon, and dropped anchor in the middle of a very hot day. It was a sight that none of them would forget, and for almost all of them it was the first sight of battle that they had witnessed. The coastline was covered in thick plumes of smoke rising hundreds of feet into the sky. Before them a line of battleships was pounding Turkish positions with high explosive shells. Behind the line of battleships sat the biggest and most modern of them all, the *Queen Elizabeth*, with great flashes from her eight 15-inch guns hurling death at tremendous velocity. Beyond the battleships hundreds of craft of all sizes and descriptions moved between the shore and the transports. Above the scene a solitary British reconnaissance plane from the *Ark Royal* buzzed about, reporting on Turkish movements.

To those who watched it from the deck of the *Seeang Choon*, the scene spelled disappointment because they thought they had arrived too late.

"Jumping Jesus! Nothing's gonna live through that hail of fire!" declared one of the boys.

"I reckon we've missed it," agreed Steve DeAraugo.

Bert was watching it too. It looked like a great bushfire to him, and yet he was drawn to it by curiosity, like that big fire at Wedderburn when he was a boy. Rob Earl held onto Bert's shoulder as he peered over him. Others were pressing against Rob, and Bert was beginning to feel squashed, but he held his tongue.

"We're gonna be the *burial* party," Bill Howard replied with disappointment.

"Well, I'm willing to bet that we'll be in Constantinople by Tuesday. Next Sunday's a cert," Rob pronounced.

"I'll take you up on that," replied Steve confidently, "because if we're the burial party, it'll take us *weeks*."

But not everyone on deck was taking the same interest as these lads. Many were deeply engrossed in card games like Banker, huddled around in circles with big mugs of steaming black tea at their sides. Up on the bridge of the *Seeang Choon* a group of 14th Battalion and 4th Brigade officers was also surveying the scene. Colonel Monash motioned towards the deck that lay below them.

"See these little knots of country chaps playing cards with big mugs of tea alongside," he said with a wry smile, "what do *they* care if the greatest naval bombardment in history is going on... When their job comes up, there'll be time to sit up and take notice."

For Captain Ferdinand Henry Wright, known to his friends as "Ferdie", this was an interesting insight into the character of the country Australian. Like the men on deck he thought that they might be too late to do anything meaningful. Captain Charles Montague Moreland Dare, the 14th Battalion's adjutant, stood next to Wright. They were two young professionals who had given up their comfortable lives in Melbourne for adventure, and a chance to fight for the Empire and Australia. Dare was an architect, twenty-six years of age, and still baby-faced. He had left his fiancée and his practice for this. Ferdie was the same age. He had left a promising career as an insurance broker, his comfortable house in the leafy suburb of Malvern, his wife Rosa, and his two children. He had even more at stake than Dare. On Easter Sunday, back in Egypt, he wrote a sealed letter to his son Harry, which was to be opened on his twelfth birthday should his father not return from Gallipoli.

Ferdie, Dare and Padre Gillison had experienced a bit of an adventure a few days earlier. Ferdie wangled a job as Brigade Censor, which had given him cause to accompany the others on a trip to the nearby island of Lemnos. One of his chief aims ashore, however, was to obtain some samples of the famous Samos wine, which retailed for a penny a glass. They had just sat down at their table at the café, when an over-friendly Greek civilian joined them and began to show an unnatural inquisitiveness about the operations of the British taskforce. He went on and on in what was extraordinarily good English, which he claimed he had acquired after a period of years of living in the United States.

They led him on for a bit and he accompanied them for a walk through the town. When he asked whether he could do them the good turn of posting the letters that Ferdie was carrying, that was the limit. He obviously knew too much, and they decided to hand him over to the French, who were policing the town, but he seemed to anticipate it and gave them the slip before they could move. They were sure that he was spying for the Turks. It also made them doubt whether the High Command had exercised any sort of control over critical information about the impending campaign.

* * *

"Look at that," said Dare softly as a hospital ship made its way past the *Seeang Choon*, steaming for Cairo with a belly full of Australian and New Zealand wounded. But it was not the ship that Dare was pointing to; it was the decks, which were overcrowded with wounded. Ferdie could see what he meant. It was a sobering sight that made everyone think that perhaps they hadn't come too late. Perhaps there would be something for them to do apart from burying the Turks? That feeling was reinforced ten minutes later, when a second hospital ship passed them in the same condition of overcapacity. A quarter of an hour after that, they began to attract a number of smaller craft that came alongside bearing wounded. Ferdie, Dare, and a number of other officers came off the bridge and crowded the upper deck. On the lower deck, Bert and many others crowded in to the railing to get a closer look. Even the card players got up to have a look.

A number of boats full of wounded were moored to the ship by ropes waiting for their turn to be carried aboard by the crudest of methods, that would have been excruciatingly painful for most of them. The sea had gone choppy and they were bobbing up and down in their small boats. All on board the *Seeang Choon* went quiet in the presence of it – the sight of blood and silent suffering. These wounded men were covered in blood, yet there was no sign of complaint. One of the men in a packed lifeboat noticed the sullen expressions of those looking down from the ship, and called out defiantly to those around him.

"Are we downhearted?"

"No!" rang out the weak but determined chorus from the wounded men in the boats. It brought a lump to the throat of many of the 14th Battalion men who witnessed it.

* * *

After the men had been fed a second hot meal for the day, at around 4.30 in the afternoon of 25 April, Lieutenant-

Colonel Courtney, the 14th Battalion's Commanding Officer instructed Captain Wright to take two platoons of A Company ashore. Wright chose No. 3 Platoon, led by Lieutenant Arthur Cox, and No. 2 Platoon, whose twenty-one-year-old leader, Lieutenant Keith Crabbe, was formerly a clerk in Melbourne's bayside suburb of St Kilda. Each man was issued with a bundle of firewood, three days of rations, and an extra hundred rounds of ammunition. It was a heavy load to bear – over 60 pounds. Bill Howard and Steve DeAraugo had been geared up and were waiting on the deck with the rest of the A Company platoons when Bert came along to wish them well, and tell them that he had volunteered to go in and help evacuate the wounded.

From the number and condition of the wounded that were being taken off the peninsula, Bert felt that things were not going well. The Turks were fighting hard, and he couldn't stand waiting around any longer. He wanted to get right into it by helping with the wounded, and was going in with about thirty others from D Company. It was the pull of duty and danger over comfort and safety – a choice that he would frequently need to make in future.

* * *

At 5.30 pm, the 16th Battalion of the 4th Brigade landed at Anzac. Among 1000 men who landed were two mates who would prove critical to the defence of the whole position, and whose names would later be held up with that of Albert Jacka in debates about who was the bravest man in the AIF. In a quiet talk that they had the previous night, they had vowed never to take an order from the enemy. They were Lance-Corporal Percy Black, an ex-gold miner, and Private Harry Murray, a sleeper-cutter. They came from Victoria and Tasmania respectively, and both had some Scottish ancestry. Murray's great grandmother had been transported from England as a convict on the infamous Second Fleet, where the chances of survival were worse than in most wars.

When their lifeboat hit a submerged rocky outcrop, Murray thought they had grounded and jumped in. He went straight to the bottom over his head. He fought his way back to the surface and bobbed around a few times before finding the sand with his feet. *Stuff this for a joke!*

They brought with them the weapon that was to prove decisive in the fight that would follow: the Maxim machinegun. As soon as they had landed, their section commander and mentor, Sergeant George Demel, gave orders to set up the guns. Black began to assemble his gun with the assistance of his Number 2, Private Harold George, while others dug a trench. It was standard practice to do this, and there was hardly anyone in the Aussie army, and very few in the world, who could harness the power of a Maxim from a standing start faster than Percy: 13.4 seconds.

Before long, the machinegun section and two companies of the 16th were ordered to follow Colonel Pope up Shrapnel Gully, to Monash Gully. Arriving at the fork in Monash Gully they were near the apex of the ground being defended by the army against a fierce Turkish counter-attack. Ahead of them was a steep rise up to a commanding ridge in the middle of the Anzac position that would be known as Pope's Hill, after the CO of the 16th. It was almost dark by the time they had clambered up the hill and began to dig in as the fury of Turkish fire rose up all around them. In the dark, and unsure of the ground, they had no idea of just how strategic their position was.

* * *

Not long after the 16th had landed, the hundred men under Wright's command were lowered into a heavy lighter that was operated by two local boatmen. They had to wait a long time in the choppy sea for a naval launch to tow them ashore, and as they waited a number of the men became seasick. At last they were away, but as they came past the *London*, an officer using a megaphone instructed them to turn back.

"Not possible!" screamed the fifteen-year-old midshipman who had command of the naval launch. "The tide is making, and I don't have the power to tow them out!"

They pressed on and were soon under shrapnel fire, which gave the appearance that they were passing through a shower of hailstones hitting the water around them. If the shrapnel burst far enough away and the force was almost spent when it hit you, you could laugh, but if you were within striking distance it would go through you like a hot poker. It flew in with a winding-down *Whizzzz*, exploded with a loud *Bang* that looked like a puff of cottonwool in the air, and then went *Swishhh* as thousands of pellets scattered in all directions. Wright was more concerned that they might be hit by a shell, which would take the lighter down quickly. Against orders he announced: "Listen to me men! I want you to remove your packs and hold them in your hands. If we take a shell there'd be no chance of getting ashore with those things strapped to your backs!"

"This way," he thought, "they at least have a fighting chance." It was starting to get dark. Suddenly the naval launch cut them loose and they began to drift. The two local boatmen were of no use, having huddled up under the armour-plated poop in the bow. They didn't even have an oar or pole with which to push the boat forward. Wright looked over the side, estimated that the water was more than chest height and didn't want to risk letting the men jump out just yet. They drifted against another lighter.

"Throw us a rope!" Wright called out.

"Don't throw a rope here, we're full of wounded," came the weak reply. Others shouted from the shore for them to jump out, but Wright held them back. Finally a British sailor from the *Drake* waded out to them with a rope and they were dragged in to the small jetty that had already been constructed by the engineers.

The men came ashore completely dry as a result, and Wright immediately reported to a naval officer, but he was fairly rattled and in a blithering state, so he spoke to an Indian Army officer who told him to form up his men as soon as he could. They did so in a scene that was indescribable. Equipment lay strewn across the beach with scores of dead and wounded piling up all over it. Above their heads screamed thousands of bullets whose movement through the air gave off a droning sound like scores of bees in a paddock of wildflowers. Shrapnel pellets and artillery shells were also coming down like rain. The noise was so great that it was hard to make out what people were saying, and the onset of darkness made it all seem even more frightening.

An animated staff officer came across to Wright and instructed him to follow him at once to General Godley's HQ on the beach. Godley was a hard-nut professional British Army officer who had organised the New Zealand contingent and was commanding the joint Australian-New Zealand Division that the 4th Brigade was a part of. His HQ was situated on the extreme left hand corner of Anzac beach, where the ridge from Plugge's Plateau comes down to meet the sea. As Wright approach Godley he saw the general looking very worried and in a towering rage.

"Who are you?" he snapped at Wright.

"Captain Ferdinand Wright, I beg to report sir!" said Wright as he saluted. "Commanding two platoons of A Company, 14th Battalion."

"Why didn't your CO or adjutant come ashore? Where's Monash?" Godley barked.

"Still on the transport, sir."

"Well, why aren't they here?"

"I don't know."

Godley looked up to the heavens in exasperation. "This is simply inexcusable! How many men did you say you have?"

"One hundred, sir."

It was now pitch black, and searchlights were ranging from the British fleet across the hills behind them looking for any movement by the Turks.

"Here's what I want you to do," Godley ordered as he pointed with his finger at Wright, then to the left of the position. "Take your men around to the northern beach there, dig in, and hang on at all costs." Wright nodded as Godley continued. "Do not retire under any circumstances if attacked, as there will be nothing between you and my Divisional Headquarters. Do you understand?"

"We'll do our best, sir," Wright assured him.

"What do you *mean,* 'you'll do your best?'" rasped Godley with suspicion, Wright quickly picked up the drift.

"We'll hold against anything they've got, sir. Nothing will come past us, I assure you."

"Good," said Godley, who was finally convinced after peering into his eyes that Wright fully understood the importance of this orders, and the gravity of the situation. What was going on around him had not changed his rather dim view of the untested fighting qualities of these Dominion troops. Inwardly, he held out little hope that they would survive the night against the concentrated Turkish counter-attack that they were now experiencing.

* * *

On board the *London*, Ashmead-Bartlett had watched the stream of wounded arriving as the day progressed, and had thought the medical preparations inadequate. "As usual, at the beginning of any British campaign," he thought, "unbridled optimism has clouded good judgment. Everything is always organised around the push forward with little thought about the consequences."

At around 9.30 pm he hitched a ride to shore in one the *London*'s pinnaces that had come off for fuel and water. Once the pinnace had stopped, Ashmead-Bartlett clambered over a number of barges, making for a drier landing on the beach, which he found to be narrow, coarse and chaotic. If it resembled anything, Ashmead-Bartlett thought, the sight of so many dead and wounded men and materials was like the aftermath of a great shipwreck that had taken place not far from shore, where the waves had brought everything into shore and dumped it mercilessly. The air was still thick with the hum of bullets, and the noise was incredible. On the ridgeline that lay above the valley, a do-or-die battle raged to hold the ground that had been won at a terrible price that day.

Along the beach he saw a group of what looked like officers standing around a smaller man who was giving them orders and pointing in a number of directions. It was General Birdwood, Commander of the Anzac Corps. As Ashmead-Bartlett approached the group, an Australian colonel attached to Birdwood's staff noticed him in his old green civilian hat.

"Who are you, and what are you doing here?" the colonel boomed. Ashmead-Bartlett was so shocked that he froze for a second.

"Seize that man, he is a spy!" ordered the colonel, pointing at Ashmead-Bartlett, and two men immediately seized him by the arms. The realisation that he could be shot if he didn't speak animated him.

"I'm Ashmead-Bartlett, the official war correspondent attached to the Expedition," he protested.

"How do *I* know who you are?" replied the colonel, looking around at his colleagues for signs of recognition. "Does anyone here know this man?" There was a spilt second of tension as Ashmead-Bartlett looked among the grim-faced officers for a familiar one.

"Yes, *I* do", announced a voice from the darkness. As he stepped forward Ashmead-Bartlett recognised Colonel Street, General Birdwood's Chief of Staff, who then took him to Birdwood and introduced him.

"How did you come ashore?" asked Birdwood.

"In a pinnace."

"Well, you must keep her here for the time being," said another officer sharply, as Birdwood returned to the task at hand. "There is an urgent dispatch to be sent off and we have no other steam launch ashore at this hour."

"Do not send your boat away whatever you do," added the British Navy's beach officer. "We have to go round to all the transports and get them to send in their boats. It is impossible for the Australians to hold out during the night. They are being too hard pressed."

The gravity of the situation was a shock to Ashmead-Bartlett. Only last night as he had watched these khaki-clad lads huddled into their units on the deck of the *London* and had walked among them, he had marvelled at how magnificent they looked, how tall they were, and fit, like athletes he thought. They were coalminers, timber-cutters, shearers and cattlemen from the country. They were also clerks, labourers and factory workers from the towns and cities. They were pioneers, and the sons of pioneers. Now he saw their broken young bodies littering the beach like seaweed.

"My God," he thought, as the hail of whirring lead and shrapnel shattered the evening sky above their heads, "any attempt to bring this army off the beach now will result in a wholesale massacre."

"Of course," he replied politely. He looked across to the officers grouped around Birdwood, who was dictating a letter to the Army Commander, General Sir Ian Hamilton. General Godley was doing the actual writing sitting on an empty ammunition box and using another as a table.

"Both my Divisional Generals and Brigadiers," Birdwood began, "have represented to me that they fear their men are thoroughly demoralised by shrapnel fire to which they have been subjected all day after exhaustion and gallant work in the morning." He looked up and quickly glanced around at the carnage that surrounded them, while Godley rested his pencil on the paper for a second.

"Numbers have dribbled back from firing line and cannot be collected in this difficult country. Even the New Zealand Brigade which has been only recently engaged lost heavily and is, to some extent... demoralised." Another pause, and Birdwood's brow furrowed as he looked down at Godley while he came to the brutal conclusion of his letter.

"If troops are subjected to shell fire again tomorrow morning there is likely to be a fiasco as I have no fresh troops with which to replace those in firing line. I know my representation is most serious but if we are to re-embark it must be at once…" Birdwood then read through and signed the note, and handed it over to the naval landing officer.

"You must take this letter with utmost urgency to General Hamilton. The fate of the whole Expedition hangs on it."

"Sir!" snapped the naval landing officer as he accepted the letter with a salute. He swung about and walked briskly towards the pinnace, with Ashmead-Bartlett in tow. They motored out to the *Queen Elizabeth*, where the naval landing officer handed the letter over to the Admiral. The *Queen Elizabeth* then weighed anchor and steamed south towards Cape Helles, where Hamilton was directing operations.

Back on the pinnace, which was bucking up and down in the choppy water, Ashmead-Bartlett turned to the naval landing officer with some trepidation.

"What is our next move?" he asked as he felt his stomach drop.

"We've got to go to every transport in turn and order them to send in their boats immediately to bring off the Australians."

"That's impossible," Ashmead-Bartlett shot back forcefully. "Not in the dark… not with all that confusion. They'd be slaughtered on the beach. The only hope the Australians have is to hold on until daybreak!"

"I know that," answered the naval landing officer coldly, "but I must obey my orders."

They made their way to the nearest transport and came up alongside. They could tell that the capacity of the ship had been overwhelmed by the weight of the wounded lying on its decks and below. Military discipline appeared to have broken down, as the naval landing officer had difficulty raising somebody on deck. Finally, he announced through his megaphone:

"Hold your boats in readiness to send them ashore at a moment's notice!"

He wasn't sure that the message had got through to someone in authority, and so it was with the other transports they visited, including the *Seeang Choon*.

* * *

Around midnight, Birdwood's letter reached General Hamilton, who was at that point contemplating the embattled position of the British troops at Cape Helles, and the fact that the troops from the transport *River Clyde* had met with disaster. Regarding the position of the Australians and New Zealanders, there was really no decision to be made, since they had no real choice. Like Ashmead-Bartlett before them, Hamilton and the Admiral of the Fleet had quickly formed the conclusion that any attempt at re-embarkation would result in a bloodbath. Instead, Hamilton ordered, and Birdwood reiterated, that they should "dig, dig, dig" into the ground that they hold, until they are safe.

By the time Ashmead-Bartlett returned to Anzac Cove a few hours later he noticed that the sting had gone out of the Turkish counter-attack, at least for the moment. Ammunition was still flying, but it was nothing like the tornado of steel that had blotted out the night earlier. He then returned to the *London* to sleep, feeling confident that the Australians and New Zealanders could hang on.

* * *

As the morning of 26 April broke Captain Wright's two platoons of the 14th were still in the position they had dug into on the northern beach. It was their first chance to get their bearings after what was for them a fairly uneventful night. They were okay except for a few slight wounds from shrapnel, and saw the Turkish trenches around 1000 yards north, with what looked like an obvious machinegun, or observation post, in the middle of it. Then a small British seaplane appeared overhead and gave off a succession of smoke signals that were picked up by the gunners on the *Queen*

Elizabeth. A couple of minutes later three shells sailed across in rapid succession, and dropped squarely onto the Turkish line. The boys in A Company were amazed by the accuracy of the fire.

A short time later some New Zealanders pulled a small howitzer onto the beach by hand, as it had been impossible to land horses. Once established they lined up the Turkish observation post and took it out with *their* first shot.

"Good shooting!" the boys yelled.

Another journalist had landed at Anzac Cove the day before. He was Charles Bean, the official Australian war historian, and during the mayhem of that first night he had fashioned himself a reasonably comfortable dugout under the circumstances. It had rained just before dawn, but a waterproof sheet over his head and a drain got the water out, and he had snatched a couple of hours sleep. When he came out he bumped into General Birdwood.

"Good morning, Bean," Birdwood said in a frustrated tone, and before Bean could acknowledge him, "I've gone all round the line last night and seen all the men. This is simply the limit if you ask me. First, there was the mistake of landing us a mile and a half *north* of where we should have landed... in this *ghastly* country... And then, there's this... this *enormous* line. The troops very gallantly took an enormous extent of country against 500 well-entrenched Turks."

"Will they hold it?" asked Bean. "Sounded as if a large number of Turkish reinforcements had arrived by yesterday afternoon."

"Oh, they'll hold it all right. I'm confident that they will," said the General. With that good news, Bean went back to his dugout and slept into the afternoon.

* * *

If Charles Bean could sleep soundly that morning and afternoon, it was inordinately due to the efforts of Percy Black, whose handlebar moustache made him a dead-ringer for Lord Kitchener. Black blasted away almost all night into the darkness, with only a brief snatch of sleep just before morning. As soon as he stirred, Black took up a rifle and dropped a sniper who had been crawling into position across a cliff face 90 yards away. But their position on the summit was not secure yet, as they had not had the chance to dig deep enough during the night, and one by one they were being picked off from… who knows where? That was the frustrating thing about it. Most of them you couldn't see at all.

Percy had set up his Maxim at the northern end of the ridge facing the Turks. On his right he could see over the heads of the Australian 1st Division boys who were holding probably the most important position in the whole line. It was the ridgeline at the centre of the ground held by the Anzacs that was to become known as Quinn's Post. He could see right over them into the Turkish held territory. "What a spot," he thought. The Maxim was watered up, belted with ammunition, and ready to fire. All he had to do now was wait.

* * *

Just before noon the rest of the 14th Battalion was being transferred to smaller ships in preparation for landing. While waiting to disembark from a destroyer a stray bullet hit and killed Sergeant W.P. Murphy of D Company. The first battle casualty of the 14th Battalion was from Warracknabeal, an immigrant who had been an old Imperial soldier. His luck had run out in this war.

Fred Anderson, his football mate Bob Earll, and the rest of A Company were put into a horse boat. The seas were still choppy, and very soon everyone was throwing up in a chain reaction, and the water around the boat became discoloured. The only thing that stopped it was the fact that they finally got going.

"Full up sir!" called the fifteen-year-old "middie" commanding the pinnace to the ship's officer in charge of the embarkation.

"Cast off and drift astern!" called the officer. They drifted astern and the young midshipman watched until the hawser that coupled the boats together stretched tight.

"Full steam ahead!" ordered the middie, and the horse boat lurched forward. He wore an old white duck suit dyed khaki, with revolver and water bottle strapped to his belt, and stood on the stern in plain view, calling out orders to a fifty-year-old boatswain who was steering the boat. Bursts of shrapnel were now peppering the sky around them and thousands of pellets were rippling across the waves. The middie's job was to steer a course through the shower of lead that was coming down.

"Hard run to starboard!" called the midshipman.

"Aye, Aye!" replied the boatswain, as the tension grew.

Fred concentrated on the boy. He's standing up there oblivious to the metal that's flying about, and the chance that he's taking. It's like he's on a picnic. What discipline there is in the British Navy! He questioned how *he* might act under fire. *It's not going to be long now. Will this day be my last?*

He clung to his rifle like it was his best friend, and winced from the pain in his fingers. Yesterday he and Bob had rowed out with six others to the *Luxor* to pick up the mailbag. There turned out to be no letters for him or Bob; all they got for their trouble was a set of blisters on both hands. Back home in the western district of Victoria he'd been a wood-chopping champion, and this would never have happened if he were still in training. Here he was going into the biggest fight of his life, and his hands were covered in blisters! The massive 15-inch shells of the *Queen Elizabeth* roared over their heads like trains on an overpass.

"Hold your course now, Mr Jessop!" the boy shouted. Then, "Cut your motor now!"

"Aye, aye, sir!"

As he did, the horse boat was released by the pinnace like a stone out of a slingshot, and drifted forward, finally running aground on a sand bar about 30 yards from shore.

"All out! Quickly!" was called and everyone hopped into the water, which for Fred was chest height, and for others was too deep. Everyone's pack was flooded with water. They tried to hold their rifles above their heads to keep them dry, but with close to 100 wet pounds on their backs it was a cold, heavy slog to the beach. The narrow beachhead was still crowded with dead and wounded as more and more troops were coming ashore by the minute. Barges and boats full of wounded men were sitting around or drifting out to sea.

Whizzzz. Bang Swishhhh. Thud. A shrapnel bullet drilled through the leg of one of the lads in A Company who was standing near Fred. As soon as it happened he dropped everything and made off with an exaggerated limp to a lifeboat full of wounded. The boys laughed at the way he was hobbling off. Tough luck, some thought. Gunner the mascot was jumping around on the beach, barking, which was what he did. They had now seen some war but were yet to truly experience it.

Fred looked at the steep hillside that led up to Plugge's Plateau. The scrub was littered with dead bodies that had been lying there since the initial attack the morning before because there were no resources to move them. When he turned around, facing the ocean he could see the flashes and smoking barrels of the guns on the British battleships, modern versions of "Nelson's bulldogs", still pasting the Turkish positions inland. It was a comforting sight.

* * *

As Fred looked out to sea, the rowboat carrying Colonel Monash was making its way to shore. Monash had his adjutant and staff officers with him, including Major McGlinn, who like Monash, was so well rounded that the boys had dubbed the pair "Tweedledee and Tweedledum". Sergeant Ernest (Ernie) Purnell Hill, who sat next to Monash, was young and athletic. Born and raised in Ballarat, he had been apprenticed to his uncle as a cabinet-maker. Having had three years experience in the militia prior to the war, Ernie Hill had met Monash before on the parade ground, when he was a Lance Bombadier. Monash still often asked him "How's my Lance Bombadier?" when they met. Now they were heading for the adventure of their lives together — a young cabinet-maker from Ballarat, and a successful middle-aged consulting engineer and businessman who lived in one of the best streets in Melbourne. Monash had his field-glasses glued to his eyes for most of the trip in, surveying the impact of the ships' artillery on the Turkish-occupied ridges.

"Effective artillery support is going to be vital," Monash said to McGlinn, who grunted agreement, as he jotted down notes in his notebook. Sergeant Ernie Hill and the other boys in the boat took heart from the calmness that Monash was displaying. They knew that the situation ashore was not good. The 14th Battalion was the last fresh chess piece on both sides to be thrown into the battle, and was badly needed to stabilise the line. Unfortunately, it was just a pawn.

* * *

The rest of Monday afternoon was uneventful for the 14th as they sat it out near the beach, except for the continuous shrapnel and occasional bullet that found its way among them. They started to take casualties from it, and there was no more laughter when someone got hit. The next morning they were ready to move anywhere. About 9 am they finally got their orders to move into the front line. They hadn't gone very far before Captain Wright and his two platoons of A Company caught up with them for the move up Shrapnel Gully to Monash Gully. It was still called Death Valley, and for a good reason: it lay directly down the Turks' line of fire at the head of the gully, and anyone in it presented a target for the scores of Turkish snipers.

* * *

Up on Pope's Hill, as the 14th made its dash through Shrapnel Gully towards Monash Gully, Percy Black's attention was drawn to a line of Turkish troops that was moving across open ground, and not towards him, but *across* his line of fire. Percy

Black's Number 2, Bert Sykes, saw them first and gave him a nudge. "What a spot of luck," Black thought, "they don't think we can see them." He ranged the sights of his Maxim, moved it across to the line of fire, cocked it — *click-click* — straightened his arms, and engaged the firing mechanism. *Rat-a-tat-tat-tat...* went the gun as he pulled it across that line of Turks, who were dropping like daisies in the field of his fire. They began to scatter, but a group of them bunched together — having no idea where it was coming from — and were blasted like ninepins.

However, Black's gun was seen by the Turks on Russell's Top, a ridge that ran roughly parallel to Pope's Hill to the west of it. They concentrated their rifle fire on him, and artillery was brought down on the position. The barrel casing of the Maxim was holed again and again by bullets, and the team was kept busy splintering ammunition boxes and forcing pieces of wood into the casing to keep the water in.

Kaba-a-a-m! An artillery shell burst close by, and Black took shrapnel through his ear and left arm, which flopped down, motionless from a torn muscle. The blood flowed freely, but he refused to be relieved. Then the Turks mounted a charge. Around seventy of them came out of a depression only 80 yards away.

"Here they come!" yelled Black, as he lay down a murderous stream of bullets, operating the Maxim with only one powerful miner's arm. Their brave attack wilted in front of him, with only one man getting within 40 yards of him.

"That's the beauty of these guns," he later told Lieutenant Colonel Pope, "you can work 'em... with one hand."

* * *

As men of the 14th Battalion began their journey up the gully they could hear the fighting up on Pope's Hill and Quinn's Post. They were soon met by wounded men making their way back to Anzac Cove, who encouraged them, telling of the urgent need for reinforcements. They soon got orders to throw off their packs,

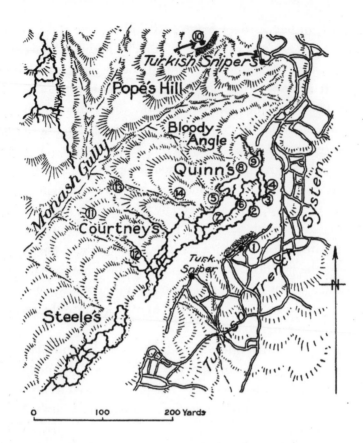

1. Turkish machinegun.
2. Captain Hoggart.
3. Cohen, Lt. Crabbe and Anderson.
4. Thompdon, Butterworth and Bowen.
5. Rations were issued here.
6. Where Captain Wright and Signaller Holmes stood when the latter was wounded.
7. New Zealand Engineers sapping here were wounded.
8. Company Headquarters – Major Rankine.
9. Turkish Snipers wrought havoc from here on our right.
10. Turkish Sniper, whose fire commanded Monash Gully, but who could not sight Quinn's Post, except at one or two isolated points.
11. Loughran – M.O.'s Dressing Station, exposed to fire from sniper at (10).
12. McDermaid's place for issue of rations.
13. Point on track down from Quinn's, exposed to fire from sniper at (10).
14. Large grave where 39 bodies were buried on Wednesday.

Quinn's Post

Source: N. Wanliss (1929), The History of the Fourteenth Battalion, A.I.F., *The Arrow Printery, Melbourne, p. 28*

which no one complained about at the time, as they weighed a ton.

When Fred Anderson's platoon arrived at the base of Quinn's Post they were told to get up to the top of the ridge. As they made their way up the winding track from the gully they passed piles of bodies, Australian bodies, which had been pushed over and down the hill – some were still quivering. Some rolled all the way down to the base, but in other places there were tidy stacks of them. There was no room for them in the clogged shallow trenches up above. Either way, it was not a very encouraging sight for the fresh reinforcements coming up into the line.

They could not go over the ridge as there were already men in shallow firing pits in front of them, so they stayed just behind the rise of the ridge and formed a line among the scrub. As the Turks were advancing Fred's platoon was ordered to fire over the heads of the men in the pits, and when they did the men below were deafened by the blasts over their ears, and screamed out the foulest language they knew for them to stop.

"This pozzie's no good," Fred thought, even though the shooting had been good, and he'd just got six Turks by his own reckoning. So he slipped down behind the ridge to tell his officer, but before he could speak the lieutenant interpreted it as cowardice, and pushed the barrel of his revolver into Fred's face.

"Get back up there... *now!*" he grunted.

As a Lance-Corporal, Fred felt it wise not to argue or the blasted thing might go off accidentally, so he kept his mouth shut, turned around and got back to the line, where around 120 men were strung across the whole ridge of Quinn's Post in a two-foot deep trench that was exposed to the enemy. Fred saw the danger, and called Bob to move thirty yards further along with him to the extreme right of the position. No sooner had they moved when a Turkish machinegunner picked up on the opportunity and rattled off a belt, sweeping along the whole line of exposed men – and boys. The 14th's sixteen year-old bugler was on the left and was one of the first to be killed. Nearly all of the men lying in the scrub on the left were killed or wounded as the machinegun rounds churned through, and swept away everything in their path.

One round hit the upper part of Fred's right sleeve, another went through his right ammunition pouch, and three tins of bully beef in his haversack were drilled through and exploded. Another bullet cut halfway through the belt around his waist. Bob Earll was a few yards down the hill, and was missed. Fred couldn't believe his luck, but was angry that the lieutenant hadn't shifted them when he came down intending to warn him, as this wouldn't have happened.

Shortly afterwards, the officer who shoved a revolver in his face called for volunteers to plug the gap that had been opened up by the Turkish machinegun. Just to show him that he wasn't a coward, Fred volunteered, and so did another digger. But as the two of them dashed back to the shallow trench, they were fired on by Turks only fifty yards away, and suddenly they were dodging bullets that kicked up soil all around them. One bullet shattered the bayonet of the digger in front, with one piece careering into his forehead, and other pieces slashing Fred below the eye, piercing his left arm and going through his right ear. Fred was knocked unconscious by the blow.

* * *

As Captain Wright made his way up the gully he could see Pope's Hill up ahead, where it was apparent that snipers were taking a toll in the open space near its base. He knew that once that clearing was reached, there would be no time to stop and think, so he approached Lieutenant-Colonel Courtney (who had proposed the toast at Wright's wedding in 1911). What Wright hated was the uncertainty of moving towards some ill-defined position in front of them.

"Sir, do you have explicit orders for me at this point?" he asked.

"Don't ask me what to do," Courtney replied sharply. "Why don't you just push on to the firing line?"

"I don't know where the firing line *is*," Wright thought to himself, so he resolved to follow the gully to where the shooting got louder – "march to the sound of the guns." To stay out of sight as much as possible Wright went over to the left of the gully with Lieutenant Cox and his platoon, and ordered Lieutenant Crabbe's platoon into the scrub on the right. When Wright's platoons got to the foot of Pope's Hill they heard fighting taking place at the summit, so they clambered up to the position that the 16th men, including Black and Murray, had held on to overnight. Lieutenant-Colonel Pope told them he didn't need reinforcements, but thought that things were in a bad way on the opposite ridge on the right. They would need to make a dash for it across the gully.

They crossed the gully and came up the other side to the ridge that would be known as Quinn's Post. There was considerable confusion when they got there, as they saw figures moving about in the distance and could not identify whether they were Turkish or Australian. They began to dig in with their entrenching tools when a sudden burst from a machinegun ripped through them from the right. A number of men were killed and wounded, including Lieutenant J. Hanby, a clerk from Brighton, and a bullet shattered Wright's rifle just in front of the magazine, grazing the fingers on his left hand, thrusting the stock against his chest, and bruising him badly. He was thrown down by the force of it, and when he got up, he saw shaken men creeping back from the inadequate cover they had formed. In one sweep of a Maxim they had lost corporals Butterworth, Bowen, Thompson, Young, Macoboy, Chisholm, Burton and Doyle, as well as privates Cohen, Wren, Gist, Greenham and Earl.

Gunner the mascot, was constantly barking at the bullets as they struck and kicked up dirt in the section of the line where Captain Wright's men were now lying. Some of the men were taking stupid risks to try to keep Gunner alive, so the dog was eventually evacuated back to Egypt. The smaller you were, the better were your chances of survival.

They were receiving erroneous messages about British and Indian reinforcements that never appeared. More confusion was caused by the Turks calling out, in perfect English, such phrases as "Stretcher bearers wanted!" or "Ammunition wanted!" Meanwhile, the machinegun that had mauled them earlier was still playing havoc, and they had not yet dug deep enough to be safe. A rumour had started about that machinegun being Australian.

"Put your caps on your rifles and let them know we are Australians," one senior officer ordered, and a number of men complied. Wright thought it was crazy. He was in no doubts that they were being pasted by the enemy. Frustrated by the continuing confusion, Captain Hoggart of B Company, decided to put an end to the rumour by rushing forward with his field-glasses and having a decent look for the position of the machinegun.

"The bloody fool'll get his blasted head knocked off," said one of the diggers. As Hoggart knelt down and put his glasses up to his eyes to get a better look, he was shot through with a half a dozen bullets. The former Master from Melbourne Grammar School was gone. When he arrived at the ridge earlier that day he had reassured the men under his command with a calm voice, "Follow me, it's all right." His death removed all doubt about the origins of the "hate" that was being directed against them, and they all commenced firing furiously. "His sacrifice was not totally in vain," Wright thought, although there were mixed opinions on that.

An injured Sergeant Reynolds came up to Wright just after Captain Hoggart's death. He had been badly hit in the jaw. In fact he had virtually no jaw left, it was so badly shot away. He was trying to say something, and Wright strained to understand him. His stomach dropped at the sight of the brave fortitude of this poor man, who was spitting blood through the raw meat that hung from his face.

"I... I can't understand what you're saying, Sergeant," the shocked and frustrated Wright told Reynolds, as he took him by the arm and pointed him towards the gully, telling him to make his way down to the dressing station below. He could not imagine what pain that man was suffering.

* * *

When he came to, Fred could hear that the tremendous noise of battle was still raging around him. He was bleeding all over the place, so he locked the safety catch on his Lee-Enfield .303 rifle, rolled back over the ridge and went down to the dressing station in the gully, where the 14th's Medical Officer, Captain Henry Loughran, put a dressing on his head. Always cool as a cucumber in the front lines, Loughran had gone from being doctor in the quiet Victorian country town of Kyneton – to this.

"You can't go back to the firing line now," Loughran said, "I've just cleaned it up, but you'll need to be evacuated to Egypt for further treatment until it heals. The fragments are still in there." But Fred had other ideas.

* * *

As the afternoon wore on things quietened down a bit, and Lieutenant Roy Cox and a young digger did some useful sniping. Captain Wright's men made no attempt to collect their dead. They had a couple of wounded Turks with them, one seriously, but it was too dangerous for stretcher-bearers to take them down the gully to the dressing station during daylight hours.

That night the Turks made a couple of determined attempts to sweep the garrison off Quinn's Post. They made a terrific noise as they attacked, shouting "Allah! Allah! Allah!" with bugles blowing.

"Come on yer bastards, I'll give you Allah!" was a common response from the men of the 14th, who probably expended more ammunition than they needed to, but they held on. Young Lieutenant Keith Crabbe did some sterling work leading his No. 2 Platoon, as did Lieutenant Roy Cox with No. 3 Platoon. When things had settled down for a short while, Captain Wright and Sergeant Dadson crawled out to retrieve Captain Hoggart's body. However, just as they got to him, the Turks noticed some movement in No-Man's Land, and commenced firing. Wright and Dadson had to beat a hasty retreat back to the Australian line.

As Wednesday morning broke, everyone on the ridge was just getting over another uncomfortably cold night, wishing they had the greatcoats that were in the packs they dumped halfway up Shrapnel Gully. Wright had just written out a message that was to be taken around to all the section heads in the trench and initialled by each of them before coming back to him. He was handing the message to one of his signallers when, *bang!* A sniper's bullet slashed through Wright's tunic between his chest and his raised arm, and crashed into the signaller's stomach, lodging in his spine. The signaller crumpled to the ground like a leaf. Captain Wright and Sergeant Little of B Company immediately pulled the signaller over to a ledge where there was some cover. As Wright bent over the signaller and took a field dressing from his pocket, *ping!* Another bullet whizzed across him, narrowly missing his head.

"Good God!"

He knew at that instant that a Turkish sniper had moved into a commanding position overnight, and had picked him out as a target. He immediately rushed over to another projecting ledge of earth, and squeezed his body and face down to the ground as flat as possible, when another bullet smashed into the earth just ahead of him, covering his head with dirt. He was scared as a rabbit as it was obvious that the sniper would not let up until he'd got him. He recalled the warnings that "Officers is their meat". Another two bullets drilled into the hill just above his head, and there was no decent cover.

He knew Lieutenant Giles's dugout was not far away, and Giles told him last night that there was room for two. It was just a hole, two feet deep, that looked something like a shallow grave. *Time to take him up on the offer*, Wright thought, so he waited until the next shot, and bolted as fast as he could. He dived into it, landing flat on top of Giles, but immediately realised that it would need another six inches to a foot to properly protect himself from the sniper. Yet another bullet whizzed across his head to confirm that, so he dragged an ammunition box full of earth across as extra protection. It was not a completely satisfactory solution. He remembered from his musketry training that a modern rifle could project a bullet through about three feet of earth, and the wider end of the ammunition box was only twenty inches long. Breathing rapidly, he drew his pistol, as he was now certain of the general direction the bullets were coming from.

"Sergeant Dadson!" he called out. "I believe the sniper is hiding in that clump of bushes that you can see over on the right! I want you to take a party of men and rush it!"

"Right oh!" replied the mature South African war veteran, Dadson. His party of men went over and prodded the bushes, but couldn't find the sniper. However, it gave Wright the opportunity to get out and find a safer position. The sniper lay low for another half an hour after that, but kept up the pressure on the battalion's water and ammunition stocks all day, and took a toll of eleven men, most of whom were killed, including the Company Quarter Master Sergeant Alston.

* * *

Over on neighbouring Pope's Hill, the machinegun crew wanted to shift to a better position, so Harry Murray went out into the scrub to find a suitably high, clear spot. Suddenly a big Turk, over six feet tall, jumped out from behind an olive tree and charged at Murray with his bayonet. He lunged forward at Murray, who deflected his blade and stepped back. Murray replied with his bayonet, and the big Turk deflected him. They danced about for a while, sizing each other up like fencers. Murray noticed that his opponent was much taller and had a foot longer reach that him. "Nah… this isn't worth it," Murray thought, so he simply pulled the trigger. When he reflected on it later, he came to the conclusion that while it was not sporting of him to have done that, his action had been justified by the fact that the Turk was now lying dead and he was still alive. He knew one thing for sure: war is not sport.

When Black's Number 2, the twenty-two year old private Harold George was killed with a bullet through the heart, Murray became Black's new Number 2, and the deadly team was formed. In the previous thirty-six hours Black had expended around 35,000 rounds of ammunition, and they had managed to live through a number of close scrapes. At one point they were shelled by friendly fire from the British Navy, and four terrifyingly loud missiles screamed their way through the air, landing right among them. The shells were armour piercing, designed to drill through six inches of steel plate on a dreadnought, and explode within. These shells drilled deeply into the earth on Pope's Hill and exploded violently, carrying up tons of earth and rubble. Men were thrown high into the air, but came down safely to earth among cavernous craters. It made them think twice about what effect the Navy shelling was actually having on the Turks.

On the morning of Wednesday, 28 April, Murray was almost nodding off from exhaustion and lack of sleep. The noise never stopped. Up to that point Murray had been a teetotaller, but Black, as a Lance-Corporal, was his superior, and he ordered Murray to take a swig of rum to wake him up. With no previous experience of drink, the stuff went straight to Murray's head, and very soon he wasn't thinking too clearly. He decided that he should get a clearer view of a Turk who had been annoying them, so he sat up on the parapet.

"Get out of that, you bloody fool!" shouted Black, as he dragged Murray down into the trench by the collar. "You won't live to see your next meal if you bob up like that again." It was a lesson that Murray would not forget for the rest of his military career: don't mix warfare and alcohol. Later that day, Colonel Pope who had observed the cool determination of this pair made a note in his diary to elevate Black to Sergeant, and Murray to Lance-Corporal.

By this time Murray simply idolised Black for his super-human bravery up on Pope's Hill. Black's Maxim finally gave up. It had been hit so many times by bullets and shrapnel that it was unworkable, so Black took it down the gully to the beach, where he thought one of the Navy armourers might be able to fix it. Rather than get it fixed, Black was presented with a brand new naval issue Maxim that had an unpainted shiny brass casing.

When Black returned to the post at the top of Pope's Hill he wore a great smile on his face as he carried the shiny brass barrel of the new Maxim on his shoulder. Murray saw him coming back up the hill that day and marvelled at the sight of him. Glorying in his physical strength and power, afraid of nothing on earth, he bore that gleaming barrel like the great bronze sword of a foot soldier on the plains of Troy. Like the mighty warrior of Greek mythology, Diomed, son of Tydeus, in Homer's *Iliad* "who went furiously among the Trojans".

"And Diomed answered: 'Come what may, I will stand firm.'"

It was an image of courage that would never leave Murray's mind.

* * *

On Wednesday afternoon, Captain Wright went out with Sergeant Dadson, Private Joseph Verswyvelt, otherwise known as "Belgian Joe", and Bugler Lyons to hunt down snipers operating between Quinn's Post and Pope's Hill. "Belgian Joe" and Sergeant Dadson each bagged a sniper, but the futility of their venture became clear to them when they realised that they were being sniped by other snipers still operating behind their lines. They retreated without solving the sniper menace.

On Wednesday night, Wright and the others on Quinn's Post came to the conclusion that the sniper who had done so much damage earlier that day must be right in front of their trenches, so they dug a "T" piece out from their own lines, and next morning they could see the hole that he was shooting from, but he was gone. "That was a plucky piece of work," Wright thought, "as the sniper would have had no chance if we had discovered him while he was there."

That evening they retrieved Hoggart's body. A burial party was ordered to dig a large grave and 29 bodies of Australians and New Zealanders were placed into it. Padre Gillison came up and read a short burial service over them. They also gave a decent burial to two Turks. Later it rained, so they spent another cold night in wet clothes, with no greatcoats or waterproofs to provide shelter. Everything was still in the packs they had been ordered to discard.

The next day they were informed they would be relieved by the 15th Battalion. Around 5 pm, a detachment of the 15th arrived, and at first the lieutenant in charge refused to enter the trenches, saying there was no cover for his men and they would be shot going in. Hearing this the young Bugler Lyons came up immediately and volunteered to show them how little risk there was. What a difference three days of war makes.

The process of getting everyone out of the trenches took longer than expected, and it was practically dusk by the time they were all out. Before leaving, the 14th's adjutant, Captain Charles Dare, looked out over the ground that lay before them. They had killed so many Turks out there over the past few days that it looked like a whole battalion was sleeping out in the open.

It was not going to be a peaceful exit though. The Turks noticed the activity and decided to shell Shrapnel Gully while the diggers made their way to the beach. Right at the bottom of Quinn's Post, Wright and another digger from the 14th were assisting a man from the 15th across the stream when everything went blank in Wright's mind. He had the feeling of falling continuously into a darkness that was bottomless and silent – then vague recollections of water being forced into his mouth at the beach.

Wright was taken to a hospital in Alexandria. He had lost the sight from his right eye, his right arm was semi-paralysed, and his right ear was being syringed every day to clean the blood and pus from it. He had suffered concussion and was declared unfit to return to his unit.

* * *

After two days of sitting on the beach, in breach of the MO's orders for evacuation to Egypt, and disgusted at finding that his pack with all his personal belongings had been "ratted", Fred went back up the gullies to Quinn's Post to find Bob. There he was told that Bob had been killed the night before, which shocked him. He and Bob had enlisted together at the start of the war and had stuck together all the way. After he got the news Fred didn't care what happened to him, and he kept on with his platoon until his wounds turned septic. He could only see a little out of his left eye, as the splinters of the bayonet were still in it and festering. His hands, which had been blistered from rowing were all swollen up. It was during this time that he was almost killed by one of his own men who let his rifle go off accidentally. The bullet just grazed Fred's head. No doubt about that charmed life that Fred led.

The following Tuesday, he was taken off to the hospital ship, the *Glouster Castle*, which was crowded with wounded. To Fred, the operating room looked like a butcher's shop, with all the legs and arms that were scattered about it. They put him on a table, unravelled the bandages and ran gauze with iodine through it. Then they bandaged him up for the remainder of the trip to Egypt. During the trip to Egypt, the bodies of 68 men were put over the side into the Mediterranean Sea. The next time his head bandage was changed was eight days later, by Japanese medical sisters on the train between Alexandria and Cairo.

In Cairo they operated on Fred's head wound twice at the Women's Hospital, and the Sudanese doctor extracted a piece of bullet and a fragment of bayonet. The Aussies called him Jack

Johnson, after the famous African American heavyweight boxing champion. He would visit every day to look over their wounds, which was often a painful experience, and in the end they dreaded the sight of him. He would undo the bandage on Fred's head, and give it a swift tug, which pulled the gauze that was stuck to the wound with iodine straight out. He never spoke a word of English, and the boys wondered if he understood any part of the abuse that they were subjecting him to, and what they thought of his parentage.

Most of the men in the ward had head wounds, and many had been blinded. One of the blind men had a bullet go right through both eyes and his nose. An English Petty Officer had a bullet in his shoulder and refused to be put under with anaesthetic. He just sat there without a murmur while they cut through the muscle of his shoulder to get it out. Again, Fred counted his lucky stars. From time to time he and some other boys would don the big loose Egyptian women's trousers, shirts and slippers that they were issued with, and make their way into Cairo.

After a couple of weeks Fred was transferred to an old hotel in Helouin further up the Nile, but he got sick of it and asked to be transferred back to his unit. They put three stripes on him and sent him back in command of forty men. Not many of the old boys were left after the defence of Quinn's, but the same spirit was there. They were now living in open dugouts on the sides of the hills, and most of their time was taken up banging the seams of their shorts with the butts of their rifles to kill the lice. Sleeping on or under a blanket was impossible because of them. The old boys smiled when they saw him, and greeted him warmly with handshakes and backslapping.

"You silly bastard," one of them said. "What did you have to come back here for?"

OF LIFE AND LOVE

4.30 pm, The hill at Kew, Thursday, 6 November 1919

A hansom cab from comfortable Kew carefully negotiated its descent into the valley of the Yarra and working-class Collingwood. On a pleasant, sunny day it was making its way to the city. Like sentinels, the towers of the Victorian mansions on the hill surveyed the river below and the suburbs that stretched out over the plain. A greengrocer's cart made its way slowly up the hill towards the shops at the Junction, while down in Merri Creek, a gang of schoolboys had just raided a Chinese market gardener's orchard. They were making away with pockets full of plunder, and he was hot in pursuit until they bolted across a fifteen-inch diameter gas pipe suspended forty feet above the creek.

"You come back… you… *baaad* boy!" he called frantically.

Undeterred by the finality of putting a wrong foot forward, they showed him their bums, and a half dozen pairs of flashing hands and feet. At the edge of the cliff the old farmer came to a sudden halt and bent over, out of breath, just as the last boy reached the other side. He shook his head as he wiped the sweat from his brow, and thought, "What fools you boys are! You don't understand your own mortality."

* * *

Four determined men, all ex-AIF, were taking on Kew hill in search of their future. Reginald Owen Roxburgh, or "Reg" as he was called, knew the Maxwell 25 he was driving could take that hill with ease, so he flattened it, swerving out to overtake the cart and then moving in to avoid the hansom cab. It was a time of rapid technological change, and society would have to run to keep up with it. He and his passengers: Albert Jacka, Ernest "Ernie" Edmonds, and Alexander Parker, were making their way up to the big white mansion of John Wren, a millionaire business tycoon of many dimensions.

Reg had been an officer in Bert's D Company. His father, Thomas Roxburgh, was a leading wheat and shipping broker and founder of Thomas Roxburgh & Co Pty Ltd. Captain Ernest Leslie John Edmonds was a commercial traveller before the war, when they were known as knights of the road; the spreaders of civilisation. He was captured by the Germans at the Battle of Bullecourt in April 1917 and spent the rest of the war as a POW. Captain Alexander Frederick Parker's father had migrated from Scotland, and for ten years prior to the war, Parker served as a clerk in the office of a solicitor.

In the back streets of the suburbs they were passing more modest merchants plied their trade. There was the milkman, the ice-man, the ice-cream cart, the "fish John", and the cry of the "bottle-o". All of their vehicles were powered by horseflesh, which provided jobs to the battalions of men who regularly swept horse manure from the streets. It was said this was the only way you could make any money by following the horses. John Wren was another exception, and Reg was concerned about whether they were doing the right thing approaching a man of his reputation. "He could pull a swifty on us," he warned.

Bert knew the story, but thought that Wren had moved on. He was a millionaire now, and the capital was now in legitimate businesses – mostly sports.

"He's not all bad," Ernie added. "He's got a reputation for giving money away to the poor in Collingwood, and he's good mates with the Catholic Archbishop."

"Well, that's a recommendation!" Reg bellowed. "Mates with mad Dr Mannix! Oh, that is just dandy – the German spy who led the campaign against conscription!"

In the debate that followed Reg made the case that Wren's first loyalty was to Ireland. Bert recalled that he had enlisted and helped the recruiting effort throughout the war, but Reg countered that he was in the army for all of five minutes, and it was just a publicity stunt.

"What do *you* say, Parker?" Ernie asked.

"I would not wish to pre-judge a man over his past indiscretions," Parker replied. "Wren has obviously learnt how to survive and prosper in the business world. He can provide advice, and some additional capital would be welcome."

"All right… All right," Reg conceded. "It's too late to quibble now. Is this it?"

"Yes."

The car entered the spacious grounds of John Wren's mansion, with its white-columned verandah winding most of the way around it. Bert led the way onto the veranda and rang the doorbell. They were surprised that John Wren himself opened the door and greeted them. Around fifty years of age, he was silver-haired and short. In the slums of Collingwood he had learned to do everything himself, and employed people to do things he couldn't do. He was not a saint, and had been a sinner, but remained a man of simple tastes. He had come up the hard way, and may have read or heard that passage in the bible about the chances of a rich man reaching heaven being worse than a camel passing through the eye of a needle. So he tried to "spread the wealth".

"Captain Jacka, what a pleasure to meet you again," Wren said with a good measure of the charisma that helped raise him to his fortunate position.

"Hello Mr Wren," said Bert formally. "I'd like to introduce my colleagues, Alexander Parker, Reginald Roxburgh and Ernest Edmonds."

"All ex-AIF I take it?"

"That's right," Bert replied. Wren smiled broadly as he shook their hands, speaking softly.

"Please."

They followed him through the entry hall into the morning room, which allowed panoramic views of the eastern suburbs of Melbourne. Two men who had been sitting in armchairs stood up to be introduced.

"Allow me to present Albert Jacka VC, and his business associates," said Wren. "This is my brother, Arthur, and Richard Lean, who manages my sporting interests."

Dick Lean was well known around town. He ran the *Stadium* for Wren, where the big fights in Melbourne were held. However, none of them knew much about John Wren's brother Arthur. They sat down and Bert kicked off: "My partners are keen to hear your proposal."

"Well, Captain Jacka," Wren began, "after what you boys have been through, I would like to help you establish yourselves in business. So please, tell me know what *you* have in mind."

"We have plans to establish an importing agency," Bert replied.

"We are the sole Australian agents for a British tonic stimulant," Parker interjected. "Fort-Reviver which we plan to make widely available throughout Australia—"

Reg cut in and talked over Parker. "Electrical goods. Electricity is the future you know. We want to fill Australian households with appliances – the best in the world." The Fort-Reviver agency was just a minor part of the plan as Reg saw it.

"Where are you to be located?" asked Wren.

"In Collins Street at the Olderfleet Buildings," said Reg. "My father's business is spread over the second floor."

"Do you have enough capital?" Wren asked.

"Not nearly enough for the scale of operation that we have in mind," replied Bert. "That's why we are here, to take you up on your offer."

Wren looked over at his brother. "We can help out the boys there, can't we, Arthur?"

"Absolutely."

"But we'll need board seats to protect our investment," continued Wren.

"We can understand that," Bert nodded.

"And Dick here will be on hand to give you advice."

"What kind of advice?" Reg asked suspiciously.

"I know my way around the traps," Dick replied.

"I'll *bet* you do," Reg thought to himself, picking up on the pun. Traps was a nickname for the police, and John Wren was known to have had several on his payroll in his off-street totalisator days.

"Now," Wren asked leaning over to Bert, "what do you plan to call this little venture?"

Parker was quicker off the mark: "Parker, Roxburgh, Jacka and Company."

"Not alphabetically, 'Jacka, Parker, Roxburgh?'" asked Arthur.

"No," Parker said. "My financial contribution will be the largest, and the Roxburgh name is well known in business circles."

"Well, it looks like you have everything under control then," Wren said, standing up and offering his hand to Parker, and then to Reg and the others. "So, we're agreed then?"

"In principle," Reg replied. "We'll need to iron out the details, of course."

"But of course!" said Wren. "Dick and Arthur will be in touch with you. They will see that the documents are drawn up. "

"We are looking forward to a prosperous partnership," Bert added.

"Good. Then we're settled," said Wren, who saw them out while Arthur and Dick continued to observe each other in silence. They heard the motor start up and half a minute later Wren returned to them.

"The problem is that the devil is always in the detail, isn't he?" asked Wren as he entered the room. He sat back in his chair, put his hands together under his own chin, as if in prayer, "So, what do you think?"

Arthur was bursting to say something, and went first. "Can you believe the impertinence of Parker and that Roxburgh fellow? What kind of businessman would miss the opportunity to put Jacka's name in front of his business? You'd put it up in electric lights, wouldn't you? I think Captain Jacka has his head screwed on, but I'm a bit concerned about Parker and Roxburgh." Wren took in his older brother's comments and nodded acknowledgement.

"Personally, I wouldn't give Parker the time of day. Dick?"

"I don't know," said Dick. "I need to spend more time with them. Edmonds hardly said a word."

* * *

Later that day, after Dick Lean had gone home, Arthur was having some second thoughts about the meeting with Bert and his colleagues, and felt he had to say something to his brother.

"You know, John, you could do your dough by getting mixed up with these boys."

"I made a promise to reward Australia's first VC winner, and I'm going to keep it."

"Yes John, but…"

"St Patrick's Day is coming up and it's going to be a big one," Wren interrupted. "The Archbishop will be the focus with thousands of Catholic diggers marching behind him. And he'll be surrounded by a troop of VCs riding white chargers. It'll put to bed any lingering doubts about Irish loyalty to this country. It'll show the public that Catholics carried their fair share of the burden during the war. We'll make a film out of it. We'll get those VCs to sign a petition to the King, supporting Ireland's right."

"Oh, that is brilliant," Arthur said, with sparkling eyes. "But will the VCs come?"

"Oh they'll come all right. My word they'll come. Sergeant Buckley is helping me with the planning. Those of Irish blood like him will come without any prompting, and I'm offering fifty pounds plus expenses. And who will lead the nation's heroes? The bravest of them all. Albert Jacka VC."

* * *

Elizabeth Street, Melbourne, Friday, 7 November 1919

The next night Bert made his way along Elizabeth Street to Sargent's Café. It was a reception of the 14th Battalion 4th Brigade and Association in honour of Bert and Sergeant Maurice Buckley VC DCM, from the 13th Battalion, who had also returned recently. Sargent's could easily accommodate well over a hundred guests in its main dining room, and the place was humming with discussion. At the head of a central table sat Brigadier-General Charles Brand, and near him were Bert's friends and comrades at arms. As Bert walked in among the tables the chatter began to subside as men recognised him.

"Over here," said Brigadier Brand, motioning towards the spare place next to him.

"Welcome back, Bert!" rang out from the rear of the hall as he took up his seat, and a loud cheer followed immediately.

"Please. Please sit down!" Brand implored the men. "You'll have a chance to hear from Captain Jacka and Sergeant Buckley presently."

Buckley's story is a remarkable one. He volunteered in 1914 and embarked with the 13th Light Horse, but was returned to Australia in 1916 in disgrace. He deserted soon after, and was narrowly missed in an army raid on his mother's house in Melbourne, but resurfaced in Sydney, where he re-joined under an alias. He came to the 13th in France as a reinforcement.

It happened in September 1918, just before the end of the war. Buckley rushed a field gun that was holding up a company. He shot the gun crew, then ran across more open ground and silenced a trench mortar crew. His trademark was to rush forward with his Lewis Gun giving them the taste of a full drum, firing from the hip. By the conclusion of the day he had rushed no fewer than six German machinegun posts and captured nearly a hundred prisoners. If ever there was a Jacka stunt, this was one, yet he was not nearly as well known as Bert. Buckley had won his VC when the war was almost over, and Jacka had been the first.

Congratulatory handshakes, backslapping and conversation flowed freely as Bert took in the comradeship of those who sat nearby, including Reg Roxburgh, and Ernie Edmonds. Captain Ted Rule came down especially from Shepparton, and Captain Fred Anderson was down from Horsham. Lieutenant Jack "the Hun Hater" Garcia was there, as was Private Alfred "Sailor" Day, a rough diamond who'd been a sailor before the war, and an infantryman all throughout it. Never far from a pub, he was ready to bet on anything from the horses to two flies crawling up a wall.

Brand asked Bert where he was living and was told he had come to a long-term arrangement with the Middle Park Hotel. It caused the Brigadier to raise an eyebrow, as he thought Bert was an abstainer. Brand still couldn't understand him. It was typical of Bert to hold on to a matter of principle and then surround himself and engage with holders of the contrary principle. He visits a bar and does not drink there. He becomes an officer and continues to fraternise with enlisted men. As a Protestant loyal to the British Empire, he enters a business partnership with a leading Irish Catholic activist. He could cut through institutional, sectarian and social divides.

* * *

Brand rose from his chair. "Gentlemen!" he said tapping a glass with his spoon. The noise died down fairly quickly as a sense of military discipline returned to the men.

"Please rise," he said, and "Attention!" was called. Chairs scraped the wooden floor as the men rose in unison. "Gentlemen, a minute's silence in memory of our glorious dead," he announced. They bowed their heads, and a pall of silence fell over them as they recalled those who had fallen in the great battles they had fought. Then came the release and the realisation that they were still here, with a second chance at life, but a life that would be different. They had changed and were different to those around them in this country, who had not been at war.

"Now… I know you have been champing at the bit to hear from our guests of honour," said Brand, breaking the silence, "Captain Jacka and Sergeant Buckley!"

"You're right, Brig!" yelled one of the men from the other side of the hall.

"So are you!" Brand called out in reply, as everyone burst into laughter and applause. It was the same old cat and mouse game that he'd played with them at the front.

"Men, I propose a toast to our two distinguished VCs. I would ask you to charge your glasses." After the clinking of glasses, he announced, "To Captain Albert Jacka and Sergeant Maurice Buckley!"

"Here! Here!"

"No Australian soldier of the Great War is better known than Captain Jacka, and you are all familiar with his extraordinary record. He is one of those versatile men who 'got there' in spite of the difficulties… He was the quickest man that I knew at picking out a 'dud', whether the dud was a general or the last reinforcement." The men laughed. "Like all good soldiers," Brand continued, "Jacka had no time for swank, eye-wash, or make-believe." The laughter grew louder, so Brand raised his hands to calm them down, as he had something serious to say.

"His Military Cross should have been a bar to his VC," the Brigadier concluded. "In fact he had been recommended for it."

"Here! Here!" the men sang in unison.

"Sergeant Buckley is a second Jacka. Again, his gallant exploits need no introduction among this group. Indeed, the Distinguished

Conduct Medal, which he won at a later date than the Victoria Cross, showed that his VC was no 'flash in the pan'. There is much to admire in these men. But in eulogising men like Jacka and Buckley we must not forget those brave men who supported them, and whose only cross is a wooden one."

Brand sat down to a thundering applause from the men. Many of them knew of the tension that had existed between him and Bert at the Front, yet all seemed to now be forgotten. When Bert rose to respond he was among his blood brothers, whom he had seen at their best, and at their worst. There was total silence as he spoke.

"I only tried to do my duty, as each and every man in the AIF had done. We few who won the Victoria Cross were lucky, but we were no different from anyone else. I do not think that a VC should be put in a glass case. He must get back to the fighting and take his chance with the others again."

"Surely there's a flaw in that logic," Ted Rule thought. "You put yourself at an uneven disadvantage in front of your men time and again. You were more than fair to the others. You often carried them. You were unfair to *yourself*."

"The name of our battalion has been made by our honoured dead who lie on Gallipoli and in France," Bert continued. "Each and all, the people who lost a son, a brother, or a husband, must feel proud at the way they died. When it's all boiled down," he said, "we were fighting the Hun for our sweethearts, wives, mothers, and sisters. We did not want to see things happen in Australia like the things we saw in France.

"In conclusion, I would like to recognise, with the utmost admiration, the women who worked tirelessly for the comforts funds. It was through their hard work that we enjoyed the few comforts we had. Every 'digger' must realise that there are no women to beat our own Australians!"

The men clapped and cheered, and the eloquence of his impromptu speech caught Brand by surprise. "Perhaps he is a talker," Brand thought to himself. "He could even make a politician if he had a mind to." There was another aspiring politician in the hall. While far junior to Brand in rank, Sergeant Allen McDonald of Winchelsea also noted the manner of Bert's public speaking. McDonald was already a councillor in the Shire of Winchelsea. After the Battle of Polygon Wood, Bert had recommended him for bravery during the taking of a couple of tough pillboxes. He had volunteered for duty even though he was a married man with children. Now he was the Nationalist Party candidate for the seat of Corangamite.

Ted Rule, Fred Anderson and Jack Garcia had not seen each other for some time. They had come out of Gallipoli as NCOs and went on to become officers in France. Fred had returned to Horsham with his English bride, and felt somewhat miffed by Bert's comments about Australian girls. Ted had married an Australian girl, Muriel Tuck, who was the daughter of a stock and station agent from Cobram. Things were rough on the marriage front since the boys got back from the war, and the law courts were now filling with divorce cases. It was always the same old story. The digger returns after a number of years and is confronted with his wife's infidelity. It doesn't take much of a spark to set fire to a marriage. It might be a whisper from a neighbour, a chance sneer that is overheard, or the chance discovery of an incriminating letter. Or there may be a child, only a few months old. Then it's off to the courts. But it wasn't always the woman's fault. The behaviour of some of the married diggers in Egypt and France was less than honourable – even Monash offended on that score.

Jack Garcia could not believe how friendly Brand was being to Bert now that they were back. "It's as if he's been reborn and sees Bert in a new light," he said.

"Because he knows Bert is no threat to him," Ted suggested. "In France his authority was challenged by Bert's popularity. Here he just basks in Bert's reflected glory!"

"I still reckon they have more in common than not," continued Jack. "Remember how Brand screamed the pants off the Yanks in the 27th Division for not mopping up the Hun remnants at the Hindenburg Line?" he said.

"It was talked about for weeks," Fred added. "The Yanks were brave enough all right."

"And suffered very bloody badly as a result," added Sailor Day.

"A bit like us at Gallipoli," Ted said softly. "Full of youthful optimism and naivety."

Ted recalled the time Brand "took" the village of Hebuterne single-handed.

"I remember that!" Sailor Day jumped in. "The British Army was falling back in disarray, and the Old Brig, he walks into their HQ and he asks about the village of Heberterne nearby. 'Occupied by the Hun' he's told. But the Old Brig he hops onto his horse, and accompanied by his Intelligence Officer, does his own look-see... The next thing yer know he's riding back from the village, having gone right through the place, and he's giving us some more of his 'dinkum oil': 'I rode right through Hebuterne, men,' he says, 'and there is not a fucking Fritz in it!'"

"Mind your language, Sailor," Ted interrupted. "We're not in the trenches now."

"It's not my language, sir. It was *his* bloody language," Sailor protested, pointing to the Brigadier.

* * *

At one point Bert was cornered by Captain Ferdie Wright, who led that first contingent of the 14th ashore on the day of the landing at Anzac Cove, and survived to organise Bert's welcome home reception. At thirty-one years of age he was Australasian General Manager of a large Dutch insurance company. A consummate socialiser, he was a Freemason, a member of the Naval and Military Club, the Savage Club *and* the Australian Club.

"You're looking a little more relaxed tonight," Ferdie said.

"Sorry?"

"More relaxed than on the first day, the frenzied reception you received?"

"Oh that, I just had to leave. I'm terribly sorry."

"I hear that you're setting up an import business at the Olderfleet," Ferdie said, rocking back and forth gently on his feet while holding a glass of beer. "That's just around the corner from where I'm located, in Queen Street, at the Batavia Sea and Fire Insurance Company. We sell insurance to importers and exporters. Look after the stock in transit and all that," Ferdie said in full flight. "You'll be needing some insurance I take it?"

"I dare say we will. Is it mates' rates?"

"Not in the insurance game, old boy," Ferdie laughed. "But we'd take damned good care to look after your interests."

Ferdie was not joking about the rates. Crucifixion would have been the entree. He would have been hung, drawn and quartered as well. Yes, it was all very chummy in Melbourne society's club land of the early 1900s, and that went for business too. Many major insurance companies from around the world had their headquarters in Melbourne, and it was all ruled over by a body called The Tariff. As a result everybody was charged exactly the same price for insurance products, so the inefficient could survive, and the larger operators could make money, hand-over-iron-fist. An older man in his late fifties, a civilian, approached them. Ferdie could see him across Bert's shoulder.

"Here's someone you'll recognise," said Ferdie. "He's been telling me about you all night!"

It was Newton Wanliss, a retired solicitor from Ballarat, who was the only non-AIF man at the function. His only son, Captain Harold Wanliss DSO, had been killed at the Battle of Polygon Wood. Newton was very close to his son, and was living in London at the time, waiting for news from the front lines. Newton first met Bert in London in 1918, when he was recovering in hospital from the gassing he had sustained at Villers Brettoneux. Ferdie had never known Harold, as he joined the 14th in Egypt after the Gallipoli campaign.

Newton gave Bert a firm squeeze with his hand. Bert liked him, and his son. He had described Harold as "the truest and best gentleman in the Battalion" in a condolence letter he wrote to Newton. Newton printed it and a number of others in a pamphlet as a collection of impressions of his deceased son by those who had known him. Of the 60,000 Australian fathers who had lost sons in the Great War, Newton was unique. So was his son.

Newton thanked Bert again for the letter. If he lived at all, Newton lived so that he would remember his son, and that Australia would not forget him as a symbol of the future the country had lost. Bert told Newton that he wished Harold might have been with them now, and Newton choked on his words as tried to talk. He simply nodded agreement. In the pause both Bert and Ferdie were feeling some discomfort, and then it came to Bert.

"There is a way for you to preserve his memory, you know," he said. "You could write the history of the 14th Battalion."

Newton was taken by surprise, but he couldn't hide the inner joy that came over him. He smiled. "But I wasn't there," he said, "and in any event, I'm not a military man."

"That works in your favour," Bert smiled back, "and you read a great deal of military history. You told me so yourself."

Newton was fifty-seven years old, and was about to re-marry in two weeks' time. His first wife Margaret, was the daughter of a squatter, John Boyd. Having given birth to Harold and his sister Marion, she died of a heart condition in September 1900, not long after Marion's arrival. Harold was still a young boy and Marion could not remember her mother. Newton had brought them up on his own, and now that Marion had left the house he was marrying again, for companionship in his older years. Coincidentally, his new bride was a Margaret too. They met at Point Lonsdale, where Newton's country house overlooked the heads of Port Phillip Bay.

* * *

Not far away Digger Brand was giving a small group the good oil on Australian politics. A Federal election was coming up and the AIF's man, the "Little Digger", Prime Minister William Morris Hughes, the man who had once been a member of the Socialist League, was having another go as a Nationalist. After the conscription debate fractured the old Labor Party, Hughes formed the National Labor Party and then merged with the Liberal Party to form the Nationalist Party of Australia. He was standing for the seat of Bendigo.

"It'll be a lively Senate with Elliott storming though it," said Brand, who knew Brigadier-General Harold "Pompey" Elliott only too well from Gallipoli and the Western Front. He had no doubts that Elliott's elevation to the Senate would put a cat among the pigeons. He also raised the candidacy of Brigadier-General Drake-Brockman, a man who was only alive thanks to the timely intervention of Private "Paddy" Reid on the first morning at Gallipoli. The diggers had given so much of themselves to the country that they believed they had earned the right to live in a society that would justify the sacrifice – a country fit for heroes.

But the main point was that they were home. A few of the boys started singing the mellow sounding song that they had sung on many cold nights in France or Belgium, huddled around fires in cosy dugouts if they were lucky, but more often out in the elements with nothing but a sheet of corrugated iron over them to keep the rain off, and a biting wind swirling about them. Soon the song was picked up by everyone in the room:

> *Keep the home fires burning,*
> *While your heart is yearning,*
> *While the boys are far away,*
> *They dream ... of ... home.*

They *were* home now, and while they had mostly left these shores as boys, they had returned, in the words of the 14th Battalion's much-loved Padre Rolland, "such men."

* * *

Olderfleet Building, 475 Collins Street, Melbourne, Friday, 20 February 1920

Bert's business was registered and launched early in 1920. An advertisement appeared in *The Argus* on Thursday, 12 February for the Fort-Reviver summer beverage. It was already available in all stores. Unfortunately, over the next few days they discovered that Captain Parker was not the officer and gentleman that he purported to be, but a big broke liar instead. The money that he had promised to contribute to the business for his share never materialised, so the company known as Parker, Roxburgh and Jacka & Co. ceased to exist, and a new company called Roxburgh, Jacka & Co. Pty Ltd was formed, with the cable address, ROJAC Melbourne, and a direct telephone line, Central 393. Dick Lean came over from Stadiums Limited that day to see how the restructured business was going.

"I advise you to quickly place another advertisement in *The Argus* for the Fort-Reviver so that everyone knows that Parker's gone and the agency is ours," Dick said.

Apart from that hiccup, things were progressing well. Reg was working all his business contacts, as was Ernie, who'd been a commercial traveller and knew just about everyone there was in the city and country. While Bert was new to the game of commerce it was exciting, and he was keen to succeed. Bert was the best-known front-line AIF personality of the war, and his name could open doors, even some he didn't want to enter. Around this time a movement sprang up to induce him to run as the democratic candidate for Ballarat West in the State elections. Nothing could have been further from his mind, as politics was not his game, he said.

"Shall we go somewhere for a drink to celebrate the start of the new business?" Reg announced.

"What about the Federal Coffee Palace?" Bert suggested, and Dick Lean nodded agreement. It was a grand but dry establishment situated on the corner of King and Collins Streets, less than a city block away.

"Come on, skipper, I want a real drink," whined Reg. "It's Friday afternoon, for goodness sake."

"Let *me* suggest something," Ernie said, breaking the deadlock. "The Commercial Travellers' Club."

"I assume they've got a bar?" asked Reg.

"We do," said Ernie with a smile.

"Well, what are we waiting for?" said Reg, flicking his hat onto his head. "Let's go and celebrate."

They were on the street in a minute and making their way to the Commercial Travellers' Club at 318 Flinders Street. It was among the most impressive clubs in the city, and for style, comfort and facilities it alone rivalled the Melbourne and the Australian clubs. Inspired by the Royal Automobile Club, London, when completed in 1914 it was among the first buildings in the city to have a revolving glass door at the front. Upon entering the building they found themselves in the middle of a large circular vestibule, with eight elegant white Ionic scroll columns that soared two floors through a circular balcony above them. The white vaulted ceiling had a complex gumleaf motif etched in plaster, and a brass and copper chandelier hanging from it. The floor was laid out in tiny cream tessellated tiles that were mostly covered by a thick Turkish carpet. On the left were the lifts, which could carry members up eight floors to the 150 hotel-style bedrooms that were used by country and interstate commercial travellers or club members when they were in town.

They were about to wheel around to the bar, when the President of the Club, Mr J.T. Pemberton, came down the stairway. Captain Edmonds took the opportunity to proudly introduce his famous VC business partner, Dick, and Reg. In the bar he found a table for four near the leadlight window, which drew light from Flinders Street.

"My shout," declared Ernie. "What'll it be?"

"Mine'll be a double shot of Harvey's Special Scotch Whiskey," announced Reg with precision. "I call it 'the shotgun'," he said with a chuckle.

"Any lemonade will do me," said Bert.

"Me too," said Dick, which caused Reg to raise an eyebrow. He hadn't picked Dick for a teetotaller like Bert. As there wasn't a waiter in sight, Ernie went to the bar and placed the order directly with the barman.

"They didn't have any Harvey's, Reg," Ernie explained when he got back, "I hope you don't mind? I ordered Joshua's Boomerang for you."

"That will do nicely," Reg replied. He wasn't the only digger to have acquired a taste for spirits during the war. They handed out rum by the barrel during those cold winters in France, and many swore they would have frozen solid without a stiff drink. The trouble was, they were no longer in the freezing trenches, but Reg was still pursuing his old habits.

"I propose a toast to Roxburgh, Jacka and Co.," Reg announced after the drinks arrived. "Long may she sail upon the high seas of industry and commerce! Peace and prosperity to all who sail in her!"

"Here! Here!" they responded, and all took a sip of their drinks. Reg skulled his "shotgun."

"I *like* this drink," said Reg, licking his lips. "It's got a certain amount of *rub* to it," he said rolling the "r".

After he had downed his beer, Ernie suggested that they move on to the club's billiards hall before the Friday afternoon rush got there. Bert was keen, but Reg didn't want to move, so Ernie told him that he and Dick could put everything on his chit, and would see them in the billiards hall when they were ready.

* * *

When Bert walked into the billiards hall with Ernie, he could hardly believe his eyes. Laid out before him in a huge auditorium were seven full-sized, top quality Alcock billiard tables. This was one of the biggest billiards saloons in the city. One of the tables was just becoming free as Bert and Ernie approached, and they were able to get on almost immediately. They selected their cue sticks and rolled the white balls down the cloth – Ernie took the spotted ball, leaving Bert with the plain. Then Ernie went over to the small marble table next to the long brown leather bench seat, and pointed to a small button.

"Reg should have come," he said with a smile. "He could have pressed this button to call for a drink."

Bert started by pocketing a loser, and went on to make a break of thirteen. In reply, Ernie managed a succession of cannons and hazards to bring up an opening break of nine.

"You've improved since the last time we played," Ernie commented. They had only played a couple of times in France prior to the Battle of Bullecourt.

"I was Sports Officer at Sutton Veny, remember?" Bert said. "It gave me time to improve my game. I also read some books on how to play for position with *mathematical* precision!"

"Have you read anything by John Roberts Junior?"

"No, but I saw him play once. Interesting stance; gets right down onto his cue, like this," Bert demonstrated by lining up a cannon.

"Have I ever told you the story about the exhibition match Roberts played in front of a group of Chinese nobles?" Ernie said.

"No, I don't think you have. That's three more, old boy, which makes seven."

"The group of nobles included some of the great men of the Celestial Empire. Well, the story goes that when Roberts attempted a fancy shot, he put some real power behind it and missed – but he split the red ball in half, driving one half of it into one top pocket and the other half into the other pocket! Yet he retained his composure as if he had *meant* to do it that way. It was all going well until the presiding prince sent his interpreter to Roberts asking that he repeat the shot."

"And? Did he?" asked Bert, as he lined up a winning hazard and potted the red for another three points.

"No. His reply was something like: 'Kindly inform his Serene Highness that I never do it more than once in an exhibition of fancy shots!'"

* * *

Once Bert and Ernie had gone, Reg called the waiter over to his table again.

"Be a good man, and get me another double Boomerang, will you?" he said looking over at Dick. "And?"

"A lemonade, please?"

"Come on Dick, Bert's gone now," Reg sighed with relief. He was sure that this tough boxing industry promoter was putting on an act to please Bert. "You can order what you like!"

"I don't care if he's here or not. I don't drink alcohol – period," Dick stated firmly.

"You heard him," Reg told the waiter.

"I was only trying to be *sociable*," Reg emphasised after the waiter had gone. When the drinks arrived Reg made short work of his second double and soon ordered a third.

"Shouldn't you try to pace yourself a bit more?"

"Oh no. I learned how to hold my liquor in France. Don't you worry about that!" Reg insisted. "Now tell me, how's Stadiums Limited coming along?"

"You haven't seen anything yet," said Dick proudly. "We have plans to go into moving pictures in a big way."

"What about the boxing?" Reg asked. "Seen any good fights recently?"

"Oh, I can tell you about a *bad one* we had a couple of weeks ago," Dick said with a smile, "it shows you the mischief that some bods in this game can get up to. I had two boxers in a preliminary bout who were announced as weighing ten stone three pounds and ten stone six. As the second boxer was clearly heavier than the weight announced, there was a roar from the crowd: 'Who weighed the bastard?' they called out, and when the 'bastard' knocked out his opponent there was a further roar of disapproval from the crowd. I rushed over to the dressing room as fast as I could and told the winner to get on the scales. You know what the cheeky bastard says to me? 'I'll lose the money if I do that.' And I say, 'You'll lose the money if you don't!' So he gets on the scales, and out goes the needle like we all thought. Then I ask the clerk of scales who weighed him, and the clerk admits that he did, but the boxer comes back at him and says, 'You're a bloody liar. You never! You weighed me twin brother, and *I* fought!' "

Reg almost fell over laughing and motioned for the waiter again.

"What about *your* boss?" Reg asked through squinted eyes, slurring his voice. "I'll bet he gets up to some tricks!"

"Oh, he's strictly above board," Dick shot back defensively. "He's got to be or we'd be out of business in five minutes. As you can see from that story I just told you, there's not much you can put over a crowd."

"The usual, old chap," Reg said to the waiter. "I meant, what's he like to work for?" Reg turned to face Dick. The last thing he wanted was to make Dick feel uncomfortable.

"What is he like to work for?" Dick asked rhetorically. He thought about it for a second. "You couldn't wish to work for a better man."

* * *

"Damn," said Bert after failing to convert a cannon.

"That's nineteen," Ernie said. "You can't be unhappy with that!" He was being beaten on his own turf.

"From the way you are taking to this club, Bert, I think you should join," Ernie said earnestly, "really you should."

"But I'm not a commercial traveller?"

"Neither am I," replied Ernie, raising his eyebrows as he sprawled across the green table to line up the red for a winner. "Not anymore at least. But you don't need to be a commercial traveller to join the club." He followed through with his shot, a gentle clip to the red ball that missed the corner pocket and opened up an opportunity for Bert to nurse a series of cannons there. "You are a merchant engaged in commerce, aren't you?"

"Yes, but only very recently."

Ernie's blue eyes beamed as he smiled. "So what's the problem?"

"All right. What do I need to do?" Bert said, cracking the ball sharply for a curve shot.

"That's three. Be a decent chap," Ernie replied while resting his hands on his upright cue, "which you *are*, of course. I'll organise the whole thing for you, and put it up to the Committee. You've met the President, and he'd be over the moon if you were to join. Seriously. We've already got one VC, Captain Grieve, but there's always room for another."

Bert was flattered by his friend's faith in him. Despite his fame, Bert felt deeply honoured to be invited to join this fabulous club and its fraternity.

* * *

When Reg arrived at the billiards hall, he could hardly hold back his surprise at the size and majesty of it. "Great Scot! There must be eight tables!" he thought. "The Australian Club, for all its grandeur, has only three."

Bert had just finished Ernie off in their second game.

"You left me in a bar with a man who doesn't drink!" Reg yelled across the hall so loudly that several players nearby stopped play, their shots disturbed.

"So?" asked Bert.

Ernie was furious.

"Well, it's not much fun… is it?" said Reg, his eyes watery.

"You're drunk, Roxburgh," said Ernie in disgust. "I don't bring my guests to my club to drink themselves under the table." He put his cue stick away. "Come on, we're getting you out of here before someone on the Committee sees you." Ernie took Reg forcefully by the arm and showed him the way to the door.

* * *

John Wren's office, Flinders Lane, 28 February 1920

There was an air of tension felt in John Wren's sparsely furnished city office. A trainer who had been disqualified for pulling up a favourite in a race at Wren's Pony Club had just burst into Wren's office, looking for blood. Wren's Pony Club was known as the "poor man's club" due to the lower entry prices. As noted by Dick, any hint of skulduggery would have demolished the takings at the gate, so Wren kept the show as honest as possible by employing stewards, who had the power to replace jockeys at a moment's notice if the prices of the odds appeared not to reflect past performance, or moved inexplicably.

"You've ruined me, and I'm going to shoot you!" the trainer screamed, pointing his finger menacingly at Wren, who was sitting behind his desk. Without batting an eyelid, Wren opened the drawer at his side, pulled out a revolver, and dropped it on the desk.

"Well, here's my gun. Now where's yours?" he said with steel-eyed determination. "You say I ruined you. I would say you sent hundreds home broke yesterday. Now what about that?"

That shut the trainer up. He had no reply, he knew that Wren meant business. Wren had pushed aside tougher nuts than this one.

"I thought so. Now get out of my office!"

The trainer disappeared through the door without turning his back, taking care to close it gently. When Arthur came in Wren was still fuming, but had put the revolver away in the drawer.

He kept it handy because of death threats he had received from the notorious Melbourne criminal Squizzy Taylor, who was ordered to stay away from Wren's pony track.

"John!" said Arthur excitedly.

"What's the problem now?"

"It's Jacka."

"What about him?"

"He's refusing to ride with the other VCs in the St Patrick's Day March."

"You must be joking?"

"I'm *not* joking. He's not taking part at all."

"Did he give a reason?"

"He said it would be betraying the King, who presented him with his VC."

This was a shock to Wren, who saw Bert as the centrepiece of his plan to revive the image of the Archbishop. He couldn't believe it, coming so soon after the financial backing he provided to Bert's business venture.

"How many VCs do we have so far?"

"Fourteen."

"Well, that will do nicely, but I was counting on Jacka. Are the horses organised yet?"

"That's been a hard slog, but we're almost there. Now, you do realise they're grey, not white?"

"Get my agents in New South Wales and Queensland going," Wren suggested. "I don't care how much they cost. Grey will do. White horses only exist in fairytales."

"John," Arthur said, fixing his brother's attention, "there's more bad news about Jacka."

"What now?" sighed Wren.

"He's a Freemason."

"You are certain of that? A Freemason?"

They were times of extreme religious sectarianism, when professional firms dominated by Protestant/Masonic partners would not hire Catholics, and vice versa. It was very common for Protestant officers in the AIF to be Freemasons. When he led the 7th Battalion at Gallipoli as a Lieutenant-Colonel, Harold "Pompey" Elliott suddenly discovered that he was the only one out of more than twenty officers in his battalion who was *not* a Freemason. So as not to feel out of it, Pompey joined up too, making a special trip to Cairo to be invested.

"We could shut his business down tomorrow," Arthur suggested, but Wren put his hands together in his praying pose, and exhaled into them, deep in thought.

"I think that's good," he said, finally.

"We close him down then?"

"No… It's *good* that he's a Freemason," Wren said to Arthur's surprise. "A man's got to be on one side or the other. Not a fence sitter. It shows character. Did you know that Dick Lean is a Freemason? That's right and he's a good man, so is Jacka from what I can see. I can understand his sense of honour to the King. He has his principles, and we have ours."

* * *

7 am, Middle Park Hotel, Tuesday, 9 March 1920

Bert woke in a cold sweat, spluttering and coughing. He couldn't shake the recurrent bronchitis he had contracted after being gassed during the war. He sat up in bed and breathed deeply to remind himself that the air *is* sweet, not drenched with poison gas. He stared at the fireplace ahead of his bed for a few seconds and the image vanished. It was still early, but he could see from the shining slivers of light piercing the drawn curtains, that it was going to be a glorious day. He slipped out of bed and drew the curtains back, letting the sun flood into the large room. Standing up made it easier to breathe, and he opened the window to let in some fresh air. The sound of carts and cars, and the occasional train, could be heard clearly now; the Middle Park station was just across the road. He glanced at his cigarette case, cursed it, as he knew it wasn't helping his cough, then placed it next to his wallet so he wouldn't forget to take it with him to work.

He walked over to the desk and checked the date on his calendar. "The interviews," he thought, "I must be at the office sharply at 9 am." He pulled on his morning robe and made his way around to the bathroom located at the end of the corridor. Having washed, shaved and dressed in his three-piece suit, he went down the winding staircase to the ground floor. The smell of last night's beer wafted through from the door to the bar on his right. He, however, was attracted by the smell of bacon and eggs that came from the dining room on his left. It lingered in his nostrils while he slipped across the road and bought *The Argus* from the newsagent/ tobacconist located in the row of shops in Armstrong Street. This was just one of the conveniences of living at the Middle Park Hotel – another was its proximity to the beach, just a few blocks down Armstrong Street.

There were only four or five people sitting in the dining room and they all looked up when Bert entered the room. Everyone who ate in that dining room always looked up when someone new came into the room, just in case it was Bert.

The waitress asked if he would be having the usual. He answered in the affirmative, and went to the table nearest the window. It had better light for reading and was generally unoccupied. *The Argus* was a broadsheet, and not easy to manage at breakfast, no matter how big the table was. You had to plough through three sheets before you got to the first news page, which was page six, and then you had to fold it once or twice if you wanted to hold it with one hand.

There were two themes dominating the paper that morning. The impending visit of the Prince of Wales was exercising people's imaginations. It was known that he would be celebrating his twenty-sixth birthday in Australia. There was speculation about whether he would be able to view the Head of the River races on the Yarra, and whether he might set a foundation stone at the site of the nation's new capital city of Canberra, which was under construction. Bert was looking forward to the Prince's visit, as he had been very cordial to him at previous meetings in Buckingham Palace and Windsor Castle.

A more controversial issue was the looming St Patrick's Day procession, which was the subject of heated debate at the Melbourne City Council. That debate had been about whether approval for processions should be the sole prerogative of the Lord Mayor, as was the current practice, or whether the decision of the council as a whole would be required. The Lord Mayor, Councillor J.G. Aikman MLC, had put the motion to his councillors in an atmosphere charged by a hostile gallery of onlookers. Bert read on.

"As you all know," said the Lord Mayor, "I have had a bad time in settling this very vexed question. The resolution I am asking you to alter was passed 40 years ago, when the streets were not so crowded."

Councillor B.B. Deveney — And there were not so many bigots about.

Several Voices — Oh, don't start that. (Hear, hear).

The Lord Mayor said that he would not have introduced his resolution had he not been assured that the coming St. Patrick's Day procession would be a credit to the city, and one of which no loyal man would have any cause to complain. (Hear, hear).

Alderman James H. Gardiner — Are you going to allow horses?

The Lord Mayor — The Union Jack is going to be carried in the very front of the procession — (Cheers) — and the Australian Coat of Arms will be carried as well. (Cheers) We have that in writing. The Union Jack, proceeded the Lord Mayor, was one of the best possible emblems and guarantees of the loyalty of the procession. The Lord Mayor added, "We have many loyal Irish citizens — some of the most loyal you could find in the British Empire. (Hear, hear) I have had a very bad time in connection with this question. I have been misunderstood, called all sorts of names, and mentioned in all sorts of ways, and I am still firm because I want to settle this trouble and bring all hearts together."

Councillor Deveney spoke against the resolution. Though much of what he said was inaudible in the press gallery because of interruption, he was heard to denounce those who were always "looking through orange colour to get a glimpse of the Union Jack," and shout the warning, "but for God's sake don't get green in it." He went on to denounce the bigotry which, he declared, had always been in evidence in Melbourne. "Today," he cried, "it is Dr. Mannix. Before he came——"

Councillor Crespin — There was no trouble! (Laughter and cheers).

Bert thanked his lucky stars that he was not part of this mess. If he had acceded to Wren's request his name would have been dragged through this circus. For his part, he had nothing against Catholics. At the war there was no time to ask a man whether he was a Protestant or a Catholic. It was enough that he was Australian.

* * *

After breakfast Bert caught the 8:35 train into the city, passing the Albert Park Lake on the way. He walked briskly down Collins Street, and into the foyer of the Olderfleet buildings. Seeing that the lift door ahead of him was closing, he sprinted the last few steps and forced the grate back, which stopped its mechanism. Once inside, he pushed the button for level three. The door closed, and the lift jerked into motion. It was only then that he turned around and saw an extremely attractive young woman staring at him.

"You're Albert Jacka, aren't you?" she asked with an elegant smile.

"Yes."

She took a step forward, almost involuntarily, as if drawn to him by a moving floor, and hugged him with both her arms. Bert was stunned. His face blushed in an instant.

"What was that for?"

"Oh, I'm sorry," she said. "I couldn't help myself. It's just that I've been reading stories about you throughout the war."

He was touched by her straight from the heart confession, and there was all round embarrassment, but he also loved being hugged by an attractive young woman. "Now here's an Aussie girl with gumption," he thought.

"Don't be," he said.

"Well, I've ruined it now, haven't I?" she said with a shrug of her shoulders.

"What have you ruined?"

"My interview," she said.

He managed a smile. "So you are one of the applicants for the typist's position?"

"Yes, I am."

"Well," Bert suggested as they came out of the lift, "why don't we just start again? Let's just pretend we haven't met." Before she could close her mouth, he walked through the frosted glass door of Roxburgh, Jacka & Co. at the end of the corridor and closed the door behind him.

"Good morning," said Ernie.

"Don't look now, but I think our first appointment has arrived," Bert said, throwing his hat up onto a hook. "Where's Reg?"

"Not here yet," he answered. There was a knock at the door. "I'll get it," said Ernie, snatching a piece of paper from a desk.

"Good morning," he said, glancing at the paper. "You must be Miss Frances Veronica Carey?"

"Yes."

"I'm Ernest Edmonds and this is my business partner, Mr Albert Jacka."

"The pleasure is all mine, Miss Carey," said Bert, acting the part.

"Would you care to join us in the boardroom?" asked Ernie pointing the way. They went through to the boardroom, which had no windows and had a central table seating eight. Ernie recorded a number of preliminaries about Miss Carey's background and experience; her ability to take down 110 words per minute in shorthand, type eighty words per minute, and type fifty-five words a minute with complete accuracy. Then they got to the bottom line.

"You do realise, don't you," said Ernie, "that this position pays three pounds a week, and that you could obtain ten shillings a week more in the Public Service?"

"Yes, I do."

"Then why would you want to work in our firm?" Ernie probed.

"Because I have heard that you are a reputable and successful firm. And there will be a review after twelve months."

"That is correct," said Ernie.

"Reputable without a doubt," Bert added, "but our success lies ahead of us. We haven't even started our full business operation as yet."

"Then... I am sure you *will* succeed," she said with a smile.

"She's very good looking," Bert thought, "and so self-possessed for her age."

"How can you be so sure of that?"

"Because you are Albert Jacka."

There was complete silence for a few seconds after she had uttered those words. She said it with complete confidence, looking straight into his eyes. It embarrassed him, and after a momentary pause a faint smile appeared in his face. Ernie's smile was much more obvious.

"How would you propose to contribute to that success, practically?" Bert asked, trying to maintain his serious composure.

"I would hope, sir, to be able to provide you with every satisfaction from my work," she stated with surety, "and I do realise that it would involve a certain amount of sacrifice."

"Are you willing to make that sacrifice, Miss Carey?"

"I do… Yes, I would, sir," she said. He wanted to tell her to stop calling him "sir", but thought it might appear too familiar and unprofessional. There was something about this young woman's manner that interested him. The immediate familiarity that appeared to exist between them did not escape Ernie, and it stayed at the back of his mind for the rest of the morning as the other four candidates were being interviewed. They went to lunch at the dining room of the Commercial Travellers' Club, where Bert's application for membership had already gone through the committee stage and was coming up for the ballot to be held at the end of April.

"Well, I can't believe the quality of candidates we attracted," Ernie announced. "That Miss Lawson we saw topped Stott's Business College last year!"

"Now, hang on a minute," Bert said, "I think I can recall her vital statistics: 160 words per minute in shorthand, 90 typed, and 70 words with perfect accuracy. How's *that* for memory?" After seeing all five girls he had his own opinion, but he wanted to hear Ernie's views, and if they were to differ from his own, he would then tackle him.

"Well, what do *you* say?"

"You know what I think?" Ernie said with a pause to draw breath. "Miss Carey by two lengths. She certainly knows how to make an impression."

"That's an understatement!" Bert said, thinking of the lift incident. "You know, I happen to agree with you. I didn't want to say it until you did. It's always better to be first for an interview, don't you think? It gives that interviewee the chance to make an impression that will set the benchmark that others are compared against." He looked at Ernie for further confirmation. "She had a certain quality about her, didn't she?"

"A sparkle, I'd call it."

"She doesn't have the technical skills of some of the others…"

"Good Lord, we won't need shorthand at 160 words per minute," Ernie cut in. "That's almost three words a second! I can't think that fast."

"Miss Carey it is then."

"What about Reg?"

"Well, he should have been here, shouldn't he?" Bert grumbled. "But he'll get his chance to vet the office boy and the commercial travellers, won't he?"

* * *

Vera was thrilled to hear she had been chosen for the job. She was barely twenty-one years of age, and still living with her parents at 67 Bayview Street, Prahran, which was something of a misnomer, given the total absence of *any* view, let alone one of the bay. It was a strange suburb, Prahran, where there was a mixture of "upstairs" and "downstairs" streets around the corner from one another. The wider streets with mansions on them tended to run north-south, while the narrow streets lined with workers' cottages generally ran east-west. Vera's parents' house was one of those wooden, single-fronted workers' cottages that had virtually no backyard.

Vera's father John had recently retired. Her older sister's name was Mary Magdalene, reflecting the family's Catholic background, but at home she was simply Molly. Already twenty-six, Molly thought she had only a few more years left in her, and then no one would want to marry her. In the last few years, as Vera had grown up, they had become very close. Vera's younger brother Jim was only eighteen, but had already left home to take up labouring jobs out in the country at Mansfield.

The first couple of weeks were uneventful, although the firm did hire an office boy, Richie, who would run errands for them around town, and a number of commercial travellers were hired on a contract basis to visit prospective customers. Vera was hard at work every day helping to build a card index system that would store the firm's client and contact names, addresses and telephone numbers. In the process she came to know the personalities of the three ex-AIF partners, but saw Dick Lean and Arthur Wren as strangers, as they visited only once during that time.

Vera thought that Mr Edmonds was very nice to everyone and would never lose his temper about anything. Bert was tougher in his business dealings than Ernie and could sometimes be heard arguing with Mr Roxburgh behind closed doors. Mr Roxburgh, she noticed, was much less regular than the other two, who appeared to apply military-like discipline to everything. Their characters were revealed in the way they interacted with her as a shorthand-typist. Mr Edmonds and Mr Jacka would dictate, and expect her to correct any little error they may have made; to clean up the "bloomers". This kept her on her toes at all times when she worked for them, and she enjoyed it. Mr Roxburgh on the other hand, seemed very jovial some mornings and depressed on other days. On those rotten days he would flush with anger if she attempted to provide the word he was looking for.

For his part, Bert enjoyed Vera working for him because she was so much fun. Spending a whole day dictating, correcting and issuing a batch of letters might have been boring if someone else had been involved, but doing it with Vera made the hours pass quickly. Every day at 3.45 pm she would make afternoon tea for the three partners, and during that fifteen-minute interval there would often be a chance for a chat that went beyond business affairs. She felt that something was brewing when she, from time to time, caught Bert stealing furtive glances at her as she worked.

One day in early April, Bert called her into his office to take some dictation, so she came in with her notebook and sat down. He often looked worried, and she was right. For the last few weeks he had been thinking of nothing but her and had kept those emotions bottled up.

"Miss Carey," he began formally. "Vera," he sighed with relief at having said it finally. "You don't mind me calling you Vera, do you?"

"Not at all, Captain, um, Mr Jacka."

"Well, in that case, you must call me Bert, and not Captain or Mr Jacka."

"But that would not seem right in the office," she pleaded. "How would it look in front of others? How would it look to Richie?"

"I see your point," he said. "In that case, I would want you to call me Bert after hours."

"But I don't see you after hours."

"Well, that's what I am getting to. I was wondering. What I mean to say is…would you do me the honour of allowing me to take you to dinner one evening?"

Vera studied him closely as he spoke and saw that he was not completely comfortable with the proposition. He was asking her very politely, yet his voice seemed to have something of a command about it too. Perhaps it was just that he had been an officer and was used to command. She couldn't deny her inner feelings either. Since the day they literally bumped into each other, and she had hugged him in the lift, it seemed that the rest of the story was pre-ordained. It seemed like destiny.

"Yes, I would like that very much," she smiled.

* * *

The memorable St Patrick's Day procession of 1920 began at 1 pm on Saturday, 20 March at St Patrick's Hall, with the marchers heading up Bourke Street, turning at Parliament House into Spring Street and finishing up at the Exhibition Buildings. At the head of the procession rode the fourteen VCs on their grey chargers to great applause, and behind them Archbishop Mannix rode in a car with several ex-AIF Catholic chaplains. Next came a column of more than 6000 ex-diggers in uniform, marching behind two large Australian flags, and after them were motor vehicles carrying nurses and wounded men. The absence of Sinn Fein colours and emblems pleased those who had been concerned about the march, but they were roundly disappointed by the apparent symmetrical absence of the Union Jack, which had been a condition of the Lord Mayor's approval.

The Union Jack was being carried in the procession, but you needed a magnifying glass to see it. Tucked away in the corner of the banner of the St Patrick's Society, which measured nine feet by twelve feet, drawn by four horses adorned in green and gold, was a Union Jack measuring twelve inches by fifteen inches. Full-sized Union Jacks were flying from flagpoles nearby, while a banner in the procession read: "Angel of Light Give Ireland Her Right." Over 2000 boys from Christian Brothers' schools marched in the procession.

* * *

At 6.30 pm Bert Jacka jumped out of a cab onto the wet pavement in Bayview Street, Prahran, and knocked on the door of Vera Carey's house. She opened the door with a big smile. Her eyes sparkled from flushed cheeks. Immediately he was struck by the scent of her perfume, which stopped his heart.

"Good evening, Bert," she said confidently.

He paused to take in a secret breath of her perfume, and was swept away by the way she looked. He had always been struck by how attractive and elegant she looked, but had only seen her in her formal business attire.

"Good evening," he managed finally, after swallowing hard.

"You must come in and meet my parents," she said, and led him into the small lounge room off the narrow passage – the only room having a view to the street. Her father was a shy man, but was thrilled that his daughter was being taken to dinner by the famous war hero and up and-coming businessman.

The Carey's were a working-class family, and Bert could certainly relate to that, even though his present situation suggested merchant middle class. If there was something that Bert and Vera shared in common, it was that they were the dreamers in their respective families. When he was still in the ranks Bert dreamt that he could be an officer, even though the odds were stacked against him. Then he

dreamt of establishing a business and it had come into being. He had
also dreamt about meeting the girl that he would marry.

As a teenage girl Vera had read about Albert Jacka VC, who
became her hero. She sought out and read everything that was
written about him, and talked about him constantly to her sister.
Since she started working for him that seemed to be all she could
talk about. Now the course of her life seemed to be flowing like
a dream.

* * *

The horse-drawn cab glided through Prahran along Williams Road
towards the St Kilda foreshore, and finally clip-clopped to a stop in
front of the magnificent Esplanade Hotel. Originally designed as
three large terrace houses, it was the epitome of elegance, standing
on a small hill overlooking the bay. Bert had first seen the hotel
in December 1914, on the day that Padre Andrew Gillison had
consecrated the 14th Battalion's Regimental and King's Colours on
the lawns facing the sea on the other side of the road. The chaplain
had laid his hands upon the Colours and said,

> In the name of the Father, and of the Son, and of the Holy Ghost, we
> do dedicate and set apart these Colours, that they may be a sign of
> our duty towards our King and Country, in the sight of God. Amen.

To Bert, the Colours, and the words, meant everything. What Bert
could not have dreamed of that day, was that six years later he
would return to this spot, to dine at this hotel with a beautiful
woman at his side. He felt proud as he led her through the dining
room to the reserved table for two near a window. He could tell
that the men in the room, and even some of the women, turned
their heads to watch her. The dining room's linen service was
heavy, and the menu extensive. They ordered their meals and
spoke generally about subjects that hadn't come up at work.

"I love the seaside," he said finally. "Don't you?"

"Oh, I love it too – but not the sea, not to swim. It's all the excitement around here that I love," she answered with a smile at a recollection. "When I was young, before the war, we lived in Seymour and we used to come here as a family in summer. Dad bought tickets for us to ride the beautifully painted horses on Weniger's merry-go-round. The music played very loudly and hundreds of glittering lights reflected from the big mirrors as we rode up and down. Mum held Jim, and Molly held me, but Dad would never ride. He just watched us from the ground and laughed at the fun we were having, and we would wait for our painted horse to come around so we could wave to him again."

"Sounds marvellous," Bert said, picturing a young Vera laughing at the top of her voice. "In Wedderburn we hardly ever got a chance to ride a big merry-go-round, unless there was a carnival on. But why didn't your father ride with you when you had come such a long way?"

"It wasn't that he didn't want to," she said sadly. "He was simply trying to save money I think. We never rode together and now we never will. He's not well. But you know, he could have ridden with us. It wasn't that expensive."

"I suppose we do see things more clearly when it's too late."

"Then a terrible thing happened during the war," she continued. "One summer's night, a mob of unruly soldiers went to Weniger's merry-go-round and said that Mr Weniger was a German, and not loyal, and that he should be closed down. There was a riot and a lot of people got hurt."

"We saw that kind of riot in Cairo, and also in England after the war," said Bert shaking his head. "There were some huge temptations acting on the boys after the war too." It was the only part of the record of the AIF that Bert wasn't proud of. Some of the boys pushed the larrikin factor too far, and it only took the efforts of a very tiny percentage to create a bad name for the vast majority who hadn't participated.

"You're close to your sister, aren't you?" he asked after a pause.

Vera thought about it for a little while before answering.

"Molly has always been a great comfort to me as I was growing up. Almost like a second mother. We would often sleep together in the same bed, and talk all night about things."

"About boys?"

"Sometimes," she said. "Sometimes I think that if she spent less time worrying about me, and more time going out and meeting people, she would be married by now."

"She will be married one day," Bert assured her.

"I hope so."

Bert listened to her, spellbound. With almost every sentence she made him smile. For the first time, with Vera, he felt completely at ease with a girl, and it was a liberating experience. While she came from a relatively humble background, Vera's vivacious qualities and charm reminded him of Lady Hallowey, who hosted him and other Australian officers when they inspected the Royal Stables at Buckingham Palace in 1917. He wanted to see her outside of office hours again.

"Vera," he said quietly, "next Friday night there is a gala performance of a new musical play called *As You Were*. I've been invited there with a few others to receive a Gold Life Pass to the Tivoli Theatre circuit."

"You're so lucky," she said warmly.

"I could get you a ticket to the show. We won't be able to sit together, but we could have dinner beforehand, and I could take you home afterwards. What do you say?"

"That would be delightful."

* * *

On the afternoon of the next day, a new Catholic church and school were opened by Archbishop Mannix in Balaclava Road, Caulfield. The Archbishop was still flushed with excitement from the activities of the previous day and applauded the decision of the Lord Mayor to allow it.

"The men who tried to prevent the procession are wiser than they were," Mannix declared. "They are now nearly as wise as I am! They will never prevent Irishmen showing their sympathy with Ireland, while yielding in none in their loyalty to Australia and to the Empire. The Lord Mayor proved himself a man with a big mind. He also proved himself a man of sanity, for while we have seen the gratifying results of his decision, no one can say what the result of any other decision would have been."

On Monday, the VCs were hosted at Raheen mansion, the Kew residence of the Archbishop. It was situated almost diagonally across the road from John Wren's mansion. Wren introduced each VC to Dr Mannix in the grounds of Raheen. The Catholics kissed his Archbishop's ring, while the Protestant VC's merely shook his hand. Then all the VCs signed the Ireland petition to the King, and later that night a farewell concert for the VCs was held at the Exhibition Building. There Dr Mannix said he wished he could confer a VC on John Wren for what he had done.

* * *

8.40 pm, The Tivoli Theatre, Bourke Street, Melbourne, 26 March 1920

The audience was packed with Federal, State, military, naval and municipal representatives. They had responded to the invitation of the British Empire League of Australia to attend the gala performance of *As You Were*. The Prime Minister, the Right Honourable William Morris Hughes sat in the front row with members of his cabinet. The Leader of the Opposition, Mr Frank Tudor, was there too. It was a busy season in Melbourne's live theatre and moving picture calendar. *Tiger Rose* was playing at King's, *Tilly of Bloomsbury* at the Theatre Royal, *Kissing Time* at Her Majesty's, and *Rose of the West* at Hoyt's Lyceum.

As You Were was an adaptation of the French show, *Plus ça change*, with music by Herman Darewski and Edouard Mathe. It began playing at the London Pavilion from August 1918, and was inspired by H.G. Wells's *The Time Machine*. The first Act opened in the year 2018, with the Great War still being fought. Sir Bilyon Boost was disgusted with the fickleness of his French wife, Sidonie, and wanted to escape to a place where there were "neither wars nor women". Professor Biscuit sold him some "transit pills", which had the power to take him to whatever country and time he pleased. Having popped the pills Sir Bilyon travelled to the France of Ninon de Lanclos, the witty and beautiful courtesan in the reign of Louis XIV, to the England of Elizabeth, to ancient Athens, and to the Troy of Helen. Curiously, he found both wars and women at the centre of affairs in all these places.

As soon as the curtain closed for the interval, Bert and his VC colleagues were introduced to some of the players, most notably Miss Vera Pearce, who was playing Sidonie, and Bert Clark, playing Sir Bilyon Boost. At the conclusion of the interval the President of the British Empire League of Australia, the Honourable Hugh D. ("Huge Deal") McIntosh MLC, walked onto the stage and recognised the prime minister, and other distinguished guests in the audience.

"We are very fortunate, indeed privileged, to be an integral part of the British Empire," announced Mr McIntosh, "which guarantees the everyday freedoms that we all take for granted. And we are proud of the part played by the Australian Imperial Force in the defence of the Empire during the last war. We are very proud indeed to have with us tonight, on this very stage, three outstanding Australian winners of the Victoria Cross, who are to receive 'Gold Life Passes', which will entitle the holders to free entry for life to all the theatres on the Tivoli Circuit."

Amid the applause Mr McIntosh called on the State Commandant, Brigadier-General Charles Brand, to introduce them: Captain Albert Jacka, VC; Lieutenant George Ingram, VC;

and Sergeant Maurice Buckley, VC. General Brand had asked Bert to say a few words on behalf of the VCs, which he did in a couple of minutes. It was a great test for Bert, as it was the first time he had spoken in public to such a large gathering outside the army, the first time he had spoken to an audience that included the prime minister, and the first time in front of Vera, who was somewhere out there in the darkness.

"…and in conclusion," said Bert, "I would ask that every time you see four ex-diggers together, you think of the fifth digger, who didn't return, and also think about the two diggers before you who might have returned, but were wounded heavily, and may be in need of assistance. We must never forget the sacrifices those men made for us."

The audience launched into spontaneous applause, and both General Brand and Mr McIntosh shook his hand, but before the clapping had died down completely, Sergeant Buckley stepped forward in a manner that suggested he too wanted to speak. This wasn't part of Brand's agenda.

"Mr Prime Minister, distinguished guests, ladies and gentlemen," Buckley began. "I also wish to thank Mr McIntosh and the management of the Tivoli Theatre for this great gift, and support what Captain Jacka has told you. We fought to bring back freedom to the states of France and Belgium – the right to live in peace in your own country. The leaders of America and the great European powers have brought freedom to many small countries…"

There was spontaneous applause for those thoughts expressed so eloquently by the young VC winner, and Buckley waited patiently until it had subsided again to complete silence.

"…I would also like to express the hope that the same rights will be granted to Ireland, which have been granted to other small nations."

This statement was met with a mixed response. While a section of the audience, including Frank Tudor, applauded heartily, there was a large group of "abstainers", in whose minds this was an unwarranted and untimely political outburst, sitting stony faced.

"Now that is a brave man," thought Bert. "There's probably a dozen men in this audience who would be happy to shoot him for what he just said." The Black-and-Tans had just been dispatched to that country, and the Irish question was a powder keg ready to explode. General Brand was very upset with Buckley's outburst, and quickly rushed back to centre stage with a smile to capture the audience's attention before a more demonstrative gesture of disapproval was evoked.

"The reason, um, that the AIF succeeded," said General Brand, "and Mr McIntosh will be able to fully substantiate this, is that it kept it's best punch for the final round, which is why I have saved some reminiscences of the Great War that I propose to share with you!" It brought some smiles back to the faces of the audience.

* * *

As she was seated near the rear of the theatre, Vera came out first, and was waiting for Bert under the bright lights outside. The crowd was still milling about discussing the play or Buckley's demonstration. Bert recognised Vera from behind and tapped on her shoulder. As she spun around with that radiant smile, she melted his heart again.

"I just saw the prime minister," she said.

"Did you enjoy the play?" he asked.

"I adored it. What about you?"

"Yes, but I had better take you home, young lady, before I shatter your mother's faith in me," he said. As she put her arm under his, she could see that patrons nearby were watching them. She was so proud of how he spoke on stage in front of the most powerful gathering of politicians and bureaucrats in the country, and so happy that he had been presented with such a wonderful prize. She was already imagining a continuous stream of theatregoing with Bert at Tivoli Circuit venues. They walked down to the cab rank at the Town Hall, and saw several cars parked there, with the horse cabs standing behind them. "Sitting on the pot" the cabbies called it. In the case of the hansom cabs, your nose told you that the analogy wasn't far from the truth. Bert decided to take a horse cab again, which he calculated was going to be more romantic, and cost less.

"Sixty-seven Bayview Street, Prahran," he said to the driver, who sat up high holding his whip. "Down Toorak and off Williams."

"Sir!" the driver acknowledged, as Bert opened the door, allowing Vera to enter first. The cab jerked into forward motion and was soon crossing the Princes' Bridge.

"What did you think of the story of the play?" he asked.

"To be able to travel through time and space like that?" she mused. "Wouldn't that be wonderful?"

"What would you do with it, if you had the power to go anywhere you wanted at any time in history?"

"I wouldn't need to go very far," she answered, after a moment's reflection, looking out as the faintly glowing street lamps on the darkened St Kilda Road, and beyond them the silent shadows of the leafy trees in the Domain Gardens, streamed past the side window. "If anything, I would like to go forward to a time not too far distant, when I am married to the man I love, and our children are around us... playing... and we are walking through the Botanical Gardens, arm in arm."

"That's a very pure wish," he said. "I've dreamt of children too, you know? Three or four of them, in fact. I can see them running about."

"Have you given them names – in your dream," Vera laughed, but Bert looked at her with feeling in his eyes, which met hers. Even in this dark cabin her eyes seemed to glow like pearls in the moonlight. There was a pause, as both of them searched for the right words.

"You know that you and I can't be just friends," he said finally. "It's never like that between man and woman. It's love or nothing, Vera. That's what it boils down to, doesn't it?"

"I know."

"So, which will it be?"

They were facing each other directly when he asked, and it was inevitable that their lips should be drawn together in their first passionate kiss. For the rest of the trip they rode sitting very close to each other, not because it was cold, but because they wanted the cuddle. Bert loved the softness and warmth of her body.

* * *

12 noon, St Kilda Pier, Thursday, 27 May 1920

What should have been a simple and triumphant entry to Melbourne by the future monarch of the British Empire was turned into something of a drama by the autumn fog that shrouded the whole of Port Phillip Bay. It was supposed to be a working day, but the whole city had stopped, and come out onto the streets of Melbourne, lining the route that would be driven by him in an open, horse-drawn carriage. Four hundred thousand people, the largest crowd in Australia's history, were in the streets waiting.

Vera and Bert were now a permanent item in everybody's eyes except their parents; those bridges had yet to be crossed. The couple were not crammed onto the Upper and Lower Esplanades, where the first sight of the Prince could be had. Instead, they were halfway up Fitzroy Street at the railway station, a position that had been agreed for the 14th Battalion. It was the first opportunity that Bert had to show off his girlfriend to his former comrades, and she captivated them all with her natural charm, which pleased Bert greatly. For most people it was a study in patience to wait for the Prince for so long without news, and as someone noted, it was "the price of patriotism". For a couple who were falling in love, being together anywhere was an opportunity to be enjoyed.

The *Renown*, the mighty battle cruiser that had carried the Prince to the Antipodes was held up at the Heads. Due to her draft she had to catch an early tide to lift her through that shallow stretch of water, and she had missed it. Meanwhile, hundreds of thousands of people waited from 10 am in one spot, with no means of knowing when he would appear. As time ticked by the program of events had to be changed slightly. As usual in the autumn, after the fog lifted, the afternoon turned out to be glorious. Providence had determined that the son of the King was brought to the New Pier at Port Melbourne at quarter past three by a destroyer bearing the name *Anzac*.

From Port Melbourne, as was the custom, he was taken by a smaller ship, the *Hygeia*, to the official welcome at the St Kilda Pier, where he landed at a quarter to four. At the end of the Pier, the Governor-General, Sir Ronald Munro Ferguson; the Prime Minister, Mr Hughes; the Lieutenant-Governor, Sir William Irvine; and the Premier of Victoria, Mr Harry Lawson were there to welcome him to the sound of the national anthem. Though small in stature, the Prince stood out among them in his youth, the gold braided admiral's uniform he wore, and the naval cockade on his head. The local welcome by the Mayor of St Kilda, Councillor T. G. Allan was brief, as was the Prince's response.

The Prince then mounted the open horse-drawn carriage at the head of two columns of Light Horse troopers. As the Prince's entourage proceeded along the Upper and Lower Esplanades, the long-waiting population of Melbourne erupted into cheers as bands played. Above them all the flags of Australia, Great Britain and the United States flew from the Esplanade Hotel and the *Arcadia Theatre* on the Upper Esplanade. As the Prince's column finally neared the position of the 14th Battalion in Fitzroy Street, they were brought to attention, and Bert snapped a salute for his Prince. After the Prince's carriage passed by, the old battalion broke up and people went their own ways.

Seeing it was such a lovely day Bert took Vera for a long walk around the Albert Park Lake. As Bert walked Vera home later that afternoon, the Prince was still being driven around the city, and through the major thoroughfares of the inner suburbs, so that the maximum number of loyal citizens could witness the heir to the throne.

* * *

10.30 am, Federal Government House, Melbourne, Saturday, 29 May 1920

Two days and many official functions later, an open car carrying the Prince drove out of Federal Government House in the Domain and made its way to the city. The Prince was dressed in mufti this time, but was so recognisable that groups of people began to cheer him at the intersections as his car drew near. Turning at the Town Hall intersection, he was driven up the hill to 36 Collins Street, and went into the Melbourne Club, followed by his ADC, Captain the Honourable P. W. Legh. They walked through the building into the garden at the back, which was not then dominated by its London plane trees, and went into the Racquets Court at the very rear of the property. For almost two hours the Prince and Captain Legh slugged it out on the court with racquets and ball. It was a game, very similar to squash, in which a white ball was belted against tall brown walls. As this was Saturday, the Prince returned to Government House using an alternative route around the city in order to avoid the crowds leaving work around midday.

* * *

Just after 5 pm that afternoon, a large crowd was waiting for the Prince as he arrived at the Commercial Travellers' Association Club in Flinders Street from the showground. Cheer after cheer rose from the crowd when he left his car holding his hat high in acknowledgement of the crowd, accompanied by Rear-Admiral Sir Lionel Halsey and Lieutenant-Colonel E.W.M. Grigg. After signing the visitors' book in the vestibule, the Prince was greeted by Bert, who stood at the head of one hundred ex-digger commercial travellers who formed the Guard of Honour.

"Captain Jacka!" he exclaimed with a smile. "How delightful to see you again, and this time in your own splendid city." He extended his hand warmly, and Bert saluted before taking it. He was shaking the hand of the next King of England, who during the last war had come to admire the feats of this hero of the Empire.

"Your Royal Highness," Bert replied. "It is a great pleasure to welcome you to Australia in a state of peace and prosperity. We have been eagerly awaiting your visit, and have assembled an Honour Guard comprising members of this club who fought gallantly for the Empire during the war.

"May I present to you the members of your Guard?" Bert suggested. The Honour Guard, which was lining the staircase to the next level filed past the Prince, with each man shaking his hand. The whole party then walked up the stairs to the main dining room, where around one thousand members of the club had assembled. In the dining room Mr W. Peirce welcomed the Prince on behalf of the United Commercial Travellers' Association of Australasia:

"It is my great honour to propose a toast to the health of His Royal Highness, and to express our members' appreciation of the honour which he has conferred upon the association by his acceptance of the badge of membership and by his presence at the club."

The President of the Victorian association, Mr Pemberton, immediately afterwards added his support: "Your Royal Highness, I fully support the sentiments expressed by Mr Peirce, and wish to assure you that an equally warm welcome would await you at every one of the affiliated clubs throughout Australia, and hope that you will avail yourself of your badge of membership in every other State of the Commonwealth."

The assembled commercial travellers then drank the Loyal Toast, and erupted into deafening cheers and the singing of "For he's a jolly good fellow...". When the singing subsided the Prince of Wales responded in kind: "Gentlemen, I am very proud to have been made an honorary member. Mr Pemberton was good enough to say that he hoped I would make use of this badge everywhere. Well, gentlemen, as you know, my program is pretty full!

"But I want to convey my best wishes to the association throughout the Commonwealth, and my warm congratulations on your splendid record during the war. It is a great pleasure to me to have had the opportunity of shaking hands with so many of your soldier members, particularly Captain Jacka, a winner of the Victoria Cross."

Loud cheers broke the rhythm of the Prince's speech, and he took the opportunity of repaying the compliments. "I will now drink to the health of the United Commercial Travellers in what I already know is a *very* good cocktail!"

Laughter and cheers followed, and Bert escorted the Prince back down the stairs into the foyer. Just as he was about to step back out into the street, he remembered that he had walked in with his hat. He turned around and pressed his way through the throng towards the Strangers' Room, where he told the General Secretary, Mr James Davies, "Why should I lose it? I only bought it this morning!"

Vera was outside in the crowd that saw the Prince leave the Commercial Travellers Association club. Bert found her afterwards and they had dinner at the Savoy Restaurant in Russell Street, which served suppers as required, even into the early hours of the morning.

* * *

When Vera got home that night her father had already gone to sleep, as he was feeling ill again, but Molly was there, having stayed on after dinner. Vera's face was full of contentment, and she told them about her eventful day.

"Guess who Bert met today?" she said matter-of-factly. "The Prince of Wales. Someday he'll be the King, and he likes Bert."

"And Bert seems to like you," her mother said, raising her eyebrows. "If he holds you in his arms against your wishes…"

"Don't you see? I want him, Mum."

"Have you thought of what that means?" she warned. "Is he willing to come into our faith?"

"Leave her alone, Mum," Molly said.

"He won't do that," Vera said with resignation. "I know him now, and he's not someone who will turn away from something he believes in."

"And you? Would you turn against yours?" her mother intoned. "It's a good thing your father's gone to sleep. "

"No."

"Well, there's no point then, is there, Rose?" "Rose" was the name that Vera was known by in the household. She was a beautiful baby with rosy red cheeks when she got that name, and had it stuck.

"Yes there is," Vera said firmly. Her mother could see there was no use. Her mind was made up, and that was it. That was how she was.

"Well, if it's that serious, Rose, you had better be getting your glory box in order."

* * *

By July, Vera's relationship with Bert had progressed to the point that it was necessary to present her to his parents in Wedderburn. They took the train out together on a wintry Saturday morning, so they might spend lunchtime and some of Saturday afternoon there, and get back to Melbourne by the evening train. Elizabeth and Nathaniel were so concerned about it that they sent Bessie off to spend some time at Fanny's house, and warned them and the other siblings not to make an appearance during the middle of the day.

Having arrived at Wedderburn, they walked along paths that had been well trodden by him as a boy, but for Vera every step was unknown. When they arrived at the house he knocked, but opened the door and led Vera inside, where Elizabeth met them in the corridor. As usual, her hair was parted in the middle and tied back into a small bun at the back. Bert gave her a kiss on the cheek first up, and then stood aside.

"Mother…"

"You must be Vera," Elizabeth began with a smile. She extended her arm, and Vera shook her hand.

"It's a pleasure to meet you Mrs Jacka," she replied with a smile. "Bert has spoken of you in such glowing terms."

"Has he now," Elizabeth said as her eyes rolled in her son's direction. "Make yourselves comfortable in the parlour. I'll see if I can find my husband."

"In here," Bert said, leading Vera to the parlour where they sat together in a two-seater divan. He put his hand on her back to ease her into the seat.

"Don't," she whispered, which made him smile. Looking around the room she focussed on the glass-cased picture of Bert and his brothers in AIF uniforms, which occupied pride of place above the fireplace. "They all looked so young and skinny," she thought. As Nathaniel entered the room she stood up.

"Miss Carey, I believe," he announced, putting his hand forward. "I'm Nathaniel Jacka," he smiled.

"You can call her Vera, Dad."

"Vera," he repeated, shaking both their hands. "Welcome home, son." The four of them sat down.

"Bill's coming back to Australia," Elizabeth began. "We've just received a letter from him. They sailed from England on 13 July."

"Which means they'll be here in two weeks," Bert calculated.

"He's thinking of setting up a dairy farm under the Soldier Settler Scheme," Elizabeth said.

"It's not an easy life."

"Your brother is capable of an honest day's work," Nathaniel said, cutting in.

"I'm yet to meet him," said Vera.

"Oh, you'll meet him soon enough," Nathaniel assured her. "So, what's on you're mind, son, that you've made this special trip out to Wedderburn?"

"Well," Bert replied. "I have spoken to Vera's father, and obtained his permission to court his daughter, which he gave willingly, and since then we have been seeing each other quite often…"

"But you work for my son, don't you?"

"Yes."

"So you would see each other every day, wouldn't you?"

"Most days. Not always on a Sunday."

"Where do you go on Sundays?" Elizabeth inquired.

"We like to go for long walks in the Royal Botanical Gardens." Bert cut in.

"And sometimes we have a picnic there and walk along the river. There are lots of families and couples there on Sundays," Vera added with a smile.

"We are seeking your blessing," Bert said, wishing to get to the point that they had all been skirting around.

"But you are of age, Vera, aren't you?"

"Yes, but—"

"Well, by law you can do anything you like," Nathaniel interjected.

"We want everyone's blessing," Bert said.

* * *

Later that afternoon, as Bert's parents stood alone on the platform at the railway station Elizabeth was genuinely worried. She was too different – too vivacious for a start. She was Catholic, which meant the children would have to be brought up as Catholics. That was the hardest thing to take; the insistence of the Catholics on appropriating the offspring with no room for compromise.

* * *

Despite his parents' concerns, Bert continued courting Vera just as vigorously as before. He followed his instincts about people, and there was no doubting that Vera made him feel happy. In fact, he had never felt happier.

Bill and his bride Joan eventually arrived in August, and stayed in Wedderburn. Joan was very pregnant with their daughter Joy, who was born on 24 August. In the course of the war, and in the period shortly afterwards, Bill's world view, and that of his older brother had diverged. Bert was frequently being requested to speak about his war experiences, but if anyone asked Bill, he would talk about the beautiful scenery in France. The slaughter of young men that he witnessed at Gallipoli and France would make Bill a pacifist for the rest of his life. While Bert sought out his mates in the 14th Battalion and the 4th Brigade, Bill sought comfort in his family. Bill had £250 that he saved during the war, and in November 1920 he had applied for a grant under the Soldier Settler Scheme to the Closer Settlement Board of Victoria.

At the annual reunion of the 14th Battalion and 4th Brigade Association at Sargent's Café on 1 November 1920, General Brand was unanimously re-elected president. There were no speeches, but Newton Wanliss gave a short account of his progress on the history of the 14th Battalion. He was corresponding with dozens of 14th Battalion veterans all over the country.

Bert had already popped the question to Vera, a month earlier. They were now making regular visits to Father Lynch, the parish priest of St Mary's Catholic Church in East St Kilda, who would guide them to the altar. During those visits Father Lynch put special emphasis on Bert's responsibilities as the father of a Catholic child.

* * *

Vera and Bert were married at St Mary's Catholic Church, East St Kilda on 17 January 1921. For Australia's most famous war hero, it was a very low-key, private affair. Bert knew that if there were any hint of what was happening, the press would have been all over it in a twinkle, and would have made a meal of it. All sorts of questions would be raised, and they would have been inundated with unwanted guests. Not all members of the Jacka family were present, and those who did come kept a low profile. Molly was the chief bridesmaid, and Vera's younger brother Jim was best man. They had to go past a long list of better-credentialled candidates for that role to get to Jim, who really liked Bert, but still didn't know him that well.

* * *

8 am, Erskine House, Lorne, 25 January 1921

Bert and Vera lay motionless on the bed, and listened to the sound of waves washing up on the beach. Bert lay on his side, looking out through the window with his head on the pillow. Outside the wet sand sparkled in the sunlight, and the waves rolled predictably on a beach that seemed to contain no rips or potholes, no surprises beneath the water. He doubted that life could be more perfect than this. He felt contentment and the future looked good.

Then he thought of Harold Wanliss. One night in France, he talked to him about Lorne and that beach. Harold told him how much it meant to him, and how that sand and water were, to him, part of the fabric of the nation. Through his field-glasses Harold had watched that beach go by for the last time from the ship that was taking him to Egypt. They were the same field glasses that he was looking through in the last instant of his life in that potted muddy field in Belgium, when a machinegun round thudded into his heart.

Bert flinched.

He felt Vera's fingers running across the depression in his upper left shoulder.

"This is one of your war wounds, isn't it?" she asked sadly. He turned around to face her.

"Yes," he answered, "a souvenir from Pozieres."

"Everything will be all right now," she assured him, and then kissed him on the cheek with compassion, as a mother would kiss her son.

1.30 pm, The Balcony, Erskine House, Lorne, 27 January 1921

Vera and Bert had spent another morning walking along the beach. During the last week and a half they had done a lot of walking, where they talked about their plans for the future. They had been out on the pier and seen the fishermen coming in with their catch. They had also been up to see the Erskine Falls, where the mist from the falling water, the cool wet rocks, and the majestic arms of the giant ferns gave welcome relief on a hot day. Vera had also done some reading in quiet moments. This was the newlyweds' second last day, and they were almost through another pleasant luncheon on the balcony overlooking the sea when a waiter arrived with the news.

"Captain Jacka, sir, there is an urgent telegram for you."

"Thank you," Bert said. He took the envelope and began to open it, wondering if this was a congratulatory telegram. "How did they find out we are here?" he thought.

"What is it?" Vera asked, seeing a sudden change of mood in Bert's expression as he read it to himself. It was like a shadow had fallen over him.

"It's from General Brand," he pronounced. "We've got to leave Lorne immediately."

"But why?" she asked. "We still have two days to go."

"We must cancel immediately," Bert replied with gravity, "because Sergeant Maurice Buckley has been killed, the funeral is tomorrow. You remember Buckley, don't you? He was the one who spoke after me at the performance of *As You Were*."

"Yes, I do. He spoke for Ireland," she recalled. "How did he die?"

"He fell off a *horse*," he said, wide-eyed with disbelief. "Can you imagine that, Vera? In the war he survived numerous charges, and he's killed by falling off a horse?" He didn't know yet that the daredevil Buckley had been trying to clear a high fence on a bet with fellow drinkers at a pub.

"That's terrible," Vera said.

"General Brand wants me as one of the pallbearers at the funeral."

"Where will it be held?"

"St Patrick's Cathedral."

"Oh," she said, barely masking her disappointment, but saying nothing against it. Vera took it pretty well considering that her honeymoon had suddenly been cut short. She didn't even know the man, and Bert didn't really know him either, yet they had to change their plans to accommodate Bert's commitment to the 4th Brigade. He was a VC, he was first among the VCs, and that was a great responsibility that he had carried on his shoulders since 1915. They drove to Colac in a Pioneer coach and caught the train to Melbourne from there. Vera still felt happy, but not as happy as she might have been if this matter hadn't arisen. She hadn't realised until now, until she had begun to live with him, how all embracing it was to be the wife of Australia's greatest front line soldier.

WAR AND POLICE

Ever since the end of the war, and particularly since he had returned to Australia, Bert was experiencing flashbacks and dreams that disturbed his sleep. One of the recurring themes during these episodes was the cross-examination he had received at the Dardanelles Commission. It was a witch hunt that targeted Winston Churchill and Lieutenant-General Sir Ian Hamilton for the British disaster in the Dardanelles. They were left carrying the can in the absence of Lord Kitchener, who should have shared the blame, but was killed in 1916 when a German torpedo sank the ship he was travelling on. Bert gave evidence before the Commission on 28 August, 1917. At the time he was convalescing in London after being sniped in the leg. It all came back so vividly in his dreams, he thought he was actually there. Bert could feel himself sliding back into the room where the inquiry was held.

* * *

"When did you go out to the Peninsula?" the Chairman of the Commission, Sir William Pickford, asks me without emotion. He's been at this for almost a year now, and there isn't much that he hasn't made up his mind about. As the Lord Justice of Appeal, he is used to seeing witnesses picked to pieces, and is an old hand at it himself.

"On the morning of the 25th we left Lemnos Harbour early," I answer.

"How long had you been at Lemnos before that?"

"Since the 13th of the month."

"You are a combatant officer I think – not a medical officer?"

"I am a combatant officer."

"And anything you did in regard to the matter of bringing in the wounded was as a volunteer?" He knows this already from my written statement, but I suppose he is trying to methodically record all the circumstances.

"Yes. Of course," I answer. "I know nothing about the medical side of the question. I can only tell you from my point of view what I saw, and I have absolutely no medical knowledge whatsoever."

"You left Lemnos in the *Seang Choon?*" Pickford says, as he takes his reading glasses off. "She was an ordinary transport I suppose?"

"Yes, just a common troopship carrying about 1200."

"Had you any horses on board?"

"No, we had a full regiment of about 1000 and other details making up I should think about 1200 men."

"I think *you,* with a party of about thirty men, left in the evening for the purpose of bringing off wounded?"

"Yes. We had been standing by all day because they could not land all the troops at the same time, and we were practically one of the last of the regiments to land. As we had been standing by all the time we could see what was going on. About that time there was some idea that part of the coast was going to be evacuated and they wanted to get the wounded off first, so they called for volunteers and I think a party of about thirty of us went, leaving the ship about 6:30 in the evening. I have told you I think in my statement what took place from that time on. Of course the whole time the work on the beach had been very hard because there was hardly a moment passed without shelling – particularly on the left side of the beach where the New Zealanders landed. That part was always swept by machinegun fire and bullets.

"Of course, throughout the day and night it was continually swept with shrapnel from… I forget the exact spot… but towards

Achi Baba, or in that direction. I think I can say that probably the last of the wounded men came to our boat, the *Seang Choon*."

My voice is echoing through the hall as I face the Commissioners who sit before me. One of them is Australia's High Commissioner, the Right Honourable Mr Andrew Fisher, who was the Labor prime minister of Australia at the outbreak of the war, and sent a congratulatory telegram to my mother.

"There had been a bit of a glut and they could not get them off," I say. "There were not enough conveyances to get them off and some had to wait a few hours, but by that time in the evening the beach was fairly clear except for a few stray men. When we first got there we could see the wounded lying on the beach, hundreds of them. That was in the morning. But they kept getting them off all day, and, to get them all off by 9 o'clock in the evening an extra party was sent out and that was what I dealt with."

"As far as you could see," probes Pickford, "were the arrangements for getting them off satisfactory?"

"They *were* and I will tell you why," I reply firmly. "If at any time the arrangements made did not prove sufficient it was always remedied by volunteers from infantry battalions. In those days, of course, we did not have the same ideas we have now and everyone used his own initiative and detailed a certain number of men to assist, and the probability is that the higher command did not know what was taking place. Nevertheless, the beach was being cleared all the time by volunteers from the infantry battalions."

"Your transport, the *Seang Choon* was not very well adapted for carrying wounded," Pickford cuts in, "*was* she?"

"No, she was just the common troopship," I agree. "She did have a hospital with somewhere about thirty to fifty beds on her. I should say the hospital was about as big as this room, but the beds were very close together…"

"About how many wounded did you get on board your ship?"

"I cannot give you the exact number, but as far as I can remember I should say 300 or 400."

"When they got on board, was there a sufficient provision of doctors and attendants to look after them?" asks Pickford.

"There were plenty of attendants, there were several R.A.M.C. men and stretcher bearers who came across in barges, and we had medical men on board our ship, but there were only two doctors."

"That was not many for 300 men, was it?" asks the law lord.

"No, but there were not so many wounded cases as the men had been bandaged up on the beach."

"Where were they taken to?"

"After we left, do you mean?"

"Yes... you disembarked after that?"

"Yes."

"And then the transport went away with the wounded?"

"Yes, as far as we knew she was going back to Egypt. We heard that the arrangements for the men afterwards were not too good, but I knew nothing about that. At the time no one was absolutely neglected, as far as getting them on the transports was concerned," I say. I'm starting to cough. "Though we heard afterwards in Egypt the arrangements were not what they ought to have been.

"Still... I think under the conditions and particularly that night, with the sea very rough, and seeing that it was rather a difficult job, it was a fine effort." Again, I'm coughing as I speak. "I think everyone thought... there was no one neglected, and no one died from want of care... or anything like that."

"Why are you coughing?" the law lord asks in puzzlement.

* * *

Bert gasped for air, spluttering and coughing.

Why am I coughing? Bert's head began to spin with the nausea of motion sickness.

Gas attack! Gas! Get those respirators out quick smart! Suddenly, his mind was in the trenches at Villers Bretonneux.

My eyes! His face was covered in a lather of perspiration.

"Wake up, Bert, wake up," Vera said, concerned, "you're dreaming. You must be having a nightmare." She put her arm over his chest and hugged him to settle his convulsions.

"Was I?"

"And coughing. You've been coughing all night. Have you got a cold?"

"No, I keep getting bronchitis from the gas I inhaled during the war."

It was something she hadn't counted on when she married the war hero. The war had scarred his mind, as well as his body. He was just coming out of a deep dream. After his gassing in France, he was repatriated to London and operated on again because some of his wounds from previous battles had cracked open. Due to his persistent coughing he had suffered a hernia and had to be operated on for that. It was now the morning of 28 April 1921, just a few days after Anzac Day had rekindled those memories for Bert, and the first time that Vera had been woken by Bert's nightmares and that rasping cough, which wasn't heard so much during the day.

3.37 pm, Australian Senate chamber, Melbourne, Thursday, 28 April 1921

That Anzac Day had sparked old memories for another outstanding hero of the AIF. Later that day, the burly, crimson-faced Senator Harold "Pompey" Elliott was making an impassioned speech in the Australian Senate chamber in Spring Street. Nominally he was a Nationalist Party senator, but his independent streak ran deep. As a left-field thinker, he was an outstanding brigadier on the Western Front, where he was instrumental in some of the most brilliant victories of the AIF. But his erratic behaviour and failure to manage up had offset the brilliance of his military mind, blocking his promotion.

Since his youth Pompey had known suffering, but even when his family were poor farmers at Charlton, twenty miles up the road from Wedderburn, he was showing exceptional talent as a schoolboy. Regardless of the talent, if his father had not persisted in his gold prospecting expeditions to Western Australia, and had not struck it rich there, he would have struggled mightily to make the most of that obvious potential. But his father did strike it rich and suddenly his life changed.

As a young Lance-Corporal at the South African War he won the Distinguished Conduct Medal for a daring raid that he devised and executed personally, resulting in the capture of a famous Boer commander. He trained the Essendon Rifles prior to the war, and was a brilliant battalion commander at Gallipoli, although showing signs of recklessness with his personal safety. Like Bert, he never sent his men out to do something he wouldn't do himself. He was "Jacka with a law degree", but even more outspoken.

"My objective is to give additional rights to officers serving in the Forces," Elliott said to the senators who had assembled to debate the British Army Act. "In the section I seek to amend, provision is made that an officer shall not be removed from the Forces without being given a chance to ascertain the nature of the charge against him... I will give an instance of the kind of thing that happens under the Army Act. Albert Jacka, who won his Victoria Cross at Gallipoli, was the first to secure the distinction, which was followed shortly after by the granting of a commission.

"He was always foremost in the fights of his battalion on the peninsula. Later he proceeded to France, where he repeatedly distinguished himself, and his name will be seen in despatches up to March or April 1917. After what was known as the first Battle of Bullecourt there was a strange silence, as his name was not mentioned in the promotion or decoration lists or despatches, although he was constantly at the Front and participating in the fighting as before. He led dozens of desperate charges, he was worshipped by his men, and, notwithstanding this, officers were repeatedly placed over him." Thus far, the Senator's speech could also have been equally applied to himself, for in his view he had had inferior men placed into divisional command above him.

"What is the reason that such a cruel embargo has been placed on Jacka, who is known by men associated with the Australian Imperial Force as the bravest of the brave?

"Honourable senators will doubtless recall that the British Tank Corps under the direction of General Monash proved a brilliant success... But the position was somewhat different when these operations were conducted by General Birdwood and General White, who, instead of providing an artificial fog, as Monash had done, sent the tanks forward when the ground was white as snow, so that every tank stood out!"

The motivation for these accusations was already obvious to Senator Drake-Brockman, who had been at Bullecourt and also knew well the poisonous relationship that had evolved between Brigadier-General Elliott and Lieutenant-General Birdwood in the course of the war. Drake-Brockman had no doubts that Pompey was using the Albert Jacka example to vent his own frustrations.

"One of the tanks suddenly blundered into a sunken road in which the members of the 14th Victorian Battalion were waiting to attack," Pompey continued. "The man in charge was so panic stricken that he turned his guns on our own men, and at a range of five or ten yards killed at least thirty. It was said at the time that if the men had a *tin-opener*... they would have murdered the man who was responsible... But he was *inside* the tank.

"Albert Jacka was the Intelligence Officer of that battalion, and as he is now in Melbourne he can be questioned. Jacka prepared a war diary, which is absolutely sacred, because it gives the history of his unit. He recorded the details of the time and place and a copy was sent to General Birdwood, who sent for Jacka and said, 'You must destroy every copy of your report sent to Horseferry Road, so that every trace of the incident will disappear.'

"General Birdwood assembled the battalion on parade, and congratulated the men on their magnificent bravery. He said:

'You fought like demi-gods. I am sure you will not be unwilling to share the glory with the magnificent men of the Tank Corps.' Colonel Peck said that it required a great effort to prevent those men from rushing General Birdwood and hooting him off the ground."

"They did hoot him off in Flanders!" interjected Senator Pratten.

"I am not dealing with that," Senator Elliott explained. "From that time onward Jacka led every charge, though he was wounded again and again. The moment he was out of hospital he went with unhealed wounds into the line."

"He was allowed out of hospital with unhealed wounds?" Senator Cox asked in disbelief. He had commanded the 1st Light Horse Brigade in Palestine during the war, and had been wounded himself.

"He led his men time after time with *unhealed* wounds," Senator Elliott emphasised. "He got away from the hospital."

"Then he was away illegally!" Senator Cox retorted.

"He chanced that. That was the sort of man he was. He has never been able to get any satisfaction."

"Jacka's case differs from that of the honourable senator," cut in Senator Foster, "inasmuch as it was a regimental matter, and he was entitled to the ordinary promotion."

"That is so, but when it suited the higher officers they abrogated all the regulations of the service."

"No wonder the privates said their prayers regularly every night!" added Senator Foster, with a dose of jocularity.

"I want honourable senators to clearly understand that my remarks this afternoon are based, in the main, on statements made to me by officers. I cannot, of course, vouch for their absolute accuracy, as I have had no means to investigate them. I only know that the statements made to me by Colonel Peck were confirmed by Jacka, and that the essential fact to be borne in mind is that, whereas Jacka, up to a certain stage in the history of the Australian Imperial Force, was marked for rapid advancement and decoration, he suddenly disappeared from the ken of the military gazettes, although he was fighting all the time in the front line.

"The Minister may deny these statements, or say that even if they are correct they do not show that General Birdwood was responsible. If this is so, it is advisable that, if ever we send our men away again, the officer in command of them should have very wide powers to refuse to carry out any manifestly impossible orders. I have heard it said that General Birdwood knew that the action to which I have referred was hopeless from the beginning, but, nevertheless, it had to be carried out."

"What has this to do with the amendment?" protested the Defence Minister, Senator Pearce.

"I am endeavouring to show the very great importance of the amendment," insisted Senator Elliott.

Senator Drake-Brockman had had enough. Of all the senators assembled, only he was there, outside the village of Bullecourt when the events being discussed actually happened – Senator Elliott was not. It was now 5.21 pm.

"I am not sure that some of the things I desire to say are altogether pertinent to the amendment," Drake-Brockman began hesitantly, "but since certain matters upon which I have a particular knowledge have been mentioned, I wish to make some allusion to them."

"If the honourable senator can connect his remarks in any reasonable way with the proposed new clause he will be at perfect liberty to make them," Senator Bakhap reminded him.

On that assurance Senator Drake-Brockman continued: "I think I can do that. In support of the amendment that has been submitted by my gallant and distinguished friend, Senator Elliott, an illustration has been drawn from the battle of Bullecourt, which he has described as one of the greatest disasters in the war. I happened to be in that battle.

"I was in command of the 16th Battalion, which was a portion of the 4th Brigade. The 14th Battalion to which reference has been made, was also a portion of that brigade. My battalion went into that action with a strength of 870 other ranks and of twenty-three officers... We came out of it with a strength of three officers and eighty-seven other ranks. I have very good cause, therefore, to remember most of the incidents connected with that battle, which took place on 11 April, 1917."

Shocked by the statistics, Senator Pratten asked, "Who was the Army Commander?"

"General Gough," replied Drake-Brockman, with thinly disguised contempt. "A comparison has been drawn between the action of the Tanks Corps when controlled by General Monash and its action when controlled by Generals Birdwood and White. However, this particular battle was not, as suggested, designed by General Birdwood or General White. It was designed by General Headquarters, and the orders were sent down through the usual channels to the 4th Division, and particularly the 4th Brigade, to carry them out.

"I am sure that the honourable gentleman did not mean to be unfair, but he has certainly been misinformed. I do not doubt that Captain Jacka is under the impression that his report upon these operations was sent forward. But I can assure the Senate that it was not, and that the report that did go forward was that which was signed by two commanding officers of the brigade, because we did not think it fair to hide ourselves behind the skirts of our Intelligence Officers when such serious allegations were being made. We demanded that an inquiry should be held into the whole thing. But it was never held. The insinuation that Captain Jacka was penalised on account of this action is certainly based on false premises.

"I wish to add that nobody has a greater admiration for Captain Jacka than myself, and I wish to say further, that he is a personal friend of mine. It has been suggested that Captain Jacka, on account of this particular incident, was superseded in respect to the command of the 14th Battalion… Captain Jacka was never superseded in my time, but what happened was this: Senior officers from outside the battalion, who were available and fit for promotion, were brought in to command the 14th Battalion.

"If it can be said that he was superseded by Colonel Peck – a very distinguished and capable officer, who took over command of the battalion – then Captain Jacka was indeed superseded. If it can be said that he was superseded by Colonel Smith, similarly, then obviously such was the case. If it can be said that he was superseded by the appointment of Colonel Crowther to take command of the battalion, then again it is self-evident that Captain Jacka was superseded.

"But all these three were senior officers, and two of them, to my own knowledge, were experienced and wholly capable to command. Captain Jacka was at best a company commander. The other officers were majors or colonels, and were specifically appointed to command the 14th Battalion."

"Did Captain Jacka complain?" asked Senator Duncan.

"To my knowledge, he has never complained officially, and I do not know that he has ever complained unofficially," Senator Drake-Brockman replied. "It has been suggested that he was penalised because he had the courage – and it has been admitted by every one that he had a superabundance of that quality – to set down on paper what he observed on the 11th of April, 1917. But he had for his battalion commanding officer Colonel Peck, one of the officers who had been brought in over his head, and who possessed enough backbone to say, 'I will not hide behind Captain Jacka, but will take the responsibility for this report myself.'"

"Order!" sounded the Chairman of the Senate. "The honourable senator's time has expired."

* * *

9 am, Roxburgh, Jacka & Co., 475 Collins Street, Friday, 29 April 1921

The next morning Bert had just come through the door of the office, and was about to sit down at his desk when his partners Ernie and Reg came in holding up a copy of *The Argus*, splashed with the following headline:

> Battle of Bullecourt. Senator Elliott's Charges. Captain Jacka Victimised.

"Have you seen this skipper?" Reg said excitedly.

"Yes."

"Well? What are you going to do?"

"Nothing."

"Nothing?" asked Ernie, incredulously.

"Pompey's gone over the top with this," Bert said with some annoyance. "He spoke to me about this some time ago, but he didn't consult me about this demonstration in the Senate." Like Pompey, Bert had spoken up on behalf of the men during the war, and there was no doubt that his rebellious nature had stopped the flow of medals and promotion that should rightfully have been his. But promotion to Lieutenant-Colonel was another thing. Even the most boyish of the boy colonels in the AIF during the war were not that young – Bert had only just turned twenty-four in April 1917. There was no doubt that he wanted it at the time though. He knew he could do a better job than some of the bods that been put in over the top of him.

"Why don't you think he called you beforehand?" asked Reg.

"Because," Bert answered, "I would have advised him not to."

"You know what's funny?" Reg said sarcastically, as he read on. "*The Argus* reckons you got the DSO! Perhaps they've found the one Brand promised you at Polygon Wood?" The phone rang just as Bert was about to answer, and Madge, the girl they employed to take over Vera's position after she had married, called out to Bert.

"Captain Jacka," she said, "I have Parliament House on the line. Senator Elliott wishes to have a word with you."

"Thank you, you can put him through," Bert called to her. "Can you excuse me please," he told Reg, who exited the office, closing the door behind him.

"Is that you, Captain?"

"Yes it is, sir."

"Have you seen this morning's papers?"

"Yes, I have, and let me say…"

"Captain, you may not agree with the stand that I adopted in the Senate last night," Pompey interjected, "but this was not just about your case. I was using your case as an illustration of a wider principle concerning the Army Act, that is currently being debated."

Bert explained that he quite understood the principle involved, but did not enjoy the spectacle.

* * *

6.10 pm, Australian Senate chamber, Melbourne, Thursday, 5 May 1921

On Thursday during the following week the Senate had already spent a long time debating the new Army Act. It was in the early evening that Senator Elliott returned to the battlefield with his new ammunition – the interviews he had conducted with veterans from the 14th Battalion. It was clear that Bert was seen as a demi-god by the boys in the 14th, and there was no doubt in their minds that he should have been their CO rather than Lieutenant-Colonels Smith and Margolin, and they told him so.

"I am distinctly opposed to any attempt to incorporate the provisions of the British Army Act in our Defence Act," Senator

Elliott said with no uncertainty, "and particularly to any attempt to do so without giving honourable senators the fullest opportunity of considering those provisions down to the minutest details. It has been said that the Army Act is perfect: that it is the embodiment of centuries of experience. It all depends on how you regard this weapon – this 'perfect Act' as it has been called."

"This perfect piece of draftsmanship?" Senator Vardon interjected.

"I might call it a perfect instrument of torture," Senator Elliott replied. "I admire my machinegun when it is in its emplacement, so that it can mow the Germans down, but I have a wholly different point of view when the German has it trained on me! *That's* how I view the Army Act."

"Does not the honourable senator recognise that in peace we are training officers and men under one system," interjected Senator Rowell, "and that as soon as war occurs we place them under another system which they have not learned?"

"A case in point is saluting senior officers," replied Senator Elliott. "The practice has not been ingrained in them as it has been in the British Army. But I observed that if a senior officer raised his arm and commenced to salute, our men would respond immediately. I suggested the adoption of this practice, and a humorous incident occurred when it first came into vogue.

"Just after the First Division had made that splendid attack on the Menin-road, and was being relieved by the Second Division, my brigade was waiting for its turn to go in. General Birdwood, who was then generally known as 'Rainbow Bill', on account of the number of ribbons he wore on his chest, was watching the First Division coming out, and was saluting in accordance with the new system that had been adopted. Of course the boys responded, but I overheard my cook, who was watching, say to a mate, 'Cripes Bill, the boys must have done well. Rainbow Bill is saluting every Aussie he meets!'"

After the laughter had subsided, Senator Elliott continued. "One never knows where he is with the British Army Act. It catches him like a boomerang. I thought I knew all the tricks that might be played under the Army Act, but Senator Drake-Brockman, in replying to what I said, showed that Captain Jacka had never been superseded in his regiment, because the matter was dealt with in a different way. A senior officer from outside the regiment was brought in and put over his head. I should say that that was even more effective than supersession to break a man's heart.

"I can cite the case of a Polish Jew who could not speak English, and who, in the three months during which he was attached to the battalion, never by any chance went near the front line. Whenever an action was imminent he developed synovitis, and his unfortunate adjutant, Captain Wanliss, one of the best officers we had, a nephew of Sir William Irvine, and a man who was dux of my own college in Ballarat, and later dux of the Hawkesbury Agricultural College in New South Wales, and who in his first action gained the DSO and was recommended for the VC, had to do the work of this unfortunate illiterate, who could not write his own orders. Captain Wanliss had to be working all day in his dugout, and then had to go into the front line at night."

"Was the Polish Jew a master of strategy?" asked Senator Foster.

"He was a major, and he was put in command of the battalion though he could not speak English," replied Senator Elliott. "Then there was a man named Smith. General Birdwood insisted on this man taking command of the 14th Battalion over Captain Jacka's head. He had joined with him a man named Thompson, who was also an utter 'dud'. This will show what may be done under the Army Act. At Polygon Wood, where Jacka distinguished himself, to cite the official account, 'by the most magnificent bravery', this man Smith disappeared for two days, and during three days Captain Jacka ran the whole show! The colonel, in disappearing, took his telephone instruments with him, and Jacka had to beg, borrow and steal telephone instruments, make a new headquarters and continue the action."

"Was this the Polish Jew?" asked Senator Pratten.

"No!" rasped Pompey. "The Polish Jew had been gotten rid of by this time. This was a permanent officer, who was subsequently whitewashed, and holds a good command here in Australia."

"Of what rank was he?" Senator Cox asked. Even as a senator he was still commanding the First Cavalry Division, so his was more than a passing interest.

"He was a colonel. I told honourable senators that I had not fully investigated Jacka's case, but I have since done so, and I am prepared to lay before the Senate statutory declarations on the subject if the Minister for Defence will promise not to institute an action for perjury against the man who makes them in order to clear up the matter and to give the public an opportunity to learn the real facts of the case."

"I should be busy for the next fifty years if I followed up all these tarradiddles," grumbled the Defence Minister, Senator Pearce. It was Senator Elliott's use of the words "real facts of the case" that finally moved Senator Drake-Brockman to break his silence, which he had kept since he laid to rest, he felt, the matter of Captain Jacka's supersession. Why didn't Pompey consult me, he thought. It was now a question of honour, and so he rose to take the floor.

"It had been my intention not to speak to this clause at all," announced Senator Drake-Brockman, "but reference has been made to an officer who served under me in France for over two years. The Jew who subsequently got into the 14th Battalion has been mentioned. Let me tell honourable senators a little about this man, so that they may have a proper appreciation of his qualities. It is true he was born in Russia. He came to Western Australia something over twenty years ago, and becoming a naturalised subject he joined our Military Forces. When war broke out he went on active service with the 16th Battalion."

"He was fighting *for* Australia," said Senator Guthrie, "not *against* us!"

"He was," Senator Drake-Brockman nodded in agreement. "He went out as a subaltern, rose to the rank of major and got the Distinguished Service Order on Gallipoli. He was my second in command in France from the time I took command... I have never served with a more gallant gentleman.

"Perhaps it is unfortunate that subsequently he was sent to the command of the 14th Battalion, because it is quite true that his method of speech was unorthodox. But this 'illiterate' Jew, as he has been termed, could not only speak English well though with a slight accent, but he could also speak French, German, Russian, Hebrew, and the Arabic language fluently!"

"He has a university education," surmised Senator Henderson.

"It is true that he was not understood by the 14th Battalion when he went to command them. It is likewise true that his characteristics were slightly different, and that he had personal peculiarities, which are not general amongst Australians."

"Personal peculiarities are present in this chamber too!" observed Senator Millen as his eyes darted in Pompey's direction.

"Yes," was the dry response of Senator Drake-Brockman, which sent the whole chamber into fits of laughter.

"Was he able to go into the line?" demanded an undeterred Senator Elliott, who raised his voice above the laughter in the chamber.

"I am coming to that," answered Senator Drake-Brockman with some annoyance at the constant interruption. "Just after he got command of the 14th, they went into the Battle of Messines, and anybody acquainted with Messines Ridge will know that it was so cut up that there was hardly a square inch that was not a hole or adjacent to a hole.

"When crossing the ridge Colonel Margolin fell into one of the holes and sprained his knee, with the result that he was sent away to the hospital, and away from the 14th Battalion. Of course he could not get up to the front line... How *could* he, with his knee swollen to about four or five times its normal size? I saw it myself.

Subsequently he was invalided out of the Australian Imperial Force on account of the injury to his knee, but he didn't want to go away while his battalion was still in Messines, as he was so anxious to make a success of his command.

"I know that Senator Elliott has not deliberately misinformed the Senate with regard to this matter. But he didn't know all the facts – I do. I have no hesitation in saying that this 'illiterate' Jew is very highly educated, he is a very gallant soldier, and a most loyal and conscientious man. Moreover, the last time I heard from him – he writes to me occasionally – this 'illiterate' Jew, as he has been termed tonight, was the Military Governor of Jerusalem. He was loyal to Australia, and loyal to me. I have the greatest admiration for him, and I should consider myself contemptible did I not stand up for him tonight."

"The fact remains," Senator Elliott insisted, "that it was most unfortunate that the Commanding Officer of the Australian Imperial Force should have sent a foreigner, a stranger, to take over the command of a battalion from a man of the type of Captain Jacka!"

Again the chamber erupted into shouting.

"Order!" called the Chairman.

"I emphasise that I mentioned no names," continued Senator Elliott, "and that the name would not have been known but for Senator Drake-Brockman. Altogether it was a most unfortunate experiment. Australians are not intolerant, but these Australians resented the introduction of a foreigner, a man from another regiment, to take command over them. Possibly they were wrong, but they were convinced that everything they told me was correct. If they have misled me – I say this in light of Senator Drake-Brockman's statements – they have done so innocently without doubt, and will any senator say that they deliberately lied to me? Whether the character of Major Margolin was such as has been described is beside the point."

At that point it was painfully obvious to the whole chamber that Senator Elliott's effort to retrieve the fiasco that had emerged a week earlier had backfired into an even deeper fiasco. Senator Millen was anxious to press the matter to a conclusion: "Does not the honourable senator think there was a responsibility placed upon him to be sure of his statements before he uttered them as facts in this chamber?"

"I am in the unfortunate position of not having been able to examine, on oath, the persons concerned," he replied wearily. It was now approaching 10 pm, and he felt completely drained of energy, and utterly alone.

"All the more reason, in my opinion, why the honourable senator should not have taken the responsibility of saying such things here," rejoined Senator Millen.

"I cited the circumstances as an example of the non-observance of the regulations, and of the failure to give those who were entitled to the chance an opportunity of making good. Senator Drake-Brockman has not refuted the facts concerning the man who succeeded Major Margolin, and who was absent for two days at the Battle of Polygon Wood. I know that the two incidents caused great dissatisfaction in the battalion. If the facts regarding Major Margolin, however, are as have now been made known, I am sorry that I was led into error."

* * *

9.06 pm, Australian Senate chamber, Melbourne, Wednesday, 11 May 1921

Matters were not to be left at that, however. Senator Pearce had been waiting for a chance to settle the score with Senator Elliott. Elliott had been gunning for him since he entered the senate, holding him complicit with General Birdwood in allowing certain British Army commanders to override the interests of the AIF. Now it was the Minister's turn. As the Army Act continued to be debated in the Senate the following Wednesday, a question arose about the safeguards available to soldiers before a court marshal in the field. Fortunately, the Senate had in its midst two members who had been both legal professionals prior to the war, and brigadier-generals during the war.

"There were in the Australian Imperial Force on active service," said Senator Drake-Brockman, "and would be again under similar conditions, gentlemen who held military rank, but who, in the ordinary sense, were not soldiers but lawyers."

"We have had a fine picture of the perfection of the military jurisdiction painted for us," Senator Elliott responded. "It must be remembered however, that the late war was exceptional in that the whole of the manhood of Great Britain of military age was conscripted. That condition of affairs did not exist in previous wars, which, in the main, were fought by the British Regular Army, the personnel of which by no means affords the same wide field of selection among men with legal knowledge."

"But we are dealing with the Australian army, which must be a citizen army," protested Senator Drake-Brockman.

"The Australian Army, at any rate overseas, will probably be recruited by voluntary enlistment, and leading legal men do not in such circumstances volunteer," said Senator Elliott.

"How is it that you got there?" Senator Senior asked of him.

"I do not claim to be one of the leading counsel in Australia."

"How did you come to volunteer?" insisted Senator Fairbairn.

"I volunteered, if the honourable senator wants to know, because the Government sent me a circular asking me to call for volunteers in my battalion, and I had sufficient sense of shame not to say, 'Boys, are you going to the war? I am not going.' I put my name down at the top and said, 'Boys, who is coming *with* me?' That is how I came to volunteer, and I lost all my legal business during my five years of absence."

Then Senator Pearce struck: "It is very interesting to me to hear Senator Elliott suggesting, defending, and advocating an appeal from the military officer per se to the Governor-General in Council in Australia," he said, "because I recently had occasion to make some inquiries… I was asking that interesting question as to whether any of our soldiers had ever been shot, or whether ever the threat to carry out that penalty was known to have been made. I was informed that it was an *Australian* officer who had once issued an order on the field for men to be shot in a certain eventuality. I had that order looked up, and have it here. The document is as follows:

EXTRACT FROM DIARY OF GENERAL STAFF, 5TH DIVISION

To Tools,
Sender's number, B.M. 383. Day of month, 24.
In reply to number AAA

50 and 60 Battalions will move at once, in accordance with B.M. 368 and 369. The right of the 56th Battalion is at O. 16B. Enemy advancing from Warfuse Abancourt. Get into touch with troops on either flank. 57th Battalion will move as soon as possible, echeloned to right rear of 59th Battalion, and ultimately attack if required along railway to right of Villers Bretonneux, clearing it by an enveloping movement. Scouts in front as soon as past Aubigny line. All British troops to be rallied and re-formed as our troops marched through thence by selected officers, and on any hesitation to be shot.

From _____ Books
Place and time _____ 10.30 a.m.

(Certified true copy, 11.5.21) Sgd A. W. Perry
Chief Librarian, A. W.M.

Before Senator Pearce had finished, Senator Elliott stood up as if he was standing in the dock of a court: "To save the Minister any trouble, I quite admit the issuing of the order."

"The order then goes on to give other directions for the battle…" continued Senator Pearce.

"It was a very fine order!" interjected the fiery eighteen stone former New South Wales rugby forward, Labor Senator Albert "Jupp" Gardiner. This debate was not at all along party lines.

"It may have been," replied the Minister for Defence, "but it shows that General Elliott was not then prepared to give even a trial. He was prepared to shoot first, and give a trial afterwards. Senator Elliott is so fond of reminiscences that I thought I would give him a dose of his own medicine…"

"I think it redounds to his credit," Senator Gardiner rejoined, but that was not enough for Brigadier-General Pompey Elliott. He had lived through hell during that war, and as the order showed, he was not willing to die without a fight. He would not give in without a fight in the Senate either.

"I think it is my duty to take this opportunity of replying to the *attack* which has just been made upon me by the Minister for Defence," Senator Elliott said. "The order to which the Minister has referred has been taken from my brigade records. I was the officer responsible for placing it there, and that fact alone proves that I was in no sense ashamed of it.

"I remind honourable senators that at that very time we had received a direct order from General Haig that every man must, if necessary, *die* in his tracks… Further, I had made representations to the British authorities that the manner in which the British troops who were holding Villers-Bretonneux were disposed would lead to sudden disaster, and it was obvious to me that they could not hold on to Villers-Bretonneux if attacked. Their position at that time was the key to the whole situation in France, and on them and us in a sense the fate of the allied armies in France in a large measure depended."

The whole tone of the chamber had now changed. The restlessness and the gloating by some senators at the veteran warrior's embarrassment was suddenly transformed. A hushed silence prevailed upon those who had not been there, and could not know how people might behave in such circumstances. The gravity of the situation that faced Brigadier-General Elliott and his men on the day he issued the order was beginning to sink in. He continued now that he had their undivided attention.

"On one hand my own brigade lay in the valley of the Somme," he said, raising his arm in an arc as if the ground lay before him, "and on the other lay the French left in the valley of the Luce, near Hangaard… If the German forces had succeeded in holding Villers-Bretonneux they would have driven a wedge between the French and the British, and the only course that remained would have been for the British to retreat to the coast, and then embark for Bordeaux and join up again with the French forces, abandoning Paris to the enemy. That… was unthinkable.

"About 4 o'clock in the morning the barrage opened up, and I issued orders for my men to fall in under arms. At that time the British troops started to stream back in utter rout, and at 9 o'clock in the morning an effort was made to stem the panic because there was a great danger of the British troops sweeping away with them many of my own men.

"Anyone not accustomed to military operations will find it difficult to realise what really happens when a panic once commences. It was necessary for a time to prevent my men from taking the law into their own hands and opening fire on the retreating men, whom they regarded as cowards. It was at that time that I issued the order mentioned, and, strange as it may seem to the Minister for Defence, we had not to fire a single shot, but merely approached the men, and in front of the pistol compelled them to fall in. They did so, and the colonel of the British regiment, who had failed to rally his men, came to me and himself recommended the two officers intrusted with the task for the Military Cross for the magnificent work they had performed in rallying his troops."

"I am not cavilling at the order issued," insisted the Minister after a moment's pause.

"It was quoted in an endeavour to discredit me!"

"It was merely quoted to show that you do not believe in a trial."

"It was my *duty* to act as I did in that instance because it was a case of extreme urgency. I was quite aware that, if my officers acted on that order, I could be tried for murder, and I mentioned that in my report. I would however, have been in a position to appeal to His Majesty the King for a remission of the sentence or for a free pardon."

"Is the British Army such a rotten army?" enquired Senator Rowell.

"The British Army is just as good as any other army, but at certain times the best of armies are subject to panic," answered Senator Elliott.

"Does it not apply to all armies?" asked Senator Rowell.

"Yes. My action was necessary at an extremely critical time to prevent the panic extending to our own troops. Those who are familiar with the history of the Peninsula Wars will remember Sir Robert Craufurd's famous Light Division, said to be the most famous body of disciplined troops that has ever existed, was on one occasion seized with sudden panic, and fled. Therefore, knowing my military history I was prepared, even with my own troops — there were none finer in the world – to act as I did, because I knew that the whole German Army was coming on, and there was every possibility of a general rout.

"Moreover, we had received an order from General Haig that every man must die where he stood rather than retreat. I took the law into my own hands although I was liable to be tried for murder."

"You didn't take much risk!" Nationalist Party Senator Charles Cox sneered. Parties had disappeared in this debate.

"I was taking a great risk under the law," replied Senator Elliott. "The order which the Minister mentioned was actually adopted by the British authorities as the order for the attack on Villers-

Bretonneux and they actually took credit for it by the publication of a congratulatory order in which it was stated that 'the idea so brilliantly conceived by the staff of the 3rd Corps (British) was ably and gallantly carried out by the 8th British Division, assisted by the Australians.'"

Now they were getting to the nub of the matter. What had been eating at Pompey was a deeply felt hurt at the appropriation of his victories by the British authorities, the British general who was commanding the Anzac Corps, and by his fellow Australians. Birdwood had been Pompey's arch-enemy, who in his eyes had blocked his promotion to the justified rank of Major-General.

* * *

9.30 pm, Victoria Hall, Charlton, 28 August 1921

The controversy that had been stirred up by Senator Pompey Elliott and embroiled Bert's name blew over. But despite his reluctance to stand for any political party, Bert was being drawn into the election campaign of Sergeant-Major Peter Hansen, the Nationalist Party candidate for Korong in the Victorian State elections. Hansen was a fine public speaker and had spoken at the welcome home for Bert a couple of years back.

This time Bert was supporting another son of Wedderburn, a political candidate who had been known to him before the war, had gone with him to that war, and was now calling on Bert's promise to help him. This was something Nathaniel preferred not to see, however, Bert's older brother Sam, and his brothers-in-law, Isaiah Olive and Alf Saunders, had come to Charlton just because they knew Bert was going to be there.

Bert sat in front of the audience by Peter Hansen's side as he vociferously denied an accusation that had just been levelled against him by a heckler waving a piece of paper. There were two things that a political candidate needed to possess in those days, and that was a voice that could carry to the back of a hall without electronic aids, which didn't exist in any case, and a quiver of quick witted remarks with which to bludgeon the heckler.

"I categorically deny the inference made in a statement circulated during the last few days," Hansen stated with great indignation, "that while I was a member of the Wedderburn branch of the Farmer's Union, I had seconded a motion in favour of a compulsory wheat pool. If my name had been inserted in the minute book, as alleged, it was without my authority. Furthermore, I was not present in any later meeting of the branch when the minutes would come up for confirmation!"

"Why did yer join the Farmers' Union then?" a droll voice from the audience asked.

"Because before the war," Hansen replied dispassionately, "I was the president of the Wedderburn branch of the People's Party. During the five years that I was at the Front, the Farmer's Union took its place. So long as the Farmer's Union stood behind the Nationalist Party it was one and the same thing, and so I threw in my lot with the Farmer's Union on my return. I remained with the Wedderburn branch until I saw that the union was sailing under false colours, and instead of standing behind the Liberal Government, it was standing for only a section of the people. I determined then that I would have nothing further to do with a body that was sectional, and untrue to its principles!"

As many of those present were Nationalist Party supporters who had known him for many years, Peter Hansen's rebuttal and later pronouncements were met with a hearty reception. Sam and the brothers-in-law were the first to come up to Bert after the meeting, while many crowded around Peter.

"Evening, Bert," said Isaiah. "Are you coming over to Wedderburn at all?"

"Of course," Bert answered. "I'm sleeping at home tonight."

"So we'll see you tomorrow then?"

"Yes, of course, give my love to Fanny and Elsie, won't you?"

After the boys left Sam gave him a dose of reality. "What does Dad say about this?" he said in a lowered voice.

"What do you think?" Bert replied with a smile. "But Mum's happy to have me home for even one night. She's even put my old slippers out for me by the bed."

Nationalist Party supporters started to gather around them and it wasn't a topic that they could discuss freely there. After some further discussion with the pundits, Bert and Sam drove back to Wedderburn together, and had a good talk along the way. When they arrived, Sam invited his brother over for a cuppa before going on to Ridge Street. Sam and his family were back in Wedderburn where they'd started, and Sam was back in the woodcarting trade. Sam's wife Elizabeth was very happy to have Bert pop in like that. Most of her seven children were asleep; only the eldest, fifteen-year-old Leslie was awake.

"Hello Bert!" Elizabeth said excitedly. "We hardly see you any more. Why don't you have a seat while I put the kettle on."

"Elizabeth," Bert said giving her a kiss. "How are you feeling? How's little Ivy?" She had only recently given birth to Ivy, and the year previously she had their fourth boy, their first since the war, who was named Albert in honour of his famous uncle.

"Sleeping at the moment," she said with a sigh that admitted her exhaustion. "Little Albert's talking now."

"Hello Uncle Albert!" said Leslie, who came into the kitchen as soon as he heard the voice of his hero uncle. He'd have a story for the rest of his class at school tomorrow. In the meantime Elizabeth put out some scones.

"Hello son," Bert said shaking the boy's hand with one hand and roughing his hair with the other. After a few minutes Sam sent Leslie back to his bedroom so he and his wife could continue their discussion with Bert. Sam informed Bert that he and Elizabeth had saved some money, and were planning to establish a new butcher's shop in Wedderburn. As he left that night Bert wished Sam luck in the business he was planning, and Sam wished Bert luck, knowing that Nathaniel was going to cross-examine him on what happened at the political meeting. Bert told him not to worry, because Nathaniel was not as concerned about it as he thinks. He had long since come to terms with Bert's political views. "You need two sides in a democracy," Nathaniel would say.

"How is Vera holding up?" Elizabeth asked, just as Bert was about to step out of the door. Of all the womenfolk in Bert's family circle, she appeared to be the most supportive of Vera. It was a way of asking whether Vera might be pregnant by any chance. Everyone had been wondering about that question. There were more Jacka children coming up by the day. Bill was now renting a 160-acre dairy farm just south of Berwick railway station, forty miles from Melbourne, and Joan was pregnant again.

"She's all right," Bert said unconvincingly, and nothing more was said on that topic.

After saying his goodbyes Bert drove over to his parent's place feeling happy that Sam and Elizabeth were going to strike out in a new family business. At least they won't have rogue partners to worry about, he thought. Bert's original business partner, Captain Alexander Parker, had just been sentenced to twelve months' jail for receiving stolen shirts. After letting Bert down almost two years earlier, he'd swung another confidence trick by getting elected to the State Parliament as Labor Member for Prahran, but was subsequently taken to court to show that he had been a bankrupt when elected. What an unholy mess Parker turned out to be... and Brand reckons I can pick a dud faster than anyone? Then there was Reg Roxburgh to worry about.

* * *

One night in 1922 Bert came home from a meeting of the Masonic Lodge at around 10 pm. The walk home only took two minutes as the Lodge was in Crimea Street, just around the corner from their rented house. It had just been established in East St Kilda as

Lodge Number 303, which was something of a coincidence given Bert's encounters with the Lee-Enfield rifle. Vera was waiting up for him.

"You're still up?" he said, as she opened the door.

"There was nothing much else to do," she replied, and asked if he would like a cuppa before bed. They went into the kitchen, where she made him the tea and sat down with him for a chat. Despite promptings, he would not be drawn into a discussion on the nature of his meeting at the Lodge.

"Well, I learnt a new song today," she said, out of the blue.

"Really?"

"Yes. It's a hymn actually."

"Which one?"

"I'll sing it for you."

On the 13th rose the ark, let us join hand in hand,
For the Lord spake to Moses by water and by land,
Unto the pleasant river where by Eden it did rin,
And Eve tempted Adam by the serpent sin...

"Stop it!" he ordered angrily. "Stop it now."

"But why?" she laughed.

"Because that's a hymn from the Lodge," he said angrily. "How did you come to learn it?"

"It was easy, Bert," she said. "I was in the backyard watering the flowerbed, and you know how the Lodge backs onto this property. It's just over the fence, and your singing carries through those walls and into our backyard!"

"You must never sing it again!" he snapped as he rose from his chair, and her smile finally disappeared. "Forget that you even heard it."

"Well, if that's what you want, I won't," she assured him without the slightest passion. Their exchange ruined their humour for the rest of the night. She felt that he was putting up barriers around her, and the Masonic Lodge was part of the No-Man's land separating the different worlds they had come from.

* * *

On 27 March 1923, Captain Ernest Edmonds married Miss Thelma Fergie at Scots Church in Collins Street. He had recently purchased a family home, Coniston, at 33 Pine Avenue, Camberwell. Thelma was the daughter of William Fergie, a well-to-do solicitor and moneylender, who lived at the fashionable end of Nicholson Street, right opposite the Exhibition Buildings. He had amassed a tidy sum of £15,000 before he passed away a few years back, leaving it to his wife and children.

Consequently, when Reg asked to withdraw from the partnership, Ernie bought out his share and became an equal partner with Bert. The firm was re-named Jacka, Edmonds & Co. Pty Ltd, even though Wren still owned the majority stake indirectly through his brother. Since Reg's father, Thomas Roxburgh, also withdrew his support, Bert and Ernie moved out of the Olderfleet Buildings, and set the new business up almost directly across the road in McCulloch's Building at 488 Collins Street.

Bert and Vera were now renting a two-storey terrace house at 41 High Street, Prahran. A tramline ran just outside their door, and it was within walking distance of Vera's mother's house in Bayview Street. Her sister Molly now rented two streets away from her mother in Lorne Road, East Prahran. Vera was still within easy walking distance of St Mary's Catholic Church.

On Bert's side, his brother Sid was now living in Alfred Street, Prahran, which was only a few blocks away. Their sister Bessie, who was putting her talents to work as a dressmaker, was living in Wynnstay Road, Prahran, not far from Vera's sister. It now seemed like there was a "Jacka village" developing in the middle of Melbourne.

* * *

Bert was in constant demand to give talks, and he gave generously. Titled, "Reminiscences of the Great War", one such talk took place in mid-August 1923 in the Lodge Room at the Collingwood Town Hall, where he spoke to the Collingwood branch of the Australian Natives Association. Illustrated with lantern-slides borrowed from the Australian War Museum, he kept the audience spellbound with his conversational and homely style of lecturing. He traced the various campaigns of the AIF in Gallipoli and France in which the Australian troops took active part, from the day of the landing at Anzac Cove to the final blow of the war struck at the Hindenburg Line in August 1918.

At the conclusion of his talk, Bert was asked what he considered was the bravest deed he ever saw during the war that was performed by another digger. Bert thought about that for a few seconds before responding. He recalled those first few days at Gallipoli.

"Among so many brave deeds that became almost commonplace during the war," he began, "it is difficult to choose the bravest. To do so would be an injustice to many others. All I can do is to describe one gallant thing, which made a great impression on my mind at the time as an illustration of cool and calculating daring. Shortly after the landing, when the 14th Battalion was in a position at the summit of the ridge that overlooked the beach, we were charged with defending the crest against the Turks, who occupied the next parallel range about 500 yards farther inland.

"As the Turks came in open order across the little plain at the foot of the hills, we potted them with machineguns. Those who got across attained safety in the 'dead ground' under our own hill, and there got ready to storm our position. At Courtney's Post, on the summit, Lieutenant Rutland of the 14th was in charge of a Vicker's gun, which he was himself firing. As the Turks advanced in short rushes he fired continually, until just at a critical time the gun jammed.

"No one could have blamed Rutland had he thrown the useless thing down. The Turks were shelling his position from the next ridge, and he was defenceless against the advance.

"Rutland did not give up. He sat down coolly in his trench and pulled the gun to pieces. He found the defect and put the thing together just in time to use it against the approaching Turks. He mowed them down, and their officer, a German, led the remnant on. To such close quarters did they get that the German made a blow at Rutland with his sword, not quite reaching him.

"The advance was stopped, but at the cost of gallant Rutland's life. He fell, riddled with a dozen close-range Turkish bullets. Ballarat has reason to be proud of such a son."

* * *

Scots Church, Collins Street, 17 October 1923

It was the season for marriages. James and Beatrice Wanliss Morrison smiled as they walked down the aisle, each pew alternately decorated with bunches of arum lilies, and white snapdragons. James was from St Peter's Pass, Oatlands, in Tasmania, and Beatrice was the daughter of Sir William and Lady Irvine. Sir William was the Lieutenant-Governor and a former Premier of Victoria, and Lady Irvine was a Wanliss. Only months ago her father, Thomas Drummond Wanliss had died in Edinburgh at the age of 94. As a young man he pushed a wheelbarrow from South Australia to the goldfields of Ballarat, where he prospered. A radical conservative, he joined Peter Lalor's committee at the Eureka Stockade, and later took a seat in the Legislative Assembly.

As the young couple emerged into the street the crowds cheered through the police barricade that held them back. Sir William stood proudly in his silk top hat, and the official cars sped the bridal party away to the reception, which was to be held at Stonington, a grand old mansion set in Malvern.

* * *

Built for a founder of the Cobb & Co stagecoach company, it was named after the founder's wife's hometown in the United States. Now it served as the "other Government House", since the original State Government House in the Domain was the Australian Governor-General's residence. The wedding breakfast was served in a marquee on the lawn and the guest list read like a who's who of Melbourne's political, business and social elite.

Most of the Wanliss clan was in the garden at Stonington that morning. T.D. Wanliss had two daughters, Lady Irvine and Mrs A.J. Fisken, of the Lal Lal Estate. Lady Irvine's brother, Captain Ewen Wanliss, was formerly the Lieutenant-Governor's adjutant. A lawyer by training, he was now an associate to Mr Justice Macfarlane, and was there with his wife Rose. Two of T.D.'s sons were colonels in the Great War, but were not at the wedding. Lieutenant-Colonel Cecil Wanliss led the 2nd Lancashire Regiment. His brother, Lieutenant-Colonel Sydney Wanliss CMG, led the Victorian 'Scottish' 5th Battalion when it landed at Gallipoli. It was an amazing family.

Neville, who was the youngest of T.D.'s sons was there with his bride of two weeks, the former Miss Helen Greene. They were a mature couple, he being forty-seven and she thirty-five. Neville was now earning a living from share trading. Earlier in life he had tried his hand at many things, including as a jackeroo on a cattle station. It was there that he discovered one night, during an electrical storm on the open plain, that he was terribly affected by the sound of thunder, and flashes of lightning. It was a wonder that Neville had volunteered for active service at Gallipoli, where the British and Turkish guns thundered continuously. On his way there he was on the *Southland*, which was sunk by a torpedo from a German submarine thirty nautical miles from Lemnos. Fourteen men were killed by the explosion, and twenty were drowned, but 1400 of them came off in an extremely calm manner, singing *Australia Will Be There*.

Neville and Helen were standing in the garden near the eastern steps of the building with Neville's niece, Dr. Marion Wanliss, and their sister in law, Rose. Marion was just fifteen years old when her older brother Harold sailed off to eternity. Despite her brother's warnings that medicine was too brutal for a girl, she persisted with her studies and was now the John Grice Cancer Research Scholar at the Walter and Eliza Hall Pathology Institute. Newton Wanliss came up to them looking for his wife.

"Have you seen Margaret?" he asked.

"No father, I haven't."

"Isn't this a wonderful wedding?" Newton commented with a cheerfulness that was now quite rare for him.

"Yes, I fully agree," his daughter replied, understanding that his praise of the wedding was code for several things, in particular the hurt he felt that Harold had not come home to be part of it. He also thought that Marion was reaching a stage when marriage would soon be expected, yet she presented a great challenge to the young men in her age group who had survived the war. She had a higher educational standing than most men, she was making more money than most men made, and she was not going to be told what to do by any man – except, her father.

Newton's brother Neville suggested that Newton have another look for Margaret in the marquee, and after he had gone, Marion voiced her concerns.

"I'm worried about him you know. He's still obsessed with Harold."

"It's understandable," Neville thought.

"And he's writing that book," Helen said, smiling.

"It's more than a book," Marion grumbled. "All he does is correspond with 14th Battalion men. There must be a hundred of them that he writes to. I feel so sorry for poor old Margaret – all she gets to do is type up his manuscript."

"Oh, don't say that," Neville said, "he's also the president of the Old Ballarat Collegians. That must divert his attention somewhat?"

"Does it?" Marion rejoined. "He's establishing an Honour Board at the school, with Harold's name is on it, and he's donating Harold's revolver to the Australian War Museum for display."

"He wants others to remember him too," Helen said.

"Well, I don't know of anyone else like him, do you?"

"That's a bit harsh, Marion," Neville said.

"It's not healthy," Marion whispered, smiling as she saw Mabel Brookes approaching them. Mabel was a whirlwind of a woman, who at the age of eighteen married Norman Brookes, thirteen years her senior, the first non-Briton to win the men's open at Wimbledon. A conservative feminist socialite, she had an organising talent that was being applied to good deeds. Having been on the Committee of the Royal Children's Hospital since 1918, she had just been appointed President of the Queen Victoria Hospital. To top it off, she dabbled as a romantic novelist.

"What's not healthy, Marion?" asked Mabel.

"My father," she answered honestly. "Allow me to introduce my uncle, Mr Neville Wanliss, and my aunts Helen and Rose."

"Delighted. How's the Walter and Eliza Hall Pathological Institute coming along? I understand that Dr Kellaway has taken charge."

"Doing a good job, I think."

"Now, I would like to talk with you about my plans for the Queen Victoria Hospital, but not today," said Mabel. Marion nodded, but had other ideas. She wasn't going to be corralled as a female doctor attending to women's issues. Her interests were broader.

"I'll give you a call during the week," she replied.

"Splendid, I'm looking forward to it," said Mabel as she noticed her friend Mrs Pitt Rivers in the corner of her eye. "Oh, there's someone I must see. Do excuse me, will you dear?" She waved to the others as she sailed off.

"Now there's a woman with spirit," Neville commented.

"I should say so."

"Have you read any of her books?" Rose asked Marion.

"No, I can't say I have," Marion shrugged. "What are they about?"

"Adventure and romance," said Rose. "Her most recent book is called *Old Desires*. It came out last year."

"Ooh, that sounds rather saucy," Marion said, permitting herself a smile.

"The title is the most saucy part of it!" Rose laughed. "It's about a young woman from Melbourne who finds herself in Cairo during the war and meets a dashing officer in the Light Horse."

"Her books are mostly about Egypt, aren't they?" asked Helen. "She lived there during the war I believe."

"I think that's right, dear," said Neville.

* * *

Newton could not find Margaret in the marquee, but spoke to his brother, Ewen Wanliss, who among other things told him about the Australian relief effort for the victims of the recent Tokyo earthquake disaster. The Argus Fund had collected £48,967 for the Japanese victims. Over 100,000 people had been killed out of a population of over 2 million.

"All of our aid is being sent over on a chartered ship," Ewen told him. "And Lieutenant-Colonel Peck is coordinating the Australian relief effort."

"He's in Melbourne then?"

"I believe he is giving a press conference soon."

Newton saw an opportunity to see him about the book. He heard good things about Peck's leadership qualities from Harold.

* * *

9 pm, St Kilda Town Hall, Friday, 3 November 1923

A month or so after the celebrated Wanliss wedding, a young man named Frederick Falkiner Knight was having a very good time at the Victoria League Ball. He saw action at Gallipoli and the Western Front, and having resumed his law course after the war, was admitted to practice in 1922. While in his late twenties, he was still living with his family at the high end of St Georges Road, Toorak, the same road that General Monash lived on. Fred's grandfather, Franc Sadlier Falkiner, was one of the big Australian land barons, who between the 1880s and early 1900s bought over a million pounds worth of sheep stations.

It was a glittering social event, with many of Australia's elite attending. The St Kilda Town Hall's large ballroom and balcony could accommodate 1000 guests. Designed by noted architect William Pitt, its vaulted ceiling could be opened at night. Stories used to circulate that the updraft created by that would suck people's hats up to the sky, so they should hang onto them.

Fred had a marvellous sense of humour, and was rocking back in his chair with laughter when a big firm hand came down upon his shoulder. The smiles disappeared from the faces of his friends around the table, and his own expression dropped as he looked up to find the huge frame of Major-General Sir William Glasgow hovering above him.

"Come with me, young man, I have something important to tell you," he told Fred sternly.

"You too," said Glasgow pointing to two of Fred's friends. They all followed him out, as if the war was still on. Out in the foyer at the base of the staircase up to the balcony, he told them.

"Now listen boys, there's a very serious situation developing in the city. Half of the police force has gone on strike, and Melbourne's underworld is taking matters into its own hands. There's a very great danger to people and property at the moment, and it is your duty to proceed to the Town Hall in the morning to be sworn in as volunteers to keep the peace."

Like Pompey Elliott, Glasgow went to the South African War as a young man, and like Pompey he won a Distinguished Conduct Medal there. They both went off to Gallipoli as battalion commanders, and both were promoted to Brigadier-Generals on the Western Front. Then on 25 April 1918, on the third anniversary of the Anzac Day landing, Elliott's 15th Brigade and Glasgow's 13th Brigade executed that brilliant pincer movement counter-attack on Villers Brettonneux that routed the remnants of three German divisions. Lauded by French Commander-in-Chief, Generalissimo Foch as "astonishingly valiant", and by General Monash as "the finest thing yet done in the war, by Australians or any other troops", it had largely been achieved through Elliott's strategic genius. Glasgow was rewarded with a divisional command soon after, while Elliott was snubbed.

Elliott blamed Birdwood and it did not escape Elliott's attention that Birdwood's Chief of Staff was General Brudenell White, who had been a long time friend of Glasgow's back in Queensland.

* * *

The police strike didn't happen overnight. The pay scales of the Victorian police had fallen out of line with other States, but that was just the powder. The match that ignited it was the spooks, the plain clothes supervisors introduced by the Police Commissioner, Alexander Nicholson, as a means of maintaining the efficiency of a police force that had been caught napping – literally. One night an inspector arrived at a large suburban police station and found the lot of them, including the officer in charge, were in slumberland instead of out there pounding the beat.

Then on the Wednesday prior to the Victoria League Ball, a couple of "spooks", Senior Constables Murphy and Tebbs, found Constables Poulter and Sutton enjoying a spot of tea at the watchman's cabin on the wharf at 5.50 pm, which was ten minutes before their appointed sign-off time and reported them. That did it.

The leader of the strikers, Constable William Brooks, declared the strikers would not parade until the spooks were withdrawn. In successive discussions with the State cabinet and Commissioner Nicholson he said he had plenty of money, and would fight this to the "last penny". Nicholson, in reply told him: "You need not think that I am going to allow you to get the impression that you are going to make me 'knock at the knees', as the Police Department will spend every penny to prevent that position arising."

"In that case," answered Brooks defiantly, "if it comes to a fight, I have a few *shillings*, and I am prepared to spend every penny of *them*."

It came to a fight all right. The 634 striking constables were dismissed on Thursday after they refused to return to work unconditionally, and on Friday morning that fact was publicised in the papers. By Friday night it was on for young and old. Even without a major riot in the city, Friday night would have been eventful. It was the Spring Carnival, and Luna Park was re-opened after massive renovations. Lit up by 40,000 electric lights, it boasted the "Big Dipper" roller-coaster ride, a new £15,000 carousel, the "Water Chute", "Noah's Ark", "Splasho" and the "Tropic Caves". At the showgrounds Wirth Brothers' Circus was presenting "The Greatest Show on Earth", while in the city every playhouse and picture theatre was ablaze with lights.

The simultaneous closing of the pubs at 6 pm on Friday night had expelled hundreds of intoxicated men of all ages into the streets. It was also late night shopping up to 9 pm that night, with the "kerbside waiters" – the boyfriends – waiting on the footpaths for their girlfriends to finish work. Smiling girls grasped their arms and peeled off down the street one by one. The saveloy van vendors were doing a brisk trade down near the clocks of Flinders Street station as thousands of people stayed back in the city, curious to see what was going to happen next.

High-pressure hoses were used continuously from 9 pm to midnight outside the Town Hall to keep the mob back. When they skittled someone with a blast from the hose it hurt as they hit the ground. At 11 pm the contingent of loyal constables from the country arrived at the Spencer Street Station and were jostled, but made it through to the Town Hall, having to bloody the crowd, including police strikers, with their batons in order to get there. An arrogant two-up school operated continuously at the intersection of Collins Street and Swanston Street adjacent to the Town Hall, with around 300 participants. In short, the mob felt it could do whatever it liked, whenever it liked.

But even a mob has to sleep.

* * *

The next morning a stream of young men, mostly ex-AIF, began to arrive at the Town Hall in Swanston Street. The main hall was buzzing with activity. Fred wondered if it was an unnecessary over-reaction, as there was no trouble outside and he was bursting to get to Flemington Racecourse. After being sworn in by a Justice of the Peace, and leaving his home phone number, he was on the next train to Flemington.

Fred himself had been frustrated by the fact that he'd not actually *seen* a Melbourne Cup since before the war. At the 1922 cup he was disappointed when everyone in front of him suddenly jumped up onto their benches, so all he saw was the back of people's heads as the horses came in. This year will be different, he thought. It surely would.

* * *

While Fred was making his way to Flemington in the morning, at 10 am the Premier, Sir Harry Lawson, and the Lord Mayor elect, William Brunton, were locked in a crisis meeting with Lieutenant-General Sir John Monash, General Forsyth, Brigadier-General Pompey Elliott, the Attorney-General, Sir Arthur Robinson, and a number of others at the Chief Secretary's city office. The Chief Secretary, Dr Argyll, was ill.

Monash had returned from war with massive prestige as the leader of the Anzac Corps, and with his reputation intact was now Executive Chairman of the new State Electricity Commission. Elliott was there because of the enormous pulling power that his reputation and personality had over the men in his 15th Brigade, many of whom lived in Melbourne.

"It doesn't take much to release the savage that lurks within humanity," the Premier sighed.

Monash agreed. "I would say that if you were to deprive a civilised man and his family of their food for a week," he said, "by the end of the week that same man would be willing to kill to save his loved ones and himself. The law of the jungle comes back to haunt us from time to time."

"But there is no hunger?" asked the Premier.

"There is human curiosity," Elliott said. "We saw it at the Wazzir riots in Cairo. It only takes a few troublemakers to start something that becomes very difficult to stop, as thousands of spectators arrive and some of them are drawn into it. And there is greed. The looting will throw open the stores to the public. Many people will find that hard to resist… Where does the Commonwealth stand on all this? Have you spoken to Senator Pearce?"

"Senator Pearce is in communication with the acting prime minister, who is in Sydney, and about to make his way here by train. I have informed the Commonwealth that we can no longer guarantee the safety of its property," the Premier said. "Chauvel is in command at the Victoria Barracks, and is now assigning troops for the protection of Commonwealth property. The deployment of troops against the mob would require an Order in Council, under Section 119 of the Constitution, declaring that a state of domestic violence exists. I believe that the Order is being drawn up as we speak… Simply as a precaution at this stage you understand…"

Monash sighed deeply. "In my opinion none of that will be necessary," he said. "I propose that we do not apply a heavy hand at this time."

"But we must protect the central institutions, and private property," the Premier said.

"They will be protected," Monash replied, "by loyal police and by bluejackets from the cruiser *Adelaide*, which is steaming here as we speak. We have already activated the plan to bring order to the streets by calling on ex-AIF men and other volunteers, and swearing them in as 'special constables'. Senator Elliott has kindly agreed to take operational command of the special constables."

Monash had great faith in Elliott as a commander of men. He was the man who stared down the German Army at Villers Bretonneux, and hadn't blinked. He was the man who personally led the 7th Battalion in their magnificent defence of Lone Pine at Gallipoli, where he was splattered with the blood and brains of a digger who had fought beside him, and where his men won four Victoria Crosses fighting a do-or-die battle in an "underground city" of criss-crossing trenches. He wasn't about to be bullied by a pack of looters. If only Monash had taken over from Rainbow Bill earlier in France, Elliott thought, things would have been different. He would have had his divisional command. If?

"We'll have to check the legality of using civilians," said the Premier.

Elliott interjected. "I understand they can be sworn in by a Justice of the Peace."

* * *

While Fred attended the Derby at Flemington, the Town Hall continued to accept recruits. At the centre of it all stood Brigadier-General Pompey Elliott, his large muscular frame barely contained in his three-piece suit, with his fedora now cocked at the angle of a slouch hat. The AIF was back. One of his

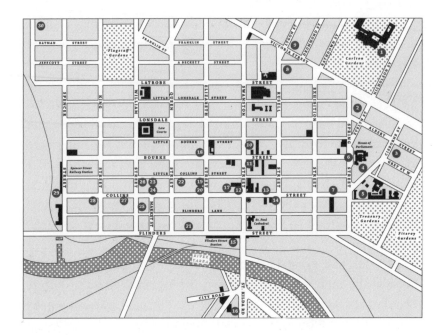

1. Exhibition Building (State Parliament)
2. Rejected site for Shrine of Remembrance
3. St Patrick's Cathedral
4. Federal Parliament House
5. Treasury Building
6. Proposed site of 'Anzac Square'
7. Melbourne Club
8. Police Headquarters
9. Trades Hall
10. Hoyts Theatre
11. Tivoli Theatre
12. Town Hall
13. Georges store
14. Anzac House
15. Flinders Street Station

16. Victoria Barracks
17. Hotel Australia
18. General Post Office
19. Jacka, Edmonds & Co 1929–30
20. Colonial Mutual Life building
21. Commercial Travellers' Association Club
22. Jacka, Edmonds & Co 1925–1929
23. Browning, Bladen & Dare
24. Scott's Hotel
25. Jacka, Edmonds & Co 1924–1925
26. Australian Club
27. Olderfleet (Roxburgh, Jacka & Co 1920–23)
28. Federal Coffee Palace
29. Spencer Street Station
30. The Stadium

Map of Melbourne circa 1919–1931

Based on a map issued to sailors on the H.M.S. Renown in 1927

Source: State Library of Victoria

former men came in with fifteen others, walked straight up to Pompey, and snapped to attention.

"Here we are again, General," he said, as he saluted. "We are ready and willing for another stunt under you."

The officers who had been his trusted lieutenants during the war – Layh, Denehy, Watson and Conder – were put into senior positions in the command structure of the Specials.

* * *

The corridors of the Victoria Barracks hummed with activity as preparations were made for the potential worst-case scenario of a total breakdown of law and order. The early morning meeting of the chiefs of the Navy, Army and Air Force decided to cancel all leave. Plainclothes members of the Australian Intelligence Corps were dispatched to act as caretakers of drill halls, and bolts were removed from the rifles there in case the mob got ideas. Almost one and a half million rounds of ammunition, and twenty Vickers machineguns were brought up to the barracks. Crews were put through refresher courses and some machineguns were mounted on RAAF motor lorries, with sandbags built up around to protect them.

They knew there were Bolsheviks in the city. All they needed was a chaotic breakdown of order, as had occurred in Russia in 1917. Chauvel put the garrison at Queenscliff on alert, ordering the issue of rifle, bayonet, and 100 rounds of live ammunition to each man. The railways were alerted to the potential need for transportation to the city at a moment's notice. All was in readiness, waiting for the order to move.

* * *

That afternoon another man who answered the call, and reported to the Town Hall was former AIF Captain, Donovan Joynt, VC. He was now in colour photography, but back in France he won the Victoria Cross for re-organising and leading the remnants of a demoralised battalion against the Germans in Herleville Wood. He got a job in the command structure as one of the three liaison officers between the loyal police and the Special Force. His task was to accompany plainclothes detectives on raids of houses in the suburbs where the looted goods were being held, and to compile a daily report.

* * *

Fred was an active member of the Australian Club, and as he neared his parent's house on the tram from Flemington, his main concern was whether he had enough time to dress for the Calcutta Dinner that night. But as soon as he came through the door his father told him that he was needed at the Town Hall. Instead of his dinner suit, Fred pulled on his worst clothes and a pair of thick boots. As he dressed, a fifty-year-old farmer from Riverslea near Sale, James Lobey, was killed outside the Leviathan store, when a sailor cracked him over the head with a metal stand. Another man died in the chaos after being hit by a motor vehicle in Swanston Street.

As Fred's father's 1907 Rolls Royce approached the city along St Kilda Road the traffic began to slow down until finally, it came to a standstill. His father bade him good luck, and at that point he stepped out of the car and into the human traffic that seemed to be drawn by curiosity to the city. There were no traffic lights (they were to come fifteen years later) and the chaos was unbelievable. The corner of Collins Street and Market Lane, which faced Scott's Hotel, was often policed by a choleric Irishman who proved to be the hero of the moment, but was well known for his intolerance of pedestrians at the best of times.

"For God's sake woman," he once cried out, "phwat are you doing wid that baby in the pram? It's nine months it took you to get it out, and now it's in nine seconds you'll be losing it!"

Due to the utter chaos around the Town Hall the Irishman came down with his red face and generous white moustache to direct traffic there. Fred watched him being jostled by the mob, but the old policeman stood his ground and was soon assisted by the Fire Department, who turned high pressure hoses on the offenders, bringing them crashing to the pavement. Seeing his opportunity Fred ran through the opening and got to the doors of the Town Hall. The Specials who had been sworn in during the day, almost all ex-AIF, were being armed with batons that had been kept in the vaults of the building since the Melbourne Wharf Labourers' strike of 1892.

"Keep your batons in your hip pockets," ordered the police sergeant. "Don't use them unless you absolutely have to. Don't strike at the head. Aim at the shoulders. We don't want to send people to hospital, we just want them to go home. And above all, make sure you stay on your feet. You'll get kicked in the head if you're on the ground." They were also advised to pack the space under their fedoras with crunched up newspapers as it would soften the impact of a blow to the head.

Once they had been armed and instructed the Specials, together with loyal police, marched out of the Town Hall in fours up Swanston Street and into the main shopping area in Bourke Street and pushed the crowd back across the intersection from London Stores and the post office at Elizabeth Street. One old woman had devised a new weapon to use against the Specials, which consisted of a loaf of bread boiled in water and held together in a brown paper bag. She threw it at one of them, and it splattered over his head, sending hot gluggy liquid running down his face.

"My God!" he yelled. "That old bitch has knocked my bloody brains out!"

"You rotten bloody scabs," some members of the mob jeered, "why don't you throw down those batons and fight man to man!"

Some among the mob distributed leaflets to the Specials and loyal police, providing a colourful definition of a scab, who fills the shoes of the worker striking for better pay and conditions. It read:

*After God had finished the rattlesnake, the toad and the vampire,
He had some awful "substance" left, with which He made a scab.
A scab is a two-legged animal with a cork-screw soul, a water-
sogged brain, and a combination backbone made of jelly and glue.
Where other people have their hearts, he carries a tumor of rotten
principles... Judas Escariot is a gentleman compared with a scab,
for, after betraying his Master, he had enough character to hang
himself, and a scab has not.*

* * *

The splintering and crashing of plate glass could be heard
everywhere. The closely packed phalanx of Specials advanced
through the crowd like the Roman turtle formation. While all
manner of missiles issued from the crowd – bottles, stones and
fragments of plate glass – they did not break. A constable was
struck from behind and fell to the ground, but he sprang back
up and having seen the culprit, lurched after him with his baton
flashing, parting the crowd with blows to shoulders. The thuds
echoed through the crowd, accompanied by wild cries and the
high pitched shrieking of women rioters.

Fred was paired up with another Special, and sent out to patrol
the side streets. At one store he caught by the scruff of his neck
a weedy looking man who was grabbing a necktie, and arrested
him. "This man's not from the underworld," Fred thought. "He's
probably got a family waiting for him at home." The crowd jostled
him roughly, forcing him to release his prisoner, but he ran like a
scared rabbit into a row of police constables who re-arrested him.
Fred had to kick his way through the crowd to get out, but by the
time he got to the police line they had pushed his prisoner into
the gutter, and released him.

"Why did you release him?" a bewildered Fred asked the
officer.

"I can't afford to hold onto him," answered the senior officer.
"I'd have to send a constable away every time I had a prisoner like

that taken to the lock-up, and frankly, every one of my men is worth seven of you."

At 8.20 pm the looters concentrated outside Salamy's in Bourke Street, where a tempting row of clocks sat high up on a shelf, still protected by jagged plate glass. In a moment looters had scurried up on the shoulders of their chums, and Mr Salamy's remaining pieces were gone. The Edmends store suffered a similar fate, as the plate glass windows were kicked in and the baying rioters made off with their loot.

At Dumbrella's Jewellry things turned out differently. As the mob smashed the window, and were about to enter, a tall man jumped out of the darkness within the store and through the broken window onto the pavement. The mob froze for a second. In his trembling right hand he held a revolver, its barrel gleaming. Nervously pointing the revolver this way and that, with his left hand he pushed them back and held his ground. Beaten back like hungry wolves they re-armed with broken bottles and other missiles, and rushed him, but he retreated to the recesses of his store, which they dared not enter.

Incredibly, while all this was going on, spruikers outside the Melba and Britannia picture theatres had continued to plie their trade, as if nothing untoward was happening.

"Come on in and experience the incredible adventures of Douglas Fairbanks in *Robin Hood*," called a spruiker.

"See the age of chivalry, romance and adventure resuscitated in this gorgeous spectacle of twentieth century realism!"

"*Robin Hood*!... Magnificent in its scenic splendour!"

"Exquisite in its beauty and artistry!"

"Thrilling and pulsating in its drama!"

"Sweetly heartfelt in its delicious love story!"

The show, it seems, must go on regardless. On this night? If you wanted drama it was out there in the streets, and it was free. Better than free.

Suddenly shots rang out, and discharged smoke from the spent cartridges rose above the thronging crowd. The crowd moved on to the gleaming section of plate glass that still stood untouched between Buckley and Nunn's and the post office. Most of the smaller items in the windows had already been removed by staff within. The shopfront mannequins, dressed in their exquisite Melbourne Cup attire, remained blissfully unaware of the danger they were in.

"Yah! Stand away and put a bottle through it!" yelled one lout.

"If you sink your boot into that, it'll come out and cut ya ta pieces!" screamed his accomplice.

"Let's have a bonfire!"

"What about having a go at the banks?"

"More bottles! Into the wine and spirit windows…"

At around 11 pm William Ignatius Spain, an ex-serviceman and railway worker was bashed to death by three youths who robbed him for the two bottles of beer he was carrying. That vicious crime occurred outside Wirth's Circus in Sloss street near City Road.

* * *

On Sunday morning carpenters were hard at work in the city, boarding up the windows of all the stores that hadn't been looted. General Elliott was at the Town Hall conducting an interview with a journalist. "The people can rely upon the sternest possible measures against a repetition of last night's disgraceful scenes," he told him.

By the afternoon the situation had changed. Elliott was discussing the progress of day's operations with his lieutenants when his wartime superior officer, Major-General Sir James McCay, arrived in the company of General Monash and they went to a room. Pompey got the point very quickly.

"Sir James has kindly offered to assist us, and I've taken him up on it," Monash said. "I've decided to undertake a re-structure, with McCay as overall commander of the Special Constabulary force, and you continuing as the 'outside commander', directing the men in the field." The news hit Pompey between the eyes.

"But we've just brought the city under control," he said, forcing a smile.

"I know that, but General McCay has strong organising ability and if he's offering it we should accept." He noticed some resistance from Elliott, so he made it crystal clear. "I take it, then, that you are happy to take orders from General McCay in the chain of command?"

Elliott looked over at McCay, who had remained silent throughout the exchange. "Yes, of course," he answered with cheeks flushed. Inwardly, however, the motivations for this outrage were clear in Elliott's mind. There was an inference of inefficiency, and Elliott knew McCay was Monash's mate from his school days at Scotch College. To Elliott it was the war all over again, like the first day at Gallipoli when McCay had overruled him in the field prior to his wounding. He was being superseded, just as Jacka had been. It was what he was talking about in the Senate debates two years ago. It was enough to break a man's heart.

* * *

When Bert arrived at work that Monday, Ernie was already reading the account of the riots published in *The Argus*. He waved the front page at Bert as he came through the door.

Mob Violence in City
Result of Police Mutiny
Rioting and Looting
Leading shops attacked
200 casualties; many arrests
Citizens rally to authority
Special Force now exceeds 2000

Ernie asked him if he had seen the headlines, and Bert told him he didn't need the paper to tell him what his eyes could see. Everyone on the tram had been glued to the papers that morning.

"What's the country coming to when you can't rely on the police?" Ernie asked.

"Well, normally they are just taken for granted, aren't they?" Bert replied. They were both happy to hear Pompey Elliott was running the show from the Town Hall. They were convinced that if it hadn't been for the old AIF, things could have been much worse. Ernie wanted to take a closer look, so he and Bert struck out along Collins Street and then turned into Elizabeth Street and Little Collins Street. It had rained overnight and the water had washed into the gutters some of the shameful leftovers from the mob's antics over the weekend. It made for a very dismal scene under the grey skies. The Specials were out in the streets in their long coats with their white armbands clearly identifying them. The scene reminded them a bit of some of the bombed-out towns and cities they saw in northern France and Belgium. In all, seventy-eight stores had their windows smashed and were looted. The loyal police and Specials had arrested fifty-five offenders so far.

The sight of this carnage hardened Bert's attitude to strikes. Bert and other AIF veterans had experienced the effects of some severe strikes, including the London police strike in 1919. At one point troops had to intervene in Scotland owing to the general strike taking place at the time. Bert's own business had been hurt by wharf and seamen's strikes in Australia too.

The two men walked along for a time surveying the damage, and neither of them spoke. "Is this what we fought for?" Bert thought to himself at times, but then he saw the volunteer spirit in the Specials, who had been willing to take risks to protect their way of life, and it lifted him up again. It was the same spirit that had fuelled them almost a decade earlier, when they had gone off to fight the war for civilisation.

* * *

The danger that the city would descend into general chaos had now subsided, and things were returning to a relatively normal pace. Most people, it seemed, had simply gone back to their day jobs – after a wild weekend of rioting and looting. Still bitterly disappointed, General Elliott attended the early morning Citizen's Committee meeting, and told General Monash that he would like to be released from duty because he wanted to participate in the hearings of the Navigation Act Royal Commission, which were being held in Queensland. Monash thanked him for his valuable contribution.

As Bert and Ernie walked along Collins Street towards the Amsterdam end, a taxi carrying Senator Elliott passed them on its way to Spencer Street Station. About the same time Captain Donovan Joynt VC was reporting to the Chief Secretary, Dr Argyll, who wanted to know what had transpired at the secret meeting of communists that had taken place the night before at the Trades Hall building in Lygon Street. A police spy had attended the meeting, which had been called to discuss the potential for revolution. Joynt obtained the police report and delivered it to Dr Argyll's office personally. The report stated that the idea of revolution had been raised, and a fiery debate ensued, but the hot-heads who might have dreamt of the Trades Hall as some kind of Antipodean "Smolny Institute" and the Town Hall as the "Winter Palace" had been overruled by their more sober colleagues, who pointed to the extraordinarily swift and effective organisation of the Special Constables. They seemed to have little idea of what would have been in store for them from General Chauvel's men at the barracks, had they been let loose.

* * *

Elliott stepped out of the taxi at Spencer Street Station. The driver came out onto the footpath and helped him unload his luggage. While Elliott was paying him, four rough-looking characters slithered into the taxi. One of them yelled out to the taxi driver.

"Get a bloody move on, mate, we haven't got all day!"

"Will you be all right?" Elliott asked the cabbie, concerned at the rudeness of his passengers. "They look like a rough mob."

"She'll be right, Guv," the cabbie assured him with a wink. "I'll drive these bods straight to the lock-up if they give me any trouble." These were mobsters from Sydney's underworld, who had arrived on the overnight train, lured by stories of looting that had appeared in the Sydney papers on Saturday. They expected there to be a free-for-all, a world in which there were no police to check the animal spirits with which they had been so generously blessed. They were to be bitterly disappointed, but they could still pick pockets at the Melbourne Cup, which was on the next day. Organisers were expecting a crowd of 125,000.

A COUNTRY FIT FOR HEROES

Lissa Thorn, 10 Redan Street, St Kilda, 14 December 1923

Newton Wanliss maintained a flat at Lissa Thorn for the times he and Margaret were staying in the city. Newton was still in the midst of an extensive correspondence with 14th Battalion veterans. It was a painful task, as every letter he received and every page he wrote brought back the memory of his son, who appeared to him in episodic flashes almost every day. Each year, on the anniversary of his son's death, he would place an "In Memoriam" notice in the papers that read:

> In proud memory of my heroic son, Captain Harold Boyd Wanliss D.S.O., killed in action, September 26, 1917. — None perhaps fell that day with more glory, yet many fell and there was much glory.

From the drawer of his desk he took out the pamphlet he had printed in England, which contained extracts from the letters of condolence sent to him after Harold's death. He found the one written by the 14th Battalion's Padre, Major Francis Rolland, MC, who took over from Padre Andrew Gillison after Gallipoli. Of all the wonderful letters he received, this was the most poignant.

You will have heard ere now of the unspeakable loss that is yours
and ours. We had no rejoicing in our splendid victory — the price
was too great. I had often intended to tell you what Harold was to
us all, but even now I cannot measure it in words... And unless I was
blind he would have been Australia's leader in days when she will
sorely need one... I need not tell you that Harold was the "beloved
Captain" of our Battalion — the best man and the best soldier and
the truest gentleman in our Brigade. I can only say that he died at
the head of his Company after gaining his objective; and though
we know so little of the afterlife, and his career seems so unfinished
here, I believe he has gained his objective there also — and his brave,
unselfish spirit, so quick to grasp new situations and outlooks, is
already at home in the wider life that God has for such as he. His
death was almost instantaneous: he died in a friend's arms. He was
buried in the position he had won.

Newton put down the letter. He wasn't the kind of man who
would ever cry, but his eyes had moistened as he read those words.
Staring into the wall he imagined his son in that encounter with
the enemy at Polygon Wood, and imagined the final moment,
when that bullet ripped through his body and exited through his
back, taking his young, promising life with it. He was so proud of
his son, and what he might have been, that the pain burned like a
candle inside him. But Newton's moment of silent reflection was
interrupted by the sound of someone knocking at the door. He
could hear Margaret walking along the corridor to answer it.

"Good evening, Captain Jacka, please do come in," she said
excitedly. She knew her husband would be delighted.

"Evening, Mrs Wanliss, is Mr Wanliss home?"

Newton came out to the corridor, and asked Bert to come
into the study, so Margaret left them to themselves. Bert had
come to deliver a copy of his Gallipoli diary. It wasn't very long,
only thirteen pages sparsely written on seven sheets, and he had
written it out with a fountain pen in his flowing cursive style on

Roxburgh, Jacka & Co. letterhead. Now that the firm's name had been changed, he had quite a few sheets of spare stationery to go through.

Newton said that he was just writing the chapters on Gallipoli, and getting some very fine contributions. He assumed that Bert had written about his VC action in the diary, and was disappointed when Bert told him it was quite brief. So Newton asked him to explain it to him. It was almost nine years since Courtney's Post, and Bert had been through so many battles since, but there was nothing he didn't remember about the morning that changed the rest of his life.

Bert explained how 40,000 Turks had attacked just before dawn, and D Company was called up into the front line. He pulled his fountain pen from a pocket, and began to draw up the positions of the forward and reserve trenches on the morning of the great attack. He showed how he flanked the Turks who had occupied a section of the Australian line, jumped into the trench and killed seven of them.

"Extraordinary," said Newton, who was spellbound by Bert's personal account.

The door opened slowly, and Margaret came in, carefully balancing some cups of tea on a tray.

"I thought you might enjoy a fresh cup of tea."

"Thank you Mrs Wanliss, that is very kind of you," said Bert.

"Yes, thank you, Margaret, you may set it down on the table," Newton added.

"How is Mrs Jacka?"

"Good."

"Margaret," Newton interrupted, "we still have some matters to discuss. We'll come into the parlour shortly." She understood his obsession about this book, and retired without saying another word. Newton opened a drawer. "I've been meaning to ask you about Polygon Wood," he said, unfolding a detailed military map of the area between Zonnebeke and the apex of Polygon Wood,

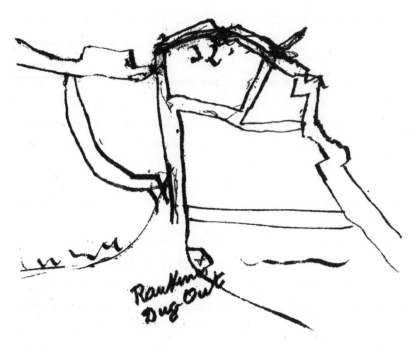

Map of Courtney's Post

Drawn by Albert Jacka on the back of a copy of his Gallipoli diary

Source: *Albert Jacka, Diary*, Source Records of the 14th Battalion by Newton Wanliss,
AWM MSS 143A

which was the area where his son had fallen in the battle. "I am trying to locate where Harold was buried in the field." As he spoke, Bert moved his teacup aside, helped his host straighten out the sectioned map on the study table, and immediately began orienting himself to the ground. The map was Sheet 28 (1:40,000).

"As you know, Lieutenant Norman Aldridge was with Harold at the time, and he later gave me the map reference J.4.b.4.3., which I passed on to the Imperial War Graves Commission, but it turns out they could not find him. I am wondering whether your recollection might assist in locating Harold... I would like to see him buried with his comrades, in a cemetery nearby, with a headstone over him. He deserves that at least, don't you think?"

"He certainly does Mr Wanliss. Leave it with me," Bert said. Bert could feel the suffering that Newton was experiencing. Newton would never feel the warmth of Harold's children.

"And how's your daughter getting on?" Bert asked, trying to look on the bright side of things. Harold had told him about his precocious little sister, who at fifteen years of age had the audacity to want to be a doctor, and hang anybody who tried get in her way.

"Oh, you know a reference to her appeared in the paper a few days ago. Did you not see it?" Newton had a copy lying nearby, and began searching through it.

"No. What did it say?"

"What did it say?" Newton asked rhetorically, as he put his reading glasses on. "I'll read it to you: 'The board of the Melbourne Hospital adopted the recommendation of the advisory board to appoint Dr Marion Wanliss medical clinical assistant, and Dr Ethel Osborne surgical clinical assistant.'" He looked up momentarily and Bert responded immediately.

"Congratulations!"

"Wait. Here's what one of the board members at the hospital, Dr McInerney, had to say about it. 'I view the appointment of so many women doctors to the medical staff of the hospital with considerable concern!'

"Can you imagine," Newton commented, "*two* women had been appointed! What calamity! Then the president, Mr A. T. Danks said, 'Your concerns are ill-founded Dr McInerney. Mark my words, I have had more experience of such matters than you. I've had just as much experience as you,' Dr McInereney replied."

"What a farce this is!" Newton added after a pause.

It was unusual for Newton to be this emotional. He was the quintessential old-fashioned Victorian gentleman, but he knew his daughter could do anything a male doctor could do, and probably do it better. Bert had felt discrimination in Egypt, when his working-class background was seen as making him unfit for officer training. He had some empathy for her from that perspective, but in his own household he would not dream of allowing Vera to get a job, and neither did Vera especially want one.

"Is your daughter very upset?" Bert asked.

"Oh, she's used to this kind of thing," Newton said with a wry smile. "It's 'character building' she says."

* * *

A few weeks later, just after Bert and Vera had returned to Melbourne after spending Christmas in Wedderburn, on the evening of 28 December 1923, a fire broke out in McCulloch's Building. As a result, the premises of Jacka, Edmonds & Co were severely damaged, and Bert, Ernie and the staff missed the rest of their Christmas holidays salvaging what they could, and reorganising the firm. They had to start over again, and this time rented space at 50 William Street, which was just around the corner.

* * *

8.30 pm, Melbourne Town Hall, 23 May 1924

Only six months after holding out against the mob, the Melbourne Town Hall hosted the quarterly "smoke social" of the Honorary Justices Association. As the special guest, Bert Jacka was making yet another presentation on the campaigns of the AIF in France and Belgium with the assistance of lantern slides.

"I propose that we drink a toast to the lecturer," said Mr T. Patterson. "We should all pay tribute to Captain Jacka's fine war service. His lecture has helped those of us who stayed at home to realise what the men at the war have suffered." The toast was supported by the Chief Commissioner of Police, Alexander Nicholson, who had been at the centre of the police strike.

"In the position which I hold," Nicholson noted, "I have had opportunities to show preference to returned men, and I do so whenever possible. That principle of preference should apply to the whole of Australia."

There was resounding support for the proposition, particularly in the presence of Albert Jacka, but Bert knew that it wasn't being adhered to in practice, and many diggers were still out of work. There was also a debate on whether women should be eligible for the office of justice of the peace. During the war women had stepped into roles that had previously been the exclusive preserve of males. Now there were even women bank clerks, which seemed unthinkable prior to the war. Yet there was no female justice of the peace, and it was an issue that was being debated by the State Cabinet.

Not long afterwards, Bert was the speaker at the Middle Park branch of the Australian Natives Association, which held an Anzac Remembrance Night at St Anselm's Hall in Langridge Street. Bert was welcomed by the president, Mr E. Goldstein, who lauded him as the epitome of the Anzac warrior. He was still heavily in demand as a speaker, since everybody knew his name would bring the public in. But every night that Bert was doing his good deeds out in the community Vera was left at home, or went alone to visit her mother. Vera's father had died and her mother was at the Bayview Street house all by herself, feeling very depressed that her husband had not lived to see any grandchildren.

* * *

7.45 pm, Ballroom, Collingwood Town Hall, 16 July 1924

That July Bert and Vera were among the honoured guests at a ball given by the Mayor and Mayoress of Collingwood. The grand Collingwood Town Hall had been built in the New Empire style and was dominated by a tall central clock tower that recalled London's Big Ben. The many windows that were cut out of its dark walls beamed streams of light into Hoddle Street.

Those taking part in the mayoral group included the Mayor of Collingwood, Councillor Tonini, and the Mayoress, the Mayor and Mayoress of Caulfield, Preston, Hawthorn and Fitzroy, and the acting Mayoress of St Kilda. Vera's frock was made of black satin, and had an overdress of black tulle with vandyked flounces edged with cornflower blue. A cluster of blue flowers was placed on the bodice. She was happy that night, as it was a glittering event, and she and Bert made a handsome and extremely popular couple. But before long they were separated, as Bert was drawn into discussions on the war.

"You are so lucky being married to such a dashing war hero," said one of the women who were standing with Vera. She smiled politely. There was no use talking to someone whose best attempt at conversation was to tell you how lucky you were to be married to your husband. "She doesn't even know him," she thought. She could just see his head among the group of people, including mayors and politicians, who had surrounded him. At least he isn't surrounded by women like this one, she thought. She was determined to continue having a good time, so she turned to another woman in her group.

"Have you seen any interesting performances at the theatre recently?" Vera asked. She was wondering why Bert hadn't taken her to any shows at the Tiv. "He's got a perpetual free ticket, and he doesn't have the time to use it," she thought.

"I haven't been to a theatre performance in months," the woman answered, "but I'm in the Austral Salon, and yesterday we had an 'At Home' at the Women's Automobile Club room at Anzac House." Founded in Melbourne in 1890 by a group of women writers, the Austral Salon was a club for the pursuit of music, literature and the arts.

"We were treated to a fascinating talk by Miss Nina Brensnall on the life and conditions of women in India… It's appalling what they have to put up with from their men."

"I pity the poor widows who are burned to death along with their husbands," said one woman.

"Beastly behaviour," said another.

"Yes, we heard all about that," said the Austral Salon woman, "apparently they are drugged, and drenched in oil so they burn faster."

"How considerate!"

"Excuse me," said Vera who was feeling her body shudder. "I think my husband needs me." She didn't want to hear any more of death. It was such a constant theme in her life with Bert that she was sick of it. He was always thinking and talking about those who had died young at the war — he just couldn't let go.

"Next week we'll be hosting some visiting artists, Mr Lenghi-Cellini and Mr Zacharewitsch," the woman continued after Vera had left them to find her husband.

During a quiet moment later on in the evening, Councillor Tonini thanked Bert again for opening the Collingwood Sailors' and Soldiers' Memorial Hall, which cost £5000, and was just a few doors down from the Town Hall on Hoddle Street. Finished late in June, it was built in remembrance of the sons of Collingwood who had not returned. It was a duty that Bert could not pass up.

* * *

The Jacka residence, Ridge Street, Wedderburn, 25 December 1924

The year had passed so quickly. At Christmas time, Bert and Vera travelled to Wedderburn. Vera still felt like an outsider and didn't look forward to these gatherings.

For the last two Christmases Bert's younger brother Bill and his family hadn't been there either. Bill Jacka and his British wife Joan had come to Australia at the end of 1920. Under the Soldier Settlement Scheme Bill began working the dairy farm they called "Tafwelton", at Berwick, about 40 miles east of Melbourne. The name reminded Joan of Taffs Well, the Welsh town she came from. Their daughter Joy was born a year later, but the time Joan spent in maternity at Nurse Mathieson's Private Hospital was hell for her because of the Matron, who had it in for British brides who in her mind had stolen Aussie boys away from their rightful owners. After that she swore she wouldn't have another child in an Australian hospital. As a result of the collapse in butterfat prices in 1920–21, Bill's dairy farm failed. To top it off Joan was feeling unwell, so they had returned to Wales.

During 1924 Bill and Joan had arrived from Wales a second time. This time they settled in Wedderburn, where Bill bought a horse and dray for £45, and started to cart wood like his father. In the same year Sam and Elizabeth Jacka had finally established their butcher shop in the main street of Wedderburn. Above the short two-posted verandah it had a big hemispherical sign, which proudly proclaimed the Jacka name. Sam also bought a small pick-up truck, so that he could make deliveries to outlying properties.

Vera found that the Christmas gathering was not as bad as she had feared. Family members were nice to her, and she found that she was getting on particularly well with Sam's wife, Elizabeth. It was quite an effort for Elizabeth and Nathaniel to accommodate their expansive family at such a big Christmas lunch. Once the big Christmas luncheon was celebrated at Grandmother Kettle's. Now the only way to deal with such a large family was to set up tables in their backyard. Several days went into the preparations, and Nathaniel, with his sons Sam and Bill knocked together some long tables – but you could never seat thirteen to a table. It was bad luck.

Except for the actual Christmas pudding, the food, decorations, and amusements had all been provided or prepared by daughters and daughters-in-law under Elizabeth's supervision. By the time Vera had arrived by train with Bert there was nothing left for her to do, which made her feel somewhat left out. Nevertheless, the Christmas spirit carried everything along, and the mood at the table during the meal was merry. The trees in the backyard had been decorated in paper-link chains of different colours that the children had made.

The thing that Bert loved was the joyful banter of the children. It reminded him of the days that he as a boy had led his two younger brothers, Sid and Bill, on adventures around town and beyond. Bert's nephews and nieces screamed with delight as they popped their Christmas crackers, and found their party hats. They all remained quiet and very attentive when the steaming giant Christmas pudding was brought out. Elizabeth cut the hot, dark, fruity pudding into portions and poured even hotter yellow custard over them. As columns of steam rose from their plates both the children, and adults began to eat in silence. They ate cautiously too, as the pudding was so hot and there were treasurers to be found. If you didn't watch out you could easily swallow something.

"I found a thruppence!" screamed Sam's seven-year-old daughter Evelyn, while Leslie spat a zac out of his mouth.

"Good for you," said Fanny. "You'll look after that now, won't you?"

Apart from coins, which the children stacked up on the table in front of them, the pudding contained silver charms. A wishbone meant you would have good luck, while the dreaded thimble meant spinsterhood for a girl.

"I hope you don't think it rude of me to ask," Vera said to Bill, "but what made you come back to Australia a second time?"

"In Wales I had a good job," Bill said, drawing breath. "I was the head weigher at a colliery near Cardiff. It was my job to supervise the weighing of the coal to fill out the coal sheet that was used to allocate pay to the miners. I got to know quite a few of the miners and I liked them, and they liked me, even though I was on staff."

"That sounds like a very good job," Vera said with a smile. "Why would you want to leave it?"

"No, it wasn't in the end," Bill replied with a frown. "I'm getting to what happened. It's important to know what I just told you, for you to understand what I'm about to tell you... There was a big strike at the Colliery, and the mines stopped producing. As a member of staff I was expected to do the work of the miners in their absence."

"I don't blame you for leaving. Coal mining must be the worst job in the world," Vera said. She seemed to the others to be so bourgeois, yet her father and her brother were both labourers. Her sister Molly was being courted by a blacksmith from Sydney – an ex-boxer named Pat Gleeson.

"It wasn't the work," Joan insisted.

"I'm not afraid of a bit of hard yakka!" Bill laughed. "It wasn't *doing* the work that would've been tough. I would have been doing *their* work. I knew them personally. I prepared the coal sheet for their pay every week, and I couldn't do that to them. It would have made me a scab. So I gave my notice, and here we are."

"A scab?" she asked.

"Bill's a Jacka," Nathaniel explained to Vera. "We don't do filthy scab work. It's not the first time that workers have had to strike to stop being ground down by the bosses."

"But in some cases, Dad, strikes are not the best way to go about things," Bert interjected. He was a Jacka too, and none of them had ever been shy in voicing their opinions. "The recent police strike showed the damage to the community that can result from strikes in essential services. Wharf strikes are much the same."

"The right to strike is the right to strike," Nathaniel insisted. "It's essential for democracy. It's sacred."

"Yes, but there should be an attempt at conciliation," Bert continued, "and all avenues should be exhausted before..."

"*Now* you're being a hypocrite," said Bill cutting him off. "You struck against Brigadier Brand before the Battle of Polygon Wood, didn't you?"

"That was against *his* command, not against the AIF."

"It was still a *strike*."

"Not the kind that compares with the police strike."

"Well, it should have been," Bill said, bitterness welling up inside him. Bill's bitter experiences during the war, and in the coal-mining region of Wales those years afterwards had hardened him as a pacifist, and pushed him further to the left. He had had enough of war.

"What are you saying?" said Bert.

"Not now," said Nathaniel, but Bill ignored him.

"I'm saying we all should have struck against the warmongers – the fat, rich, men who started that filthy war in the first place. They didn't pay. No, not them. It was the poor people who had to pay for it with their blood – and their taxes."

"That's not true," Bert insisted. "The British upper classes lost many sons fighting for France and Belgium's freedom. Their fathers didn't pull their sons off the playing fields of Eton for them to die in the Belgian mud just to turn a profit! Good God, I can't believe you just said that."

"But you wouldn't deny that the slaughter at Gallipoli was just a British grab for oil would you?" Bill persisted.

Tense, everyone was looking at Bill now.

"You volunteered for it!"

"I was young and naive. We all were!"

"Speak for yourself." Bert answered acidly. He was beginning to lose his temper.

"I said *enough*!" Nathaniel shouted. "It's Christmas for God's sake, and I'll not have you two going at each other over the table like that. Not here. Not today." Everyone went quiet at the table after Nathaniel put his foot down

"Aren't these peaches lovely!" interjected Sam's wife Elizabeth, after a moment's silence.

"I agree," said Vera. "Perhaps you should try one, Bert?" She, like Elizabeth, and the other wives was keen to turn the discussion away from politics.

"What about that peach tree down by the old railway workers' houses?" commented Sid, who had remained quiet up to that point.

"It's still there," said Bert. "Right next to Sergeant O'Brien's place."

"We used to keep a good eye out for those peaches," Sid explained, "and when they were nice and ripe we'd be over there to pinch a couple."

"You did what?" Vera chuckled in utter shock, as she knew Bert was such a stickler for complete honesty.

"Everyone did," shrugged Bert, looking around at the others.

"Remember Sergeant O'Brien?" Bill asked with a smile.

"My word I do," Sid replied.

"I'll tell you a story about Senior Constable Joyce, who was O'Brien's offsider," Bill continued.

"It's not about pinching fruit is it?" Vera asked.

"Well, you may say it's about pinching forbidden fruit," Bill said with a grin. He had calmed down since his spirited exchange with his brother over the causes and consequences of war, and everyone was listening to him now. "Anyway, I thought it was sort of cute. The owners of the Saw Mill at the time were the McLennans, and Senior Constable Joyce was quite keen on their daughter, Mary. We'd often see them rolling by the old house in Newbold Street in a gig. Well, one day the Cameron brothers and I were out in the bush picking wildflowers and doing a bit of bird nesting when we came out onto a track, and saw the two of them kissing in the gig." The others laughed, as most of them knew the couple concerned.

Vera was amazed at how quickly all the tension between the brothers had dissipated.

"They hadn't seen you?" Vera asked.

"We were standing twenty or thirty yards behind them. They had no idea until one of the Cameron boys stepped on a branch, which cracked and gave us away."

"What did they say?" asked Fanny.

"Ohhh, they just sped off."

"I'm not sure that this is a discussion to be had on Christmas Day in front of children," the elder Elizabeth announced from behind the table.

"Wedderburn was a gold town, wasn't it?" Vera asked.

"It was," said Bert.

"In its hey day there were thousands of diggers, but it all died out," Nathaniel said.

"Tell them about the incident involving Mr Duckett," Bert suggested.

"Oh, it's nothing much really," Bill began with a smile. "Mr Duckett sank a shaft right in the middle of Godfrey Street, near Grandmother Kettle's house. He asked me to tell grandmother to come and see what he's got in his wheelbarrow. I went up to her and she replied in her English way, 'Indeed? And what do you think he wants to show me?' She was quite suspicious."

"Did you say I was delicious?" Grandmother Kettle asked from not far away. She was eighty-eight, had lost much of her memory and was becoming deaf.

"I said you were *suspicious*," Bill explained with another smile. "Anyway, she finally came to the gate, and he lifted a hessian bag off the wheelbarrow to show the gold nugget that lay below."

"How big was it?" Vera asked.

"I'd say it would have to have been worth £500 or £600."

* * *

As Bert and Vera sat on the train going back to Melbourne they were both quiet for a long time. Bert was often quiet, it was a family trait.

"What's the matter?" Bert asked finally.

"Your family…I don't think they fully accept me," she said. "Not that I mind, you understand."

Bert thought about that statement for a while, tossing it around in his thoughts before answering.

"How do you know that?" he asked finally.

"Did you notice how hardly anybody wanted to speak to me unless I asked a question. That's why I kept asking so many questions. I felt so foolish. And when I suggested we play a game, they all looked at me as if I was being stupid. 'Games are for children', was their attitude. And you said nothing."

"No one knew your game."

"You're all boring, you lot. That's what you are."

* * *

8.45 pm, Dining Room at Scott's Hotel, Friday, 3 April 1925

Apart from giving talks on his war reminiscences, and less frequently at the opening of a new building or monument, Bert was also being called on to chair business functions around town. He was a comfortable and accomplished public speaker now, and people knew that his name added lustre to any event. On this particular night he was chairman of a dinner that was being given for Mr Frank J. Boileau in appreciation of his services on behalf of taxpayers at a prestigious hotel, Scott's, which was located opposite the corner of Collins Street and Market Lane.

Bert tapped a glass with his spoon and brought them to order. He put one hand in his pocket when speaking in public, leaving the other free.

"Gentlemen," he began in his usual manner, "many of us have known Frank Boileau as a prominent stock and station agent around town, but his recent inspired actions on behalf of the taxpayers of Victoria deserve special recognition." Frank Boileau was in line to a baronetcy, and came from a family that had contributed to French and British history for over 700 years. A Boileau had secured the Rock of Gibraltar for Britain.

"Gentlemen, please charge your glasses." After drinks had been poured and they became upstanding, Bert continued.

"When the State Ministry announced its original taxation proposals to impose an unwarranted increase in State income taxation, Mr Boileau convened a meeting of protest, and started a process for which taxpayers owe him a debt of gratitude. The Allan-Peacock Ministry had had the audacity to adopt the Labor Party's extravagant proposals, and it is in great measure due to the alertness of Mr Boileau that the proposals have been rejected."

"Hear, hear!" they chanted.

"Had the Labor Party continued in office, taxpayers would have expected to fight against an unscrupulous onslaught upon their savings. The meeting that Mr Boileau convened brought capable and enthusiastic supporters to his aid, and they fought the issue until the Legislative Council was induced to reject the measure... To Frank Boileau!" said Bert raising his glass.

"Frank Boileau!" cried the participants, who after downing their drinks erupted into applause. A smiling Frank Boileau rose to respond.

"Thank you, Captain Jacka, and thanks to all of you, gentlemen," he began, getting to the point immediately. "Something had to be done. The action of the Allan-Peacock Ministry in adopting practically holus-bolus the budget proposals of the socialistic Labor Ministry was outrageous. The taxation proposals were unjust and unnecessary."

He picked up a piece of paper from the table then continued, glancing down from time to time. "For the nine months of this financial year the revenue exceeded that of a similar period in the last financial year by £866,406. Railway revenue was greater by £516,457 and excise by £579,410, a total increase of £1,095,887. The Liberal-cum-Country Party politicians have been financing on the blind, and no attempt at economy has been made.

"What happened at the Farmer's Union conference held a few weeks ago proves that composite ministries are doomed, and that they are doing incalculable harm to the Liberal cause. Liberalism is by no means dead."

He was interrupted by an extended applause.

"A bold and vigorous Liberal policy, advocated by men of principle, will prove victorious at the next election!"

Among the audience that applauded there was an architect, Charles Montague Moreland Dare, who had just entered into a partnership to form the firm of Browning, Bladen and Dare, with offices located at the Stalbridge Chambers, 443 Little Collins Street. A graduate of Melbourne University, he had also studied English and European architecture, and was recently appointed as an architect to the Federal Government assisting with the building of Parliament House in Canberra.

Dare had miraculously come through a hail of bullets on several occasions at Gallipoli without a scratch, but Brigadier Brand pumped a silver bullet into him in France, relieved him of his command, and sent him packing. He had recently written to Newton Wanliss giving his side of the story. Brand had criticised him for holding the line too thinly at Pozieres and allowing the Germans to puncture it. In Dare's opinion it saved lives. Then General Cox gave him what in his view was an unfair straffing for not deepening the trenches in the 14th Battalion's sector. How could they, when the German artillery was demolishing them faster than they could dig?

It was ironic how the tables had now been turned. Dare used to be the one out in front, when Bert was an NCO, and now Bert was the man every one wanted to know. Newton was not convinced in any case, as in his opinion the young Lieutenant-Colonel Dare had not been fair to Bert, and there were other negative opinions he had received from 14th Battalion officers.

* * *

10 am, The Heads, Port Phillip Bay, Thursday, 23 July 1925

The first fleet Bert ever saw was the Australian fleet that he was in, which gathered at Albany late in December 1914 and carried him and the rest of the Australian army to the war. The second great fleet he had seen was the one that was formed at Mudros Harbour in preparation for the assault on Gallipoli. For many Melbournians, Vera included, the impending visit of the American fleet was a novelty that was creating the same level of excitement as the visit of the Prince of Wales in 1920.

The fleet was led through the Port Phillip Heads by Admiral Robert E. Coontz in his flagship, the four-funnelled light cruiser *Seattle*, which was followed in single file by the light cruisers *Richmond*, *Marblehead*, *Trenton* and *Memphis*. Then came twenty-eight destroyers and six auxiliaries. Bringing up the rear were the three great modern battleships, the USS *Oklahoma*, the USS *Nevada*, and the USS *Pennsylvania*, which waited back in case the depth of the harbour was not sufficient. The battleships and the *Seattle* docked at Prince's Pier, while the destroyers, parked side-by-side like sardines packed into a barrel filled up the whole of Victoria Dock. Among the many functions that first night the Returned Sailors' and Soldiers' Imperial League of Australia (RSSILA) put on a "smoke night" for 500 petty officers and men at the Exhibition Building. The Presbyterian Ladies' College Old Collegian's Association invited thirty-five junior officers to a dance at the St Kilda Town Hall, and there were numerous private dances held for them in large mansions around the city.

On the first morning Admiral Coontz and his Vice-Admirals, all in formal gold braided uniforms, were brought ashore at St Kilda Pier, where they were welcomed by the Mayor. A few days later two thousand men and officers came ashore with rifles and paraded down through the city to a huge, rapturous crowd. So excited was the crowd that too many climbed onto the Hoyts Cinema verandah in Bourke Street, causing it to collapse. Fortunately, no-one was killed. The next two weeks was to be a kaleidoscope of activity, as the visitors engaged with the locals in The Star-spangled Banner Ball at the St Kilda Town Hall, three-day trips to Alexandra, Shepparton, Echuca,

Bendigo, Ballarat, Camperdowne and Geelong, baseball matches at the Melbourne Cricket Ground, rifle matches, motor picnics, symphony orchestra performances, and boxing matches. There was something for everyone.

The US sailors were known colloquially as "GOBs", or God's Own Boys, and officers were paid in gold sovereigns. Now 30,000 of them, all thirsty refugees from the *Volstead Prohibition Act*, were about to be unleashed on the city. Recently married, Fred Knight and his wife entertained some of them in their new house in Toorak, and R.A.D. Hood, a grazier from the western districts told him that at one of the dances he had seen a couple of ensigns down their glasses of neat whiskey in a single gulp.

"Don't you want a chaser with that?" Hood asked them.

"That's real kind of you, sir," they said as they poured themselves another couple of glasses of whiskey and demolished them in the same fashion. At Fred Knight's party one of the guests, a lieutenant-commander, made advances to one of Fred's wife's unmarried girlfriends, and when she asked him whether it was true that he was married he replied, "I sure am – but I'm not a fanatic!"

* * *

1.45 pm, Dining Hall, Commercial Traveller's Club, Friday 24 July 1925

Bert Jacka and Ernie Edmonds had come to the dining hall of the Commercial Traveller's Association Club to hear the address that the Admiral was scheduled to give. In the last years Bert's orientation had moved away from this club to the one that was establishing itself as a force in St Kilda, the St Kilda Army and Navy Club, which had completed the construction of the St Kilda Soldiers' and Sailors' Memorial Hall in Acland Street in November 1924. The prime mover behind the building of the Memorial Hall was a forty-nine year old St Kilda councillor and accountant, Thomas Unsworth. Born in Warrington, Lancashire, he had been to the Boer War as a young man, and as a captain in the AIF was quartermaster of dental supplies in England during the Great War. There was going to be a dance at the club that evening, and twenty US officers had been invited.

Commencement of the Commercial Traveller's Club function was delayed for a time due to the accident in Bourke Street, but it did nothing to dampen the applause as Admiral Coontz led the procession of his fellow officers, Rear-Admirals Marvell, Ziegemier, Leigh, Magruder, Cole, and Schofield, and a number of staff officers into the grand dining hall. After the main course had been eaten, the President of the Commercial Travellers Association, Mr J. Glen, kicked off the official welcome with more than a hint of drama.

"The American Fleet!" he began, and paused. "I couple with it the name of the commander in chief, Admiral Coontz. I tender to him and every member of his great company an enthusiastic welcome to these shores. I wish to express the delight of our members at having a second opportunity to offer courtesy and hospitality to the representatives of the American Navy. The previous occasion was in 1908, when we had a similar memorable function in our club. Events since 1908 have brought Australia and the United States closer together. We used to call Americans our cousins, but now we call them 'big brothers'."

Senator Thomas Crawford, the Assistant Minister for Defence, and simultaneously President of the Queensland Sugar Producers' Association, supported the toast: "There are no other countries in the world that are as self-supporting and self-contained as the United States and Australia. Australia hopes one day to realise the great resources that are in our keeping, and if we ever grew weary of the task, the success of our American brothers should inspire us to persevere in our endeavours to prove ourselves worthy of our opportunities."

"Here, here!"

"Australians have admired the Americans for their great achievements, loved them for their many splendid personal qualities, and now rejoice at being given the opportunity of meeting so many of them face to face."

"Oh there'll be more than a face to face meeting next week," Ernie Edmonds whispered to Bert, in reference to the exhibition boxing matches against the Americans at the *Stadium*. Their business associate, Dick Lean, had given them a number of free tickets to it.

"More like a fist in your face," Bert whispered back with a smile.

"Although America and Australia are separated by a wide ocean," Senator Crawford continued, "the peoples cannot regard one another as aliens or foreigners. Far from it, for we are blood relations, kinsmen descended from the same stock, speaking the same language, and inspired by the same ideals."

"Here, here!"

"Those ideals will be held at any cost, as has been abundantly proved by the gallantry of the naval, military and air forces in the last war, and by the sacrifices uncomplainingly borne by the people in connection with the same stupendous conflict. Americans, like Australians, hate monopolists, and therefore I must not accompany any more of your time!"

He sat down as the audience laughed. The Premier, Mr Allan then rose.

"I am not a commercial traveller," said the Premier. "I am stationary in a good position, and am going to stick there."

As the audience laughed, he asked rhetorically, "Why… is the American Fleet in the bay today?"

"To lend us twenty million pounds!" shouted a voice from the audience, and more laughter followed.

"The Americans have lent fifteen million in an hour, and they can be assured of repayment."

"Here, here!"

"The fleet is here because of the friendship between the two English-speaking nations."

His speech was again broken by applause, but he may not have been fully aware of the battle for world naval supremacy that Britain and the United States were in the midst of as he spoke. While Admiral Coontz and his men were English speaking, it didn't prevent them from preparing war plans against the British Fleet.

"If an enemy had entered the Heads last night," the Premier continued, "Admiral Coontz would have said, in effect, 'If you fire on Melbourne, you fire on the American Fleet.'"

Even at this time it was not merely a theory, as certain long range plans had already been set into motion. Only three months earlier a couple of Japanese freighters were discovered acting suspiciously off the coast of BHP's Port Kembla steel works north of Sydney, and an Australian pilot who boarded one of them noticed a strange map that was quickly removed from sight. Just over a year earlier a Japanese training squadron comprising the cruisers *Asama*, *Yakumo* and *Iwate* had entered the Port Phillip Heads on a similar goodwill visit. As they departed, Vice-Admiral Shichigoro Saito recalled Australia's response to the Tokyo earthquake. He wrote a letter to the Lord Mayor, Councillor Brunton, thanking the people of Australia for their "promptitude and generosity in forwarding relief to my country. I can assure you that the people of Japan will never forget this." One day the captain of the *Iwate*, Mitsumasa Yonai, would deliver on that promise.

The silver-haired, gold-braided Commander in Chief of the US Fleet was greeted with prolonged applause as he rose to speak.

"One would be a poor soul," he began, "if he did not appreciate the warmth of the greeting that you have given us today. We are simply overwhelmed by the kindness of the reception of the American Fleet. People are talking about the loan, but I had not heard of it before I began the tour... Yes, yesterday we obtained two million dollars of Australian money and are going to spend it here!"

He continued through the applause as it subsided.

"I can talk not only as a naval officer, but as a businessman, for I have been interested in enterprises such as daily newspapers and life insurance concerns. References have been made to trade routes and the necessity for keeping them open. The developments associated with trade are wonderful. As we came to Australia from San Francisco, Honolulu and Samoa our radio talked to amateurs all over the world, and we began to wonder whether some of those messages did not come around by way of the South Pole in order to get through the shortest way!

"The more civilised people become the more they want, and that is where the demand for trade arises. As the fleet has moved along in its tour of the Pacific, I have wondered when the islands of the Pacific would be exploited for further trade. I have also thought of the requirements of China, India and the Dutch West Indies, and when thinking of the possibilities of the future in these and similar respects I have considered that Australia could satisfy their demands.

"The Suez and the Panama canals are open, and possibly in a few years there will be great aerial lines of commerce. That is where Australia's chance arises. We in the United States want to see that. We want to see the world prosper, and everyone happy. That is the American view of the millennium."

"Here, here!"

"I can tell you that I belong to several chambers of commerce, but I have to admit that I really want to get through and go to some of those dances at St Kilda!"

* * *

"Hear that, Bert?" Ernie said nudging his partner. "Exercise or get old." The only exercise Bert was getting was rushing from meeting to meeting, presentation to presentation. The worst thing was business lunches like this one, where the food was high quality and difficult to resist. Bert, now thirty-three, was starting to pile on some pounds, and had begun to look the part of the "prosperous businessman". The test came a couple of times a year when he would have to put on the uniform he wore as a fit twenty-five year old.

"That was a wonderful speech by Admiral Coontz," Bert replied. "Don't you think?"

"I agree with the general sentiments," answered one of the businessmen at their table, "but I'm concerned about the debt. We have something of a boom in this country at the moment, but I fear that it is being bought at the expense of future generations."

"How so?" asked another at the table.

"Well, I'll tell you how booms are produced," he answered. "They are generated by uncontrolled borrowing, and there's far too much of that going on at the moment. We have Prime Minister Bruce over in England spruiking further loans, and commodity prices are high at the minute. But the moment those prices fall, mark my words, we will have a hell of a time paying back all that debt. It will be left up to our children."

Bert told them that something needed to be done about the unemployment situation. The rate of unemployment had not been less than 9 per cent since the conclusion of the war, and many of the down and outs were returned men. He also told them that the Soldier Settlement Scheme had been a dismal failure, recalling the bitter experience of his brother Bill, and his old trusted lieutenant, Ernie Hill who was struggling to make ends meet in Lemnos, the soldier settlement east of Shepparton.

Ernie Hill had said that the government expected him to run water uphill, and then – "walk on it". He wasn't joking. A canal ran between the two properties he had, and his requests to build a bridge linking the two fell on deaf bureaucratic ears. So in summer, when the canal was flush with water he put a bridge across that sat just under the waterline so it couldn't be seen. He had to train his horse to make that "leap of faith" when it came to the edge, but it too had learned to "walk on water".

"It's not dissimilar to what has happened to many of the British migrants who have come to Australia on the promise of land and sunshine," said the businessman. "They often end up with either sandy soil and drought or an infernal bog. The next thing you know they're joining the swelling ranks of the unemployed."

The discussion put a dampener on the table after the optimistic "big picture" of future growth prospects painted by the Admiral. Bert knew all about debt at the individual firm level — his firm had tons of it. He had plans to expand into the retail arena, where he could eventually build up a whole chain of Jacka, Edmonds & Co. stores. But first he had to prove the formula in one store and pay down some of the debt that was owed.

* * *

7.15 pm, The Stadium, Wednesday, 29 July 1925

Everyone was fight crazy in the 1920s. Pugilism as a sport was supported by patrons representing the whole cross-section of society, particularly the military. The premium entry ticket for a ringside seat was ten bob, which was about fifteen times what it cost to see a movie. Even cheap seats were five times the cost of a movie.

Bert had finally convinced Vera to come along to the "House of Stoush". She had heard about it from Molly, who had been a few times with her new husband Pat Gleeson, and hadn't liked what she heard. But there was a festival spirit in the city and this was being promoted as a series of exhibition matches with the Americans. Dick Lean met Bert and his party in the foyer, which was bobbing with bluejackets topped with white US sailor caps. Bert introduced his party to Dick.

"Welcome to the Stadium," Dick said to them. "Follow me, I'll show you to your seats."

"I haven't seen you for ages, Pat," Dick asked. "What have you been up to?"

"Staying out of trouble, Mr Lean," Pat answered. "I'm working as a blacksmith these days." Molly squeezed her husband's arm supportively when he said that. She was furious with the Stadium for what it had done to her husband, but he had been so keen to come tonight. The beatings to the head that he had sustained in his fighting days left a legacy that she was now suffering too. Her sister Vera was in a similar position; her husband had been traumatised by battles of a different kind.

"I believe this is your first fight, Mrs Jacka?" Dick asked.

"That's not entirely true, she's gone a few rounds with me," Bert joked, but Vera ignored this.

"My sister has told me something about it," Vera told Dick flatly, "and much of what I've heard hasn't been to my taste, to be perfectly honest."

"Oh, I think you'll find it's not as brutal as you might have imagined, Mrs Jacka," Dick assured her, looking over at Pat and Molly. He was confident in his prediction, as most of the program was devoted to sparring matches with the Americans. As they walked into the stadium the brightly illuminated ring, about twenty-feet square, dominated the darkened seating area that surrounded it. Again, the sailor caps of the Americans were dotted throughout, like white confetti that had been sprinkled across a dark blue floor. The young Americans were keen to see their boys in action against the "Orzies", who were an unknown quantity to them. Vera sat next to Dick, with Bert on her left and then the others in their party.

"One thing that has always puzzled me," Vera asked Dick, "is why this *square* platform they fight on is called a ring?"

"That is a good question, Mrs Jacka. I believe that it dates from the time when there was a small ring drawn in the middle of the fighting area, and that was where the contestants would begin."

Bert tapped Vera's hand to get her attention.

"That's John Wren across the other side of the ring," he said. "Second row, sixth man from the left."

"Yes, that's right," added Dick. "He has his own seat near the ringside."

During fights at the Stadium, Wren would make the moves of a fighter as he sat in his seat cheering them on. He may have been small, but you didn't want to pick a fight with him, as he could use those fists. One time a big bloke knocked on the door of the Wren mansion at night, and one of his young sons went to see who it was. "Can I see your father?" he asked, so the lad sent him in to the dining room where his father received him. Later on the lad saw his father accompany the visitor up the driveway to the gates, where a fight broke out. Wren knocked him down right there and then. When he returned to the house his hands were bleeding as the veins on the backs of his hands had burst from the fight. The lad asked his father why he took the stranger up to the gates for the fight. "I didn't want to worry your mother," was his reply.

A loud group including a couple of wealthy young graziers, Dan Langdon and Percy Powell, who were wearing dinner jackets, came into the Stadium just before the first fight, and sat right in front of Dick and Bert. It was common but not mandatory for those at the ringside to wear dinner jackets, but since the seats cost a pound a piece, which was more than opera tickets, they thought you might as well. These boys were not just theorists either. One of them, Percy, had been the Victorian amateur middle-weight champion. They had obviously been to dinner prior to the Stadium, and their exuberance suggested that a significant component of their meal had been liquid. While pubs stopped serving at 6 pm, drinks could be taken with dinner up to 8 pm.

On a previous visit to town one of these graziers had landed into a lot of hot water. Sometime after midnight Percy got into a barney with a saveloy merchant who stood with his horse and cart under the clocks at Flinders Street Station. Percy was not happy with the quality of the saveloy that had been offered to him, so he lifted up the tail of the horse and deposited the red-hot saveloy, causing the horse to rear up in a frenzy, and bolt down Swanston

Street towards the Town Hall, dragging the unmanned cart behind it. Not being built for speed, the cart discharged boiling water, hot saveloys and bread rolls onto the street as it sped away. The police recovered the horse and cart from somewhere north of Bourke Street, but by the time they had returned it to the merchant, the lad had fully compensated the merchant by pulling a hundred pound roll from his pocket and depositing it into the merchant's hand, which changed his expression in an instant. Thank God for the wool price!

There were a number of preliminary six-rounders between Australian fighters and the American sailors. Billy Fieney of Australia defeated "Ike" Rovan of the United States, while "Patsy" Mozier from the fleet defeated George Gray of Australia on points. The main problem was that while the fleet men boxed well, they were inclined to spar rather than actually fight for all they were worth. This annoyed Dan and Percy, who kept turning back to Dick, bitterly questioning the reality of what they were watching.

"Come on, Dick," said Percy. "This is not worth the quid we paid for these seats. There's more excitement in boxing yer own shadow!"

"Wait for the main event, boys, will you?" Dick snapped back. "It's 'Snowy' Christensen and Chris Jordan."

The next fight between Christensen and Jordan did keep them quiet for a long time. Jordan, who was about ten pounds lighter than Christensen, defeated him on points after twelve rounds. It was a particularly painful fight for Pat and Molly Gleeson to witness. As lightweight champion of New South Wales at the end of January 1920, Pat met Jordan, who was the Victorian lightweight champion, in what was effectively the Australian lightweight title fight. It was the first time that Bert had laid eyes on Pat, and he never imagined that night that he would be best man at Pat and Molly's wedding a few years later. Unfortunately Jordan laid his gloves on Pat that night – repeatedly. Jordan had come out aggressively and for a while, Pat had avoided getting plastered owing to his fancy footwork. He got loads of cheers for his spunk when he rallied in the eighth round, but after that he weakened and Jordan kept closing in, eventually knocking Pat out cold in the eleventh round.

After the Jordan fight there was another lull in the excitement as another exhibition match with the Americans was put on. It was a middle-weight fight in which Bob Stewart of Australia defeated Bob Jones from the fleet on points. The graziers began to drone on to Dick again.

"These fighters are pussy-willows!" Percy said, swinging around.

"Why don't you bloody well get up and show us how it's done then," Dick replied disdainfully. It was just the cue the two troublemakers were waiting for.

"More than happy to!" Percy shot back, nudging his partner. "Won't we, Dan?"

"I'm ready when you are, Percy," he said eagerly, thrusting out his fists in a flurry of imaginary blows.

"All right, wait until the stadium clears," said Dick, accepting the challenge. "I'll see what we can do." At the conclusion of the evening the hall began to empty, but Dan and Percy and a few of their friends stayed on, as did the gentlemen of the press, who promised not to report on what was going to happen.

"I would prefer to go home," Vera told Bert.

"So do I," said her sister. "I've had enough for one evening."

"But this could be interesting," he pleaded with a smile.

"I want to go home right now," Molly insisted.

"All right," Bert agreed finally, "if that's what you want." He turned to Dick Lean and thanked him for the seats, and they began moving out.

"Did you enjoy it at least?" Bert asked Pat.

"Not really. I wanted so see him go down."

"Jordan?"

"Yeah."

Meanwhile, Molly was quietly complaining to her sister.

"I wish we hadn't come, Rose."

"I couldn't agree more," she whispered back.

When they came out of the hall it was difficult to hail a taxi as they had all been taken. Standing on the dark street corner they could see a spectacular display of shafts of light criss-crossing in all directions into the crystal clear night sky, like a duel in white laser beams. There was absolutely no wind, and even though they were wearing their winter coats, they were shivering. Steam issued from their mouths as they spoke.

"Look at those beautiful beams of light!" Molly cried, pointing towards the sky.

"That's the searchlights on the battleships berthed at Prince's Pier," Ernie explained.

"They *are* beautiful! Why don't we take a cab down to the Pier and have a closer look?" Vera suggested.

"No we won't," Bert cut in sharply. He was in a bad mood, and agitated. To him the searchlights were not beautiful – to him they meant war, and some memories of ships' searchlights at Gallipoli flashed across his mind in that instant. "You all wanted to go home, and that's exactly what we'll do."

Ernie and Thelma took a taxi to Camberwell, while Vera and Bert, Molly and Pat squeezed into one taxi together.

"Forty-one High Street, Prahran, thanks," Bert told the driver abruptly.

* * *

Back inside the empty stadium, Dan and Percy shed their dinner jackets, took off their stiff collars and starched white shirts, as well as their shoes. They entered the ring wearing their dress trousers, and their silk singlets. Dan was wearing a pink one and Percy had his blue one on. They danced around sizing each other up while their braces trailed behind them on the canvas. The staff of the Stadium came in closer, as they wanted to see some toff blood spilt by these boys.

For a while they kept parrying each other's attempts to get through their guards. The boxing style was extremely vigorous, and a couple of good hits to the body were being made. Then Dan sent over a heavy right, which landed on Percy's shoulder. He came back with a solid left to the nose, sending Dan reeling back to the ropes, blood pouring from his nose. Then Percy came in with a relentless flurry of blows that left Dan, bleeding and helpless on the ropes until…

"Ouch!" screamed Percy. "I think I've broken my bloody thumb on you, yer bastard!"

"That's enough!" called the referee. "Fight's over."

Percy had not broken his thumb; it was just dislocated. He and Dan engaged in a good deal of celebrating later that night, which left them worse for wear in the morning, but in their minds they had finally experienced a decent fight.

* * *

Everyone remained very silent in the taxi as it drove down St Kilda Road to Prahran that night. Vera was annoyed that she had agreed to see the fights in the first place, and had been disgusted by the violence she had witnessed. Molly kept comforting her husband Pat as their outing had re-kindled memories of his fighting career, particularly that knock-out by Chris Jordan five years ago. Bert was annoyed that he hadn't been able to see the private fight between the larrikin graziers.

There was little talking that night as Bert and Vera prepared for bed. They were both a little headstrong at times. In Vera's mind her husband was not being as generous as she had hoped. On their first wedding anniversary he had given her a vase as a present, but for the last few years he hadn't bought her anything. He was very frugal with the household budget, wanting to pour all he could into making the business a success. Vera turned away that night and dreamed of a life that she wanted. At least it was pleasant. He turned away and saw in his dreams a time when searchlights spelled danger.

* * *

Reserve Gully, Gallipoli, 6 August 1915

It was a crystal clear night, moonless and perfectly still. As the stars twinkled above, the men of the 14th Battalion fell in quietly at the foot of Reserve Gully. There was excitement in their hearts, though. Finally, they could see that a serious push was being made on several fronts, including an assault on Lone Pine earlier that day. Each man had a white calico patch sewn onto his back and another on his arm, so he would be visible to his own men from behind. Some of the men were sick with dysentery.

The whole 4th Brigade of 4000 men under the command of Brigadier-General John Monash was now assembled and given the order to march north and outflank the Turks. They were part of a force of 12,000 men, including Australians, New Zealanders, Brits, Gurkhas and Sikhs. They moved in ascending order with the 13th Battalion, and then the brigade headquarters leading the 14th, 15th and 16th battalions. The magazines of the men's rifles were not charged, in case someone got trigger happy, and gave the game away. Strict orders were given against smoking and talking, as silence was required to surprise the Turks. But the night was far from quiet, being sharply punctuated by the sound of incoming Turkish shrapnel shells directed at British howitzers near the beach. Some early casualties were taken there as they marched past them.

Forty-seven year old Major Robert Rankine was now in command of the 14th Battalion due to the retirement through ill health of its original CO, Lieutenant-Colonel Courtney. Major Charles Dare, the young Melbourne architect, was his second in command, and was positioned at the rear of the column together with Padre Andrew Gillison and the battalion's MO, Captain Henry Gerald Loughran. A senior doctor at the Kyneton Hospital south of Bendigo, Loughran had been to the South African war as a young man, and his calmness under fire was legendary among the men of the 14th.

When it reached the beach the column wheeled north along the main sap and began to penetrate enemy territory for the first time in months. Bert marched quietly, but was increasingly frustrated by the snail's pace of the column. Scouts from the Light Horse were somewhere up the front giving this unwieldy queue some direction, but he was not convinced they were getting anywhere. Out at sea a British destroyer was ranging its searchlights over the Turkish positions in the hills, and shells were sailing over their heads in both directions.

As he marched, Bert recalled some of the notes he had prepared on the subject of column marches. He had a sergeant's stripes in his sights, and he was studying hard to get them.

The advance guard is a body of troops put out for the protection of a force when on the march. Its duties are reconnaissance and resistance. The OC of the advance guard has a very difficult job. He must have plenty of dash and at the same time must not get too heavily engaged with the enemy. If he does, the OC of the main body may have to deploy to get him out again, and by doing so he might be forced to fight on unfavourable ground. The scouts should be deployed in an arc 300 yards ahead of the advance guard platoon, with the three platoons of the main guard placed 400 yards behind them, and the main body 400 yards behind them. The duty of the scouts is to look into places the enemy might hold and be on the lookout for ambushes...The pace is regulated by the main body...The rear guard is to protect a retiring force and to hold up the enemy and make him deploy so as to gain time for the main body to get away.

As the long thin column marched on quietly through the night, shrapnel whizzed in and exploded above them, and each time one exploded with a bang and the swish of pellets, the boys could not help themselves flinching, even though they knew what to expect at the end of the *Whirrrrr*. Not once did Bert take the slightest notice of the sudden ear-splitting bang high above them, or the pellets that rained down. Private Norm Folks, a blacksmith from Bonnie Doon, who was marching next to Bert felt ashamed for being so jumpy, but then, almost everyone was jumpy.

The Turkish shells continued to fire at the British destroyer, and the air was soon thick with smoke. As the column reached "Number 2" outpost, which sat on the closest spur jutting out towards the sea, the order was given to halt and rest, while the British 40th Brigade crossed their front. Suddenly, the ship's searchlights dipped, and bathed the whole column in light, making everything appear as bright as day. The unease of the exposed men could be felt, as they must surely now be visible to the Turks on the heights. "Bloody idiots," Bert thought as he glanced out to sea. It was 9.30. Then the destroyer's searchlight was just as suddenly killed, and instantly a huge cheer was heard over the hill behind them, causing everyone to turn their heads. The Auckland Regiment was clambering into the Turkish trenches at the old Number 3 post, taking it with cold steel.

The 4th Brigade marched further into the night – slowly. At 11.30 pm the brigade turned into a valley and was split into two columns, with the 13th and 14th making up the left flank, and the 15th and 16th taking on the right. They were guided by Captains Overton and Eastwood of the 13th, and the advance guard was engaging in skirmishes with pockets of the enemy. At each one of the halts, the men of the 14th would take cover in the nearby scrub. Men were dropping out of the line, claimed randomly by shrapnel or fire from snipers, whose positions were given away by muzzle flashes that stood out against the blackness. Each time a man fell Captain Loughran would arrive to administer first aid or morphine.

Sometime after midnight the 13th was held up and scattered in front of the 14th, which came to a halt again. Brigadier Monash came up, ordering the 14th to push on, as the whole brigade was now well

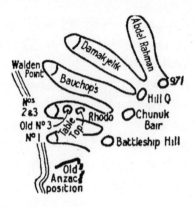

Night March, 6th August, 1915

The 4th Australian Infantry Brigade marched along the coast from the Old
Anzac position, skirting the five ridges, to dig in on the Demakjelik Bair,
6th–7th August, 1915

Source C. E. W. Bean, The Story of Anzac, Angus and Robertson, Sydney, p. 657

behind time. They entered the Aghyl Dere Valley and then went
into a northern offshoot valley. As the morning dawned they could
hear the 40th Brigade digging in on their left, so Major Rankine
decided to dig in as well, but the men were exhausted after their
long night march. Soon after they began digging, they saw a group
of about 50 Turks being driven towards their position by the 15th
Battalion. Around twenty were killed or wounded, and twenty-one
were taken prisoner, but the remainder melted into the scrub and
inflicted a number of casualties that day. As he watched the 15th in
action, Bert reflected on the bad blood that existed between it and
the 14th Battalion. It seemed to permeate right through the ranks
from the COs, and MOs, right down to the privates. He hoped that
it wouldn't cause any real strife on the battlefield.

   During the day, Bert and others digging in on the ridge were
constantly worried by sniper fire. Often the Turks fired "on spec"
into the bushes on the ridge, because they knew the Australians
would be digging in close to it. Captain Loughran and the stretcher-

bearers were running up and down the ridge all morning, making themselves targets. At one point the MO was binding up a man's leg behind a bush when a bullet crashed through and broke the man's arm. Even the sight of an entrenching tool above the line of vision attracted an instant barrage of bullets, so most men just lay in their shallow trenches all day with the sun beating down on their backs.

Having covered miles up and down the ridge all morning, by 3 pm Loughran was "all out" and retired to a little nook where Major Rankine had established his HQ, leaving it only twice in the afternoon: once, to attend Corporal Davidson, whose arm had to be amputated; and to treat a D Company signaller, London-born Private H. Schmidt, who was down with an abdominal wound. When he heard that Captain W.E. "Teddy" Groom had been hit, Loughran began to make his way towards him, but returned when he learned the officer had died. When he got back to the HQ completely exhausted, he grabbed a couple of hours sleep.

By the end of the day, despite the fact that they had not yet met the enemy in any force, eleven men from the 14th Battalion were dead, including Privates H. Caley of Ballarat and N.J. Veal of Bendigo, Driver L. Williams of Stawell, and Private G.W. Preston of Ararat. By a cruel twist of fate Private Augustus Frederick Boden, a twenty-three year old iron driller from Williamstown, was also killed that day; a short man of heavy build, he was carrying a wounded Turkish officer to the beach when he was cut down.

* * *

At dusk on 7 August General Godley sent Monash a couple of messages urging him to push the 4th Brigade on to the summit of Hill 971:

The G.O.C. wishes you to close the troops... well up the slopes towards the enemy during the preliminary bombardment of the position, so as to be ready to reach the crest as soon as the gunfire

stops to-morrow morning. The assault should be carried out with
loud cheering. I feel confident that, after today's rest, and starting
comparatively fresh, your brigade will make a determined effort to
capture the key of the position... selecting it for this task, I had the
original brigade in mind...We all expect the reconstituted brigade
to live up to the traditions of the original.

Monash was concerned that Godley thought his brigade was fresh – it was not. The men were exhausted before they began their punishing trek, and had hardly slept in the last 48 hours. The hot day had been followed by a cold night, which left the men shivering and sleepless, as they had been ordered to leave their greatcoats back at Anzac. Nevertheless, Monash sent for the COs and adjutants to assemble at his Brigade Headquarters. As adjutant of the 14th, Captain George Cooper accompanied the acting CO, Major Rankine to the meeting, where they were to receive their orders for the operation.

"Gentlemen," began the brigadier at 7.45 pm sharp, "this brigade is to form part of a force having for its objective Hill 971, the remainder of the force being a brigade of British Infantry on our left, and the 29th Indian Infantry Brigade on our right. The troops are to be clear of their trenches by 3.00 am and to move out over to the Abd-el Rahman Bair to the north. It is not a steep slope. It is rather gentle. Your guide will be my own Orderly Officer, Lieutenant Locke, who earlier today made a reconnaissance of the position. The attacking force will be comprised of the 15th, 14th and 16th Battalions, with the 13th remaining in reserve in the trenches. Are there any questions at this point?"

The most crucial assumption in the plan was the present position of the 4th Brigade, which the brigadier thought was a spur of Abd-el Rahman Bair. It was the fatal flaw. They were on a parallel ridge, situated a mile further away from Hill 971 than he thought. The second flaw was halting the Brigade's progress the evening before, when Hill 971 was less strongly held. If there was ever a hope of taking Hill 971, it had passed as the sun rose over it that morning.

While the brigadier and his battalion COs conferred at Brigade HQ, Loughran was out on the ridge again, searching for wounded. At 10 pm he was told that Major Rankine wanted to see him back at HQ. There he found the assembled 14th Battalion officers huddled around the confined space.

"Is everyone here?"

"We can't find Major Dare and Captain Hansen."

Not wishing to waste any more time Rankine began the briefing, giving them the "cheery news" that their brigade had been ordered to take the highest hill on the peninsula in the morning.

"We are to move out by 3 am," Rankine explained. "We are to be supported by an English brigade on the left and an Indian brigade on the right, and advance in columns of platoons."

Loughran was not happy about the orders, which seemed to throw responsibility for the whole Gallipoli campaign on the shoulders of the 4th Brigade. He knew how exhausted and sick the men of the 14th were. He had been treating Major Rankine for dysentery for more than a month. He thought of Tennyson:

> *"Someone had blunder'd,*
> *Theirs not to make reply,*
> *Theirs not to reason why..."*

* * *

Since most of the damage had been done by snipers from the rear, Major Dare and Captain Hansen were sleeping on the enemy side of the parapet they had constructed above the shallow trenches. They knew nothing of the revised plan to attack Hill 971 until they heard the last platoon of the battalion moving off after breakfast. The 16th Battalion was now moving up behind their trenches.

"What's that?" asked Hansen as he sat up.

"What?" asked Dare.

"It's the battalion. They're on the move!" They scrambled to get their gear together and catch up to the rear of the column. It was the day of destiny for Dare, and he almost slept through it.

"Where is the column heading?" Dare asked an officer in the tail of the column.

"We're attacking Hill 971."

"When was the order given?"

"Late last night. We couldn't find you."

"What's the matter?" asked Hansen, who could see Dare's distress at the news.

"We won't have enough time to get into position before daylight. That's what the matter is!"

"What do you mean?"

"I had this out with Major Rankine and Colonel Cannan yesterday morning, but they wouldn't believe me." He noticed that the column was winding back towards the beach, instead of heading for the summit, which only convinced him more. "That's Hill 60, across the riverbed, not Abd-el Rahman Bair, and it's a good deal further from the summit of Hill 971 than they think!"

"God, it's too late," Dare thought. "We've started too late, and we'll be caught out at first light."

The pace of the column was not more than one mile per hour, and it had wheeled back towards the beach because of a narrow path that had been found on the other side of the Kaiajik Dere leading up to Hill 60. At 4.15 am, just before dawn on 8 August, the 15th Battalion was already on the oatfield on the exposed ridge, which everyone called "the cornfield". The British bombardment of Hill 971 had just ceased, which was the signal for the brigade's final assault, but it was hopelessly out of position. The 14th Battalion was still in the dry riverbed of the Kaiajik Dere. Worse still, the fall of the "cornfield" plateau across which the 15th battalion advanced

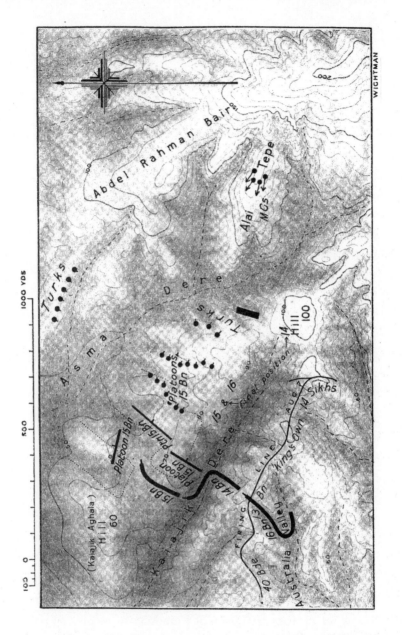

Attempt by the 4th Australian Infantry Brigade to reach Hill 971 by way of
Abdel Rahman Bair, 8th August, 1915

Source: C. E. W. Bean, The Story of Anzac, *Angus & Robertson, Sydney, p. 655*

was like the slope of a slice of cheese that was tilted to the north, where the Turks lay waiting.

* * *

As the day dawned, the men of 14th walked out into the stubble on "the cornfield" and the pinnacle of Hill 971 still loomed far away. The battalions advanced in columns of platoons, and they had to walk around the freshly cut hay that still stood about piled into stooks. The 14th Ghurkas advanced on a ridge to their right, but the British troops that were meant to be advancing on their left were nowhere to be seen. Bert stared at the pretty yellow glow that came off the stooks in the morning light as he recalled a passage from his notebook on military tactics:

> *In these days it is very difficult to see the enemy. Invisibility is brought about by the colour of the clothes and the likeness of everything. The only way to overcome this is to practice using the eyes. Visual scanning is like a general reconnaissance, quickness in detecting objects and quickness in judging distance. So recognise point of aim in collective fire. So align sights on the mark, and so observe the strike of bullets. Men from the city have not the same powers of observation as men from the country. Men without training will find it almost impossible to pick up a man in khaki at 400 yards...*

But if they are German-trained Turkish men from the country, and the enemy dressed in khaki is advancing in thousands across the broad crest of a ridge bathed in morning light and covered in freshly cut stubble, they *will* be seen – and fired upon. Overnight the Turks set up four batteries of four Maxim machineguns on Abd-el Rahman Bair, beneath the peak of Hill 971. With each machinegun capable of firing at a rate of 750 rounds a minute, the combined firepower of these batteries was roughly equivalent to three modern Black Hawk helicopters armed with Gatling miniguns, each spitting out 4000 rounds a minute. As they opened up on the field the sound of the machineguns was like the whir of an electric motor whipping up a storm that hit the men in the stubble field like a tornado of steel. They had wandered into the jaws of death.

"Advance at the double!" was called, and they began to scatter. Clouds of dust rose from the field as the machinegun rounds churned the ground, and the yellow stubble was splattered with red blood as men fell as stalks to the scythe. Sergeant Ernie Hill, the Lance-Bombadier who had come ashore sitting next to Monash on 26 April, ran the gauntlet out in the stubble field that day, and had his rifle disintegrate in his hands as a machinegun round smashed into it. The force of it gashed his finger, releasing blood, and the spent hot shell ricocheted up his right arm to the elbow, leaving a thick and painful burn scar.

The 15th Battalion ahead of them was taking even more of the heat. Captain Loughran saw a line of Australians drawn up ahead charging towards the scrub on the left. He and his stretcher-bearers ran for their lives towards scrub on their right, where one of his men drew his attention to a small red flag tied to a bush. It was the brink of a small dere (or gully) that was a tributary of the dry river bed of the Kaijaik Dere, and indicated the dressing station of Captain John Luther, MO of the 15th Battalion. Born and educated in Ireland, he was a doctor in Bundaberg prior to the war, and as brave as they come.

Loughran set up his dressing station in the gully a bit nearer the enemy than Luther's station, and before long was dealing with a stream of casualties. Almost all his stretcher-bearers had departed down the gully carrying wounded men, leaving Loughran and Corporal George Michie on their own. The 14th Battalion's signallers set up a post not far away from them. Shortly afterwards Major Rankine arrived with the assistance of his batman, looking pale and in a very weak state. His batman explained to Captain Loughran that Rankine had fainted from exhaustion while crossing the Kaijaik Dere. Loughran poured him a tot of rum from his flask, and continued working on his wounded cases. Rankine's adjutant, Captain George Cooper then struck out to inform Major Dare that he should assume command of the battalion.

As the 15th Battalion had withered under intense fire ahead of them the lead companies of the 14th, C and D companies, and with them Bert Jacka VC, came into direct contact with the advancing Turkish force and held them back as A and B companies arrived in support, with the Sikhs on their right, who had come to a standstill. Dare, who was now at the head of the column, took command of the 14th when informed by Cooper that Rankine had dropped out. The 15th was in trouble from the losses it had sustained and had to deploy on its left in order to meet a flanking movement by the Turks. Leading platoons of the 14th were rushing across the southern edge of the stubble field, getting onto Hill 100 and firing at some Turks who were fleeing across the Asma Dere.

Then the Turkish machinegun posts on Abd-el Rahman Bair caught sight of them and cut into C and D Companies, causing numerous casualties. It was here that a handful of C Company men, who had forced their way into the Turkish position, were cut off and killed. The commander of C Company, Lieutenant Warren, fell mortally wounded, but ordered Lieutenant Luscombe and his 9th platoon to push on. Luscombe went down in a hail of machinegun bullets a few moments later, and was captured. Another handful of men built a barricade out of Turkish ammunition boxes and fought desperately until all but two had been killed or wounded. The thirteen survivors were taken prisoner by the Turks.

At this critical point Dare was shocked to see that the Sikhs on his right were now retiring, so he went across to them and got a Sikh machinegun officer to post a machinegun on Hill 100 to support the 4th Brigade's left. It was around 7.30 am. Captain

Cooper was down on the left flank at this time among the half demolished and scattered 15th Battalion.

"Where's your CO, and the guide, Lieutenant Locke?" Cooper asked the 15th men.

"The last we saw of them, they were heading for the dere."

After giving them orders to hang on, Cooper went off to search for the CO, while Dare received a message that he and the remnants of the 14th should retire. Dare responded that he could hold his ground on Hill 100 as long as his left flank was supported.

* * *

The little dere occupied by the dressing stations was visited by Lieutenant Colonel Cannan of the 15th, and Lieutenant-Colonel Pope and Major Margolin of the 16th, who were in communication with Brigade HQ, about a mile and a half behind them, by means of runners. However, by the time Captain Cooper got there Cannan was already gone, so he reported to Pope just as a signaller arrived, dragging a telephone line from Brigade HQ. Lieutenant-Colonel Pope got on the line and spoke with Monash, who told him that Lieutenant-Colonel Cannan and Lieutenant Locke were already at HQ with him. Then Monash, who had already received permission from his superior, Major-General Cox, ordered Dare to withdraw. By 8.30 am Pope had communicated Monash's order to retire to Dare, who was still out with his battalion. Dare sent his men out to collect wounded and the bolts from rifles that couldn't be brought back. At 10.30 am Captain Cooper visited Loughran at his dressing station a short distance away.

"The situation is very dangerous," he said in a low voice. "I can tell you confidentially, that the brigade is about to be withdrawn. Say nothing to the men, but I urge you to evacuate all the wounded as soon as possible. And can you... quietly... inform Luther of this."

Soon afterwards Loughran went over to Dr Luther's dressing station to inform him of the potential move.

"Who did you get the message from?" was Luther's barbed, sleep deprived response.

"George Cooper."

"Oh! It's only a bloody rumour invented by the 14th! They always want to withdraw." This incensed Loughran's pride. He had always tried to be friendly to Luther, and had always thought there was no reason for the MOs to be at it, even if there was bad blood between their battalions. He had had just about enough of Dr Luther at this point.

"All right! I've told you."

"And I, refuse to take any notice of you!"

That did it for Loughran, who spun around on his spot and marched straight back to his own dressing station without saying another word to his learned colleague. He was still seething when a 16th man burst into his dressing station in a panic.

"Look out, the bloody Turks are on us!"

Some of Loughran's stretcher-bearers were there and they all looked straight at him. He could see the fear in their eyes. For the first time ever, he felt they might be getting ready to cut and run. They started to make preparations to move.

"Wait a moment…" he said, holding up his hand. "I'm going to take a look." He went up the little gully to the brink of the plateau that was around ten feet above them to sneak a look. Across the stubble field, among the scrub he could see Turks moving west. *They look like they are trying to move towards the beach to cut us off from Suvla*, he thought. *Or, they might be forming up into a line to charge us across the stubble field.*

There were a number of signallers nearby who were watching them too.

"Why don't you open fire on them!" Loughran called out to the signallers.

"We've got no ammunition, sir!"

They were wearing full equipment, but carried not a round of ammunition in their leather pouches – too much weight to move

Capt. Albert Jacka, VC, MC and Bar as
he looked when giving evidence at the
Dardanelles Commission, London, in 1917

Australian War Memorial neg. no. AO2868A

April 1919 – Capt. Albert Jacka with prizewinners at the AIF's Sutton Veny camp, England

Australian War Memorial neg. no. PR84 333 004

June 1919 — Capt. Albert Jacka (foreground), was best man at the wedding of his brother, Capt. William ('Bill') Jacka, to Joan Jacka in Taff's Well, Wales

Courtesy of Josephine Eastoe and Don Llewellyn

October 1919 — Upon arrival at Port Melbourne, Capt. Albert Jacka was met by Brig.-Gen. Charles Brand (right)

Courtesy of the State Library of Victoria from The Herald

Mechanics Institute Wedderburn — William Dowsett (left, whose daughter married Albert Jacka's nephew, William Jacka Olive) digging for gold during the Great Depression

Courtesy of Val and Jason LaMacchia

Artist's impression of Albert Jacka's counter-attack on Pozieres Ridge, France — many thought a second VC should have been awarded

Courtesy of the State Library of Victoria from Smith's Weekly

L-Cpl. William ('Bill') Howard

Courtesy of Aileen and Marie Howard

Lt. Steven DeAraugo

Courtesy of Vin and Chris DeAraugo

Capt. Ferdinand Henry ('Ferdie') Wright

Courtesy of Steven Marriott

L-Cpl. Frederick ('Fred') Anderson

Courtesy of Stuart Anderson

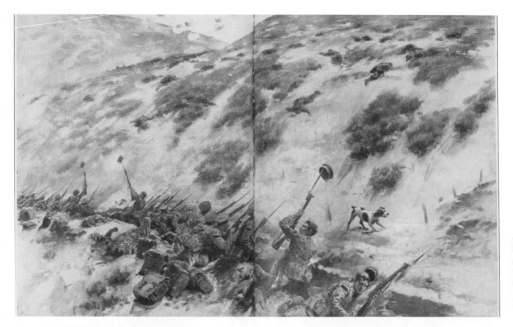

Artist's impression of 14th Battalion's defence of Quinn's Post, Gallipoli, with its fox terrier mascot 'Gunner' in the foreground

Courtesy of the State Library of Victoria from London Illustrated News

Brig.-Gen. Harold ('Pompey') Elliott

Australian War Memorial neg. no. A02607

Lt. Harold Wanliss

Courtesy of Tom Wanliss

Archbishop Daniel Mannix, John Wren, Sgt. Maurice Vincent Buckley, VC, DCM

Australian War Memorial neg. no. P01383.018

Frances Veronica Carey ('Vera') at the
time of her marriage to Albert Jacka

Courtesy of Betty Jacka

Bourke Street — Archbishop Mannix and 15 mounted Victoria Cross winners during the 1920
St Patrick's Day procession

Courtesy of the National Library of Australia

Vestibule of the CTA club, where Albert Jacka greeted the Prince of Wales in 1920 — now the Rendezvous Hotel, Flinders Street

Courtesy of the Commercial Travellers' Association

Frederick Falkiner ('Fred') Knight when admitted to the Bar in 1922

Courtesy of Judy McKechnie

Captain Albert Jacka with subalterns in France, including Lt. Ernie Hill (standing at centre)

Courtesy of Barrie Hill

Police and Special Constables charge rioters in Melbourne during the Police Strike of 1923

Courtesy of the State Library of Victoria, from The Age

Sailors march past Federal Parliament House, Melbourne, during the visit of the US Pacific Fleet in July 1925

Courtesy of the State Library of Victoria from The Argus

The 'Angel of Mercy' statue stood in the archway of the Colonial Mutual Life building (corner of Collins and Elizabeth streets), which was demolished in 1960

Courtesy of the National Library of Australia

Albert Jacka addresses the Advertising Institute of Victoria on the meaning of Anzac Day in 1927

Courtesy of the State Library of Victoria from The Argus

Jacka, Edmonds & Co. Pty Ltd — 'three doors down from Collins Street' in Elizabeth Street, opposite the Block Arcade

Courtesy of the Victorian State Archives VPRS 12903/P1

April 1927 — The Duke and Duchess of York welcomed at St Kilda Pier by Mayor, Cr. Burnett Gray as Town Clerk Frederick Chamberlin reads the Proclamation

Courtesy of the State Library of Victoria from The Argus

VCs at Government House on Armistice Day 1929. (sitting from left) Capt. Albert Jacka, VC, Maj.-Gen. Sir Neville Smyth, VC, Lord Somers, and Lord Stonehaven. Capt. W.D. Joynt, VC standing first on the left

Australian War Memorial neg. no. A05537

The Soldiers' and Sailors' Memorial Hall in Acland Street, St Kilda

From Cooper 'History of St Kilda'

December, 1914 — The Governor General, Sir Ronald Munro Ferguson presents the King's Colours to Lt. W.H. Hamilton of the 14th Battalion on the St Kilda foreshore

From Cooper 'History of St Kilda'

April, 1930 — The Regimental and King's Colours of the 14th Battalion were placed in the foyer of the St Kilda Town Hall

Courtesy of Port Phillip City Collection

Vera and Albert Jacka in formal attire as the Lady Mayoress and Mayor of St Kilda

Courtesy of Port Phillip City Collection

Albert Jacka with his daughter Betty, at the beach in St Kilda/Elwood in the summer of 1928-29

Courtesy of Betty Jacka

St Kilda Council, 1930-31. Standing — Cr. G.H. Robinson, J.P., Cr. J.B. Levi, Cr. T. Unsworth, J.P., Cr. F.L. Dawkins, J.P., Cr. R.T. Taylor, Cr. R.H. Morley, J.P., Cr. H. Moroney, J.P.. Sitting — Cr. G.B. Renfrey, J.P., Cr. E. O'Donnell, J.P., Cr. A. Jacka, V.C., J.P. (Mayor), Cr. B. Gray, M.L.A., Cr. G. Cummings

From Cooper 'History of St Kilda'

Two minutes silence at Anzac House. Left to right from Commander Harris (in white) — Brig.-Gen. Jess, Brig.-Gen. Brand, Col. Lavarck, Rev. T. Watt Leggett, Rev. F. Rolland

Courtesy of the State Library of Victoria from The Herald

The funeral procession of Capt. Albert Jacka, VC, including eight VC pallbearers, makes its way through Melbourne to the St Kilda Cemetery

Courtesy of the State Library of Victoria from The Herald

May 1932 — Vera and Betty Jacka watch Brig.-Gen. Charles Brand unveil the Albert Jacka memorial at the St Kilda Cemetery

Courtesy of the State Library of Victoria from The Argus

for no good purpose. Well, there was purpose now. It was then that Birmingham-born Sergeant-Major Frank Warburton, who was in the dere, shouted in a stentorian voice:

"Signallers! Fix! Bayonets!"

It steadied the signallers, who then pulled out their bayonets, the only weapons they had, and fixed them to their rifles.

"Spread out along the edge of the dere!" he called out. "And make sure your bayonets are sticking up over the brink so the Turks can see them!" While they clambered up to do that, he broke open some boxes of ammunition, and moved along the line supplying them.

"Fire at will!" he ordered, and they inflicted some heavy casualties, which dispersed the Turks.

* * *

Shortly after this, the 14th Battalion's rear guard was being pursued across the stubble field by a strong party of Turks. They were just about to be overwhelmed when the 4th Brigade's machine-gun company, led by Captain Rose, sprang into action from the ridge ahead of them. The machinegunners had been in retreat accompanied by several platoons looking for a place with a commanding presence over the battlefield. It was Percy Black and Harry Murray in their element again, saving this day, as they had many days previously at Anzac. The four machineguns that were unleashed against the Turkish attackers instantly changed the balance of the equation, inflicting heavy casualties, and causing them to retire.

Father Bowen, the 4th Brigade's Roman Catholic chaplain was attached to the 15th Battalion, and was a great friend to both Loughran and Luther.

"When will you retire," Loughran asked him.

"When Luther does," was the chaplain's response.

"So am I," said Loughran, giving full credit to Dr Luther's bravery, but also out of pride in the 14th. He wasn't going to give

Luther the pleasure of saying: the 14th always want to withdraw –
look at their MO. So he waited, but before long he saw that Luther
was moving off in an indifferent manner with his stretcher-bearers
carrying wounded. Loughran had only two stretcher-bearers and
Corporal George Richie, so the four of them followed, carrying
two wounded men as they went. On getting into the Kaijaik
Dere they fell in with Captain Henry, and the rearguard of the
14th Battalion, and the brigade. Henry was irritated by the slow
rate of withdrawal, which was due to carrying the wounded men.
Nevertheless, they soon made their way through their original line
that was now being held by the 13th Battalion in reserve.

* * *

Back in their old trenches around what later came to be known as
Australia Valley, Bert drank what remained of the water he had in
his flask, and contemplated what had just happened as he wearily
watched Captain Loughran and his stretcher-bearers bringing in
those last couple of men. It was then around 1.30 pm. Loughran
had left the hopeless cases back at the dressing station, but some
machinegunners who acted out of pity had brought them in with
them.

Out on the stubble field and in the scrub were lying hundreds
of dead and wounded diggers. The 14th Battalion alone had over a
hundred dead, with another 400 wounded and missing. "What
a useless bloody stunt that was," Bert thought. Still, he was lucky
to have come through without a wound. Lieutenants Warren,
Curlewis, Harris, Hill and Mathews were gone. Sergeant Twose
was gone, as were corporals Hope, Smith, Minogue, privates
Folks, Sheehan, Miller, Pither, and many others. Private Schmidt,
the signaller who was shot in the stomach and attended to by
Captain Loughran, didn't make it either. Lance-Corporal Frank
Hewett, the twenty-year-old bricklayer from Wedderburn was
mortally wounded, and died two days later. In the Will he signed on
25 April 1915, he left all his effects to his father, Ezekiel Hewett,

who was president of the Mechanic's Institute in 1913. There were too many to remember; too much pain to forget.

Soon Bert's heavy eyelids closed, and he gave way to the sleep of exhaustion. Since 6 am on 6 August, over the past three days, he had had only a couple of hours sleep.

* * *

The 14th Battalion worked hard after that, digging day after day to fortify the position around Australia Valley against any possible attack by the Turks. They dug so hard along the ridgeline they made it impregnable to attack. As they dug they noticed that day after day the Turks were digging just as hard on the other side of the dry riverbed of the Kaijaik Dere. The Turks were up on Hill 60 now, digging, making it impregnable to attack from the south. One day, even Lieutenant-General "Rainbow Bill" Birdwood would come to understand that, but there was more slaughter to come at Hill 60.

For Brigadier-General Monash, the "Bloody Eighth of August" was the worst day of his military career. It was the low point from which he would climb, over the next three years, to command the Anzac Corps on the Western Front as a Lieutenant-General. Ironically, three years later, on this same day, he would lead the Australians in a battle that would practically decide the outcome of the war. It would be something to be proud of.

THE CRASH OF '29

The influence of Alfred Charles Burnett Gray on Bert was to be profound. Bert had continuous contact with him through their membership of the Freemasons Lodge No. 303, and the St Kilda branch of the RSSILA.

Burnett Gray was born in Geraldton, Western Australia, and was educated at Prince Alfred College, Adelaide, and Wesley College, Melbourne. He was assistant secretary of the Royal Children's Hospital in Melbourne, and for a time tried his hand as a miner on the Bullfinch and Ararat goldfields. In 1911 he returned to Melbourne, became a merchant/salesman in the bayside suburb of Elwood, and married Miss Queenie Hilary Margaret Smith. Driven by his extraordinary level of community spirit, he sought election to the St Kilda Council, and in 1915 had sufficient spirit left, at the age of thirty-one, to volunteer for duty with the AIF.

When he came back, Gray launched himself into the St Kilda Council again, and added returned soldier causes to his expanding list of activities. He became a Progressive Liberal, a small party formed late in 1926, whose motto was that "commerce is the great instrument of civilisation, and an inspiration to praiseworthy human activity".

Gray saw his opportunity to wrest the State seat of St Kilda from Mr Frederick Eggelston, a conservative who supported the coalition of Nationalist and Victorian Farmers' Union members that kept Labor out of office. Eggelston's undoing was his support for the Motor Omnibus Act, which sought to curtail and regulate the private buses serving St Kilda, partly as a means of protecting the businesses of the state owned transport system. Gray opposed the Act as a travesty that "struck a blow at the very principle of private enterprise". He campaigned for all-night trains and trams, for housewives to have an influence in municipal government, against increases in parliamentary salaries, and for State public services to be organised on business lines. His package struck a chord with electors, and suddenly he was the local member of the Legislative Assembly, as well as the Mayor of St Kilda. However, as one reporter saw it:

> *Mr Gray beat Mr Eggelston on the buses issue. Mr Eggelston took away the buses. Fivepence into town in 20 minutes, and now you have to pay 7 pence, wait for a train, and take 40 minutes to be dumped into the central railway station. Now St Kilda has neither buses, nor Mr Eggelston.*

In the period between the wars, some people shifted to the left and others to the right in search of the answer to challenges such as unemployment, and the best way to harness the benefits of a technological age.

Early in 1925 Bill sold the horse and dray, and left wood carting to join a railway gang, but after a period of hard work on the line he was offered a supernumerary position at the Wedderburn Railway Station. With his innate intelligence he soon passed all the necessary exams and became a permanent railways man, never wavering from his Labor upbringing, and the cause of the union. His famous brother's business, by contrast, was being affected by a crippling maritime strike, during which the Australian Seamen's Union demanded the legislative abolition of the Casual Waterside Workers' Union. By September 1925, the country was a mess, and the importers, exporters and others affected by the shipping crisis called on Bert to chair another meeting at Scott's Hotel.

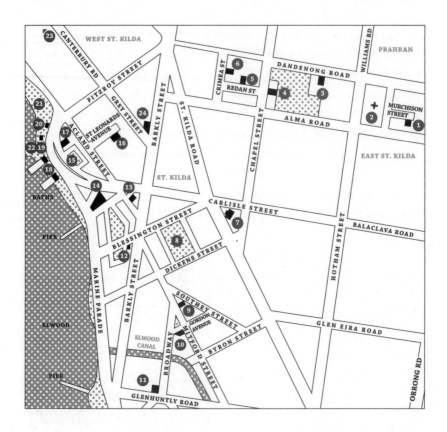

1. 23 Murchison Street, East St Kilda

2. St Kilda Cemetery

3. St Mary's Catholic church

4. St Georges Presbyterian chruch

5. 10 Redan Street, East St Kilda ('Lissa Thorn')

6. Masonic Hall (Lodge 303)

7. St Kilda Town Hall

8. St Kilda Botanical Gardens

9. 'Ma' Futcher's house, Mitford Street, Elwood

10. 'Narooma' corner Broadway and Gordon
    Avenue

11. Maison de Luxe dance hall, Elwood

12. 60 Chaucer Street, St Kilda

13. St Kilda Soldiers' and Sailors' Memorial Hall

14. Luna Park

15. Alfred Sqaure

16. 'St Leonards', 10 St Leonards Avenue, St Kilda

17. The Esplanade Hotel

18. St Kilda baths

19. Royal Melbourne Yacht Club

20. Cenotaph

21. Catani Gardens

22. St Kilda Pier

23. Middle Park Hotel

24. Old St Kilda Court House and Council
    Chambers

Map of St Kilda and Elwood, circa 1919–1932

In 1925 Bert and Vera purchased a brand new Californian bungalow at 23 Murchison Street, East St Kilda, which ran parallel to Dandenong Road and faced the St Kilda cemetery. They chose the middle one in a row of three bungalows built by P. S. Walsh. It boasted six rooms, a dark wood panelled corridor, indirect art deco lighting fixtures, and all the latest American labour saving devices. It had a garage at the back of its generous allotment, which was slightly elevated.

Vera could finally enjoy a bay view, even if it was just a sliver of blue on the horizon. Due to the elevation of the house at the rear, there was plenty of storage room underneath for the laundry and its double concrete basins. Steam issued from the room, where Vera used a long stick to push the clothes she was washing down into the boiling water of the copper. They now had room for a garden, too, but Vera's great passion was reading.

Vera's mother, Catherine, moved into the new house to live with them. Since Vera's father had died, and both James and Molly had married and moved away, Vera was the only close family she had left. She was now suffering from uraemia (an illness that accompanies renal failure), which gave Vera some additional work in looking after her, including visits to her GP, Dr Wilson. Near the end of the year, Bert's younger sister Bessie finally got married to Harold Dowrick. She was the last of the seven children that Nathaniel and Elizabeth had married off. Mission accomplished, but not for Bert and Vera – their mission had not even begun.

* * *

By 1926 Bert had relocated the business to the corner of Briscoe Lane and Little Collins Street, just east of Queen Street. He was now just a few doors down from his old adversarial CO, Lieutenant-Colonel Dare, whose architectural practice was located at the Stalbridge Chambers. Occasionally Bert would bump into him in the street. This wasn't a main street location, but it was ground floor, and the showroom now catered for retail customers too. The modern household appliances they were importing were all the rage.

It was cloudy that afternoon, late in October 1926, with a spring shower threatening. Bert and his business partner Ernie Edmonds were walking east along the north side of Collins Street. As they neared the intersection with Elizabeth Street, the massive edifice of the Colonial Mutual Life building loomed ahead. The most impressive business building in the country, it had been commissioned by the American Equitable Life Assurance Company, and built between 1890 and 1896 as a symbol of permanence.

From the beginning that building was a disaster. Seven men were killed during its construction, and one of them had nothing at all to do with it. On 8 August 1892 a compressor high up on the half finished building exploded, projecting a clump of metal that sailed across Collins Street and the buildings opposite, came down in Flinders Lane, and sliced straight through Ellis Plasterer. He had just collected his pay and was walking east towards Elizabeth Street with his young daughter along the south side of Flinders Lane, which ran parallel to Elizabeth. He let go of his daughter's hand as he slumped to the ground, and died in hospital the following day.

The main archway of the building was dominated by a set of twelve-foot high bronze statues, which sat on a granite platform that was held up by two massive forty-foot high red granite pillars. The statues were cast in Vienna, at the Imperial Art Foundry of the Austro-Hungarian Empire, and it was ironic that they depicted an angel of mercy protecting a widow and her two children. This dramatic entry to the building was framed within a great stone archway that was about eighty feet high.

As they walked, Bert was quiet. He had lost the spring in his step, and that eternal optimism that Ernie remembered from their time together in France during the war. Nevertheless, Ernie persisted in talking about his experiences as a POW in Germany during the war.

"…Then there was this Hun corporal who spoke good English, or should I rather say, 'bad English'. He had obviously spent a few years in London before the war, and from the way he swore, I'd say it was probably Whitechapel! He told us that our blankety navy was starving them, and we would blankety have to starve along with them! Still, he didn't do too badly for us. Then there was the time he marched us through town playing *Tipperary* on his mouth organ. Can you imagine that?" He saw that Bert's expression was blank. He seemed lost, far away in his thoughts. After a few more seconds of silence Ernie stopped walking, forcing Bert to stop and people to have to walk around them. It began to drizzle.

"Bert, you're not listening to a word I'm saying, are you?"

"What?"

"What's the matter, mate? Not all of you is present and accounted for. Let's duck over here for a bit," Ernie suggested, guiding Bert under the great archway. They stood looking at each other, eye to eye, as the raindrops darkened the grey walls of the monolith.

"Well, I'm worried about Vera," Bert muttered. "We've settled into the new house and I thought that would make her happy."

"What's wrong?"

"Her mother is sick and it's all rather depressing, and… something's missing."

Ernie knew what he meant, as he and Thelma had discussed a number of times that a child was needed to balance Bert and Vera's union.

"It's a child isn't it?"

After a short pause Bert agreed. "Yes, that's what it boils down to, I suppose."

"Then the answer's simple. You need a child."

"Don't be funny, Ernie."

"I'm not being funny at all. I'm suggesting adoption."

"Adoption?"

"That's right."

Bert paused again. "To be honest, it has crossed my mind, but I've been loathe to bring it up with Vera. I don't know how she would react."

"Well, I think you owe it to yourselves to have this one out with her."

Bert knew that Ernie was right. They needed to do something.

* * *

That afternoon Bert thought about Ernie's suggestion, and he came home with the intention of raising it with Vera at the appropriate time. He was quiet all throughout dinner. He didn't want to raise it in front of his mother-in law in the kitchen, so he waited until she had gone to bed, and they were alone, listening intently in the lounge, as the sounds of wood cracking in the art deco fireplace punctuated the classical music program playing on the radio.

"What's wrong, Bert?" Vera said, finally. "You hardly touched your dinner, and you didn't say a word to me or Mum all night."

"I had a talk with Ernie today."

"Yes?"

"About us."

"What in particular?"

"Well, I told him that we were not happy. That we want a child… and he suggested that we adopt one."

"Why does Ernie have to know all about our private affairs?" Vera whispered.

"It's not half obvious is it?" Bert shot back.

"Lot's of people don't have children, Bert, you've said that yourself many times."

"Well, that's true, but still…" Bert grasped his wife's hand on the divan and squeezed it firmly. He wasn't good at showing emotion to her, but this time he looked her straight in the eyes. "Damn it, I thought you wanted to have children. So why don't we adopt one?"

It was like a thunderbolt for Vera. While she was not pining for children, she felt it was her wifely duty to give him a child, which she knew he was keen to have. She felt guilty about it, but so did Bert. For all he knew, the bullets, shrapnel and gas had taken their toll. All he knew was that there's a problem and here's a solution. He looked at her in silence as she thought it through. She took a deep breath.

"All right," she said finally. "We'll adopt a child. We'll do it." She stood up and smiled. "Goodness me, are we really going to do it?"

* * *

Children's Welfare Department, Railways Buildings, Flinders Street

The corridor of the Children's Welfare Department building was spartan, giving the impression of a hospital ward decorated in browns. Bert and Vera were well dressed for the interview. After spending some time in a waiting room, they were met by a social worker, who invited them into her office.

"First of all, Captain Jacka, let me say what an honour it is to be meeting with you and Mrs Jacka, and assisting you in this matter." She felt she had to say that, but she was determined to deal with this famous man and his wife on a strictly professional level. Having seen the file, she was absolutely confident that there would not be any problem with such an upstanding couple. They had all the credentials: they were young; they had a nice house in a good suburb; he was a decorated war hero, heavily involved in community activities and a partner in a successful business; she was a well-spoken, healthy young woman. They had the means to give a child in need all the benefits of a good home.

"Thank you for agreeing to meet with us at such short notice," Vera replied. It was yet another reminder that the Jacka legend still carried a lot of weight in Melbourne.

"So, you wish to adopt a child," said the social worker, looking from Bert to Vera and back again. "First of all, you must be aware that this is a lifelong commitment. There can be no going back for you. Just after the war we saw some very fickle foster-parenting. A couple would adopt a child, and then abandon it two years later after a baby of their own had been born."

"There's no chance of that here, I can assure you," Bert added, which brought a stare from Vera.

"There are risks, you know," said the social worker.

"What kinds of risks?" asked Vera.

"I must also make you aware that as the Victorian law stands at the moment, there is nothing that prevents the parents of an adopted child from claiming it back at some time in the future."

"But that's ridiculous."

"It's the law."

"Then it should be changed."

"There are moves afoot."

"When?"

"We've been trying to get new legislation for years. Some say it could be raised in parliament as early as next year."

Vera cut in. "So let me be sure that I understand it. As the law stands at present we could adopt a child, love it, care for it and have it taken away from us on a whim?"

"Yes, that is correct. The real question is whether it's a commitment you are willing to make, and a risk you are willing to take?"

Vera looked at Bert. He could see in her eyes that she was ready for this. Over the years he had sensed her disappointment when it became obvious that they would not be able to have their own natural-born children. They both spoke almost simultaneously.

"Yes."

"Yes, we are prepared to do whatever is necessary," Bert repeated more formally. "What then is the process we need to go through?"

"Well, it currently falls under section 67 of the *Neglected Children's Act*. An adoption order needs to be obtained from a police magistrate, and a number of consents are necessary: the consent of the guardian of the child to be adopted, and the consent of the husband of the woman who wishes to adopt the child. That's you, Captain Jacka."

"Do we have *any* protection under the current law?" Bert asked.

"The only real protection you have is the cost of a legal process to reverse the adoption. The matter could end up in the Supreme Court. The problem is, as I have already explained, that the process is somewhat informal in the absence of specific legislation."

"Well, there's some comfort in that at least," Vera muttered to herself.

"Just a final word of advice, before you plunge into the role of foster-mother, Mrs Jacka. If you are expecting that after years of taking care of your child, feeding and clothing it, educating it and seeing it through to adulthood that that child will say to you: 'Thank you darling foster mother, for your gentle care', you are likely to be disappointed. Your adopted child will have nothing to be grateful about because love, food and shelter are every child's birthright. Your reward will be found in the act of giving those things to your adopted child."

Vera smiled at the social worker, acknowledging her point. She looked at Bert, and saw he couldn't stop himself from smiling. Vera was happy too. She was confident that she had the strength to take on the responsibility of parenthood, and had the capacity for unconditional love.

* * *

On a crisp Wednesday morning in the week before Anzac Day in 1927, the powerful British battle cruiser HMS *Renown* broke through the mist that hovered on Port Philip Bay and berthed at Princes' Pier, Port Melbourne. As was the custom, the *Renown*'s valued passengers, the Duke and Duchess of York were transferred to the Royal Barge, and made their way across the bay to St Kilda Pier, where thousands of people were waiting to welcome the royal couple that had captured the imagination of the public at home and abroad. Light rain and a cloudy day didn't dampen anyone's spirits, and given that they had just sailed from Sydney, some wit on the Esplanade put up a sign reading, "Welcome to the Sunny South."

First to welcome the royal couple at the pier was His Majesty's representative in Australia, the Governor-General, Lord Stonehaven, and the Mayor of St Kilda, Councillor Burnett Gray, MLA, dressed in his robes. The Duke was dressed in a gold-braided naval uniform, just as his older brother had been seven years earlier. The Duchess was a "girlish vision in blue", wearing a frock of soft blue georgette and a greyish blue coat wrap embossed in a metallic design. She soon showed her captivating smile that was charming crowds across the globe. Then the presentations began, with Lord Stonehaven presenting the Governor, Lord Somers, and Burnett Gray, who in turn presented his councillors and the Town Clerk, Mr F. W. Chamberlin, who read the proclamation of welcome.

* * *

On the Friday leading up to Anzac Day Bert addressed a luncheon of the Victorian Institute of Advertising. A photographer from *The Argus* snapped him, capturing the dark bags under his eyes that spoke of the sleepless nights he was experiencing.

"Whenever you see four returned soldiers you should think of one more soldier who did not return," he said. "It is a fact that for every four soldiers who returned one was killed. Out of the four who returned three were wounded, and of those three, two were wounded at least twice. I do not think that the public takes into account the tremendous effect that the war had upon the men who returned. More than 22,000 soldiers have died since their return, and this is some indication of the terrible effects. Thus, when you see a returned soldier in a court, or 'down and out', do not judge him too harshly, but remember the terrible experiences through which he has passed."

*   *   *

Saturday night was the eve of Anzac Day, and the most extraordinary Annual General Meeting and dinner that the Victorian Branch of the Returned Sailors' and Soldiers' Imperial League had ever held, or ever would hold, was taking place at Anzac House. One extraordinary thing about it was the assembly of thirty-two Victoria Cross winners in one place – which was claimed to be the largest gathering of VCs in history. The guests of honour were the Prime Minister, Mr Stanley Melbourne Bruce, and Sir John Monash, while the many delegates included Senator Harold 'Pompey' Elliott, from the Camberwell branch.

Among the VCs was Captain Donovan Joynt. After his brief spell as liaison officer for the Special Constabulary force during the police strike, he had applied himself to a number of causes outside his printing and colour photography businesses. One was a touring display of photographs from the Great War, and another was Legacy. An organisation of returned servicemen who were now in business, Legacy sought to alleviate the suffering of families that had been disadvantaged by the war. Now Legacy had a brand new cause, and Joynt was implementing it, moving around in the hall and speaking to those he knew he could count on.

The issue of a monument commemorating the sacrifices of Victorians in the Great War had been simmering since 1921, but had come to the boil in the months leading up to this Anzac Day. The original plan was to build a Shrine of Remembrance in the Domain Park on St Kilda Road, and an international competition for its design was won by Messrs. Hudson and Wardrop. Conveniently, they were Melbourne architects who had been to the war. Their design for the Shrine was based on the Parthenon in Athens and the Mausoleum at Halicarnassus, one of the seven wonders of the ancient world.

By 1926 the idea of a shrine at the Domain had been superseded by the concept of an Anzac Park, which was to be carved out of the buildings opposite Parliament House in Spring Street. This view held that the shrine building was ugly, drab and sombre, while a park at the end of Bourke Street would beautify the city. Anzac Park had been promoted by the managing editor of the *Herald* newspaper, Keith Murdoch, who was so successful that State Cabinet and the RSSILA had already given their approvals. It was now the eleventh hour, as a Bill had already been drawn up to requisition the properties in the area at the top of Bourke Street between Exhibition and Spring Streets.

That night at the dinner there was a short break, and the speeches were about to begin. Joynt VC took the opportunity to approach Sir John Monash.

"Sir," he whispered, "tonight would be a splendid occasion for you to make your pronouncement regarding the Shrine, because all the delegates from all the branches are here and they will all listen to you and I am sure they will move to change their decision regarding support for the Anzac Square if you give them the lead."

"Say that again, Joynt?" Monash asked as he looked around the room.

"I said, sir, that tonight would be a good time to make an announcement about the Shrine. All the delegates are here, and they hold you in extremely high regard. If you were to come out publicly in favour of the shrine, they would reverse their previous decision on Anzac Square. With your endorsement, we would have the numbers."

"Well, I'll consider it," Monash replied. It wasn't the answer that Joynt was looking for, but it was better than nothing. Joynt went back to the table with the VCs, and sat down next to Bert.

"Get ready for Sir John's speech," Joynt warned them all. "If he mentions the War Memorial in his speech, start clapping."

"Has he been fully briefed?" Bert asked.

"Oh yes, we visited him in his office a few weeks ago – Kem Kemsley, Blackett, Doolan, Meldrum, McCrea and myself. We told him that if we all continue to fiddle, Rome will burn, and what we'll get is a nice big expensive square at the top end of Bourke Street. The Parliament will dominate it, and within a generation people will forget what it was put there for…"

"And what was his opinion?"

"We couldn't quite tell. It looked as if he was in agreement with us, but for some reason he felt he couldn't make his views public."

"Do you think he'll do it?" asked Lieutenant R. Moon VC, who was listening in.

"Well, we won't have to wait long to find out," Joynt surmised, as Monash had just stood up, apparently to give his address. Turning around to face Sir John, he added, "We have to be ready, just in case he does."

Sir John did not begin his speech immediately, but instead raised a toast to the good health of the prime minister. After it had been drunk, Mr Bruce responded.

"I have not come to this gathering as the prime minister, but as a soldier, and an extraordinarily incompetent one!" he said, which drew laughter from the audience.

"But," he continued in a more serious vein, "it is fitting that at a gathering representing the returned soldiers of Victoria, the prime minister, representing the nation, should demonstrate in person the nation's gratitude to and interest in the men. The commemoration of Anzac Day should live for all time, because it is essential for Australia's greatness that the ideals and principles which guided its sons from 1914 to 1918 shall be preserved and maintained.

"Nothing is ever accomplished unless there is behind it sentiment. Sentiment counts for everything. Australia's war effort was based on sentiment, tradition, and patriotism, the greatest factors in the making of a nation. They were appreciated in those dark days of war, but are Australians not now inclined to forget them? Are we not tending to forget all but our own selfish ends? Soldiers will never accomplish anything in the realm of party politics. It would be disastrous if they tried. But they can influence the outlook and sentiment of the whole of the people. The influence of returned men in Australia has been a steadying one.

"Deep down in all Australians there is not only sentimentality, but a certain disreputableness which will never let us lose our sense of humour, and will force us on with the job. Every Australian can be relied upon to find a way out of his difficulties. In this job of mine, which is far more rotten than the job that any one of you has, one suffers disappointments and rebuffs. One wonders whether one is doing any good, and whether things are worthwhile. Then I go back to my war memories – the recollections of gallant deeds and uncomplaining heroism, which I witnessed there, and think of the manner in which those Australians carried on in the face of almost insurmountable difficulties. And with those thoughts, one cannot fail to be inspired to renewed effort."

There was hearty applause at the conclusion of the prime minister's speech, but it only heightened their anticipation of what General Monash would say. While it was heartening to the State RSSILA leaders to hear these fine sentiments of the prime minister, there were a few words they were waiting to hear from Sir John, who used to say that he only had to raise his little finger for the AIF to spring into life again. He had done it in an emergency in 1923, and hoped that his little finger would not be needed again.

"Many of you have heard my voice before," he began amid laughter, when replying to a toast to his health. "When I threatened you with an additional half-hour's drill." Again there was laughter.

"But times have changed! This gathering is the most representative of the Australian Imperial Force that I have ever attended. I have had thrust upon me much credit and reward which was due to the whole of the Australian Army Corps. Great honour has been bestowed upon me by the Government of Britain and by the Allies, but all these, I feel, have been only because I was the leader of, and the spokesman for, a great fighting force.

"My work in France gave me the opportunity of judging the work of other army corps, and I consider that the Australian Army Corps was the most formidable instrument of war that any war has ever produced. Its features were that we were all men of one nation, and all volunteers." As he spoke there was a round of applause and cheers, which subsided as he continued.

"No other military machine could have been more powerful or more invincible. In the last few months of the war I was able to recommend twenty-five men for the Victoria Cross. Their acts of gallantry were almost superhuman... We soldiers have got the destiny of this country in our hands if we speak with one voice, and if we show the same principles of comradeship and devotion which actuated these Victoria Cross winners and indeed all Australians in the war. There are plenty of disruptive forces, and it is our business to prevent their operating, and ensure the happiness and prosperity of our community." Again he had to pause for the audience's enthusiastic response.

"With the commemoration of Anzac Day, one naturally thinks of Victoria's war memorial." This was the section that Joynt and the others were waiting for, and they sat on the edge of their seats as he continued. "I was a member of the committee of assessors which selected the design for the Shrine of Remembrance. It is my firm conviction that that is the only proposal worthy of the support of the soldiers of Victoria. When the time comes I can give you one hundred good reasons why you should not consider any other form of memorial, why you should not support plans for the beautification of Melbourne at the expense of the soldier and of his war record."

Joynt, Jacka and the other VCs rose from their seats, started clapping for all they were worth, and shouted their approval. The whole body of returned men stood and clapped, and shouted and cheered. Above the din of this spontaneous demonstration, those present struggled to catch the last few words of Sir John's speech.

"An Anzac Square is out of the question for many reasons, among them that of finance. Keep your judgment in reserve, and when you are able to make it let me come and tell you in detail why you should support only the Shrine of Remembrance."

The applause kept going as Sir John stood there to acknowledge it, and only gradually subsided.

When Sir John finally sat down, the Returned Services president, Ernest Turnbull, leaned over and invited him to attend a conference of RSSILA delegates in two day's time. After the function, Sir John came over to Captain Joynt, told him about the invitation he had received, and asked him to come along to assist with information. The outcome was a reversal of the RSSILA's position back to its original approval of a Shrine of Remembrance at the Domain.

* * *

The Anzac Day that followed was the most successful ever. Thirty thousand diggers, led by Sir John Monash, marched in front of a crowd of around half a million. They formed up at the start of St Kilda Road, crossed the Princes' Bridge, marched up Swanston, Bourke, Exhibition and Collins streets, and then wheeled into Spring Street, where a temporary cenotaph was set up in front of the Federal Parliament building. At Parliament House Sir John fell out of the parade to take the salute with the Duke. Dressed in his captain's uniform, Bert marched past and gave his salute with the large group of VCs.

* * *

"We'll be among some class tonight," Bert said into the mirror in their bedroom the following Tuesday night as he battled to fix his white tie to his heavily starched shirt. "Blast this thing!"

"Here, let me help you with that," Vera said, as she sorted out the jumble Bert had created. She and Bert had never been on better terms, as everything was now travelling smoothly. His business was doing well in Briscoe Lane, and Vera had been floating on air ever since they had worked through the adoption papers. They had received the wonderful news that their daughter had already been born a week or so earlier. All Vera had to do now was wait for the initial period of breastfeeding by the natural mother.

"Excited?"

"Very much," Vera smiled as she re-tied the knot.

"There," she said with a sense of achievement at having tied the knot backwards.

* * *

As Bert drove up to the Watch Gate in the Domain, Vera could see the lights in the 145-foot tower of Federal Government House shining high above the trees. While it was not quite Buckingham Palace, it was a worthy palace nevertheless.

A line of guests had formed inside the main entry, as they were all being presented to, and greeted personally by Lord and Lady Stonehaven. The royals were still at a dinner at Federal Parliament House, and would not be arriving until about half past nine. A London-born Scot, in his youth Lord Stonehaven had spent time as ADC to the Governor of New South Wales. Later he became a conservative party politician in England, and was chosen by Mr Bruce from a list of candidates.

"Captain Albert Jacka VC, and Mrs Jacka!" was announced, and they stepped forward and were greeted by Lord and Lady Stonehaven.

* * *

Sometime later, in the ballroom, Bert and Vera came across a couple that they knew quite well from St Kilda.

"Your Worship," Bert said.

"Evening."

"Good evening, Queenie," Vera added.

"Captain and Mrs Jacka, how are you?" Queenie replied. "Isn't it a perfectly stunning evening?" Having been married to Burnett Gray since before the war, when he was a young councillor, she was used to the public life.

"What a gorgeous room," Vera commented.

"I can tell you the last few days have shot past like a dream," Bert said. "It's hard to see where the time went. Say, have you heard any more news about the accident?" Bert was referring to the air accident that was witnessed by thousands on the day the royals arrived. A formation of DH9 aeroplanes that had escorted the royals was suddenly caught in a tangle as one of the machines had unexpectedly risen up and bumped into the one flying above it. One of the planes crashed through a garage roof when it came down, and four men were killed.

"Nothing more than I've read in the papers really," said Gray.

"I heard that three of the men were married," added Vera.

"They didn't need to go to war," said Queenie sadly.

"The weapons of war are inherently dangerous," Bert said, "even when only training or demonstrating their capabilities. It's a unique job."

These comments reminded Mayor Gray that returned soldiers have special needs. "I meant what I said at the dinner on Saturday night," Gray said turning to Bert. "I want to form a soldiers' party composed of all the diggers in the House. We need to get sympathetic consideration of all problems affecting returned men. We should constitute a power in the House, and obtain for soldiers prompter legislation for their needs."

Queenie and Vera were starting to lose interest in the direction of their husbands' discussion. Whenever they got together, somehow things always seemed to gravitate towards a discussion of the war, or what could be done for down-and-out returned soldiers, or what could be done to remember the glorious dead. This evening they were already at it. Fortunately Lady Stonehaven came by and invited the ladies to come with her.

"I couldn't agree more," said Bert. "Sir John said something similar on Saturday night too, if you recall. I was at a function with Police Commissioner Nicholson a few years ago, and he assured everyone there that preference would be shown, but there's nothing of the sort."

"I know. Another issue is the Metropolitan Gas Company, which is working under an Act passed in 1878! It's clear to me that this legislation is too antiquated to protect the public's interests."

"What's wrong with it specifically?"

"For a start, the company is restricted in the expansion of its activities. There have been special committees set up, recommendations made, but nothing seems to happen. You're smiling?"

"Oh nothing," Bert replied. "It just reminds me of a debate on the merits of the Metropolitan Gas Company that we had in France."

"You debated this in France?"

"There wasn't much that we *didn't* debate in France," Bert laughed. "Our Padre used to organise them. We even had a mock parliament once."

"So you do have some interest in politics," Gray shot back. It was a lead he needed, as he had been working on Bert for years. He saw a natural politician in him, but Bert just wouldn't be convinced. He continued to see himself as the businessman.

"That's not politics," Bert insisted. "It's business."

"It's the same jolly thing. Don't you see? Your experience as a businessman would make you all the more valuable as a politician."

"I just don't want to be in a political party."

"Then join us in the council!" Gray implored. "There's lot's to do. I know your concern about the unemployment situation. If unemployment were to rise any further, we could be in for a revolution that would make the Police Strike look like a walk in the park. We can't afford to gamble with the socialistic and communistic forces in our midst. If successful, they would eventually disrupt our society, and subvert the individual rights and freedoms and liberties that we take for granted."

* * *

To Vera's great delight, elsewhere in the ballroom Lady Stonehaven was presenting her and Queenie to the Duchess, and they were now locked in discussion. Vera was struck by how cool the Duchess appeared to be, despite the heat that had built up in the ballroom over the evening. There was not a hint of anxiety — just her natural dignity, calm nature, and beaming smile. Queenie had already been presented to the Duchess the previous Friday at Parliament House, and recalled an incident there. A curly headed boy of about three had accompanied his mother to the presentation, and had completely innocently blown the Duchess a kiss, which she responded to immediately by blowing a kiss back.

"We were all delighted by the way Your Royal Highness blew a kiss back to that little curly headed boy," Queenie recalled.

"He was such a darling. The children of Melbourne have been altogether wonderful in their welcome to us. It touched us deeply to see and hear the cheers of the little ones as we passed the Children's Hospital on the way to Parliament. They seemed so brave."

"How is her Royal Highness Princess Elizabeth faring?" Queenie asked.

"Very well," the Duchess smiled. "The Princess has just had her first birthday, but she was far too young to bring with us on a long sea voyage."

"What is your Royal Highness intending to do with all the toys and presents that the people have asked you to accept on behalf of Princess Elizabeth?" asked Lady Stonehaven.

"Well, it is a dilemma isn't it?" the Duchess replied. "If I take them to the Princess, she wouldn't know what to do with it all;

and if I leave them here, perhaps with the children at the hospital, they would be put to good use. But the people who passed them on would be roundly disappointed, wouldn't they?"

Rather than dwell on that moral dilemma any further, Vera decided to ask the Duchess something that she had been bursting to ask ever since she had been presented, and now was an ideal opportunity.

"Your Royal Highness," she said, "I have been meaning to ask you something."

"Please do."

"I am about to have a baby daughter in three weeks' time, and I would like to name her Elizabeth, after the Princess. Would your Royal Highness mind at all if I did that?"

"Why not another Elizabeth?" replied the Duchess enthusiastically. "We would be delighted." As she said that, the eyes of all the women around Vera, including those of the Duchess, gravitated downwards to her stomach, and noticed it was flat. Vera caught onto the body language implied by their gaze, and hastened to explain.

"Oh, I am *adopting* my daughter," Vera added with a smile. "I'm sorry, I forgot to mention that." With that, the Duchess beamed her broad smile again, and relieved smiles appeared all round. Vera could breathe again.

* * *

8.30 pm Iona, St George's Road, Toorak, 8 August 1927

An interesting commonality between the Duke of Wellington and Sir John Monash was that each man was perfectly fluent in the language of his enemy. The former had been sent as a young man to train for the army in a French military academy, while Sir John's parents had migrated from Prussia in 1860, and as a boy he used to write in German to his father at Jerilderie. Monash was, in any case, fluent in French too, and Latin for that matter, but at times the German-Jewish ancestry had made things difficult for him at the beginning of the war.

The Duke of Wellington maintained a tradition of inviting his senior officers to a dinner at his home each year on the anniversary of the Battle of Waterloo. While the dining room at Sir John's house, Iona, was nowhere near as grand as the one at Apsley House, No. 1 London, it is said that the punch, being a mixture of whiskey and brandy, was far more potent. In 1921 Monash first invited his eight most senior officers residing in Melbourne, and their wives, to a dinner that commemorated the great victory of 8 August 1918, when the Australian Army Corps, the Canadians, and the British Tank Corps smashed the defences at the Hindenburg Line so hard, that Field-Marshal Ludendorff described it in his memoirs as the "black day of the German Army in the history of the war".

To Monash there was nothing wrong with a victory dinner held in private, but he was against a public memorial that had any hint of "victory over the conquered". That is why he supported a memorial of remembrance rather than an "arc of triumph". By 1927 Monash had widened the group of attending officers to twenty, without wives. The generals and brigadiers attended in dinner jackets without medals. When they filed into the dining room from the parlour they crossed the wide passageway displaying Monash's butterfly collection of 600 German battalion lapel insignia encased in glass, which gave the impression of a museum. Throughout his life he was a great collector of everything from native spears to the autographs of the Crown Heads of Europe.

The host raised the first toast of the night to The King, and the second was to "Our fallen comrades". The third and final toast was raised by General Sir Cecil Brudenell White to "Our Leader, Lieutenant General Sir John Monash". The event was, as usual, accompanied by a great spirit of fellowship that was born out of the tremendous ordeal that they had passed through during the war years, when in the midst of the filth and squalor, the death and destruction, they had rallied together and prevailed against a most skilful and determined enemy. As a result of this shared experience there had developed among them a very deep and lasting bond. In the cordiality of this evening, among the singing of the old marching songs, even the old protagonists would sometimes find a moment of reconciliation.

Monash knew the old antagonisms, too, and saw to it that at the start of the evening at any rate, the seating arrangements would not grate on anyone. After that, he could not control what was going to happen. So, at one point Lieutenant-General Brudenell White, now Chairman of the Commonwealth Public Service Board, but during the war Chief of Staff to Lieutenant-General "Rainbow Bill" Birdwood, found himself sitting right next to Senator Elliott. Despite having a few years ago publicly accused Brudenell White of incompetence in the application of tanks at Bullecourt, Pompey immediately turned to him.

"I don't suppose you've had the opportunity to read Major Liddell Hart's most recent book, which he has titled *The Remaking of Modern Armies?*"

"I have not had the pleasure."

"I have an arrangement with a bookseller to receive all the latest books from London."

"He's keen on this perception of tanks as the new cavalry, isn't he?" suggested Brudenell White, who had heard of Liddell Hart's imagery of the tank as the new knight in shining armour, but much more potent. It was amply demonstrated during the war in a hollow between Cachy and l'Abbe Wood. Seven British whippet tanks with twenty-one men on board got in among three battalions of German troops and had ridden over and gunned them down mercilessly. According to Liddell Hart the tanks returned to base "spattered with blood", but the German attack had been "nipped in the bud".

"That's the main theme of the book," Elliott agreed, "but that impudent fool has had the audacity to suggest that it was the commander of the Third Corps, General Butler, who designed the brilliant counter-attack at Villers-Bretonneux in April 1918."

"So, he denied your role?"

"Denied my role?" Elliott said, raising his voice. His old colleague Major-General Drake-Brockman, who sat on the other side of the table, knew his voice well and turned his head. So did Brigadier-General McGlinn, who unlike Monash, had retained his hefty "Tweedledee-Tweedledum" figure from before the war.

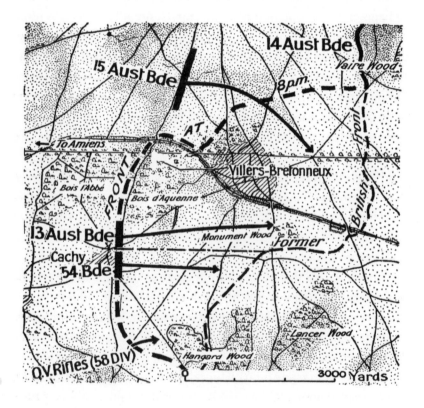

Villers–Bretonneux, 25 April, 1918

Source: W.D. Joynt, VC, Saving the Channel Ports, Wren Publishing, 1975, p.22

"My role," Elliott continued in a whisper, "was to conceive the whole method of attack from start to finish. I immediately sent my plan up to division and it was delayed there for a while. But by God I got the authority back in time to execute it. It was based on my recollection of the Battle of Cannae in 216 BC, when Hannibal routed the Romans by driving his cavalry around and behind the Roman legion." As he spoke he described the movements of his and Glasgow's brigade to Brudenell White on the tablecloth, with each brigade represented by an index finger, and his cup representing Villers-Bretonneux.

"I'm familiar with the Battle of Cannae, as is Liddell-Hart I'm sure."

"As if that wasn't enough," Elliott continued. "He goes on to make an allegation in his book that an unnamed Australian brigadier... And let's face it, there's a choice of only two isn't there? This unnamed brigadier is supposed to have changed the orders that he was *given* by higher command, and almost bungled the whole show by wheeling one of the pincers in too sharply and allowing some of the trapped Germans a way out!"

"You see, this is precisely what has always annoyed me most about you, Elliott," Brudenell White said glibly. "You interpret everything you see as a slight against *you* personally, when to a disinterested observer it would look completely different."

"What do you mean?"

"Well, it could simply be ignorance or incompetence on the part of Liddell-Hart?"

"Then was it ignorance or incompetence that inspired Birdwood to overlook my achievements when the divisional commands were being determined?"

"Look," said Brudenell White, "I can tell you quite categorically that it was not my decision. But if I had been him, would I have promoted you over Glasgow?"

"Glasgow was your mate up in Queensland before the war wasn't he?"

"I hope you're not suggesting that?" Brudenell White recoiled crossly, looking down his nose at Pompey. "Don't you understand? Monash, Glasgow and the others in this room got promoted because they were competent in every position they occupied, and, importantly, they didn't burn all of their bridges on the way through, as you did. When Birdwood suppressed your Polygon Wood report, he was not trying to hurt you. That report was going to be even more damaging to your reputation."

"Monash had enemies too. Bean, Murdoch and you I dare say?"

"We were competitors, not enemies. I saw what he accomplished with the Anzac Corps in France. He should have been commanding the whole Fourth Army, not Rawlinson. Monash designed the Battle of Hamel, and then Rawlinson implemented Monash's plan on a larger scale on 8 August. Now Rawlinson generally gets the credit for it, and we have an annual dinner because we have a different recollection. Sound familiar?"

"Monash wrote to the newspapers and he wrote his book to set the record straight."

"Yes, but unlike you he's not obsessed by it, he gets on with his life. And yes, you could say that I was superseded by Monash for the Anzac Corps commander's role, but you won't find me dwelling on it."

"You are right, I suppose," Pompey sighed in reluctant agreement. "I suppose you could say the injustice of my supersession has coloured my whole post war experience."

It had coloured Pompey's whole post war view of the world, but his hatred of General Birdwood, and the British mismanagement of the war at Gallipoli and on the Western Front hadn't made him anti-British — he was quite the opposite. His great grandfather had fought alongside Nelson at Trafalgar. In August 1927 he took on the role of president of the Pendulum Club, which had as its aim to "keep the Pendulum of Reciprocity swinging from Australia to Britain and back". Sir John Monash was vice-president of the club.

* * *

While Pompey Elliott and Brudenell White were having a rapprochement of sorts about events in Europe a decade earlier, on the other side of the table there was another discussion that centred on events closer to home. One participant was the Chief of Police in Victoria, who had been appointed to the role by Dr Stanley Argyle in the wake of the police strike, at a salary of £1500 a year. Thomas Blamey had landed at Gallipoli on the first day as a Major on the staff of General Bridges, who commanded the First Division. He had risen to the rank of brigadier as Sir John's Chief of Staff, and had never been backward in coming forward. Like Bert he was of Cornish stock, and liked to make his opinion known.

Engaging Blamey in discussion was George Jameson Johnston who was the managing director of a furniture store that bore his name and was located in Gertrude Street, Fitzroy, and lived only two blocks away from Bert in East St Kilda. On the first day of the Gallipoli campaign he landed as a colonel commanding the 2nd Field Artillery Brigade, and a geographic feature, Johnston's Jolly at Lone Pine, was named after him.

"He's a great leader and a gracious host, but sometimes I don't understand Sir John," Johnston complained. "You were at the Anzac House dinner this year when Sir John spoke of the disruptive influences that need to be kept in check if this country is to prosper, weren't you?"

"Yes?"

"I thought he said it was the duty of the AIF to regulate matters. Yet when I wrote to him during the police strike and suggested that the wonderfully fine body of men who constituted the Special Constables should be made a permanent force, he baulked at the suggestion. Said it reminded him of the Italian Fascists, or the Ku-Klux-Klan, and told me that no Australian government would countenance it."

"Well, the prime minister said as much in his speech at the same function, didn't he?"

"He did, but I still think there are circumstances in which such a force would be needed to break strikes and protect loyal workers," Johnston insisted. "We know that communist cells are attempting to control the unions. They're behind these strikes, and if matters were to get worse, what then?"

"Are you inferring that the police force is not capable of doing its job?" was Blamey's retort. "I can assure you that we are investigating the communist ring leaders, and will descend on them with appropriate force when and if necessary."

"But what if we had an extreme case of a national emergency, the 'disruptive influences' were at the point of open and armed rebellion, and the police force was not sufficient to cope with it?" Johnston pressed.

"Well, in that case, we would have to wait and see how the AIF would respond, wouldn't we?" Blamey replied, looking him straight in the eye.

"Care for some more punch?"

* * *

Roslyn Road, Belmont, Geelong, Sunday, 22 April 1928

Eight months later Bert's extended family gathered in Roslyn Road Geelong, to pay their respects to Nathaniel's mother Elizabeth Jane Tremewan Jacka, nee Bottrell, who had died the previous Friday morning at the age of ninety-three. She was born in Cornwall in 1836, and her father, Nicholas Tremewan Bottrell, was born in 1796 during the Napoleonic wars. In 1854, she had married Bert's grandfather, Josiah Jacka, at St Buryan, Cornwall, which lay near Penzance, in the very tip of the boot of England. If you fell into the sea there, you were already swimming for Australia! Almost immediately after marrying they sailed to Australia, with their first child, Sophia Jacka, being born in Adelaide in 1855.

After the funeral service there was a great gathering of the family in Roslyn Road, Belmont, where Elizabeth had lived. Nathaniel was one of Elizabeth's eleven children, most of whom had survived to adulthood and been married. Not all of the surviving children were able to come to the funeral in time, but there was no lack of numbers, as the family had grown large. They didn't realise it at the time, but this was to be one of the last great gatherings of the Jacka family before it became too big, and cousins went their own ways. If each branch of the Jacka and Bottrell families was a balloon, the old lady who passed away that year was the frail hand that held those balloons together, and her passing would soon disperse them to the winds.

Bert was, as always, the star attraction at these gatherings. He was popular not just because of his outstanding war record, but also for the perceptions of the interesting life that he led. They would often read about him in the paper. He had not brought Vera with him. She had her hands full with her sick mother and little Betty, who had just turned a year old.

One of Nathaniel's younger brothers, Charles Hamilton Jacka had a daughter, Irene, who was only eighteen at the time, and she brought with her an autograph book that she used to collect memories from family, friends and the occasional person of note. When she saw her cousin Albert she had all three of the above, even though in truth she hadn't seen him for years.

"Hello Irene," he said. "You've certainly grown up since I last saw you."

"My dear cousin Albert!" she said excitedly. "You're my favourite cousin you know..."

"Shhh," he whispered.

"I don't care if they all hear me. You're the bravest man in the world, and you are my cousin... and I'd love to have your autograph for my book," she said as she opened up the book at a blank page.

"So you think I'm not afraid of anything?" Bert said, smiling at her blind adolescent faith in him. He took hold of the book, pulled a pen from his pocket and scribbled something down.

"There."

"Thank you very much," she said. Then she looked at what he wrote.

"Only fools are never afraid"
Your cousin, Albert

* * *

Not everyone subscribed to the Anzac legend, and some interpreted it in different ways. Membership of the RSSILA had been massive at first, but by the mid 1920s it had slumped to less than a third of the original number. Many old diggers who couldn't sleep at night because of nightmares or the recurring pain of trench feet, wanted nothing to do with it. Nor could the young communist idealists subscribe to what Monash had called the "great Anzac tradition" that the young nation should live up to. During the 1928 Anzac Day March, eighteen-year-old Judah Waten, a writer with a vision, and nineteen-year-old Ernest Smith were arrested in Swanston Street for distributing pamphlets deemed offensive to the Anzac Day spirit. These young communist activists associated Anzac Day with a spirit of bourgeois militarism.

By May 1928 it was announced that the Fund for the Shrine of Remembrance had reached £136,543. As usual, Bert was right in the thick of the fundraising. When a special session of community singing was held at the Theatre Royal during lunch hour on 17 May, scores of people could not be admitted because it was announced that Captain Albert Jacka would speak. A collection was taken up to assist funding of the Shrine campaign, and after several songs had been sung, Bert gave a short address on "The Landing at Gallipoli". He recalled the details of the first Anzac Day, which the AIF commemorated in Egypt, and then concluded with a deeply held conviction:

"Everyone would agree that on that day Australia was lifted from an obscure Dominion to being one of the front-rank nations of the world. Thousands of young Australians were killed then and at later times, and they set for us traditions that must be lived up to. It is for us now to do something to keep evergreen the memory of the fine men who died."

A month later he appeared at Mason's Theatre in Chelsea, where the war memorial committee organised a very successful "pleasant Sunday afternoon" gathering. There he addressed the large audience on the meaning of the Shrine of Remembrance, and explained the principal battles fought by Australian troops during the war. Later in June, he and the organising secretary of the Freemason's appeal for the Shrine, Mr G.N.S. Campbell, travelled to Heathcote to attend a concert at which further funds were raised. It pleased Bert to see that at the end of August, his brother Sam had donated 10 shillings to the Shrine appeal. It was difficult to part with money when you had seven children to feed, but Sam did.

Vera's mother Catherine died at 23 Murchison Street on 2 September 1928, aged 67. She had suffered badly from uraemia during the two years she had lived with Bert and Vera, but it was a heart attack that finally claimed her. It was sad, but she had suffered in those last few months. Molly and Pat Gleeson were now living in Sydney at 33 Payten Street, Ryde, and couldn't come for the very simple, private funeral that was held at Fawkner Cemetery the next day. With both her parents gone, with Molly living in Sydney, her brother living in the country, and Bert out in the community so much, Vera drew closer to Betty.

On the same day that Vera's mother died, Lieutenant-Colonel John Peck, then the officer in charge of military training in

Brisbane, died from acute nephritis – a kidney disorder. In 1923 he had organised Australia's aid for victims of the Tokyo earthquake disaster, and in 1927 was Chairman of the Appropriation Board of the mandated territory of New Guinea. Bert was saddened to hear that his cheerful ex-CO, a man who had been so full of life, and had inspired the men of the 14th with his wit and humour, had been cut down so prematurely, leaving a wife and children. Of all the COs Bert had served under, he was the one who understood Bert best.

* * *

23 Murchison Street, East St Kilda, Saturday, 5 January 1929

A short sharp burst of crying woke Bert early that morning, as it had on many previous mornings. It was going to be a clear warm summer's day.

"Mummy? I believe that's for you," he said to Vera. She sprang up from the bed, wrapped her morning coat around her and quickly made her way around the corridor to her daughter's bedroom. While Vera's mother was alive, Betty's cot used to be kept in the lounge room. As she walked into the room she saw Betty giving her a big broad smile from her cot. It was always a bit cooler in Betty's room in the mornings as it didn't get the sun until late afternoon.

"Oh, you're awake now," she said with a smile.

"Mummy!"

"Now let's get you dressed and ready."

She loved dressing Betty, who was now a cute little toddler, and afterwards brought her into the kitchen, where she gave her breakfast. The jolly, rotund King Willie smiled at Betty from the side of the Weeties packet as she ate her porridge. Bert was already drinking a cup of tea while listening to the radio in the lounge room. Radio had first burst onto the scene in Melbourne in 1923, and the city now had two radio stations, 3AR and 3LO, and the ability to listen to Sydney's 2FC and 2BL, Adelaide's 5CL, and Brisbane's 4QG. Jacka, Edmonds & Co Pty Ltd was capitalising on the radio craze by selling The World brand of compact five valve wireless sets direct to the public. Bert was glued to reports of the Third Test that was being played at the Melbourne Cricket Ground later that day.

"Would you like to have your breakfast now, dear?" Vera asked.

"In a minute," he answered, but it was a good ten minutes before he made his way into the kitchen.

"I thought we could all go for a long walk after breakfast," Vera announced cheerfully. She was still grieving for her mother, whose memory during a quiet moment would often bring a tear to her eye, but she owed it to Betty to look forward in life. Her mother's passing emphasised to her that beautiful days like this one should not be passed up.

"I was hoping to listen to the Test from midday," Bert said.

"Today is going to be so beautiful, and the Test will still be on when we get back, won't it? I'm making us some sandwiches for a picnic lunch..."

"A picnic?" he asked blankly as he felt an instantaneous flashback to his cross-examination by Sir Thomas McKenzie at the Dardanelles Commission Hearings in London. *You did not expect it to be a picnic, did you?*

"Yes, a picnic," Vera laughed. "I thought we'd take out the pram and walk to the beach. We can have our lunch afterwards in the Botanical Gardens."

"England needs to get 332 runs today to win, and they might just do it."

"And there's nothing you can do about it," she said with a smile. Vera never took any interest in sports.

"But England will retain the Ashes if they win today."

Bert knew that this was the most important day in the whole Ashes series, and he was bursting to listen to this exciting match, which had seesawed day after day. It had also seen the re-introduction into the Australian team of a new brilliant young player, Donald Bradman, playing at number six, who was hitting the ball with astounding maturity. In the first innings he smacked a useful 79 runs, and in the second innings, had top scored with 112. Then England's J.C. White got the tail-enders, Grimmett and Blackie, out cheaply. England's main bowling weapon, Harold Larwood, was being rested.

"It's going to be over 80 degrees today you know," Bert continued.

"It will be cooler nearer the sea. Come on."

Bert really wanted to hear the Test, but he could see that Vera had her heart set on this outing. It was true that ever since Betty arrived they had stopped doing many of the things they had previously done together. Vera packed their picnic basket after breakfast and they set off behind the high wicker pram on what would be a six-mile round trip. When they came to the foreshore there was a slight breeze blowing in from the sea, which provided relief. The water was quite calm, but the breeze was pushing the white yachts around in the bay like swans gliding across a pond.

They were too late to see the tiny "bottle-o's" who mopped up the beach after these hot summer nights to collect money on discarded bottles. Due to competition from their peers those children were out on the beach at first light pushing billy carts made of old crates and discarded pram wheels, collecting bottles that had been thrown away by party-goers the night before. They sat down to rest on one of the park benches that faced the sea, and Bert smoked a cigarette there, which made him cough. "It's impossible to believe," thought Bert as he looked at the huge crowds of people, "that there is an economic depression going on." His own business had never seen a slower month.

The gardens of the St Kilda foreshore, designed by an Italian engineer, Carlo Catani, were now well developed, with trees and palms that were getting taller. During the war he lost one of his sons, Lieutenant Enrico Catani, who died in the ranks of the AIF at Pozieres. Carlo was a native of Florence, and wanted the St Kilda foreshore to reflect the ambience of the famous Italian beachside resorts.

They entered the St Kilda Botanical Gardens and found a spot on the lawns near the duck pond. He didn't tell Vera about the pain he was experiencing in his feet. His feet had swollen so much he thought he would have trouble taking his shoes off later.

"There were a few hot heads among that crowd on the beach," Bert commented as Vera placed the blanket on the lawn. Bert then lifted Betty out of the pram.

"How's my little girl?" he asked, setting her down on the blanket, and she smiled back at him. Betty was delighted to see the ducks and swans swimming around in the pond and waddling about on the grass. Some time later she threw something in their direction.

"Uh-oh, don't feed them!" he called out to her, but it was too late, as a whole webbed squadron had already set sail across the pond.

* * *

Bert did have time for his family, but he could never say "no" to any approach for him to appear at a function that would raise money for the Shrine, or otherwise preserve the memory of those who had made the supreme sacrifice. One Sunday in March 1929, Bert spoke at the "Pilgrimage to the Soldier's Memorial" at Trafalgar.

Later that year Councillor T. G. Allen of the Central Ward of the St Kilda Council died, which left a vacancy that Councillor Burnett Gray, Councillor Thomas Unsworth and others felt Bert could fill. On 27 August Bert announced his campaign for election to the St Kilda City Council in the extraordinary election that was to be held on 13 September. Bert told the reporter from *The Herald* that it was only the night before that he decided to nominate for the election, and that his friends had been pressing him to do so for some time. At first he said, he had not been particularly keen about seeking municipal prominence, as he was in business in Briscoe Lane, and emphasised that he had no quarrel with the present Council.

* * *

It had been a while since Bert paid a visit to John Wren. Now Bert felt the need to go on the front foot in a tight situation. Wren was well aware of the economic downturn and the effect it was having on the unemployed. When his horse "Muratti" won at Flemington in the winter of 1928, he had donated the £356 stake he collected to the Mayor of Collingwood for the use of the unemployed relief committee.

"Captain Jacka," Wren said with a smile, "please, come in and sit down." Wren's office hadn't changed at all since Bert had last visited him some years ago – still the same austerity, economy in furnishings, and sporting pictures on the walls.

"Thank you," said Bert, pulling his chair a bit closer to the desk.

There was a moment of awkward silence, and just as Bert was about to open his mouth to speak, Wren put out his hand in a "stop" fashion and pre-empted him.

"Arthur and Dick, have kept me fully informed about the progress of our enterprise. I understand that it is now clear that the move to Briscoe Lane has been less than rewarding?"

"We've put everything we could into it, but we can't survive much longer unless we move to an alternative location."

"What's wrong with where you are?"

"We're located in a laneway with insufficient traffic to attract passers by."

"Does that matter?" Wren asked, raising an eyebrow. "I thought that most of your business is selling to the trade."

"It wouldn't matter if times were different. Take the Silent Vortex vacuum cleaner, which we are the Victorian agent for. We supply Chandler's, Myer's, John Danks', O.J. Nilsen's, and others. The economic downturn has put people out of their jobs, and demand for household appliances has withered. Retailers don't want to hold stocks until they need them, and we can't move them from the warehouse. They are shifting the cost of holding inventory back to us.

"That's why we have to open at the retail level. It would provide a higher margin, and reduce our costs, especially if we could move the stock faster. We have to continue in the wholesale market, where we are the agents, but we've got to be in the retail market as well. If we need to discount from the retail price, we would still be making more than we do by selling to the trade."

"I see," Wren nodded slowly. He brought his hands together again, as if in prayer, and exhaled. "But I've already advanced £6000 above my initial investment, and the accounts give no indication that I'll ever get it back," he said squinting. "Well?" said Wren after a period of silence.

"We've cut all of our expenses to the bone."

"Have you heard the talk about the tariff on imported goods to protect Australian jobs?" Wren asked. He knew all about it, as he had been vigorously lobbying for a tariff on imported spirits, which would help his own liquor company's fortunes.

"It would be a disaster for my business, but it's a chance I'm willing to take."

"With my *nicker*?" Wren emphasised.

"I've been to the National Bank, and they have indicated their willingness to advance a considerable sum, if it can be secured with some further guarantees from you." The chief manager of the bank, Sir Ernest Wreford had just decreed that no new lending should be undertaken. He considered Australia was "financially sick, and will not get well by drinking the Champagne of further borrowing". His response to the evolving economic crisis was to batten down the hatches. Sir John Grice agreed; he had been on the board in 1893, when a run on the bank's head office in Perth was ignited by a rumour that there had been a run in Melbourne. He was now chairman of the board almost forty years later.

"Of course they would," Wren grunted. "Grice knows I'm good for it." He thought about it for a couple of seconds, then looked at Bert. "And if I was to agree to your plan. What *is* your plan, exactly?"

"I have identified new, larger premises at 101 to 103 Elizabeth Street – between Collins and Bourke streets. The front of the store is glassed and opens directly onto the entry to the Block Arcade. All shoppers coming out of the Block are forced to look across the street, and if we mount a significant advertising campaign, and prominently display discounted bargains in the window, it should attract many more sales than we have at present."

"What's there now?"

"Carters men's clothing and accessories. They have another store in Bourke Street, and they're closing this one down."

"Well, that's an omen," Wren said sarcastically.

"They had a fire last year. If we don't act now, we'll be closing down too," Bert said with his determined look. Wren stared at him. He admired Bert's enthusiasm and pluck. Bert continued: "I will be putting my own money in too."

"You don't have any!" rasped Wren.

"I've sold my car, and I'm moving my family into a flat. We'll rent our house out and live on the difference. That way I can cut my salary from the business in half, and provide more cash to service the interest."

Wren nodded agreement. Despite his scepticism Wren found it difficult to resist Bert's logic, and the personal sacrifices he was willing to make in order to survive. He had a soft spot for Bert, and agreed to this last ditch plan, but warned that he wasn't a bottomless pit. If he couldn't make it work in Elizabeth Street there would be no more loans, no more moves, and no further bank guarantees. Bert went away with renewed confidence. At least he could give it a good fight now.

Bert had always been good at winning too, which the council election results bore out. Bert got a primary vote of 1578 and 1859 after distribution. Harry Raymond Johnson came second with a primary vote of 1189 and 1560 after distribution. Frederick Newman Levin came last with 652 primary votes.

* * *

8.45 pm, Anzac House, Collins Street, 25 September 1929

On the eve of the twelfth anniversary of the Battle of Polygon Wood, over 300 men of the 14th Battalion and 4th Brigade Association gathered for their annual general meeting. As president of the Association, Brigadier-General Brand, who was currently Quartermaster General of the Australian Army, delivered his annual address. Brand opened by stating that when the Australian War Memorial committee asked him which battle he would select to immortalise the deeds of this famous brigade he had replied firmly.

"Bullecourt, 11 April 1917, I told them. No greater valour and self-sacrifice were shown than in this operation. Without artillery support, without tanks, and acting on misleading information supplied by outside sources the 13th, 14th, 15th and 16th battalions, together with the 40th and 47th battalions of the 12th Brigade broke through the Hindenburg Line. Overwhelmed on three sides by the enemy, and in the midst of a snowstorm, the remnants of these gallant battalions fought their way back to the original jumping off line under terrific German artillery fire. The 4th Brigade's losses were seventy-five officers and 2661 other ranks.

"I can tell you that Captain Jacka and I periodically inspect the Bullecourt model now in preparation by Mr Les Bowles of the War Museum in Nicholson Street. This model is about fifty feet square, which gives some idea of the stupendous task set by higher authority. It was a task that, if successful would have had an important bearing on the 3rd Army's great battle of Arras, a few miles farther north.

"I am also delighted to announce that the first instalment of the *History of the 14th Battalion* by Mr Newton Wanliss has been quickly disposed of. However, I understand that copies can still be obtained from Captain Jacka, at 397 Little Collins Street," he said looking in Bert's direction. "I also believe that Captain Jacka has a motion that he wishes to put to you."

At the conclusion of the applause Bert rose to his feet to put a matter of some importance to his old comrades in the 14th Battalion: "Some of you in this room were on the St Kilda foreshore in December 1914, when the first Padre of the 14th Battalion, the Reverend Andrew Gillison consecrated the Regimental and King's Colours, and we watched as Lieutenant Hamilton received the King's Colour from the Governor-General. When the battalion sailed for Egypt the Colours were left behind for safekeeping in Padre Gillison's parish at St George's Church, in East St Kilda. Neither the Padre nor Lieutenant Hamilton returned from Gallipoli.

"It has recently occurred to me that for future generations to remember the 1000 Australians who gave their lives in the ranks of the 14th Battalion during the Great War, we should place the Regimental and King's Colours in a public place of honour, so that current and future generations may be reminded of their sacrifice. The foyer of the St Kilda Town Hall would admirably achieve that purpose.

"I therefore move the following motion, 'That the Regimental and King's Colours of the 14th Battalion AIF, at present in St George's Church, Chapel Street, East St Kilda, be presented to the municipality of St Kilda to be placed in the foyer of the Town Hall, St Kilda.'"

The motion was carried unanimously.

* * *

A conference was being called by the City of Preston for 14 November to discuss strategies for the unemployed, and the issue was debated at length in the St Kilda Town Hall's council chamber in mid-October. Councillors Dawkins and Renfrey argued that battling the effects of unemployment is a governmental function, and not the preserve of local councils, but Burnett Gray disputed that view.

"There should be coordination between the various municipalities and between the municipalities and the government," Gray said. "I move that two representatives be appointed."

"I agree with Councillor Gray," Bert said. "The extent of unemployment in Melbourne is an absolute tragedy. Every day in the city we find diggers who are down and out. There are also thousands of others who are not returned soldiers in the same plight." Gray's motion was agreed to and both he and Bert were appointed to represent the council at the conference.

* * *

A few days later, Bert and Ernie approached the corner of Collins and Elizabeth streets as the paperboys sang their usual song.

We are the Herald boys, the boys of Flinders Street,
We're always up to mischief, no matter where we meet.

They stood among fresh stacks of newspapers, held together by wire, which had just been delivered by a lorry and dumped on the pavement. The smell of newsprint that was barely dry hung about them that afternoon, and the boys were doing a brisk trade.

"Prime minister forms new ministry!" they cried. "Get your *Herald* here! Prime minister forms new ministry!"

It was Tuesday, 22 October 1929, and a few days had passed since the Bruce Government was swept away from power by Labor in a Federal election. The prime minister who had just formed a new ministry was the Right Honourable James Henry Scullin, the former grocer from Ballarat. He was the first Catholic in the job, and the first Labor prime minister who was native born.

"Give me *The Herald*, son," said Bert handing over a coin.

"There you go, sir," said the boy, doing his mental arithmetic very quickly and getting the right change back to him in half a second. Before Bert could open it, Ernie had grabbed the paper away and was scanning all the headlines.

"This morning I heard a radio report about the collapsing stockmarket in New York," said Bert pocketing his change. "What does Mr Murdoch say about it?"

"There's nothing on the front page."

Bert grabbed the paper back from Ernie and thumbed through it. "Here it is," he announced. The headings read "£500 million market value lost" and "Frenzied wave of liquidation".

"Looks serious," Ernie said.

"It's been serious for quite some time. You saw last month's sales – the worst month we ever had. The last thing you want to buy when you're unemployed is a vacuum cleaner," Bert said in exasperation. "You know what people are buying now?"

"What?"

"Books!" he said.

"Cheaper than a picture show and they last longer," Ernie smiled back. "I think we're done for."

"Not yet, mate. Not yet," Bert replied with that determined look. "We move into Elizabeth Street next week."

"Just in time for some Christmas sales."

Bert still had some of that old optimism that got him through the war, but they were in the midst of an economic slide. The Crash of '29 should have been called the "smash", because the whole country had been in free-fall for two years, and Bruce couldn't do a thing about it. Over to Labor – except that as Frank Anstey, Scullin's newly appointed far left Minister for Health saw it, Labor was "sitting on the eggs of a serpent".

* * *

On the eve of the 1929 Melbourne Cup, the St Kilda Council was locked in a protracted debate over a proposal to erect enclosed baths for men and women on the foreshore, at an estimated cost of £45,000. The debate followed the receipt of a letter from Mr Angus, Minister of Lands, which said the Ministry was not prepared to make a substantial grant, or to provide a loan at a low rate of interest for the construction of a new baths. It would make £4,500 available provided the council constructed them rather than an outside body.

"I am pleased that the letter from the Minister of Lands has come before the Council, if only to clear the atmosphere," declared Councillor Thomas Unsworth. "I am a believer in private enterprise, but there are public utilities which should not be controlled by private enterprise. The control of baths should be vested absolutely in the council."

"Here! Here!" was heard in the gallery.

"I move that we accept the terms relating to the borrowing of the money," Unsworth continued, "and that the council proceed with the construction of the baths."

"I second the motion," said Councillor O'Donnell.

However, Councillor Moroney moved that all the correspondence should be read, including that received by private bodies, before voting on Councillor Unsworth's motion. After the reading of the full correspondence, Councillor Jacka rose to speak.

"I move an amendment that the matter be referred back to the Minister for Lands, with a request for the sole lease on the beach, with power to sublet for building by private enterprise," Bert said. "The council is suggesting building baths at a cost of £45,000 pounds, and will probably not be able to cope with the number of bathers desirous of using them. On the other hand, we have the proposals of Bobringer, Taylor, and Johnson for baths costing £100,000, and Councillor Frank Beaurepaire's proposal for a modern pool to cost from £15,000 to £20,000. If these people could give the necessary financial guarantees nothing could be better! But I will not be a party to handing over the control of bathing facilities to private enterprise unless the council is the controlling lessor. The proposed site of Councillor Frank Beaurepaire's pool adjacent to the old men's baths is only a rubble heap, and the pool would be a great asset to St Kilda."

Councillor Moroney seconded Bert's amendment motion and it was put to the vote, but was lost by a margin of six to five. Bert's push for a partnership between the private and public sectors was defeated.

* * *

The following Friday night there was a display of war medals, including Bert's VC, at the Fete held at the St Kilda Soldiers' and Sailors' Memorial Hall. Bert was on the organising committee and when Councillor Burnett Gray MLA opened the fete he referred to the necessity to reduce the £32,000 debt on the Memorial Hall, which had been erected by the citizens of St Kilda in memory of the soldiers who fell in the war. The president of the Memorial Hall Trust was Councillor Thomas Unsworth. While Bert had disagreed with his ex-AIF colleague on the baths question, in the broader scheme of things they were on the same page.

* * *

Being so fresh in people's minds, Armistice Day was an extremely solemn affair in the 1920s. The city actually came to a standstill at the eleventh minute of the eleventh hour, and thousands of people and troops assembled in front of Parliament House to hear the *Last Post* played. That evening the Governor General, Lord Stonehaven, in the company of the Governor of Victoria Lord Somers, again welcomed Bert to Federal Government House for a dinner with other Victoria Cross winners. At the same time Lady Stonehaven was attending the 11 November Ball on board the HMAS *Australia* together with 400 guests of Rear-Admiral Evans and Captain W.S.

Chalmers. The guests, including Mr and Mrs Norman Brookes, and Lieutenant-General Sir Harry and Lady Chauvel, had boarded the vessel along gangplanks decorated with Japanese lanterns.

Among the eleven VCs present at Government House, Bert and Major-General Sir Neville Smyth were the only two who came dressed in white tie, and they sat together for the official photograph. Sir Neville, his wife and young family had settled as New Australians, among the hundreds of thousands of immigrants from Britain who had been attracted to Australia by Prime Minister Bruce's drive for "men, money and markets". After suppressing the slave trade in the Sudan just prior to the Great War, Smyth was ordered to proceed to Gallipoli, where he commanded the 1st Australian Infantry Brigade at the Battle of Lone Pine between 6 and 9 August 1915. On the Western Front he commanded the 2nd Australian Division, and considered the Australians were the finest troops with whom he had ever served. So much so, that he now wanted to live among them.

"Captain Jacka, I'm pleased to see that you know how to dress for functions at Government House!" Sir Neville said in a spirit of jocularity.

"Sir Neville, I'm never concerned about being over-dressed," Bert winked. "The alternative is far, far worse."

"Oh, I couldn't agree more," Sir Neville chuckled. He was the first who earned his right to sit among the other VCs at Lord Stonehaven's table that night. As a young lieutenant he was orderly and intelligence officer to Major-General Sir Archibald Hunter who was commanding the Egyptian division at the Battle of Omdurman in September 1898. One of the Mahdi's dervish warriors had broken through and was about to spear two war correspondents when Smyth dashed forward on horseback, and despite being severely wounded in the clash, shot him dead. That's how he won the VC, but he continued to live up to it when he later captured the Khalifa Muhammad al-Sharif and two of the Mahdi's sons. During the South African war he was at one point cut off with a small group of men. Rejecting the option of surrender, he escaped on a horse belonging to the Boer commander.

Lord Somers joined them, and now two tall men stood over him.

"You two know each other I take it?" said Sir Neville.

"Oh yes," said Lord Somers. "Good evening Captain. Are you keeping well?"

"Yes, thank you, Your Excellency," Bert said – it was far from the truth. Despite his aristocratic background, Lord Somers had a good deal in common with Bert as well, and was testimony to his respect for the British aristocracy, which had sent so many of its favoured sons to the killing fields of France along with the grocers' sons. The Duke of York served in the British Navy, and was in a turret gun crew during the Battle of Jutland. Lord Somers was twice wounded at Ypres, and in 1918 commanded the 6th Battalion of the New Tank Corps. He was awarded both a Military Cross and DSO. Lord Somers and Lord Stonehaven were respectively the Grand Master of the United Grand Lodge of Freemasons of Victoria and New South Wales.

Writing to his nephew in England earlier that year, Lord Somers thought it difficult to describe Australians. "There are all sorts," he wrote. "One common trait is hospitality, willingly even anxiously extended, and a real desire to be welcoming. There are many well read and erudite but few with culture. We are so far from any older civilisation, that our only standard, except what we form ourselves, must come from memory or illustration. Neither can be relied on." What he privately thought of Prime Minister Bruce could not be repeated in polite company, so he kept it to himself. What Lord Somers hated most about Australia though was the summers, when the wind is "like a blast from the furnace", and Lady Somers would have to resort to sitting under a sprinkler in the garden at Stonington, clad in her bathing dress.

Another friend who caught up with Bert at the function was Donovan Joynt, VC. Joynt noticed a significant deterioration in

Bert's physical appearance, but said nothing. His face had bloated up and he was greying at the temples. The pressures of home, work, public appearances and community activities were beginning to weigh down heavily upon him. He still could not sleep well for the dreams that took him back to Gallipoli and beyond. Joynt, by contrast, was still dark haired and looking much more virile.

At dinner that evening a message from the Prince of Wales was read:

I am glad to hear that Your Excellencies and State Governors are entertaining Australian holders of the Victoria Cross on Armistice night. Please convey to them my best wishes, and say that their fellow V.C.s dining in London on Saturday night will be thinking of them.

Edward P.

The return message read:

Eleven VCs united here tonight are very pleased to receive the gracious message from Your Royal Highness. They respectfully send you their loyal and hearty thanks and their good wishes.

Stonehaven Somers

* * *

9.12 pm, Australian Senate chamber, Canberra, Thursday, 21 November 1929

"My party has always honoured the principle of preference to returned soldiers," Senator Elliott declared in answer to the Labor Party's Senator Rae, who stated that the former Nationalist Government had honoured the principle more in breach than the observance.

It was a debate about the new Governor-General, Sir Isaac Isaac's speech. Prime Minister Scullin had been hard pressed to get an Australian-born man into the position, and had to confront the King in person about it. The King's own choice had been none other than Field-Marshall William Riddell Birdwood, or Baron Birdwood of Anzac and Totnes, or "Rainbow Bill" as some diggers liked to call him. And if the King had somehow persuaded Prime Minister Scullin otherwise, the debate that ensued would have been much hotter.

"What about the returned soldiers on the Port Adelaide wharves, who were dismissed and replaced by 147 Europeans!" interjected Labor's Senator O'Halloran.

"Even returned soldiers have to obey the law of the land," Senator Elliott said in a regretful tone. "If they refused to work on the wharves naturally others had to take their place. However, I leave Senator O'Halloran to settle that matter with the State authorities.

"With Senator Sir William Glasgow, I regret exceedingly the abolition of compulsory military training. Senator Hoare has interjected that during the recent war, with a little training, Australia produced the finest soldiers in the world. Nothing could be further from the truth! At Broadmeadows they had merely the veneer of the soldier. That was about the end of August. Steady training was continued until the middle of October, with drill every day and even at night. The men were drilled all the way to Egypt and when they arrived there on the 6th of December they were drilled morning, noon and night in the desert until the following April when we set off for Gallipoli and delivered the attack that made the name of Australia famous.

"Even then these men were not trained soldiers. Had they at that time acquired the absolute mastery of the art of war which they had gained by 1918 when I led them at Villiers-Brettonneux, their casualties would have been nothing compared with what they were at the landing. They attempted to do things which in France they would have recognised as impossible or as requiring other means of achievement. They were the First Division, a body of absolutely picked men, the cream of Australia, whose appearance and intelligence were favourably commented upon by everyone who came into contact with them, but at the end of nine months they were still raw.

"It is said by Senator Daly that war is becoming more scientific. Of course it is, but that does not mean that soldiers can do without training. As a matter of fact it means that they require more training. The greatest advocate of a mechanised army, Major Liddell Hart, is of the opinion that by reason of the scientific training required, all armies should now consist of regular soldiers."

"What's wrong with training soldiers for peace?" asked Senator Barnes.

"Unfortunately," Senator Elliott sighed, shrugging his shoulders, "people like the Kaiser insist on having war, and in those circumstances what can a man do? I had no wish for war, but when Mr Andrew Fisher sent along and said, 'Colonel, your men are wanted. Will you put up a notice and ask for volunteers?' I did the one thing it seemed possible for me to do in those days. I put my name at the top and said, 'Boys, who is coming with me?' I find that most of the people who are so enthusiastic in asking for a volunteer system are those who want the other fellow to volunteer."

* * *

11 am, Dardanelles Commission Hearing, London, 28 August 1917

Bert was dreaming again about the hearing back in 1917. Many times he was drawn back to the past, usually triggered by an event or a comment that would have him thinking and almost reliving previous events.

Sir William Pickford is not letting any ball slip through to the keeper as he interrogates me. He is determined to find some scapegoats to pay for what happened at the Dardanelles, and his voice is echoing through the hall.

"About how many wounded did you get on board *your* ship, the *Seeang Choon?*" he asks.

"I cannot give you the exact number," I answer, "but as far as I can remember I should say three or four hundred."

"When they got on board, was there a sufficient provision of doctors and attendants to look after them?"

"There were plenty of attendants," I reply. "There were several R.A.M.C. men and stretcher bearers who came across in barges, and we had medical men on board our ship, but there were only two doctors."

Then Sir William's right eyebrow rises up at me. "That's not many for three hundred men, was it?" he says in a mildly sarcastic tone.

"No, but there were not so many wounded cases as the men had been bandaged up on the beach."

"Where were they taken to?"

"After we left do you mean?"

"Yes. You disembarked after that?"

"Yes."

"And then the transport went away with the wounded?"

"Yes. As far as we knew she was going back to Egypt. We heard that the arrangements for the men afterwards were not too good, but I knew nothing about that. At the time no-one was absolutely neglected, as far as getting them on the transports was concerned, though we heard afterwards in Egypt the arrangements were not what they ought to have been. Still, I think under the conditions... and particularly *that* night, with the sea very rough, and seeing that it was rather a difficult job, it was a *fine* effort. I think everyone thought there was no-one neglected, and no-one died from want of care or anything like that. We, as soldiers, have heard all sorts of remarks, and we have followed what has happened at the Dardanelles Commission as far as we could, but I think everyone would share my opinion."

I have said that with utmost sincerity, but I don't think Sir Thomas McKenzie is convinced.

"You say *no-one* died from lack of care?" he asks in incredulity.

"Not as far as I know."

"But I suppose you *would* take the evidence of a man like Colonel Begg, who was there at the time?"

"Well... he would know something about it."

"He makes this statement," says Sir Thomas. He fits his reading glasses to his nose and reads the statement out: "'The barges available were so much required for the carriage of stores, ammunition, etc., that patients had often to be detained for long periods on the beach. The beach was quite exposed, and no arrangements were possible at first for operation on urgent cases ashore. The delay was so great that very few of the abdominal cases survived after operation on the ships... This cost many lives?'"

"As I told you, I did not take a hand in the actual matter till 6.30 pm, so I did not see that."

Sir Thomas sits up and leans forward in his chair. He plucks the reading glasses from his nose, to add some theatre to the point he is about to make. His eyebrows fall and he squints down his nose at me: "But you are giving evidence that everything in the garden was lovely and that the arrangements were good and satisfactory, while *we* have evidence here of quite another kind?"

"I am sure you can get tons of evidence the same as my own," I reply, but that doesn't stop him. He knows he can't let this go, and he comes back at me.

"Your evidence is the first I have heard of the nature you suggest," he says disparagingly. He puts his glasses back on and continues to read from the page, "Then he says, again: 'As the picket boats would never wait, it was necessary to load the wounded on to the barge and allow them to remain there under heavy fire till the picket boat arrived. A system of signalling was adopted later, after many protests, but was never satisfactory... The sufferings of the wounded on the transports on the way to Alexandria was very severe.'"

"Is that dealing with Anzac?" I ask.

"Yes, with the first landing. Then we had Surgeon-General Howse..." Sir Thomas adds with a further dose of sarcasm. "Would you consider *his* evidence on the point was a little valuable?"

"Yes."

"He was asked by Mr Fisher, the High Commissioner for Australia: 'Did you consider the arrangements made were adequate?' And he says: 'I did not. I considered, to put it broadly, that the arrangements as far as the Australian troops were concerned, were so inadequate that they amounted to criminal negligence!' You are an Australian, are you not?"

"Yes," I reply, as if that isn't half obvious. "I do not know, of course, what the arrangements were. I am simply telling you what I know was done afterwards."

"At what *date*?" he asks me sharply.

"On the night of the 25th," I say. "I can quite understand that they did not have half enough staff in the first place, but, of course, they never bargained for anything like what they got."

"*Why* did they not?"

"That is something I do not know, of course, and nobody else knows. We never thought we were going to stay on the beach for seven months for instance."

"You knew that you had to fight the Turks?"

"Yes."

"And you did not expect it to be a *picnic*, did you?"

"But you must remember that they only had past wars to go upon," I reply, "and in every war up to that time I think the ordinary arrangements had carried them through."

"I am afraid that is not so," Sir Thomas interjects. Again he peers down into the statement he is reading from. "Then he says: 'There was great difficulty during that day' — that is the 25th, *and* on the 26th, 'in finding ships to put them on, and when they were put on the ships there was no available medical attendant to treat them.'"

"There were two doctors on our boat," I hasten to add.

"You did not see any men lying on the beach in the heat of the day and cold of the night for thirty-six hours without attention?"

"No, I did not," I reply firmly, "and I think I might contradict that because I am absolutely certain no man lay there for thirty-six hours, unless of course, it might have been considered he was beyond help and could not possibly recover. I have seen that even now when the doctors have thought they have had no chance of living."

But Sir Thomas continues as if I am saying nothing: "Then I think statements were made by General Howse that many men were lying on the beach for a long time and some back in the gullies as well. Did you see anything of General Birrell at all?" He is losing sight of the fact that I was a private at the time.

"No," I answer. "On the morning of the landing it is true it was a rather gruesome sight to see the men lying dead on the beach with their packs and so on, but the next morning they were not to be seen at all, and everyone remarked upon it. There was a terrible lot of suffering for the first few hours naturally, because there were so many casualties until they started to get them on board the transports it seemed to be bad."

* * *

"Why does your cough seem to be so bad?" Vera asked. Bert had been tossing and turning and coughing all night again, and was all sweaty. He was dreaming again.

"My cough?"

"Yes, your cough," Vera said. "You really should see a doctor."

"Well, it's the bronchitis isn't it?" Bert answered, coughing. "I've had it ever since the war."

"I'm telling you it's too persistent to be bronchitis."

It was their first morning waking up in their small flat at Narooma in Elwood. She stared at the ceiling denying the fact that they had been displaced from the house she loved in Murchison Street. It had just been rented to a commercial traveller, Mr Jad Louis Blashki.

"I don't like it here," she said. "It feels strange to be away from our home."

"How do you think I feel?" he shot back. "I've got John Wren breathing down my neck. I've got the bank, and the creditors nipping at my heels, and the people on the payroll to look after, and a bad bout of bronchitis to top it off!"

"Sshh...You'll wake Betty," she said quietly. "Why did you take on the St Kilda Council then? You're torturing yourself."

"Because, there's a lot that needs doing, and someone has to do it."

"But why you?"

"That does it, I'm getting up," he announced, as he threw the blanket off and went into the bathroom, still coughing. He looked at himself in the mirror and wondered where the young man had gone. It seemed like only yesterday that the sun shone in a blue sky, his whole life lay ahead of him, and he felt he could do anything. Now his hair was greying and his face was bloated and sagging.

They were in the middle of what was the first great apartment block development in Melbourne. Since 1917 Elwood had been developed with two- and three-storey apartment blocks built in Tudor, functionalist and Art Deco styles. It was still quite convenient. An electric tramline to the St Kilda station ran down Broadway via the Elwood Junction, only the 1906 vintage Rickety Kates (as the trams were called) woke them in the mornings. On the other hand, Elwood had all that was needed in the way of shopping facilities and entertainments, including the *Broadway Picture Theatre* and the *Maison de Luxe* dance hall.

They only occasionally saw Bill and Joan, who were living on the other side of Melbourne in Footscray. Work at the railways was being rationed, and Bill was only getting two weeks' work in three. Many fortunes were reversed during the Crash – even the sons of T.D. Wanliss suffered. Newton's brother Neville lost most of the value of his share portfolio, which was his livelihood, and had to rent out half of his house as a flat. In effect, it was the same strategy Bert was applying.

* * *

At the council meeting a week after Armistice Day Councillor Unsworth proposed a motion to accept the proposal of the 14th Battalion and 4th Brigade Association to present the 14th Battalion's Colours to the St Kilda Town Hall at the next Anzac Day. It was seconded by Councillor Dawkins and passed unanimously. A vote of thanks was then made to Bert for sponsoring the idea, and Bert in turn presented the municipality with a signed copy of Newton Wanliss's *History of the 14th Battalion*.

At the next council meeting, at the beginning of December, Councillor Thomas Unsworth spoke on behalf of the public works committee. He raised the prospect of a loan of £70,000, with £45,000 being spent on rebuilding the men's and women's baths. He was challenged by Councillor Cummings, who felt it was unwise to encumber the municipality further.

"I see no objection to the council borrowing money for other works in the schedule apart from the baths," Councillor Moroney added. "If money has to be borrowed for the baths at a high rate of interest, probably 6 per cent, with a capital cost of £45,000, I am totally opposed to it."

At a special meeting of the council held on 19 December 1929, a motion was put up for the council to borrow £66,700 subject to permission from the ratepayers being obtained. The main work included in the rate schedule was the construction of the St Kilda men's and women's baths at a cost of £45,000. Councillor Moroney was opposed to the baths, but said he would vote for the schedule as he was in favour of every other item on it. Councillor Cummings also said he was opposed to the baths item, but when the vote was taken it was found that Bert had not voted.

"Councillor Jacka, you must cast a vote," said the Mayor, Councillor Robinson.

"I am opposed to the item for the reconstruction of the baths," Bert replied tersely, but when the vote was taken again, he too voted for the schedule. The only dissenters left were councillors Cummings and Dawkins.

* * *

In February 1930 Bert took on the chairmanship of an organising committee to put on an All Nations Fair in the Town Hall over the first three days of May in order to raise funds for the Alfred Children's, the Austin and St Vincent's Hospitals. Vera assisted by leading the organisation of a Cinderella Dance at Ormond Hall in Moubray Street in aid of the Children's Stall at the Fair. While they danced, decisions were being made in Canberra. On 12 March, Prime Minister Scullin announced a general increase in tariffs, which meant imported goods would be much dearer, which meant that Bert's business in Elizabeth Street was doomed.

THE "BIG DIPPER"

It was another sleepless night for Vera. Bert had been coughing again, and turning over and over in the bed all night. It was almost light now and she lay there, staring at the ceiling. Bert had finally stopped, and she sensed that he was awake.

"Are you awake?" she asked.

"Yes."

"Why don't you see a doctor?"

"It's that damned bronchitis again," he replied, starting to cough again.

"That persistent cough. And these dreams or nightmares… they're happening more often. Did you know that?"

"All right, all right…" Bert coughed, then lay there for a few moments staring at the ceiling, trying to suppress the coughing. He could never put Gallipoli out of his mind.

"I'm getting up," he announced suddenly.

"The sun's not up yet," she said, "and you'll wake Betty."

"No I won't," he whispered, then coughed. "It'll be up soon, and I've got things to do. You know what day this is, don't you?"

Vera just turned over in bed, knowing there was nothing she could do.

Every day Bert felt it was getting harder to lift his aching body out of the bed. As winter approached there was stiffness and pain in his left shoulder that sent a shiver through him every time he got up. In the bathroom he pulled out the razor and sharpened it on his leather strap. He lathered up the horsehair brush, and stopped to look at himself in the mirror. He could see that Vera was right – he looked so knocked out, he could hardly recognise himself. His stomach protruded from what had once been a very athletic body. The bloom of youth had disappeared so quickly, he hardly had time to blink. But while his body had aged, he felt the same man inside. He still had his old fighting spirit, and there was much left to do.

He came back to the bedroom after shaving, and pulled his old uniform out of the cupboard. It wasn't creased, but the brass wasn't up to scratch, so he polished it with *Brasso*. He brought the billycan of milk in from the front porch, and after putting it in the icebox, he decided to clean the stove. He laid out a number of sheets of *The Argus* on the linoleum floor in the kitchen, then pulled out the grate and brushed the ashes into a dustpan.

Not long after the sun had risen, Vera got up, then woke Betty. Vera prepared a healthy breakfast for Bert and Betty. She wanted to tell him that he had not bothered to look at her when he came back to the bedroom to fetch his uniform. *All he seems to care about is that uniform.*

* * *

2.30 pm, St Kilda Town Hall, 27 April 1930

Bert, Vera and Betty arrived at the Town Hall a full hour before the ceremony was scheduled to begin. Even though the Mayor, Councillor Robinson, was to take on the custodianship of the 14th Battalion's Colours, no one doubted that it was Bert's show. He had conceived the idea and had pushed it through at Anzac House and at the Council.

Four massive white columns dominated the portico that had recently been added to the front entrance to the Town Hall. The portico stood out from the original building, which had never been rendered. The grand dome had never been built either – the crash of '93 had seen to that. The original building was now an unsightly combination of unfinished raw red bricks covered in dark green creeper vine. When the ceremony was about to commence, the mayor and the councillors took up their positions between the middle columns.

The service began with an organ recital by Raymond Fehmel, assistant organist of St Paul's Cathedral, followed by introductory remarks by the mayor. "Attention!" was called as dozens of young 14th Battalion (CMF) men with fixed bayonets marched in along the gravel path and stopped in front of the portico with the Regimental and King's Colours in the lead. The organist played, and a hymn was sung.

The flag bearers stood between the central columns of the portico, while the soldiers formed up in two lines against the background of the building with rifles on shoulders. The bearers of the Colours faced the crowd, which showed its approval with a lengthy applause. The Reverend J.J. McCall from St Bede's Anglican Church in Elwood stepped forward holding some typewritten pages. Looking like a pale English vicar whose hair was too long, he read a prayer that was most prescient for the times:

"O Thou who are our Deliverer and our Hope, forgive all forgetfulness of Thee, all ingratitude, all worship of Mammon, all refusal to seek the best and highest, all proud boasting of our strength, as though we could do without Thee, till as a people and as an Empire we seek Thy will in everything, and Thy blessing on all our undertakings.

"O Father, who has blessed us with this good land, look in Thy mercy upon us. Show us the folly of selfishness; the folly of warfare between man and man, and class and class, and party and party, so that our life be not disturbed and we be not hindered from fulfilling our trust as stewards of this great heritage."

When the Anglican minister had finished, the Lessons were read by the Reverend Jacob Danglow, VD MA. Having served in France in 1918 as Jewish chaplain to the Australian Imperial Force, he wore his medals proudly.

"Come behold the works of the Lord," he said, "what desolations He hath made in the earth. He maketh wars to cease unto the end of the earth; He breaketh the bow, and cutteth the spear in sunder; He burneth the chariot in the fire. Be still and know that I am God..." It was all fire and brimstone. It preceded and contrasted with Captain R.H. Hunt's reading of gentle Psalm 23: "The Lord is my Shepherd; I shall not want..."

After the reading of Psalm 23, and further hymns and prayers all joined in the Lord's Prayer, and finally the National Anthem was played by the St Kilda City Brass Band. Bert felt a great sense of relief. He had closed the circle that began with the consecration of the Colours on the St Kilda foreshore fifteen years earlier. The Colours had been consecrated by the Padre of the 14th, the Reverend Andrew Gillison, who in fulfilling the tenets of his faith, gave up his life for another at Gallipolli. The Colours that had been accepted from the Governor-General by Lieutenant Hamilton all those years ago were now in a safe place, where people would see them, and remember. Hamilton died defending Courtney's Post at Gallipoli, only a few feet away from Bert that fateful morning. Bert had avenged him, and won the Victoria Cross in the process.

* * *

The presentation of the Colours was one of the few positive glimpses of life that Bert saw in 1930. The new location of the store in Elizabeth Street did not stem the flow of red ink. Ever since the previous November, when they moved into the new premises, Bert and Ernie had conducted a sustained advertising campaign supported by price cuts. In December they advertised "Practical Gifts for Xmas!" In early January it was a "New Year Sale", and in late January the "Final Days" of the "Jacka-Edmonds SALE" was heralded, but in April a "Clearance of English Sanitary Ware" was announced. Prices dropped by 30 to 40 per cent. The *Silent Vortex* vacuum cleaner that was selling for £12/10 shillings in February 1928 was now on sale at £8/8 shillings. Even that was still two weeks' wages for most people, and in the worst economic depression on record, no one loved his wife that much.

Margins were being squeezed as demand dried up, and a couple of months later the winter came. Now hardly anyone was shopping in the windy city streets. Bert came down with a severe bout of influenza and bronchitis that kept him in bed for a whole month. While he was off ill Ernie could only raise funding to support a couple more months of advertising. In late June 1930, they gave it their last advertising shot. They announced their "Stocktaking bargains", including the Australian-made Supreme electric iron for 19/6 pence, which had been on sale at 15/9 pence a few months earlier. The Supreme bath heater was down, roughly 20 per cent cheaper than a few months earlier.

When he came back on board at the end of June, Bert could see that there was no hope of the firm trading out of the mountain of debt – a financial reckoning was coming at him like a steam train. One night at the St Kilda Soldiers' and Sailors' Club, he confided to his good friend Burnett Gray his doubts that the firm could last much longer, and then he too would be joining the ranks of the unemployed. Gray shuddered at the thought, and suggested a possible solution, even if it was just a temporary one. He would support Bert for the position of mayor, which carried a £500 salary.

It wasn't usual for councillors to be elevated to the mayoral position after only one year's service, but Bert had impressed with his contributions to the Health and Widening High Street sub-committees, and in general council meetings. Gray said he would talk to some other influential councillors like Thomas Unsworth, but warned Bert that it would not be easy, particularly if he was still expecting to run the business in Elizabeth Street.

* * *

Betty screamed with excitement when she saw her father walk through the door that evening. Bert picked her up and gave her a big hug. She was already dressed in her night-shirt, ready for bed.

"Have you been a good girl for Mummy?" he asked, and Betty responded by nodding "yes". She hadn't been seeing much of him in recent months.

"I wasn't expecting to see you for dinner," Vera said, feeling embarrassed that she hadn't prepared a meal.

"That's all right, I can wait," he replied. He spent some time with Betty that night before she went to bed. While he was doing that, Vera prepared a meal for him. After he had dined on his own and Betty was safely tucked away in bed, Bert spoke to Vera in the kitchen.

"Several of the councillors have expressed support for me stepping into the role of mayor for the next term," he said.

"This is quite a surprise," she said. "You've only been a councillor for a short time."

"I've got the numbers, apparently."

"But we hardly ever see you as it is."

"The firm is going broke, Vera," he said quietly. "It is about to go into voluntary liquidation, which means that everyone in it will lose their job, including me. No one is hiring people at the minute. The position of mayor pays an allowance of £500, as well as use of a car. It will give us a chance to see things through."

The councillors were confident he would succeed in the mayoral role, and they had every confidence in Vera too. As a councillor's wife she was a vice-president to Mrs Hallerstein on one of the ladies' committees, and they were currently organising a *café chantant* to help pay down the debts on the Soldiers' and Sailors' Memorial Hall. She quite enjoyed this social activity, and was good at it.

"I can't do it without you," he said honestly, and there was silence as she thought further about it. "We'll be able to move back to the house," he added as a sweetener. She knew that she couldn't change his mind on something even if she insisted on it. Once his mind was made up, that was it. But she was not too different really. Still, she was quite excited by the idea of being the Lady Mayoress of St Kilda. Now that the firm was being liquidated it could give them both the social visibility that could help launch Bert into a new career after their term had expired.

"All right," she said with a half smile that betrayed some lingering doubts. "All right."

* * *

Bert often took to standing outside the Elizabeth Street store, where he spoke to passers-by. He was looking quite sad when Donovan Joynt VC came across the street from the Block.

Joynt was shocked at his appearance. "Bert," he said. "What's the matter? You're looking very downhearted."

"I'm being closed down," Bert said. "Wren, thinking that he's bought me, wants me to take a course of action politically, but I refused to do so. Then he said, 'All right, if you don't, I'll close you down,' and I told him 'Close me down. I prefer to be closed down.'"

"That's terrible news. Can you avert it?"

"It's hopeless. The creditors are screaming for their money, there are few sales, and the bank is demanding its payments."

Joynt instantly recalled walking down Queen Street from his office each night with men every five yards asking him, "Can you give me the price of a feed mister?" Joynt told him how sorry he was that things had gone so badly, and asked if he could help, but Bert assured him there was nothing anyone could do. Joynt had a lump in his throat, so shattered was he by the news. This is Australia's greatest frontline soldier, he thought. He couldn't bear it. As soon as Joynt had walked off down the street Ernie came out of the store.

"Was that Joynt?"

"Yes."

"You didn't tell him about Wren's decision did you?"

"It'll be out soon anyway."

"Perhaps you *should* take Wren up on his offer?" Ernie urged him. "Don't worry about me and the staff, we'll get by. You've got to look after yourself and your family. What's wrong with Wren's offer anyway?"

"No, Ernie," he shot back. "They are not my style. And if I did accept, they'd say, 'Look at Jacka — failure in business, he climbs into a safe job as an MP.'"

It was never going to be on. To join the Labor Party would have made Bert look like a hypocrite given his RSSILA and business activist background. He had campaigned for the Nationalist Party on several occasions. Then there was the question of whether Wren could actually deliver him a seat. Labor was on the ropes politically, and in the current job market, the few sitting members would not be standing in line to give their seat up for him, war hero or not.

* * *

Bert did actually climb into a fairly safe job as Mayor of St Kilda when he was voted in to the office unopposed on the first day of September 1930. The £500 salary would take care of his family's current needs, but it was only a temporary solution. It was as if he was walking the plank on a pirate ship surrounded by sharks, and the plank had just been extended by a year — at the end of it there would be another reckoning. He pushed all that to the back of his mind, and very quickly fully immersed himself in the role of mayor. As always he felt that he would be judged on the last thing he did, and that thing would have to be done to the best of his ability. It was no good being a celebrated war hero one minute, and a dud the next.

* * *

St Leonards, 10 St Leonards Avenue, St Kilda, 16 September 1930

Being of a similar energetic and sociable temperament as Bert, Vera quickly and effortlessly threw herself into the role of Lady Mayoress. Almost immediately, she was hostess of a card party and *café chantant* that was held at the St Leonards boarding house owned by Councillor George Cummings and his wife Maud. The *café chantant* idea was borrowed from Continental Europe, where it had been popularised as a form of light-hearted outdoor cabaret. The aim of the party was to reduce debt on the St Kilda Soldiers' and Sailors' Memorial Hall.

St Leonards was a massive Victorian period house with a three-storey tower set on a very large block of land that accommodated two tennis courts. Miss Myra Marsh organised a tennis tournament, and there were numerous stalls that sold jams, pickles, and home-made cakes that had been donated by volunteers. George Cummings was an architect by profession, and had been Mayor of St Kilda in 1922–23 and 1925–26. Mrs Maud Cummings was an experienced former Lady Mayoress, and therefore felt she could offer Vera some advice.

"How are you finding the role of Lady Mayoress?" she asked Vera that afternoon as she stood in the shade of the large verandah watching the tennis.

"There are so many functions in our calendar."

"This is just the beginning," Maud said. "I was fortunate that I could share being Lady Mayoress with my daughter."

"My daughter is still a toddler."

"Yes, I know," Maud said with a smile. "That's her over there with Mrs Futcher isn't it?"

"Yes."

"Dear child."

"Poor Mrs Futcher," Vera sighed, as she waved to Betty and her minder. "She put so much work into organising this function, and now she's following Betty around. Betty calls her Ma Futcher, you know."

"Well, dear, I'm sure that Mrs Futcher will look after her well," said Maud tapping Vera on the arm, "and I'm sure that Alison will help you out whenever she can too. She is so energetic and idealistic."

"Yes, I'm sure she will," Vera said with a strained expression. She was uneasy about Miss Alison Cummings, who was about the same age as she was. She was one of the army of young women who seemed to have missed out on marriage as a result of the war. Instead, she lived close to her family and devoted herself to charitable causes. How was she going to meet a husband that way? At functions like these, or at committee meetings perhaps? Both of Alison's brothers were architects like their father, and both had gone off to the war. Now they all lived together at St Leonards. To Vera, Alison appeared very confident, and very interested in working with Bert on all kinds of projects.

During the afternoon hundreds of guests were entertained by a number of artists, including soprano Christine Nasson, tenor John Cook accompanied by Herbert Preece on piano, and Marion Lightfoot, who played some tunes on the banjo.

* * *

The bridge party continued into the night, while Bert and other members of the St Kilda Army and Navy Club arranged a billiards tournament. Bert got through a couple of rounds before being eliminated. When he wandered back to the bridge room he bumped into Alison.

"How is the tournament coming along?" she asked.

"Which one?"

"Billiards, of course!"

"It's a lot quicker than the cards, I'll tell you."

"Is my little sister annoying you again?" Howard Cummings intervened. He had also been eliminated in the billiards, and noticed that she seemed to hover around Bert at every opportunity, but she wasn't the only one. Even though he now looked middle aged, looking older than than he was, the aura of Bert's reputation still held a fascination for many women.

"Not at all," Bert hastened. "You want her back do you? Well, I'm afraid the municipality needs her. She's doing lots of good work for us."

"Not to mention father dear," she added.

Bert had known Howard since they came back from the war together on the *Euripides*, so he knew that he was a bit of a handful. Bert was the ship's adjutant, and was made aware of Howard's condition. A six-footer, Howard was working as an articled pupil for HW & FB Tompkins, Architects, in Elizabeth Street when he joined up in March 1916. His younger brother Cliff had joined six months earlier, and needed his mother's permission because he was only nineteen and a half. Cliff was wounded in France, and came back as a corporal.

When Howard joined up at the Melbourne Town Hall Depot he insisted on being sent to the prestigious Australian Flying Corps, but ended up as a driver in the first Auxiliary Mechanical Transport Company Reinforcement. Perhaps it was the disappointment of it that got him into trouble before he even left Australia's shores. After going AWL he was confined to base and fined. Upon arrival in England he earned seventy-two hours detention and another fine for using obscene language to an NCO while on parade. After six months at the front in France he was sent back to England on leave, and must have loved those girls, because two weeks later he was in hospital, sick with a dangerous infection in the nether regions. His medical condition kept him in England for almost a year after the war had ended, and that's why he came back on the same boat as Bert late in 1919.

* * *

Later that night Bert slumped into a large sofa patterned in green floral motifs in the lounge at St Leonards. Thoroughly exhausted from the day's activities, he engaged in a conversation with the host, Councillor George Cummings. Cummings was now sixty-eight years old, and as a retired architect, was devoting most of his time to community affairs. His ruddy complexion was complemented by his neatly combed white hair, and matching heavy white moustache.

"Thank you so much for making your house available for this function, George."

"It's the least we can do," smiled Cummings. "But tell me, how are things going at your end?" Bert knew he was referring to the business, but just as he opened his mouth to answer, Burnett Gray placed his hands on the back of an empty sofa chair nearby.

"Mind if I join you?"

"Please do," said Cummings.

"The creditors' meeting is being held next month," Bert continued. "It's been a shocking time for all of us." He had already been through this with Burnett Gray, who knew what he was talking about.

"I can well imagine," said Cummings, staring grimly.

"The only good news is that we are moving back to Murchison Street shortly, although we did enjoy Elwood in the end."

"You know," said Cummings leaning over. "It's quite the worst thing I have seen in all my years. The crash of '93 was disastrous, but not like this." There had been a run on New York banks in 1893, and in Melbourne the forty-year long speculative housing and investment bubble that was born in the gold rush finally burst. After a run that saw its coin reserves severely depleted, the National Bank had closed its doors for some weeks. Bert was only a baby then, but George Cummings was a young man, and he remembered it well.

"I've been thinking about what we can do to alleviate the situation facing the unemployed in our municipality," Gray said.

"Tell us," said Cummings.

"One of the essentials that people forget about is footwear," Gray began. "Unemployed men can't look for work or earn sustenance wages if they can't afford shoes. Back in '23 I ran a campaign to gather used footwear from householders, and we distributed the shoes among the unemployed through the St John's Mission."

"That's a very good idea," Bert said. "Decent shoes are just as important to the unemployed as a square meal. I'll keep that in mind."

"Agreed," said Cummings. "You can count on me to help out whenever required."

"Another idea I've had," Gray continued, "is to fit out unemployed men for some gold fossicking – I've done it myself!"

"That's what is happening back in Wedderburn, where stories abound of people digging up nuggets in the streets." Bert said. "They're digging for gold as we speak."

"But that's in one's own town," Cummings added in a cautionary tone. "It is one thing to dig for gold in the main street of your own town and be able to sleep at night in the comfort of your own bed. It is quite another matter to be out in the wilds, having to feed and support oneself. You need capital for that. Has anyone in Wedderburn found anything that would make the effort worthwhile?"

"Not as far as I know," said Bert. "But I understand that the main street is looking a little worse for wear!"

Gray laughed with them, and was happy to see that Bert's spirits seemed to have revived.

"Nevertheless," Gray said seriously, "I feel that financing some fossicking is something the council should pursue."

"I quite agree," said Bert, who believed in men working for a living rather than being provided with plain sustenance.

* * *

On Saturday evening a few days later Bert attended a farewell function that was given for the Governor-General, Lord Stonehaven, by yachtsmen at the Royal Melbourne Yacht Club smoke night. Bert was standing on the deck at the back of the building overlooking the famous St Kilda Pier. The white-hulled yachts bobbed gently at their moorings, reflecting the lights from the clubhouse, stood out starkly against the dark water in the bay beyond. It was quite chilly, but he preferred it to the smoke filled main dining room, which had started him coughing a little earlier. The worst thing about a smoke night was the smoke. He used to enjoy them, but now wished he had never touched the things. Internally he was feeling downhearted about his business, but the small group of yachties around him couldn't detect it through the optimistic energy he was displaying in the mayoral role. The chatter subsided when it was announced that the Governor-General was about to speak, and they moved into the main dining room of the luxuriously appointed club.

"Having lived in Australia for five years now," Lord Stonehaven began, "I feel that I have accumulated enough experience to speak with some authority on the problems and prospects that you now face. I want you to understand that we in Britain will be watching you with sympathy and interest, and that we want you to realise that the difficulties which are confronting you are causing the greatest anxiety to your fellow countrymen. The very life of the Empire depends upon its various units standing firmly together; the ties of Empire are just as strong as the ties of blood.

"It has been a tall order to be ordered to represent the King, when one really understands what the King stands for. It means, for one thing, that one had to be on good behaviour for five years!

"Governors, however, are merely human, and being of good behaviour is not sufficient occupation, and so I have taken up yachting. My old friend Lord Forster wrote to me saying that he had two yachts that he would dispose of on very advantageous terms... As a Scotsman, I bought only one of them!

"I am very proud to have been a member of the crew of my own boat. I remember one occasion when I asked the skipper, Angus McIntyre, for a cigarette. The skipper's expressions, while particularly appropriate to that occasion, were not couched in terms suitable for a Governor-General to recount! Nevertheless, I respected the skipper all the more for that!"

At the conclusion of the applause for Lord Stonehaven's heartfelt and very tailored talk, he presented trophies to a number of yachtsmen. Speeches were then made by several distinguished guests, and Bert gave a speech in his capacity as Mayor of St Kilda.

"We are all saddened by the news that Your Excellency is to complete this term as Governor-General of Australia. Your support for the cause of returned men over the years has been greatly appreciated. As the newly elected Mayor of St Kilda I see a number of important things we can do to beautify this city, while at the same time alleviating distress.

"One of the big issues in our local area is that the council's baths building program is carried to a satisfactory conclusion. This and other tasks will require manpower, which will provide jobs to the unemployed. The council needs volunteers to help us achieve our goals, and I am sure that they can be found amongst the yachtsmen present here this evening."

Bert was congratulated afterwards by Councillor George Cummings, who was also a keen yachtsman, had been a member of the Royal Melbourne Yacht Club for many years, and was a man who had unfurled every yard of canvas for the community.

* * *

The following Monday night a deputation from the unemployed of St Kilda placed a number of requests before the Council. In reply Bert said that a council official would be placed in charge of the odd job bureau in the Town Hall, however, the Town Hall could not be placed at the disposal of the unemployed committee. In response to concerns that the council was providing jobs to unemployed from other areas, Bert noted the city engineer's statement that of the thirty-two men employed on the baths construction, nineteen were residents of St Kilda. He also outlined a program of relief entertainments, which the committee had drawn up, and which would be activated almost immediately. As Mayor, Bert allowed his name to be used as Patron of the St Kilda Unemployed Organization, which was provided with printed stationery.

* * *

On 25 September Bert and Vera attended the Fleur-de-Lys Ball at the St Kilda Town Hall. The sponsors of the ball, the St Kilda District Rovers and Rangers, had asked the Art Student's Association to prepare a number of large "luministic panels" that were hung across the stage, and joined to form a canopy over the orchestra. More than 400 tickets were sold and a considerable sum was raised for the unemployed relief fund.

The very next day was the anniversary of the Battle of Polygon Wood, and it was not without irony that on that day Mr J.P. Hughes, ACA, Liquidator, signed the order announcing the meeting of creditors of Jacka Edmonds and Co., which was to take place on 14 October. The advertisement appeared in the Judicial and Law Notices of *The Argus* the day after, and two days after that it spawned a news article titled, "Firm of Jacka, Edmonds & Co has decided to go into voluntary liquidation".

That night Bert was at the annual meeting of the 14th Battalion and 4th Brigade Association, where it was announced that he would be the future president of the Association, since Brigadier Brand had accepted the position of Patron. At the meeting Brigadier Brand recalled to the men's memory the former Surgeon-General, Sir Neville Howse, VC, who had recently passed away in London. He asked them to remember the great work that he had performed among the wounded on the beach at Anzac Cove in the critical hours after the landing, which jogged Bert's memory of that day, and the grilling he had received later at the Dardanelles Commission.

* * *

At 8 pm on the eve of the meeting of creditors that was to pick over the bones of his firm, Bert chaired a public meeting to discuss the establishment of an unemployed relief committee. Vera was there too, in her capacity as Lady Mayoress.

"I have called this group together," Bert said, "to see if it is possible to form a permanent committee that will function throughout my term of office. We should have one central body to handle the whole of the distress, and particularly with regard to unemployment relief. We have many representative people with us, and I think we should now consider what can be done in St Kilda towards the relief of distress caused through unemployment. As the council has only just taken over control of the Odd Job Bureau, I am making an appeal to place men. We sincerely hope you will ring up. We are getting an extension from the Town Hall phone to the Old Court House. In the meantime, the unemployment has been supervised under the supervision of the Ladies' Benevolent Society and is collecting food which is being distributed every Saturday afternoon. I want to take this opportunity of thanking the business people of St Kilda for their support.

"We have with us Mr Stenning, Secretary of the State Relief Committee, and the object of this meeting primarily is to form a committee to look after the interests of the men who are out of work. In the course of the next few months we will also have to supply funds for the L.B.S. for the relief of distress. Finally, before we come to the appointment of committees, one big thing we have in mind is the organisation of a carnival for the month of December."

"Less than three months ago," Mr Stenning began, "it was my privilege to preach the gospel of 'safety first' to railway men, and tonight I am speaking in the same way. The supply of foodstuff is a matter of life and death to many of the citizens, especially children. The State Government has instituted what is commonly known as the State Relief Committee, firstly to provide sufficient food and clothing to augment the supply already being made available through the various municipalities to the citizens in need of help, and secondly to cooperate with the relief funds. In most municipalities up to date we have been able to form a subsidiary committee, and I must say that we have been requested to do the same for your Mayor, a gentleman like Captain Jacka... He certainly has very persuasive ways about him!"

It made everyone laugh, as they knew his "crash through" nature. Stenning continued.

"I have come here mainly to persuade you to form a subsidiary committee to the State Relief Committee from the charitable committees existing in St Kilda at the present time. With one committee under the control of the Mayor, you will to a large extent keep out the overlapping and the imposition. If you should run out of the necessities, the State Relief Committee will supplement your wants. I have come here in a constructive kind of way, not to criticise, but to be of direct assistance in the formation of a committee desirous of being established."

"Thank you, Mr Stenning," Bert said at the conclusion of his opening remarks. "The citizens of St Kilda have been well looked after. The stallholders of the market have been particularly generous. Bakers have given daily donations of bread. The Colonial Meat Company has also given a large amount of meat. We have, as far as possible, endeavoured to do everything possible in St Kilda. We want to get as much food in St Kilda as we can, and then draw on Mr Stenning's organisation for the remainder. Last Saturday Mrs Vale and Mrs Couchman of the L.B.S. came along and supervised the distribution of the food, and everything appeared to be in order. The L.B.S. is the only body in St Kilda who could carry out its work permanently, or at least right through next winter.

"I would also remind those present," Bert added, "that Miss Cummings has arranged a bridge afternoon and tennis tournament at St Leonards for 12 November next." Here we go again, thought Vera, another evening with Miss Alison Cummings at St Leonards. She was becoming more and more concerned about Bert and the ladies who liked to hover around him.

The outcome of the evening was the formation of a new relief committee, with all St Kilda councillors as ex-officio members, and a ladies sub-committee was formed by the Lady Mayoress. The new committee met immediately to discuss arrangements for the

Lord Mayor's Hospital Appeal, and to organise a beach carnival in December to aid in the relief of distress.

"Is the beach carnival organiser to be in an honorary capacity or in a paid capacity?" asked Dr Levin.

"I want to make it quite clear that the Organising Secretary is for the carnival," Bert stressed.

"I have pleasure in moving that Mr I.P. Levoi be appointed Honorary Organising Secretary," Dr Levin said. Mr Harlem seconded the motion. Ioris Philip Levoi was in the 59th Battalion, and was currently Secretary of the St Kilda Army and Navy Club. He was a good mate of Bert's, which everyone knew. Levoi worked as an insurance agent in the city and was located just across the street from Bert's store. Bert used to pop across every second day to say hello. That's one reason he was there.

The carnival date was set for the week of 24 to 31 January 1931.

* * *

11 am, Boardroom at Collins Gate, 377-378 Little Collins Street, 14 October 1930

Mr W. Mc Adam presided at the meeting of creditors convened to consider the voluntary liquidation of Jacka, Edmonds and Co. Limited, merchants, of Elizabeth Street. A reporter from *The Argus* obtained details of the meeting, as this business failure among the thousands taking place at that time was particularly newsworthy. Mr J.F. Hughes, Public Accountant and Liquidator, read a statement showing that at the date of voluntary liquidation, 22 September, amounts estimated to be owing to unsecured creditors totalled £21,289. The estimated amount available to meet unsecured creditors was £1347 after deducting £262 due to preferential creditors. Therefore, the estimated deficiency of assets to meet liabilities was £19,942.

Mr Hughes submitted a further statement showing the unsecured creditors, the principal being the National Bank of Australasia Ltd, which was owed £11,544, John Wren's advances and interest, £6051, KFB Metters Pty. Ltd. £654, KFB Foundry Ltd. £408, McCulloch Carrying Co. Ltd. £274, Condor Lamps Ltd, £174, and Lava Manufacturers £173. A committee representing the principal creditors was appointed to act with the liquidator. In his article the reporter wrote that the committee represented the National Bank of Australasia Ltd, John Wren, KFB Metters Pty Ltd, and McCulloch Carrying Co. Ltd.

The news about Bert's financial demise spread throughout the city carried by the article in *The Argus* and by word of mouth. In the same issue there was news from Germany that the Nazi Party was taking on the communists in the Reichstag. The Nazis would march into the parliamentary chamber two-by-two wearing their brown-shirt paramilitary uniforms. Since the wearing of uniforms in the streets was banned, the Nazis had to wear overcoats, or get changed in the corridors of the parliament building. That's why the communists laughed at them and pelted them with inkwells as they marched in. While the Nazis screamed "Heil Hitler!" the communists chanted, "Down with him!"

While those mad scenes were taking place within the Reichstag building thousands of Nazi Party supporters gathered outside in a huge demonstration shouting "Awake Germany! Down with the Jews!" The police had all been drawn into defending the Reichstag, while mobs rampaged through Berlin attacking all the shops, cafes, hotels and large stores that were supposedly owned by Jews. Australians were coming around to the conclusion that the war hadn't solved anything.

Two days later it was cryptically announced in *The Argus*, that while the National Bank of Australasia Ltd held no securities from Jacka, Edmonds and Co. Pty Ltd for its advances, it was otherwise fully secured as regards its claim against the estate, and further, the bank's name had been withdrawn from the committee appointed by the meeting to act with the liquidator. How could the bank have been "fully secured"? It was not obvious to the public that an anonymous donor had put up security for the £11,600. That donor was John Wren, who had lost around £20,000 on Bert's business venture, at a time when an average house in the suburbs cost approximately £1500.

* * *

In October 1930 communists were a visible presence in Melbourne too, and police detectives were actively investigating unemployed worker groups who might be infiltrated by them. Their publications trumpeted an aim to "establish a workers' and peasants' republic in Australia", which suggested some foreign input at the drafting stage. When Senior Detective Dunn of the St Kilda police force led a raid on their headquarters at "communist hall" in Exhibition Street, he arrested around forty people, many of whom were an "Internationale" hailing from Germany, Italy, Canada, England, and Scotland. Hidden under the floorboards were batons made from short lengths of water-pipe, or metal conduit, with holes at the end to take a loop of cord. They were described by the defendants as defensive weapons.

There were some violent hotheads among them, who were busting for armed revolt, but most Australian communists were planning to convert the population via the drip method of propaganda. There was no better time than the present, with more than one-third of the working population unemployed. Most of their publications came out of Sydney, and with titles like *Dock Rebel* (Mort's Dock), *White Bay Dynamo*, and *Bridge Hammer*, they read like a league of Soviet soccer teams.

* * *

That evening Bert took part in a mini-golf challenge against the Mayor of Melbourne, Councillor Harold Luxton, as part of the Lord Mayor's Hospital Appeal. The event took place at the

"Top-Hole" course in St Kilda, and the fact that Bert was playing attracted a large attendance. They were all square at the fourth hole, but then Bert forged ahead, winning the match by five holes. All the takings of the Top-Hole course for four days would be devoted to the appeal fund. The next night both Bert and Vera appeared at a dance at the St Kilda Army and Navy Club, for the Soldiers' and Sailors' War Widows Provident Fund. They left Betty with Mrs Futcher again.

On Saturday, 1 November 1930, the Lakes Golf Links were opened at Beaconsfield Upper, and Bert proposed a vote of thanks. A few days later Bert attended a function for the Lord Mayor's Appeal for combined charities under the patronage of Councillor Harold Luxton. Bert was Honorary Treasurer, and Miss Alison Cummings was organiser. He was seeing quite a bit of Alison lately.

* * *

"What do you mean, you're not coming?" Bert asked Vera as he changed out of his business suit. It was mid-November and they were both due to appear at the Unemployed Charity Ball that night at the St Kilda Town Hall. "You put a lot of effort into organising it, and you should be there," he insisted.

"No, I'm staying home with Betty."

"But I thought we had arranged for Mrs Futcher…"

"Betty is not feeling well. She's a bit congested, and Mrs Futcher was part of the committee, so she should attend."

"All right, Mummy, you stay home with Betty then," Bert relented, after hearing about Betty's illness. "Have you let Mrs Futcher know?"

"I did that this afternoon, and she is happy to have a night out."

* * *

At the function later that night, Bert had to explain that unforseen domestic issues had intervened, and the Lady Mayoress was unable to attend. Back at the Elwood flat, Vera was putting Betty to bed. She made up a mixture of olive oil and camphorated oils, and rubbed her daughter's chest with it. Betty giggled, and it brought a smile to Vera's face to see her daughter laughing like that after feeling miserable and congested all afternoon.

"Now say a prayer before going to sleep, won't you?" said Vera, and Betty knelt on her bed, putting her hands together in prayer. After the prayer Betty quickly slipped back under the sheets, and Vera tucked her in. She gave her a kiss on the forehead, which was hot and moist from the fever she was running.

"Another story, Mummy?"

Vera looked at her lovingly, and couldn't resist her pleading. She had been reading her a different story every day, and Betty had come to expect it.

"Please?"

"All right then, just one more story, then you'll have to go to sleep."

Betty nodded agreement, and Vera found an Aboriginal story translated by Daisy May Bates, who had worked as a writer, anthropologist and social worker in central and north-west Australia for the previous thirty years.

"This is a story that the Aborigines tell about a willy-wagtail called Jitti-jitti, who lived in the Nyitting times, the times of the cold and ice of long ago, when there was no sea, only lakes and swamps. Jitti-jitti the Wagtail had his kalleep…"

"What's a kaleep?" Betty asked.

"His kaleep was his home, and it was built beside a great lake, where there were plenty of good things to eat: fish and roots and fruits and honey from the Banksia trees. One day Jitti-jitti said, 'I will go north', and away he went, travelling a long, long way from his own kalleep.

"He stayed away a long time, but by and by his heart became hot inside, and he said 'I will go to my kalleep'. While Jitti-jitti was travelling a great number of invaders came on his home ground and made bush shelters, and caught fish and ate all the good things they found on the country belonging to Jitti-jitti, and got fat and grew strong with the good food. One day they looked north and saw Jitti-jitti coming home.

"'Here's a kalleep-gur coming' they said, and they went and caught some good fish and cooked them, and offered the fish to Jitti-jitti, but he was so angry with them for trespassing on his own kalleep without his permission, and sitting down upon it as if it were their kalleep, that he would not touch the fish they had brought and cooked for him. He did not speak to the invaders, but went over to the beena (that's a lake) where they had caught the fish, and, taking his biggest spear he thrust it into the middle of the lake down and down and down, and then splashed the water all round and about. As he splashed the water it rose higher and higher and came up and caught the invaders as they were running away, and drowned them, every one of them, all who had invaded his kalleep. And the water rose and rose and covered all the country.

"Woggal, the great magic snake who was Jitti-jitti's great friend, came along and made great hollows with his great long body, and the hollows he made became rivers and creeks, and the waters followed Woggal along all the hollows into a big big hole, which turned into the great sea that the Bibbulmun call 'Wadidarn'.

"And Jitti-jitti's kalleep, which was called Jittarning had always plenty of fish and honey, and the waters of the great lake of Jittarning always rose up high and high if any strangers came near, and frightened them away. So Jitti-jitti sat down at Jittarning in his own kalleep, and Woggal the magic snake always looked out for his friend Jitti-jitti."

Vera had finished telling the story and put down her book. Betty was already asleep. *I hope she's not dreaming about magic snakes*, Vera thought. Perhaps that story was a little too vivid for such a young child she thought, but at least it imparted some worthy values about friendship and the evils of stealing. She gently covered Betty over with the blanket, and turned off the light as she left the room.

* * *

In France in December 1930, a father sued a teacher who had told his son in class that Father Christmas was an invention, and that his parents were actually the ones who filled up his Christmas stocking with presents. The father said he wanted to maintain the boy's illusion longer.

On the Saturday morning just before that Christmas, Vera had gone into the city early to do some Christmas shopping, as there were some good bargains to be had, and she now had a bit of money to spend at last. She asked Bert to bring Betty in on the tram by 10.30 am, as she wanted to buy her some new shoes, and to see Father Christmas at the Georges store in Collins Street. They had moved back to their house in Murchison Street on 27 November, and it was only a short walk to the tram stop on Dandenong Road. At first Betty sat on Bert's knee. Then she stood up on the bench seat next to him and looked out of the window full of curiously. She pointed to a sign with her finger.

"What does it say?" she said.

"Don't point, dear," he said, bringing her hand down. "It says, 'Three miles to the city.'"

"How far is it, Daddy?"

"Not far. We'll be there soon." Bert smiled to himself. She was full of curiosity about the world, like he had been as a young boy growing up in Wedderburn. Only Betty had a much bigger world to start with. When he was her age he lived on the very edge of a small country town. For Betty the city must seem like a never-ending expanse of roads and buildings.

"Daddy, your fingernails are too long!" she said, pointing to his fingers.

"I need to cut them. Can you remind me when we get home this afternoon?"

As they neared an intersection cars honked their horns.

"Hear that?" Betty asked.

"We are near the city," Bert answered. "There are lots of motorcars in the city."

"Where is our car, Daddy?"

"It's getting fixed." It was actually the mayoral car, and Bert had allowed the Unemployed Association to use the car to help people get jobs. It was too hard to explain.

"We there?"

"Not quite. We are getting closer though."

"Going to the city?"

"Yes we are. We are going to meet Mummy. She's going to buy you some new shoes." Betty looked down at Bert's fingers again and tugged at the skin on the top of his hand.

"What's skin for, Daddy?"

"It does its job."

"Skin doesn't do a job!" Betty beamed with incredulity. She was feisty, and already had her own opinion on things.

"Yes it does. It holds my body in. If you didn't have skin you wouldn't stay together."

"One two three," she counted. "I see motor cars."

"Sshh... now," Bert said in a whispering tone. He noticed that everybody else on the tram was quiet, and was listening in to their conversation. He was impressed with her counting, which her mother had taught her. "She's a smart little girl," he thought, and reminded him of how he was at her age. She's curious, just like I was. And brave. He loved her very much.

"One two three ... Daddy, you look on there and count," she said pointing to the windows on the other side of the road.

"Hold on round the curve!" the conductor shouted, so that all the passengers would brace themselves as he was, clutching his big leather bag full of money and tickets.

"I told you not to point, Betty," Bert said.

"Daddy, why don't we go in that street?"

"Because there are no tracks going down that street. A tram needs tracks to run along, dear, and that street doesn't have them."

The city was full of Christmas decorations, which didn't give the impression of a city on the verge of economic collapse. Bert brought Betty to the main entry of the Georges store in Collins Street a few minutes early, and they waited there watching the trams go up and down the hill. Betty was getting more and more anxious about her mother, and was very relieved to see her.

"Mummy!" she cried.

"Betty dear," Vera said. "Now, we're going to take you to see Father Christmas in here first. Won't that be nice? Here, take these," she said to Bert, handing over a shopping bag. "After that, we'll buy you a new pair of shoes."

"There's a big sale on at Myers," Bert suggested.

"I know, that's where we are going after Betty sees Father Christmas."

"Isn't there one at Myers?"

"Yes there is, but the queue there is dreadful." It made sense, and Bert was pleased that Vera was going to do the shopping at Myers, because its owner, Mr Sidney Myer, was sponsoring a free Christmas banquet for 10,000 unemployed men and their families at the Exhibition Building. The banquet was to be served in five sittings of 2000 people drawn from the inner suburbs. His only disappointment was that the unemployed of St Kilda had missed out when those across Dandenong Road in Prahran got to go. Perhaps it was St Kilda's "patricians village" image that had done it?

He thought about how lucky they were that they all had a roof over their heads, and could still afford to buy new shoes for their daughter this year. Last year they had no money at all for presents. Next year, he thought, the unemployed in St Kilda won't miss out on their Christmas dinner, because I'll see to it that they have one.

* * *

Prospect Hill Road, Camberwell, 5 February 1931

The Great Depression, like the Great War before it, left deep scars on Australian society, destroying jobs, businesses, families, and people. For those who had fought the Great War to save civilisation, and thought they had won it, the bitter harvest of The Depression was hard to take. Re-armament was already taking place, and a disarmament movement was gathering momentum.

The mood of pessimism that permeated the world during these times was reflected in the contemporary sci-fi novel, *Last and First Men* by University of Liverpool philosopher, Dr Olaf Stapledon. It foreshadowed hundreds of years of wars to follow the Great War, beginning with France defeating Fascist Italy over lands in North Africa. The infuriated Roman mob puts its leader to death. Then France and Britain go to war in the air, with death rays destroying both London and Paris. In the east, Germany and the Soviet Union go to war destroying Berlin, Leningrad and Moscow in the process. Weakened Europe cannot resist the onslaught of the United States, which has become 100 per cent American (by losing its British roots), and while Australians remain neutral (not through cowardice, but a "conflict of loyalties"), the New Zealanders hold out against the Americans in their mountainous regions. Then, the Chinese are "awakened from their long indifference" and go to war with the United States over the oil-fuel question, ending up dividing the world between them – and that was just the beginning of the story.

Pompey Elliott wore a grim expression that afternoon when he stepped off the 5.15 at Camberwell Station, and began the walk up Prospect Hill Road. He was now fifty-two years old, and his mind wandered on that walk, back to the fateful day of 26 September, 1917 at the Battle of Polygon Wood, and his brother, Dr George Elliott, who was MO of the 56th Battalion. A few months before the battle, when his brother spotted Pompey engaged in a serious discussion with a group of senior officers, George had given him a sharp brotherly tap on the shoulder. Not knowing who it was, Pompey swung around fuming at the impudence, and George saw it written on his face.

"I don't care a damn who you're talking to with all those ribbons on your chest," he said to Pompey defiantly, "you should be glad to see your little brother!" He loved his younger brother dearly. Then, at the moment of his victory at Polygon Wood, Pompey received the shocking news that "Geordie" had been mortally wounded by a shell fragment to the skull. He could not even leave the battlefield to see him. During the same battle he received news that his legal partner, Glen Roberts, had sent the firm broke in dubious ventures, which made Pompey liable for large debts he had nothing to do with. After the battle, General Sir Herbert Plumer, commander of the Second British Army congratulated him for saving his army from disaster, but that was no consolation to his general depression. After his brother's death Pompey had written to his wife Kate saying, "I would gladly have welcomed a shell to end me." Twice he walked up and down the front lines in full view of the German machineguns, but no one on the other side had bothered to pull the trigger.

* * *

His wife Kate, and his sister-in-law Belle both thought he was acting strangely that night. He didn't say much at dinner, and after dinner he handed the children's insurance policies to Belle, with the comment, "You might need the money". She told him not to say that because he was still healthy as an ox. He had altered his Will the day before, but didn't tell her that. Belle was so troubled by her brother-in-law's curious frame of mind that she didn't go to bed until after midnight, and lay awake, tossing and turning for some time. Then she heard a door open, and the sound of footsteps coming down the corridor. It was Pompey – she knew it. The footsteps were much too heavy to be one of his children. She listened as the door to the kitchen closed. She was so on edge that she lay perfectly still, straining to hear any sound.

Finally she could bear the silence no longer, and got up. Stepping into the dark corridor she could see a light coming from under the kitchen door. She quickly tiptoed down the corridor to wake his children Violet and Neil, and together they went to the kitchen. As the door was opened it hit them.

"Gas!" The room reeked with gas fumes and Pompey sat slumped back over a chair with his legs sticking straight out. His head had fallen back and his arms lay dangling at his sides. The stove *hissed* gas…

"Harold, wake-up!" Belle screamed as Violet rushed over to the kitchen stove holding her nose and turned all the knobs off.

"Harold!"

There was no response from Pompey as Violet and Neil darted about opening all the doors and windows. With all the noise, Kate had woken up, and rushed into the kitchen.

"Good heavens!" Kate cried, as she slapped his bloated red face and shook him for all she was worth. "Wake up!"

"Daddy, wake up!" Violet said bursting into tears.

"I'm calling an ambulance," Kate said.

"That… won't… be necessary," Pompey blurted out, half conscious. They had come just in time. When Pompey was fully revived, they all went back to sleep, and he went off to work the next day as if nothing had happened. His family was distraught at this near-miss nightmare. Then a week later Neil caught him entering the toilet with the cord from his nightgown, and raised the alarm. This time he was taken to the Alfred Hospital by ambulance, and stayed there for over a month.

* * *

By March the Federal Government of James Scullin had plunged further into the abyss. In New South Wales the Labor premier, Jack Lang, was threatening to repudiate the interest due to London's bondholders on 1 April. On Friday, 6 March 1931, debate around the *Fiduciary Currency Bill* descended into chaos. Far from Canberra, a Tasmanian MP inaugurated a movement for secession of the State from Australia. In New South Wales huge rallies were taking place in Wagga Wagga, Narrandera and Cootamundra. The Riverina Movement, which had been formed by local businessmen and farmers, was serving an ultimatum to the Lang Government: unless its demands were met, it would hold a referendum in the Riverina for secession from New South Wales, and the creation of a new State.

Across the border in western Victoria on the same day, wild rumours were circulating about a communist insurrection that was meant to be sweeping down through the northern region of the State. Rumour had it that more than 600 unemployed men in a camp at Mildura had been turned by communist agitators in the Unemployed Workers' Movement. There was also confusion in Victorian country towns as rumours of Catholic treachery spread. In Donald, armed Catholics waited in a convent fearing an attack by the Protestants. Protestants on the other hand feared a Catholic attack – the local Catholic priest, Father Coghlan, had been seen driving communists into town. The local Catholic dentist, Dr Flanagan, had been seen delivering a carload of hand grenades packed in crates. It was only some time later revealed that the communists were actually a pair of swaggies, while the two crates delivered by the dentist contained nothing but tomatoes.

In Bert's hometown of Wedderburn two middle-aged men spent that Friday night hanging onto their rifles halfway up a gum tree near the town's water supply. It was a precaution just in case the rumours of a Catholic-Bolshevik plot turned out to be correct. They were told that they were part of a secret White Army of loyal citizens who stood in the path of the Bolshevik onslaught. It was rumoured that the chief of police himself, Thomas Blamey, was the leader of the White Army, and that it had been going for years. By 3 am only the crickets had turned up, so the two men in the tree literally gave up the ghost, and went back to one of the houses for a drink, and a bit of a laugh. The matter was soon forgotten in Wedderburn.

In New South Wales on the other hand, where Jack Lang's stand on repudiation was considered a matter of national life or death, things took a more dramatic and public turn. Eric Campbell, a thirty-eight year old lawyer and former officer in the AIF, formed the New Guard, which was to organise large public rallies at the Sydney Town Hall, divide Sydney into four geographic command zones, stock up on weapons, and throw the gauntlet down to the Lang Government.

* * *

It was in the midst of these real and imagined threats to the Australian way of life that Bert received a phone call from Ernest Turnbull late in March. An Australian Citizens' League had originated in Melbourne in February. This "All For Australia League", was a movement that had been started in Sydney and soon amalgamated with Melbourne's Australian Citizens' League. In Melbourne, Turnbull was elected president, Mr G. J. Coles and the managing director of Myers, Mr E. Lee Neil, were made vice-presidents, and Mr Staniforth Ricketson of the stock broking firm of JB Were and Sons was made honorary treasurer.

Turnbull explained that the All For Australia League was seeking to establish a branch in St Kilda, and wanted to book the Town Hall for a public meeting. The League was backing Joseph Lyons as the next prime minister. He stressed that at the next election there will be no reason for Australians to vote for parties along religious lines, because both candidates will be Catholics. The biggest issue, according to Turnbull, was whether the country wants a responsible government that will restore Australia's honour. The Town Hall was booked for 9 April and Bert agreed to chair the meeting.

* * *

Pompey was still deeply disturbed when he came out of the Alfred Hospital. A psychiatrist, Dr J.F. Williams, found him to be suffering from a "definite form of nervous disorder", but not to the extent of being clinically insane. Pompey had read about the collapse of Bert's company, and was troubled about the state of his own finances, which were actually quite sound. He talked negatively to his mother about how he wished he had never been born, and told his wife, Kate, he was done. Dr Williams arranged for Pompey to be admitted to a private hospital in Malvern, and visited him there at 7 pm on 22 March 1931.

To Dr Williams, Pompey appeared to be resigned to his stay, but he did grumble that he could not afford it. Williams assured him that was something he need not worry about. When he left Pompey that night Dr Williams ordered that he be confined to his bed, and watched regularly. The nurse checked him at 2 am and at 3 am, and reported him to be sleeping peacefully. When she returned at 4.25 am the bed was covered in blood, and a razor blade was found deeply embedded in his elbow. It was too late. The staff had not taken the obvious precaution of removing his shaving kit from his side.

At the funeral Bert reflected on the sad passing of this seemingly indestructible Australian hero of the Great War, who had character to spare. At last his troubles were over, a remarkable life had expired. The newspaper reported his death as being due to a "haemorrhage while undergoing treatment in a private hospital", but the news got out about what really happened. There had been many suicides in recent times. He was one more unrecorded casualty of the war, as Bert had previously noted in his speeches. It just took a little longer to get him.

* * *

7 pm, St Kilda Town Hall, 9 April 1931

Nearly one thousand people crammed into the St Kilda Town Hall to hear about the All For Australia League. The stage was dominated by two large flags, the Union Jack and the Australian flag; to have displayed the latter without the former would have been considered an act of disloyalty. In the centre above the stage was a sign that read, "National Integrity, Security and Service." The large crowd was welcomed by Bert, who received a rousing cheer. These were times when Australia needed a hero.

"The All For Australia League has been formed with the aim of stabilising the country's finances," Bert began. "The Victorian president of the movement, Mr Ernest Turnbull, who is well known to us as the former State President of the Returned Soldiers', Sailors' and Imperial League of Australia, has been heavily involved in the building of the Shrine. Please welcome Mr Turnbull!"

Applause greeted Turnbull as he approached the lectern and opened up his speech notes. "Ladies and Gentlemen," he said. "It is my pleasant duty to address you on behalf of the All For Australia League, which is playing a not insignificant part in the affairs of this nation.

"Australia is in a serious plight, and we are here today to sink our minor differences in an effort to help her out. You, who are Victorians, hardly know the full force of the disaster which has befallen New South Wales under the dictatorship of Mr Lang. Listen to this description from the Press of the condition of thousands of homeless people in Sydney.

Driven from their houses through inability to pay rent, many are building shacks on any available area of land which looks as though it belongs to the Crown. Others have taken possession of the famous Domain, and around the waterfront on the Wooloomooloo Bay side there have been built humpies which defy description...

Around the rugged foreshore of Middle Harbour and higher up the harbour to the Parramatta River and Lane Cove River every cave and every ledge of rock where there is a projecting rock overhead is occupied.

"In this land of limitless opportunity we have men searching vainly for the privilege of earning a living by work! We have 'illimitable natural resources' and 'untold natural wealth' – how glibly the phrases come from our tongues – and yet we have so mismanaged them that we have over 360,000 workers compulsorily unemployed.

"What we want is, first, the restoration of confidence. The first step in the restoration of confidence is to dethrone those politicians who stand for the dishonest policies of repudiation and inflation, and to put at the head of the Federal Government a man in whom the people of Australia and investors oversea have complete confidence. Such a man, we believe, we have found in Mr Lyons, and for the present the activities of the League are being concentrated on placing him in power.

"Let me take your minds back for a moment to the days of the Great War. We were obsessed then with the one idea of winning the war, just as we should be obsessed now with the one idea of saving our country from dishonour. We have not yet won that war. Some of the men who fought and suffered physical injuries and privation in the conflict are now suffering starvation. The war is not won until we have remedied that, and extricated our country from the current mess."

The next speaker introduced by Bert was Mr E. Lee Neil, the managing director of Myers, and after him the Reverend Jacob Danglow, and Councillors George Renfrey and Robert Morley spoke. At the conclusion of the meeting a motion was agreed to form a branch of the movement in St Kilda.

* * *

One of Vera's roles as Lady Mayoress was to take on the president's position at the St Kilda branch of the Homeopathic Hospital Auxiliary. While Bert had been busy helping with the organisation of the All For Australia League, she had organised a card party in the afternoon and evening at St Leonards Cafe on The Esplanade, which was held a few days later. With thirty-five tables sold by the ladies of St Kilda, it was another great success for Vera.

Saturday, 18 April was Betty's fourth birthday, which was a great thrill for her, because she was old enough to know she would get presents. Being so close to Easter, chocolate Easter eggs were available, and Vera bought some for her birthday. Both Vera and Bert were shocked to discover that their daughter hated chocolate! They could not understand it. "What child hates chocolate?" they asked.

* * *

The following Friday night, on Anzac Day eve, Bert met all his old comrades again at the 14th Battalion and 4th Brigade Association reunion dinner. Bert was now president of the Association, and while Lieutenant-Colonels "Ferdie" Wright, and Robert Rankine were present, Lieutenant-Colonel Dare was not. The next morning at 11 am, Bert in his capacity as Mayor, and in the presence of councillors and hundreds of onlookers, placed a wreath at the cenotaph located at the end of Fitzroy Street.

Not long afterwards, at a meeting of the council Bert replied to a letter from Mr G. Dunn of the Unemployed Workers Organisation of St Kilda. Despite repeated requests, Dunn had argued, the Mayor and Town Clerk had failed to produce a balance sheet of the carnival held around the previous Christmas. Dunn claimed that as a result sustenance accounts were being held up, and many of the unemployed hadn't worked for eight or nine months.

Bert was unequivocal. "An interim balance sheet *has* been prepared," he emphasised, "but an outstanding amount from a raffle has yet to come to hand. Once it has, a balance sheet will be submitted to the carnival committee. I emphatically deny that I, and the Town Clerk have given evasive replies regarding the balance sheet. It is apparent that Mr Dunn, who has been dismissed by the Council, and in the following week has been dismissed by the unemployed themselves, has directed the criticism against me."

Mr Harris, a deputised representative of the Unemployed Association who was in the gallery asked to be heard. "I would like it placed on the record," Harris said, "that the Unemployed Association of St Kilda disassociates itself from anything Mr Dunn has said. Our organisation has every confidence in the Mayor."

"Thank you," Bert said. "I would add that the council has made an application to the Ministry for £1000, which with a further £500 will be expended on labour in the municipality."

* * *

As the winter of 1931 approached, Bert's cough worsened. It got so bad that Bert finally went to see Dr Crowe at the Repatriation Commission, and recounted to him the troubles he had with influenza the previous year. During the examination he was coughing badly, and listed his various ailments that could be traced to his war service. He had frequent attacks of heart palpitation, and was experiencing shortness of breath at the slightest exertion. During the winter he felt an aching stiffness in his left shoulder from the bullet that had gone through it at Pozieres. On the other hand, the doctor found that the scar from his hernia operation was well healed. His eyes were not giving him any trouble from the operation he had in England to stitch up the rips caused by steel fragments, although he had slight conjunctivitis in both eyes.

Bert's general condition was assessed to be flabby, and his abdomen was found to be protuberant. However, the chest X-ray showed that there was no trace of TB. The doctor assessed that his physical condition as "20 per cent impairment" due to his gassing during the war, which would attract a part pension. He recommended a review be undertaken in a year's time.

* * *

10 am, St Kilda Town Hall, Saturday, 4 July 1931

In the depths of Melbourne's winter, Bert stood in front of several dozen volunteers outlining the plan of attack, as if it was a military operation. He had a map of the municipality on display, with sections of territory drawn out for his troops to cover. He was putting "SOS Week" into action – the plan to gather boots and clothing from the community and distribute them to the unemployed. The volunteers included Councillors George Cummings, Robert Taylor and Robert Morley, the St Kilda Scout Troop, around thirty unemployed men, and women from the Ladies Benevolent Fund.

A circular had been mailed to each householder in the community to advise that a collection would be made during the week. The Automobile Club had provided stickers for motor windscreens to advertise the drive, and twenty-five motor cars had been pledged by residents to help make the collections. Each of them would have two people on board to bring in the goods.

Councillors Cummings, Taylor and Morley worked every day during that week bringing the shoes and clothes in. In the end the drive collected large quantities of men's suits, and women's dresses; as well as hundreds of pairs of men's, women's and children's boots and shoes. When he made his report to the council at the 13 July meeting, Bert said that the great proportion of the clothes was in first class order, and practically 90 per cent was useful and serviceable.

"It has all been brought to the Town Hall for distribution to the unemployed," Bert said. "We had hoped that by last Wednesday the whole quantity of clothing that has been so generously donated by the residents would have been given out, but it proved too big a job for the men handling it. In fact, there still remains a portion of the municipality from Brighton Road to Elwood that has not been touched. One lady has even sent along a big parcel of *Weeties* breakfast food, and jams! The ratepayers have responded splendidly, and have appreciated the opportunity to assist their less fortunate fellow citizens."

* * *

In the middle of July, Newton Wanliss received a letter from Bert, together with a narrative that Newton had written about the Battle of Polygon Wood. Newton had finally convinced Bert that his biography should be written, and that the battle was a key part of it, since it was the pinnacle of Bert's success as a front-line commander. Newton thought there was a danger that his leadership abilities would not be recognised by future historians unless he set out the facts of the battle, and Bert's pivotal role in securing victory in the 14th Battalion's sector. By June he had written up a narrative of it, and posted it to Bert for his review.

23 Murchison St
St Kilda
18/7/31

My dear Mr Wanliss,
I suppose you must be wondering what has happened not having had my reply to your letter of the 20th. I put your letter aside the day it came with the object of replying to it by return but unfortunately it got mislaid & we could not find it anywhere. I was just at the point of writing to ask you to send another copy and the wife found it under a wardrobe.
I am returning herewith the narrative and after reading it through, I think it covers all that I could say. You will notice I have slightly altered your sketch of the Coys in the advance & that A & D Coys had practically the whole front between them. As a matter of true fact C & B Coys were really behind A & D during the greater part

of the advance. I am enclosing herewith rough sketch of the front line & Block Houses. The positions are of course approx. & from memory, but I think they are fairly accurate. The German Mortar fired from behind the first B. House from the group of houses from the position indicated by a circle. I think the gun crew were shot by Harold's men from A Co sector. You will notice that A & D again had the lion's share of the front line even after the objectives had been taken.

I was very interested to read your remarks re the Canadian Bn History. I will watch for your article in Reveille. Thank God my term of office as Mayor ends at the end of August & I am hoping that I will be getting another start in life then. I have every hope of getting started with the Shell Oil Co & that is the reason why I have not yet asked you to write to Gen. Monash.

I will be interested to hear of Joe Mackay. I understand he had a bad nervous breakdown. Well dear Mr Wanliss I have no more news so will close with kindest regards to yourself and Mrs Wanliss.

Your sincerely,

Bert Jacka

Bert is so courteous, just like Harold, Newton thought. His mention of Lieutenant Joe Mackay sparked Newton's interest. He was sure that Mackay had convalesced with Harold at the Wandsworth Hospital in London in 1916. Everything seemed to remind him of Harold.

* * *

A few days later Vera woke up in the middle of the night. She felt something was wrong as she couldn't hear the resonating sound of Bert's heavy breathing. She could not feel him beside her in the bed either, so she switched on her bedside lamp. The bedroom door was closed, but a dim light shone through from the other side of the house, and she could hear muffled coughing sounds. She slipped on her dressing-gown and walked across the corridor into the lounge, and found him poring over a number of handwritten

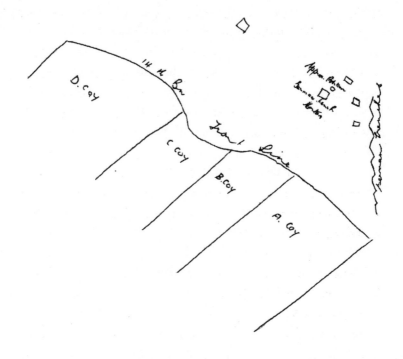

Map of 14th Battalion front-line at Polygon Wood,
26 September 1917

Drawn by Albert Jacka as part of a letter to N. Wanliss dated 18 July, 1931

Source: Source Records of the 14th Battalion by Newton Wanliss, *AWM MSS 143A*

pages on the dining room table. She glanced over at the clock on the wall, which said 2.30 am.

"What are you doing up at this late hour, Bert?"

"It's a report…"

"It's for the council, isn't it?" she sighed.

He nodded.

"Mummy, you needn't worry. I've just been offered a position with a new soap factory in Footscray."

"You didn't say anything."

"It hasn't been fully confirmed yet."

She exhaled after a short period of silence. "You can't keep going at this pace, Bert. You might have to leave the council for a while."

"I have no intention of doing that," he said, adamant.

"What about your health and your family?" Vera pleaded. "What about Betty, who has an absentee father? You spend more time with Alison Cummings than with your own family."

"Oh, that's ridiculous!"

"Oh? She's 'just a friend', I suppose?"

"She's a colleague in committees!"

"There's no such thing where a woman is concerned," Vera thought. She went back to bed without saying another word, but in her own mind Bert had broken their trust, which in her view was the most important part of a marriage.

*   *   *

At the last council meeting on 28 July, Bert presented his report on the progress of the boot repairs. For the week ended 6 July, ninety-five pairs of boots had been soled and heeled, and seventy pairs had been patched. Similar work had been undertaken during the following two weeks, which meant that the majority of unemployed men had comfortable footwear.

"We still have some more footwear left over from the SOS Drive, which are to be handed over to the unemployed. Very shortly," he said, "it might be necessary to apply to the council for a further grant. I assure councillors that all the money voted so far has been wisely spent."

*   *   *

Early in August, Bert's mother came to Melbourne and stayed with her youngest daughter, Bessie Dowrick, who, with her husband, had bought a house in Bealiba Road, Caulfield East. She left Nathaniel to fend for himself at their six-roomed house in Wedderburn, and it turned out to be near fatal. At 3 am on

Tuesday 11 August, Nathaniel was sleeping in the house when it caught fire and burnt down completely. Thankfully Nathaniel escaped almost unscathed, but when he tried to save the trunk in the bedroom he singed his hair and moustache. The trunk, which contained all of Bert's letters from the war and other Jacka family memorabilia, was destroyed. It was not all that was to be lost around this time.

* * *

8 pm, Leonard's Café, The Esplanade, St Kilda, 1 September 1931

Bert and Vera's terms as Mayor and Lady Mayoress of St Kilda expired at the end of August, and by this time Vera had made it clear that she was leaving. The St Kilda Younger Set got in touch with her, as they wanted to show their appreciation for the support she had given their organisation during her term of office. They asked her what present she would prefer, and she told them she needed money, as she would be leaving soon to make her home in the country.

The evening was organised as an informal party with games, competitions and dancing. The newly elected Mayor, Councillor Moroney and Mrs Moroney were there, as was Bert, who had to act a part. The evening was organised by the Younger Set Committee's president, Miss Yvonne Levin, and secretary Mr Leon Silberman. The girls who made their debut at the Younger Set's first ball in the St Kilda Town Hall presented Vera with a handbag, and the members of the Younger Set presented her with a cheque.

* * *

On 12 September Bert attended the opening of the new Anglo Dominion Soaps Factory in Footscray, which was a joint venture between Australian Soaps Limited of Sydney, and William Angliss

& Co. The factory was opened by Councillor E. Hanmer, the Mayor of Footscray, who knew Bert through municipal circles. The Minister for Trade and Customs, Mr Forde, was on hand too, as this was exactly the kind of import substituting business the government liked to see. At peak capacity the factory could churn out a hundred tons of laundry and toilet soap a week. Actual production was still a couple of weeks away, however.

Bert was grateful for the opportunity to start as a commercial traveller with the organisation, seeing it as a stepping-stone to greater things in the William Angliss empire. Bert was optimistic that once he had proven himself and understood the business well, he would be promoted. He had obvious management and leadership skills that could be well utilised by the vast William Angliss organisation.

One day Vera brought Betty out to see her father leave for work and he quickly glanced back at them, waving as he accelerated down the road.

"All gone Daddy," Betty said, as he drove off.

When he returned home that afternoon, they had left.

MARS REJOICES

4.30 pm, The Venetian Court, Hotel Australia,
Thursday, 1 October 1931

The Hotel Australia was situated on "the Block", in Collins
Street, between Elizabeth and Swanston streets. With a stately
entrance that was complemented by a warm and luxurious
interior, the hotel enjoyed a strong reputation for delectable
cuisine, delicious meals and efficient service. The set minimum
serve for dinner was 3 shillings, and 2/6 for lunch, but upstairs
in the Venetian Court, light refreshments were served from
one shilling. It was at the Venetian Court, that Vera found
employment as hostess, and today she was having a major
function – the parade of new season's lingerie, rest suits and
ensembles cut on the sailor styles that were coming into vogue.
In addition they were presenting the new season's Klingtite
swimming suits by L. & E. Marks, and Saulwick Pty Ltd in
conjunction with Australian Knitting Mills.

As the models walked out onto the floor, the female compere
of the parade spoke to the ladies with a voice that carried through
the room without the aid of a microphone.

"These charming girls," she announced, "are demonstrating for
you the principle of 'contour alignment' upon which the Klingtite
suits are designed. By the scientific use of motifs, figure defects
are disguised. Remember ladies, every Klingtite model is made

in a range of colours to suit blondes, brunettes and Titians…"
Of course the "charming girls" had no "figure defects".

The ladies seated around the floor at tables were showing interest in the exclusive Kayser creation known as Nite-Jamas, which were designed to give a pair of pyjamas the effect of a nightdress. While the compere spoke, the waitresses circled around the tables delivering drinks and nibbles. Bert suddenly entered the room straight from work, scanned the many women's faces, and picked Vera out very quickly. He made his way towards her. She had changed her hairstyle from the conservative soft curls that she used to wear as the Lady Mayoress, and now had the fashionable Eton crop, made famous by the American actress Louise Brooks. To Bert she looked slimmer and younger than before. Vera saw him coming. His face was flushed with discomfort.

"I've got to speak to you," he demanded, as she glanced hesitantly from side to side.

"Come with me," she whispered, leading him out into a corridor via a side exit door before speaking again. "What are you doing here?" she said once they were alone.

"I want you to come home," he said.

"Yes, we can wait for you there, can't we?" she said sarcastically. "I can't do it. Life is slipping by."

"It won't *be* like that."

"Yes it *will* Bert," she said, tears welling up. "Let me ask you one simple question. Are you prepared to resign from the council and show more affection and commitment to your family?" It stopped him cold, and he thought about it for a few seconds before responding.

"I can't resign just now! I'm still chairing committees… I'd be letting everybody down." His heart raced uncontrollably as he said it.

"You don't seem to have any difficulty letting Betty and me down."

"Why in heaven's name can't you wait until the end of my term, when I can stand down honourably?"

"Because I know you won't. They'll convince you to keep going, and it will all be the same again."

"You don't know that."

"I know *you*, and that's what you'll do. I just know it." Just as she said it the compere came through the door.

"Oh!" she cried, startled to find Vera with a strange man in the corridor, and looking obviously distressed. "The first segment of the parade has concluded," she said uncomfortably. "People are asking for you."

"Ahhm...Yes...Thank you," Vera said, trying to retain her composure. "I'll be there in half a minute."

"Are you getting enough sleep?" she asked, noticing the bags under his eyes. He didn't reply. "I... I have to go now," she said. There was a part of her that wanted to come back to him, but she knew there was no use.

"Give my love to Betty, will you?" he said forlornly. She stopped, and looked him straight in the face as tears welled up again.

"You showed me no affection Bert," she said as she walked off.

* * *

Bert sold the house at 23 Murchison Street and considered himself lucky to have come out of it without owing the bank any money. He rented a house at 60 Chaucer Street, on the corner of Blessington Street, for 60 shillings a week. It sat opposite a park, and was only two streets away from the beach. From the front window he could see the Big Dipper ride at Luna Park, only a block away on the right. Young riders in search of thrills would be winched up to a commanding height, with great views out over the bay, and then, hanging onto their rail car for dear life, would suddenly plunge back to earth down a precipitous slope. At night, the screams of teenagers and courting young adults could be heard across the tin, slate and terracotta rooftops of the neighbourhood.

Another St Kilda councillor, George Renfrey, lived only two doors down from Bert at 64 Chaucer Street. But not everyone in the neighbourhood was so community minded. A few doors along from Bert's place in Chaucer Street, some events had recently taken place that were worthy of a Canterbury Tale.

On 6 August, Harold Percival Pleydell, aged forty, had been shot twice through the chest by his eighteen-year-old nephew, Walter Herbert Nixon, who lived in a sleep-out in the backyard. St Kilda Market stallholders saw the lad run around to Acland Street, and mount a motorbike that had a flat tyre. He then wheeled the motorbike around into Barkly Street and attempted to inflate the tyre at Nathan's Motors, but it had a puncture and kept deflating, so he ran around to another service station less than 100 yards from the scene of the crime, where he rang a friend to ask if he could borrow his car. He was still on the phone when police from the St Kilda bicycle patrol arrested him, and found a pistol in his pocket with two spent cartridges in its chamber. Pleydell was a thief, the police later discovered, as under his bed were a set of golf clubs and trophies that had recently been stolen from the East St Kilda house of the Victorian amateur champion, Mick Ryan. The only reason Bert heard about it was that the men at the St Kilda Soldiers' and Sailors' Club were describing it as the most botched getaway in criminal history.

On 8 October, Sir John Monash died of heart disease and pneumonia at the age of sixty-six. Three hundred thousand mourners lined the streets, and at the Brighton Cemetery the Reverend Jacob Danglow delivered his eloquent tribute, declaring that "a prince and a great man has fallen". Australia's legends of the Great War were falling, one by one.

* * *

The annual meeting of the St Kilda branch of the Homoeopathic Hospital Auxiliary was held at the Wentworth tearooms, Collins Street, on Friday, 16 October with a card party and *café chantant*.

The new mayor, Councillor Moroney presided, and on behalf of the committee presented Vera, as the retiring president, with an inscribed fountain pen. Posies were presented to the president of the central auxiliary, Mrs Carnegie, Mrs Moroney and Vera. As was the custom, the new Lady Mayoress, Mrs Moroney, was elected president, while Vera, Mrs Susan Futcher, and Miss F. Jenkins were elected as vice-presidents. Bert was still upset from the last meeting he had with Vera, and couldn't take time off as the firm was preparing for production and needed orders. Both Vera and Mrs Futcher could be at this function together because Vera had placed Betty at the Catholic convent of Notre Dame Sion at Box Hill, where she started school early and would have to learn to speak French at every meal time.

* * *

3 pm, Collins Street, Saturday, 24 October 1931

It was a glorious sunny afternoon, and the newly crowned Queen of Flowers, blonde Miss Mervyn Pitt, waved graciously to the crowds from her flower encrusted throne on a lorry drawn by four white horses. Planes flying overhead dropped confetti and flower petals on the city as Collins Street was transformed into a war zone. People who had bought bags of flower petals in aid of the Lord Mayor's Hospital Appeal were pelting each other in a frenzy of laughter. The Queen's float, which had been prepared by the Royal Horticultural Society then crossed the Prince's Bridge, and was carried along the St Kilda Road, where people cheered from the balconies of their mansions. In the Queen's wake followed kilted pipers, tableaux and floats displaying the products of firms such as Electrolux, Bryant and May and Robur Tea.

Upon her arrival at Alfred Square, St Kilda, the Queen declared that Melbourne's winter had ended, and that Luna Park was now open for the summer session. She forgot to declare an end to the Great Depression, but on this day almost everyone forgot the troubled times the country was passing through. Miss Pitt was greeted at the Square by the new Mayor of St Kilda, and other councillors, including Bert. The St Kilda Beach Festival was opened and would continue for another week.

Soon afterwards, down on the Lower Esplanade, the battle of petals that had begun in Collins Street was in full swing again. Members of the Royal Melbourne Yacht Club, dressed as pirates, had raided the petal ammunition dumps of their rival community clubs and were showering everyone with them. The foreshore was decorated in thousands of flags and bunting, and many people were in fancy dress. Squeakers, funny noses and masks were purchased at the stalls on the Esplanade as the Hawthorn Banjo Club hammered out tunes on the piazza in front of the Baths.

Bert came home early that night, as he was exhausted and not feeling well. He had not eaten a thing all day. Having just poured himself a glass of cold milk from the ice-box, he heard muffled explosions outside. Taking the glass of milk with him, he went out onto the front porch overlooking the park, and took a sip as he watched. It was the fireworks display, which was being launched from boats moored in the bay. As the rockets went up and colourful stars exploded and fell from the sky, it immediately brought back memories of the war, when rockets had been used to call for a supporting artillery barrage. On his right he could see the Big Dipper and Scenic Railway rides, as well as the arabesque domes of Luna Park that were etched against the dark sky in thousands of bright lights. Young boys and girls were walking around enjoying their Coney Island "crispettes".

Bert stood there thinking, as the fireworks continued to explode in the sky. He felt so tired. He stared into space against the background of those explosions, and reflected on the sense of loss he had felt that day watching families with young children having a wonderful time. He thought about what Vera had told him on their first date about her father, who had held back on enjoying the carousel at St Kilda. Her father had not taken full advantage of those precious moments with his "Rose" – his pride and joy. Bert felt sorry that he had not spent more time with Vera and Betty. "Perhaps if I had tried harder on the home front," he thought, "this would not have happened? Am I going to miss my times with Betty?"

* * *

The lights flickered across Bert's face as he watched the fireworks exploding in brightly coloured starbursts over Port Phillip Bay. The starbursts reflected in the corneas of his eyes, and the sounds carried him back to that early morning at Gallipoli as the shrapnel burst over Courtney's Post, and 40,000 Turks bravely, insanely, charged the Australian line. Suddenly, Bert was transported back to the trenches to face them.

* * *

"Allah! Allah! Allah!" screamed the Turks, as a line of blazing muzzle flashes from Australian rifles and machineguns were illuminated in the night against the backdrop of bugles, bands and general mayhem.

"Bombs!"

"Look out!"

Eight grenades went off with a ferocious *Kabam-bam-bam-bam!* in the next bay, shaking the earthen and sandbagged walls around Bert with ferocious power. He was half deafened by it. Looking over to the right, he saw a dark cloud of dust rolling down the communication trench, with a couple of wounded diggers bursting through it as they ran back towards the reserve trench. Lieutenant Boyle was just coming up to the front line to check the state of the ammunition, and passed the wounded diggers on his way to corner of the front trench. Fearing the worst, he quickly glanced around the corner.

Bang! A Turk had shot him through the ear, spraying blood over the trench wall.

"They've got me!" Boyle screamed as he ran back down the communication trench holding his head. "Turks are in the trenches!"

But Bert didn't run. He moved in under the cover of the haze of dust and took up a position behind a sandbagged traverse. He watched as Lieutenant Hamilton, the tall young "Duntrooner" who had received the King's Colour on the St Kilda foreshore came running up the communication trench towards him firing his automatic pistol, trading shots with more Turks who were shooting back at him from above the parapet. Hamilton brought down two of them.

Then *Bang!* A Turkish bullet smashed into Hamilton's head, instantly knocking him to the ground. Jacka kept firing down the trench at the Turks, but he couldn't get a clear shot as they had taken cover behind a series of traverses. *If they find out I'm alone… they'll rush me*, he thought, so he fired another couple of bullets in rapid succession to make it look like he wasn't.

"Officer needed on the right!" had been called, and in response Major Rankine sent Lieutenant Keith Crabbe up to the front line. He crept forward cautiously with his service revolver drawn. When he reached Hamilton he felt for a pulse. There was no pulse, although Hamilton's automatic was still in his hand. Crabbe looked over at Bert and began to walk towards him. Bert pointed with his finger towards the Turks.

"What's the matter?" asked Crabbe.

"Back out!" Jacka yelled. "Turks in here!" Crabbe immediately shuffled back against the trench wall. He thought about the situation for a few seconds.

"Would you charge the Turks if you had some men to back you up?" he asked.

"Yes," Jacka answered.

Crabbe backed off down the communication trench. Just past the junction with the reserve trench he met a number of his A Company men who had been sent up to help hold the line.

"I need volunteers to back Jacka up and charge the Turks," he announced. The boys from Bendigo who knew Jacka were the first to raise their hands.

"I'll do it," said Lance-Corporal Bill Howard.

"You can count on me," said Private Frank Poliness.

"Me too," said Lance-Corporal Steve DeAraugo.

Crabbe needed to be sure.

"Will you charge?" he asked. "It's a tough job. Will you back Jacka up?"

"It's sink or swim," Poliness reaffirmed.

The men all fixed bayonets in preparation for the charge. From his position behind the traverse Bert watched them come up the communications trench until they were just across from him. Howard and Bickley were closest to the corner of the trench. Howard came out first and was met with a volley of bullets just as surely as if he had been lined up by a firing squad. Three bullets thudded into him, and he dropped like a stone. Poliness and DeAraugo stopped in their tracks.

Bert's eyes flashed down at Bill Howard's body. *Poor old Bill. This is going nowhere!* he thought. He peered cautiously around the traverse and could just see a Turk's rifle aimed at the opening to the communications trench, waiting for the next attacker, but not anticipating a jumper from his side of the trench. It was an opportunity that had to be taken.

Bert jumped across Howard's body, as a stream of bullets zapped behind his back, and drilled into the corner of the trench wall. *Phut... phut... phut.* The Turks hadn't counted on that move.

DeAraugo, Poliness and Crabbe took Howard by the legs, and pulled his body into the safety of the communications trench. Dislodging these Turks was not going to be easy. Crabbe thought that they should attack the Turks from both ends of the trench at the same time. He ordered another digger, McNally to get some bombs from Major Rankine at the Company Headquarters down the track.

"I'll try the other end," Bert said.

"Righto...."

Before Crabbe finished giving his instructions, Jacka had run off down the reserve trench, and was soon looking down the parallel communications trench. At the end of it he could see a short sap, jutting out into No-Man's Land, where two AIF machineguns were located. A key part of the 14th Battalion's defence of Courtney's Post, they rattled away oblivious to the danger of the Turkish party that was only a few yards away from them. Bert could see it. All the Turks needed to do was come around that corner, and shoot the machinegunners in the back. That would cut the Battalion's firepower in half, and open the door to an avalanche of Turks. They would get the Post in minutes.

Jacka waited for the bombs. He pulled the bolt of his .303 back, and slammed it forward, arming the chamber with a bullet. *Crabbe said there would be bombs. Where are the bombs?* He gripped the stock of his rifle in anticipation, while his feet rocked back and forth, like a sprinter taking up his starting position for the Stawell Gift. The machineguns kept up a steady rate of fire, and the noise of everything happening at once was creating an atmosphere of surreal drama and confusion. Death floated in the air, and waited at every turn for its victim. *The machineguns are exposed. When's Johnny Turk going to wake up to this?*

Kabam-bam! The bomb thrown by McNally exploded with a gut-wrenching noise just above the trench line near the Turkish held section of trench – throwing dirt and debris high into the air. The force of it jerked Jacka into action, like a starter's gun, and he took off down the trench at full speed, holding his rifle out in front of him. In seconds he crossed the main trench behind the machinegun post, and leapt up onto the parapet and out into No-Man's Land. Instinct guided him. A few more steps up along the parapet, and he jumped back into the murky section of trench occupied by the Turks – all so fast that the dust had not yet settled from the explosion.

As soon as his feet touched the ground he fired into the mass of Turks ahead of him, *re-load – fire! re-load – fire! re-load – fire!* At point blank range he couldn't miss. The element of surprise that he created by jumping in from the rear had created a panic, and the Turks were scrambling to get away. One by one they fell. In around 10 seconds five of them had fallen. Then a Turk swung around, and lunged at Jacka with his bayonet. There was no time to re-load – instinct took over again. Jacka deflected the blade, kicked him down to the ground and dug the blade into his chest, slicing straight through. He twisted the blade and yanked it out in regulation style, just as the drill sergeant had ordered: "into the Turk… and twist!" The blade slipped out quickly, covered in blood.

Two more shots rang out nearby. It was Poliness, who had just downed two Turks trying to escape over the parapet above. Their bodies rolled away into No-Man's Land. Another Turk who had been planning to escape saw them get shot, and turned around to meet Jacka, but he jumped at the Turk with lightning speed, and thrust his bayonet through him. It was all over in a matter of less than 20 seconds.

His face was flushed, and he was exhausted by the ordeal. When Crabbe and the others came around the corner of the trench, Jacka was standing among a pile of Australian and Turkish bodies. He was leaning back against the trench wall, and had just put an unlighted cigarette into his mouth.

"Well… I managed to get the beggars… sir," he told Crabbe.

* * *

In spite of his health and domestic issues, Bert kept his head down and continued working at a feverish pace as a commercial traveller by day, and by night, and during weekends, as a St Kilda councillor. Launching a new soap brand into the market presented a challenge, which gave Bert ample opportunity to try out his persuasive skills on shop owners.

On 3 November he gave notice that he would move at the next meeting that mixed bathing should be permitted in the women's section of the new St Kilda Baths during restricted hours that were to be decided by the council. It was another one of the progressive ideas that Burnett Gray had tried to carry through prior to the war. Now that the war had shaken things up, and women's hemlines had risen precariously anyway, it was felt that society should take the plunge together, so to speak. The 16 November meeting was important because this and two other potentially divisive social issues were to be decided. They were whether public amusement could continue beyond midnight, and whether tennis could be played at council courts on Sunday.

On social issues there were two groups among the councillors: the social liberals, who included the three AIF men (Jacka, Gray and Unsworth); and the social conservatives. The existing regulation required that halls be closed at half past eleven on weeknights, and quarter to twelve on Saturday night, except when special permission was granted. Councillor Robert Morley opposed going beyond midnight, on the grounds that St Kilda was essentially a residential area. "I do not wish it to become the Paris of the south," he said. Councillor O'Donnell spoke in support, declaring: "I am not in favour of late hours. 11 o'clock is late enough!" which caused the gallery to erupt into laughter.

As Bert came late again, only eleven councillors voted on the first issue, but the late night motion was carried by six to five. The Mayor's casting vote wasn't required as the otherwise socially conservative Councillor Levi voted with the social liberals (who had been to Paris). The council had previously decided to rescind all motions prohibiting tennis on municipal courts on Sundays. As a result a deputation representing 13 Protestant churches in St Kilda argued that Sunday tennis would mean dishonouring God, as it would lure people away from church. Councillor Morley could see how the vote was going to fall, and maintained that the Mayor's casting vote should be in favour of retaining the existing order.

He was supported by Councillor Levi, and Councillor Taylor, who said he saw this vote as so important he had returned from New South Wales just to vote on it. As expected, the vote was tied, and since the Mayor had the casting vote, the motion to stop Sunday tennis was negatived.

Shortly before midnight, the council began debating Bert's motion that mixed bathing be permitted in the women's section of the St Kilda baths during restricted hours. Councillors who opposed the motion warned that the lessees of open sea baths would be seriously affected by the motion. Immediately a councillor gave notice that he would move at the next meeting that the decision be rescinded.

It was around 2 am in the morning before Bert got to sleep, and he had difficulty rising for work the next morning. He was wheezing and coughing all night again, only this time he was alone. When he was shaving in the morning he suffered another coughing attack, and coughed blood into the hand basin. After steadying himself, he turned the tap on and let the water wash it down the sink.

* * *

On 7 December Bert's plans for an aquatic carnival on the night of the federal election were announced to the media. The federal election was to be held in less than two week's time on Sunday, 19 December. Tensions on the political front remained high, as the United Australia Party of Joseph Lyons challenged James Scullin's Labor Government, which had been battered by just over two years of depression economics.

The Labor Government was not as battered as the Toorak house of Sir Stanley Argyle, the Leader of the Opposition in the State Parliament, which sustained a bomb blast a month earlier, or the house of Senior Detective H.S. Dunn, whose house in Somers Street, St Kilda was badly damaged by a bomb on the morning of 8 December. Senior Detective Dunn was the one who was struck on the head by communist demonstrators outside Parliament House, and was responsible for the raids on the Communist Party headquarters, and associated arrests. The bomb tore a large hole in the cement floor on the veranda, knocked down the glass front door and ripped off large sections of plaster in the main entry hall. Fortunately, Dunn and his entire family were sleeping together in a single room at the back of the house.

During his speech to the Constitutional Club only a day earlier the Prime Minister, Mr Scullin, had spoken of a need to "combat communism in the country, and the way to do it is to make conditions which cannot breed it. When you have 300,000 people existing on a pittance, you find the feeling that anything is better, and nothing could be worse. These people are wrong both in their analysis and judgment, but desperate times breed desperate remedies."

* * *

8.30 pm, St Kilda Town Hall, Council Chamber, Monday, 14 December 1931

This was the last council meeting before Christmas, and in that spirit it had none of the divisiveness of the previous meeting, which had split the council on social issues. Bert was holding to the promise he made to himself a year earlier – that the families of the unemployed in St Kilda would not miss out on a decent Christmas dinner.

"In conclusion," he said at the end of his report, "I would like to remind councillors of the Carnival to raise funds for the unemployed Christmas dinner, which is to be held this coming Saturday evening. The number of entries to the various competitions has been very encouraging, and an attractive program is promised."

"Thank you for that reminder Councillor Jacka," the Mayor said. "I am sure all councillors will see to it that they vote early, so that they and their families may be in attendance. That concludes tonight's agenda, bar one item… I now have the pleasant duty to present an illuminated address to Councillor Jacka in recognition of his good services as the outgoing Mayor of this municipality." The illuminated address contained copies of the 14th Battalion Colours, and a photograph of the new baths construction in progress.

"Councillor Jacka has ably upheld the tradition of the city during his term in office," Councillor Moroney continued as he made the presentation to Bert. "He has occupied the mayoral chair during a very stressful time, and has acquitted himself with credit. In addition to the anxieties and worries inseparable from the erection of such a fine building as the new baths, in which Councillor Jacka displayed tact and resourcefulness, the City of St Kilda, like every other suburb of Melbourne, has been faced with the problem of helping the needy unemployed, and in this regard Councillor Jacka has proved himself quite equal to the occasion, and has earned the goodwill of this fine body of men.

"I desire to couple the name of Mrs Jacka, the ex-Lady Mayoress, with all that has been accomplished during Councillor Jacka's term of office. This lady has been a bulwark to Councillor Jacka, and I would ask Councillor Jacka to convey to Mrs Jacka the collective thanks of the councillors and officers for the fine work she has accomplished during the period." It struck at Bert's soul to hear that reference to Vera's work as Lady Mayoress. It was true that she had put her heart into the role, and had charmed many of the councillors and constituents with her bubbly personality. Unfortunately, the experience had pushed their personal relationship beyond the brink. The Mayor's comments were received with a hearty applause by the councillors and Bert rose to respond.

"Thank you, Your Worship," he said, slightly bowing his head in recognition. Burnett Gray was struck with how washed out Bert looked. He seemed to be actually grimacing with pain as he spoke. For his part Bert was saddened by the fact that Vera was not there to hear these words of recognition for the work she had put into the community, but the councillors knew full well the unfortunate domestic situation now faced by Bert.

"Mrs Jacka and I thank you for your flattering remarks," Bert responded, "and to all councillors for your hearty approval. In the year 1914 I had little dreamed that after fighting in the World War, I would return to St Kilda and in due course be elevated to the position of Mayor. My term as Mayor has been an experience for me, and I trust that I have carried out the duties appertaining to the office to the satisfaction of the council and ratepayers. Of Mrs Jacka I can say that she has proffered great assistance to me during my period as Mayor, but I can truly say the position was too big for even the two of us!" God how he wished it was still the two of them, he thought, while the councillors and the gallery laughed, many unaware of the sad irony of those words.

"I thank the councillors and their wives, and the officers of the council for their whole-hearted assistance; and I thank also the public, who have helped me considerably on many occasions. I will conclude now, by thanking the Mayor and the councillors for this handsome present, and assure all of you that both Mrs Jacka and I will always treasure it."

All councillors and the whole gallery then erupted in a standing ovation for the Gallipoli legend, who had always been in the front ranks when the stuff was falling, and never shirked his responsibilities to the community and the underprivileged in the role of Mayor. As Burnett Gray listened, he was sad to see Bert was still maintaining the public façade that he and Vera were together. *Ever the optimist*, he thought.

Councillor Renfrey responded to the Mayor's Season's Greeting to councillors and staff, and the Mayor then invited councillors, officers and the Press representatives to his office for a "social glass".

* * *

The next morning Bert could hardly rise from his bed. His temperature sky-rocketed, and he barely made it through the day at work. He was running a fever. He had hardly slept at all on Tuesday night, and his eyes hurt. On Wednesday morning he telephoned Anglo Dominion Soap in Footscray to say that he couldn't come to work, and would be visiting the doctor at the Caulfield Military Repatriation Hospital.

The hospital sat behind a wall of massive pine trees along Kooyong Road, and behind them was a row of grey-green plane trees, heavy with bright new season's leaves. The hospital consisted of a grand old main building, with many single level "temporary" ward blocks, very similar to the blocks that were constructed around London's Wandsworth Hospital, where Bert spent times convalescing between 1916 and 1918. The Caulfield wards were set among lawns and gravel paths, with overstuffed flowerbeds that seemed to be growing over them. The asbestos sheets used to construct the low-rise wards were considered the last word in efficient insulation. Inside the complex was like a maze of long corridors, and connecting covered pathways, which left you totally confused unless you had been there often.

There were men in those wards who had been convalescing there since the end of the war, and would never come out. Blind or limbless, they were rolled out once a year to the Anzac Day marches through the city, except that they were driven at the back of the parade. In some ways, they were now better off than many of their "healthy" ex-digger mates who were out of work. Hundreds of them had strung hessian sheets up against the railway fence that ran down Wellington Parade from the city to Jolimont. That was the only roof they had over *their* heads.

After waiting for over an hour he was finally seen by Dr Reuben Rosenfield. A short man of Jewish religion who was Russian born, he had become a naturalised Australian citizen before the turn of the century, and by 1909 was a Medical Officer of Cadets with the rank of captain. He volunteered for service in 1915 and served with the AIF in the Middle East, where he attained the rank of major, and at the Sutton Veny camp in England.

Dr Rosenfield was an oculist, and during a retinal examination found white haemorrhages and white patches in Bert's eyes. He also found very heavy albumen, and much blood in his urine. On testing Bert's blood pressure he found it to be markedly elevated at 220/150, which suggested extreme hypertension, so he referred him to his colleague, Dr Montefiore Silberberg. In line with accepted medical practice of the day, Dr Rosenfield withheld the actual blood pressure reading, as it was felt that too much information would itself accentuate the hypertension. Dr Silberberg was a graduate of the University of Melbourne, who served as a captain in the AIF in the Middle East, but had suffered enteritis, appendicitis, and an irritable heart, which cut short his service.

On listening to Bert's chest, Dr Silberberg found that a gallop rhythm was present in his heart rate. Through his stethoscope he could hear a very accentuated blurred aortic second sound, and thought it was a possible aortic dilation. Bert explained that recently he was feeling exhausted with the least exertion. He had seen enough, and after Bert had dressed again, he told him the result of his examination.

"It's not good news, Captain Jacka," Dr Silberberg began. "You are suffering from nephritis, in combination with cardiovascular degeneration."

"What is it exactly?"

"…It's an inflammation of the kidneys. You also have high blood pressure, which is affecting your eyes."

"What can be done for it?"

"You must be admitted to hospital as soon as possible," Dr Silberberg replied. "The only thing for you now is rest in bed, and vigorous treatment. I'll make arrangements for you immediately."

"Immediately?"

"Yes. I will send my report through to the Administration Office today… I should think you could be admitted by Friday. You are on a 20 per cent pension aren't you, Captain?"

"Yes, it's 17 shillings a fortnight for me and 5/6 for my wife. My rental is 60 shillings a week. How will I pay it when I'm in hospital?"

"Don't be concerned about the rental. You can fill out an application for payment of sustenance allowance once you have been admitted, and your degree of debility has been appropriately adjusted. You should not go back to work tomorrow."

"Can I report on Saturday morning instead?" Bert asked, lapsing into military speak.

"I wouldn't recommend it…"

"There are two reasons for my request doctor," Bert explained. "I have an important committee meeting at the Town Hall on Friday evening. We will be making the final arrangements for the beach carnival to be held on Saturday. And secondly, I should like to vote on Saturday morning prior to going in."

"I still wouldn't recommend it, Captain," the doctor argued. "You need complete rest in hospital."

"I can rest at home on Friday, prior to the meeting," Bert pressed, and in his usual convincing manner was able to persuade Dr Silberberg to allow him to report on Saturday morning.

* * *

St Kilda Town Hall, Friday, 18 December 1931

Not long after the meeting at the Town Hall had begun, Bert began to feel severe discomfort. Perspiration trickled down his temples, causing him to pull a handkerchief from his pocket several times to soak it up. The back of his neck was sticking to his shirt collar, and he thought of unbuttoning his shirt and removing his tie, but felt he couldn't in the circumstances. He could hardly move, and it was getting worse by the minute. He told the committee he was pleased to see the proposal to hold an aquatic carnival at the new ladies' baths had been taken up with such enthusiasm. He also announced that he would not be there for the actual carnival, which was to commence at 8 pm, as he had arranged to be admitted to the Caulfield Repatriation Hospital after casting his vote in the morning.

In addition to Bert, the committee comprised Mr A. P. Newey, Honorary Secretary, the Town Clerk, Mr Frederick Chamberlin, Treasurer, and Mr Jack Irvine, Publicity Officer. Since 1924 Jack had been the Secretary of St Kilda Football Club. By trade he was a tailor who ran his business (and the club) from his house at 345 High Street, St Kilda. He described the advertising campaign for the carnival that had been run throughout Melbourne, but particularly in St Kilda. He had with him a copy of that day's *St Kilda News*, where he had placed a half page advertisement for the carnival.

"As you can all see," Jack said, opening up the newspaper and spreading it on the meeting table, "we have featured the speedboat racing, and the fact that the progress of the election results will be broadcast to those present."

"It could turn into an election party for some," Chamberlin added.

"And an election wake for others," Jack replied. "There's no doubt that Jimmy Skullin's gone, is there?"

Chamberlin wore a worried expression. "Are you all right, Captain Jacka?" he asked thoughtfully. He had been following Bert's obvious discomfort throughout the meeting, and felt he had to say something.

"It's all right," he said, attempting a smille. "I'm going into the hospital tomorrow morning."

"You don't look well," said Jack, seeing that he was obviously short of breath. "Perhaps you should go to the hospital now."

"That's a splendid idea," Chamberlin agreed. "I'll run you down to Kooyong Road myself," he said to Bert.

"I'm not that ill," Bert emphasised. He had been through much worse in the war he thought. His head felt like it was going to explode, and his pulse was racing. Chamberlin persisted, and convinced Bert that the meeting should be brought to an early close, as all was in order, but Bert should go to the hospital immediately. Even Bert could see there was no point going home now; he should get to that hospital in a hurry.

"Thank you gentlemen," he said, bidding the committee members goodnight, and thanked them for their work. Even walking out of the Town Hall to his car was exhausting. He eased himself onto the seat, and swung the car out into Carlisle Street.

* * *

Ward 5, Caulfield Military Repatriation Hospital, 20 December 1931

When Vera and Betty walked into Bert's ward on Sunday afternoon it was already teeming with family members, and there were also visitors seeing other patients. Elizabeth and Nathaniel had come with Bessie and Harold Dowrick. Since the house in Wedderburn burnt down they had collected the insurance money and now lived in a house just a few doors up the street from Bessie and Harold. Bert's brothers Sid and Bill were there with their wives and children, and when Vera and Betty walked in everyone went quiet, staring at them flatly across the shiny dark brown linoleum floor. "What is *she* doing here?" some thought with indignation when they first saw Vera come through the door. She had deserted him in his hour of need. They were convinced that her disloyalty had contributed to the rapid deterioration of his health. As she approached the bed Betty felt the weight of all eyes upon her, and thought the bed was so high she wouldn't be able to reach her father.

"There's my little girl!" Bert said as cheerfully as he could. "Now give Daddy a big kiss." Vera lifted Betty up so she could kiss her father.

"It's lovely to see you here, Mummy," he said.

"Oh, Bert," Vera said, fighting back tears. It was what she had always suspected would happen only it happened much sooner than she had thought.

"Now, now, there's no need for that," he said, taking her hand, "I'm still here."

Bill's daughter, eight-year-old Josephine wondered to herself what her Uncle Bert saw in Vera. "That Eton Crop hairstyle makes her look so ugly," she thought. The discussion that followed was rather stiff and formal.

As the adults talked, young Josephine was holding onto a penny that her uncle had given her "for being a good girl". She was already thinking about what she would spend it on. In a discussion on the side Nathaniel and Bill expressed their disappointment that Scullin had been defeated in the election. He didn't stand a chance they said, having been bitten by the now fully hatched serpent of depression, which had emerged from the "egg of debt" they had inherited from Bruce's conservatives in the twenties.

* * *

It was a very sad Christmas for the Jacka family later that week. Bert was kept in bed and put on a strict diet that included fresh fruit and abundant vegetables. There was no drug available that could control hypertension. The only treatment available for acute nephritis was a combination of rest and diet. A maximum intake of one and a half pints of fluid per day was imposed, comprised of a fruit juice-glucose combination, or milk. However, there was an alternative view that all fluid and liquid should be withdrawn, so that no pressure at all would be placed on the kidneys.

On a subsequent visit the following Sunday, Bert had all three of his brothers standing around his bed. Sam had closed down the butcher shop in Wedderburn, and had moved with his family to a dairy farm in Liverpool Road at Kilsyth. There was some reminiscing at Bert's bedside about the old times in Wedderburn, since almost all the family had now left. Only Fanny and her family still lived there, in the same house on Kerr Street near the Anglican Church.

"Wedderburn's not the same as it used be, before the war," Bill said.

"Nothing's the same as it was before the war," Sid rejoined.

"I remember the first car."

"Josh Gray's motor buggy," Sam said. Josh Gray was the Korong Shire Secretary who was based in Wedderburn and took over from Samuel Rinder. He was an American from Ohio, who had come for the gold rush and stayed.

"On Sundays Jack would drive up Main Street, with Josh sitting next to him in the front, and Mrs Gray and young Clarrie sitting in the back," Bill recalled. Jack was the Grays' son, and Clarrie was their daughter.

"That was when you used to spend quite a bit of time in Main Street knocking about with your mates," Sid said.

"Oh… there were a few of us there: Fred Saunders, Frank Hayes, Howard Smith, Albert and Fred Kirk, Peter Alexander, and a few others. We used to give the Grays a big cheer as they drove past," Bill continued as Bert and the others listened. "It didn't matter if they were going up the Charlton road, or the St Arnaud's road. Either way they would still drive up and down Main Street, and we would cheer them on."

"You couldn't cheer every car that goes down that road today," Sid added.

"You'd run… out of … breath…" Bert laughed through another coughing fit, as he saw the irony of his own remarks.

"Don't you talk, Bert," Bill said in a concerned tone. "You should be resting."

"I wish I had gone to Repatriation before this," Bert said, returning to his present situation. "If I had, perhaps I wouldn't be in this condition today. I know I am not walking out of here."

The brothers were surprised at how nonchalantly he said it. He was displaying the same stoicism that he had always displayed in the heat of battle, and he now knew that this battle would be his last.

* * *

One day Bert was visited by his colleagues from the council, including councillors Gray, Unsworth and Cummings. They informed him of the great success of the Beach Carnival, and how much the unemployed and their families had enjoyed the Christmas dinner that was funded by the proceeds. The discussion turned to the great issues of the day, and the future of Australia. The Japanese Army had invaded Manchuria, and was aggressively pursuing its imperialistic designs.

"I'm glad that Lyons got up," Bert said. "Now… the country has a chance to pull through, I think."

"It's been the reverse of '29," Cummings noted.

"I'm afraid the UAP's victory bodes ill for me," Burnett Gray lamented.

"Really?" Unsworth asked with surprise. He thought Gray was impregnable in St Kilda given his high public profile.

"At the next State election they'll be in a prime position to take St Kilda. Menzies has kept up his attacks against me in the Parliament – calls me a socialist. *Me?* In my heart I feel I've always voted in the best interests and welfare of the people, and that has meant voting with Labor on those occasions when they *haven't* been socialistic." Menzies' view was that those occasions were too frequent. In a recent speech in the State Parliament attacking Burnett Gray, it had been noted that he voted with Labor seventeen times, and voted with the Conservative Opposition only six times.

As they spoke Thomas Unsworth looked around and noticed that Ward 5 was not behaving like a normal ward at all. Everybody's attention was directed at Bert, as the celebrity patient, and it was extremely crowded. The other patients and their visitors would either remain quiet, listening in to all the conversations Bert and his visitors were having, or openly discussing Bert and his war record amongst themselves. People had to be told that Bert could not sign any autographs, and they constantly pestered Bert's visitors for information, even in the corridors. Then there were the reporters from the press.

Later that afternoon Councillor Thomas Unsworth telephoned the hospital and complained about the unacceptable conditions Bert was suffering in Ward 5. According to Unsworth, Bert was being "held up as an exhibit" by the other patients and their visitors in the ward. He suggested that Bert be moved to the Austin Hospital, where he could be placed into a private room. An internal minute based on his conversation was typed up, but nothing happened. On 7 January 1932, Bert was put on the critical list.

* * *

Bert had already lasted longer than the doctors had anticipated. He was now completely blind from the hypertension, and wore dark glasses when visitors came. It was a horrific ordeal for the family, but one that brought them closer together than they had been since before the war, when everything was less complicated. Suddenly subtleties in religious and political orientation did not matter much, as the most celebrated member of the family, who was loved and respected by everyone, was suffering what was now understood by all to be a terminal condition.

Vera sat next to the bed and took Bert's hand, which brought contentment to his face. Bert could no longer see her, but he knew the feel of her hand, the scent of her perfume.

"This is a rough spin, but we've been through many rough spins together. I'm afraid, Mummy, you'll have to struggle on alone. I feel I'm done."

"Don't say that," she said, trying to turn it around though tears welled up in her eyes. "We've had a rough spin, but it's been good in parts."

"Yes, Mummy," he replied, "it was good in parts."

* * *

Elizabeth and Nathaniel were devastated by the events of the past few weeks as the prospect of their son's death loomed closer. Probably the worst experience possible is for parents to bury their own child, as it goes against the laws of human nature. It was a travesty for their most famous son to find himself in such a perilous state when he had not yet reached forty years of age. Elizabeth was inconsolable, and Nathaniel brooded in his grief. He cursed the war that had destroyed so much, and turned what remained upside-down.

Nathaniel had always loved Bert dearly, and was proud of Bert's achievements during the war and afterwards, but hadn't told him the full measure of his pride because it wasn't in his nature to brag or throw compliments about. Burnett Gray and Thomas Unsworth told him all about the good work Bert had been doing for the unemployed in St Kilda.

"I heard from your councillor mates that the families of the unemployed in St Kilda had a decent Christmas dinner this year thanks to the carnival you organised," he said.

"They missed out... the year before," Bert said weakly.

"Son, I've watched what you've done for the unemployed these last couple of years," Nathaniel said with uncharacteristic emotion in his voice, then paused. "It made me... It made me very, very proud to be your father," he said finally.

"It was my duty."

"Shhh... Save your strength now, and rest..."

"I'm still fighting, Dad," he whispered.

* * *

Ted Rule's farm, Shepparton East, 10 January 1932

Ted Rule had risen from private to captain under Bert's tutelage, and had followed him from Gallipoli to the Western Front. After the war Ted went back to being an orchardist in Shepparton, and became a major in the Citizens Military Force. He often used to have his officer mates from the 14th, Ernie Hill, Les Ebbott and their families over for Sunday lunch. It was after lunch now and the three former diggers were quietly reading newspapers in the lounge as Ernie's two daughters, Doris and Elvie, were playing a game on the floor with Lieutenant Ebbott's children.

Colonel Ernest Purnell Hill, MM, ED was a 14th Battalion original who trained at Broadmeadows, and landed at Gallipoli in the same boat as Monash. As a sergeant he was in the front line of the trenches on the morning of the big Turkish push against Anzac – the morning Bert won the VC. Later he won a Military Medal for leading a section of men during the ill-fated charge at Hill 60. Soon after the 14th was transferred to the Western Front in 1916 he collected a clump of shrapnel that opened up his gut. He now called the massive scar that wrapped around from his stomach to his back his "Map of France", and if anyone thought it didn't look like France, he insisted: "I got it there!" As a lieutenant he commanded the "lucky 13th" platoon in Bert's D Company, and according to his men was able to achieve the impossible – for one thing he convinced them that the number 13 was lucky.

They loved reading the newspapers to find out what their old comrades from the 14th were up to in civilian life. Ernie had been elected to the Shepparton Shire Council back in 1928, just before Bert went into the St Kilda Council in 1929, and used to stop in to see Bert when he was in Melbourne. When the phone rang, Ted threw the paper aside and picked up.

"Hello, hello," said the operator from the Shepparton East exchange, "Melbourne calling".

"Hello, is that you Hill?" enquired the voice at the other end. The call had originally gone through to Mrs Homewood, who operated the Lemnos phone exchange from her house. Finding that no one was at home at the Hill residence, and suspecting they might be at the Rule's, she diverted the call to the Shepparton East exchange.

"No," Ted replied, "but if you hang on a minute, I'll get him." He pointed the receiver at Ernie, who was sitting down not far away and peering over the top of his paper.

"Here you are, Ernie, someone wants to speak to you from Melbourne." Ernie got up from his chair and came over to pick it up, as Ted and Les told the children to keep their voices down.

"Captain Mitchell speaking," said the voice, which was clearly audible to everyone in the room. Mitchell was one of the four company commanders of the 14th Battalion at the Battle of Polygon Wood, and now ran a foundry business in Melbourne. "I've rather unpleasant news for you," he said. "Jacka's in the Caulfield Military Hospital, and not expected to pull through. In fact, the doctors have given him a couple of days to live. If he passes out it has been decided to give him a military funeral, and we're making arrangements accordingly. We want you to act as one of the pallbearers. They're all men picked from the survivors who landed with him on Gallipoli. There's no need to tell you that we expect all 14th men in your locality to attend. I'm afraid the funeral may be as early as Sunday."

Ernie's stomach dropped. "What happened?"

"It's his kidneys."

"And the gas?" Ernie had received what he considered a light dose compared with Bert, but was still constantly bothered by copious phlegm and coughing.

"No doubt."

"Poor Bert."

"Stand by for my call, will you?"

"Of course," Ernie muttered, as if he had just seen a ghost. "Of course you can count on us... Thank you for letting me know. It's a great honour."

When he put down the receiver there was a feeling of disbelief among his friends. Their leader who was their inspiration during the war was close to death, and they received the news in silence. Ernie put down the receiver and sat back in the sofa.

"You heard?" he said, finally.

* * *

As Bert drifted into unconsciousness, many thoughts crossed his mind about Vera and Betty, his parents and his family, and the friendships he had known. Despite the difficulties he considered himself privileged to have had the good fortune to survive the Great War, to have had the mates he had, to have met the people he got to meet, and to have done what he managed to do. He thanked God for those countless blessings, and his thoughts turned back to Gallipoli, to the thinly held ridgeline at Courtney's Post, where it had all begun that fateful day in May 1915. As the sun came up that morning, he found himself surrounded by the bodies of young Australians and young Turks who had fallen in the fight. They had not lived to see their future wife and daughter as he had.

He thought about the boys from Bendigo who had backed him up that morning: Bill Howard, Steve DeAraugo and Frank Poliness. They volunteered their lives to help a mate. Poor old Bill was shot in three places, and it was a miracle that he had not been killed. One bullet smashed a rib but glanced away from his body, another hit the proverbial "book in the pocket" and was similarly deflected; while the third passed through his hand, delivering only a flesh wound. Because it was already daylight when it was over, Bill couldn't be taken down to the dressing station at Anzac Cove – the risk from snipers was too high. Instead, he would have to survive the day while he bled in a dugout on the ridge, and be taken down in the evening under cover of darkness. Bert heard that Bill was lying wounded in a dugout and later in the morning found him lying there.

"G'day mate," he said softly as he squatted down next to Bill. A shaft of light penetrated the dugout, and it took a little while for Bert's eyes to focus properly on the inside.

"G'day Bert," Bill replied weakly.

Bert lit a small paraffin candle, and they could now see each other better in a soft yellow glow. "Sorry for the way things turned out. How are you holding up now?"

"Oh… I'll be right, how about yourself?"

"I was lucky… and Lieutenant Crabbe reckons I'll be recommended for something."

"The boys told me what you did," Bill whispered quietly. "How could you have done that?"

Bert thought about that for a second before answering. "Ooh. I reckon I did my bloody block!"

That's what he told Bill, and he often reflected on the sight of Bill Howard lying in the dugout that morning, and the conversation they had together. He thought he had known Australian men when he sailed off to Gallipoli with them in December 1914. Words often failed him when had tried to talk about the men of Anzac, about their spirit – how they strived to do their best in the common cause, for an idea, even in the face of a "noble defeat" that was not of their making. They were great men, every one of them: tough, brave, industrious, and kind-hearted. They were his mates, and he loved every one of them. He found out then that he had not really known Australian men until those glorious days at Gallipoli. Better men never lived; they were born fighters, who knew no fear – men who didn't know what turning your back to the enemy meant.

* * *

From the time Bert had been placed on the critical list, Vera had hardly ever left his side. As Sunday morning dawned on 17 January she sat in a chair by his bed as always, and prayed that by some miracle he might still be spared. She felt so guilty now that she had left him just when he had needed her most. He must have been suffering while he lived alone at Chaucer Street without even telling her. Of course she would have come back if he had told her there was a problem, she said to herself. Why didn't he tell me? She now wondered like the others about whether she had contributed to his illness. His breathing was heavy as he slept – rhythmical and monotonous like the tones of a Gregorian chant. She had heard it for so many years now that she was impervious to it, like people who live near a train line and don't notice it anymore.

She looked up and saw that the sun's rays were illuminating the curtains, so she stood up and walked over to the window to draw them back, and let the light enter the room. He didn't stir at all.

"It's morning, Bert," she whispered to him, but she knew he couldn't hear. Or could he? He seemed to be in a deep sleep. "It looks like it's going to be a beautiful day today," she said to him with a brave cheerfulness, just in case he could. "You know what day this is?" she asked, and paused. "It's our anniversary," she said with a half smile as tears welled up in her eyes, and she blew her nose into a handkerchief. It was the day he always seemed to forget, she thought, and she could not forgive him for that. It was as if he was trying to put it out of his mind – but why should she worry about that now?

The rhythm of his breathing hadn't changed in some time, and she could see his chest moving up and down as his damaged lungs took in and expelled the air. She sat down again next to the bed, and closed her eyes. The rhythm reminded her of the countless sleepless nights she had endured, when he had snored and breathed so heavily through those countless dreams and nightmares, "He had suffered so much for that blasted war," she thought. It made her very angry. People didn't realise how much he had suffered, because he wouldn't complain. Everyone just saw him as the hero who had "made it". But she knew better than anyone else that he hadn't.

She stopped thinking for a second, and sat there silently staring into space for a little while before she realised that there was no sound. He was no longer breathing. She looked over at him, and saw him lying perfectly still.

"Nurse! Nurse!" she called, bursting into tears.

It was 11.15 am.

* * *

11.20 am, Anzac House, 151 Collins Street, 19 January 1932

The old digger, looking more aged than his years, hobbled into the hall with his walking stick, wearing an army tunic that was dyed black. He won the Great War, but in latter times had been overrun and defeated by the economic war that followed it. He shuffled along in the line that wound around Bert's coffin, which lay in severe splendour at the centre of the hall. At each corner of the railing that surrounded it, a soldier in the catafalque party stood like a statue, his hands resting on his upended rifle, his head and helmet leaning forward in sorrow for the fallen warrior.

Down from the walls of the hall stared large paintings of war-ravaged Western Europe: the skeletal remains of the Ypres Cloth Hall; and other sites that Bert had seen during those years. Their starkness contrasted with the hundreds of wreaths made of bright fresh flowers that were piling up around the coffin. Upon the casket lay the colours of the 14th Battalion that had been specially brought from the St Kilda Town Hall. His slouch hat and officer's sword now rested on the Union Jack.

The old man paused and looked at the felt hat, and its rising sun emblem, and the flowers piled high all around. He thought back to those times, and the legend of "good old Bert" who had seemed so invincible that his very survival had given them hope. He wiped one cheek with the cuff of his sleeve, and then wiped the other cheek, and hobbled on quickly. At the door he was stopped by a reporter.

"Excuse me sir? I'm Hugh Buggy from *The Herald*. Could you tell me, in a few words, why you have come here this morning?"

"He's a man's man, who made himself... That's why I'm here."

Hugh wrote it down in shorthand. He was a journalist's journalist, with printer's ink coursing through his veins. He declined editorial roles, as he wanted to be close to the action that he loved. He covered the police strike of 1923, and the fatal shoot-out between the rival criminals "Squizzy" Taylor and "Snowy" Cutmore in 1927. In 1928 he covered the arrival of Kingsford-Smith at Brisbane in the *Southern Cross* after his epic flight across the Pacific. He didn't just cover a story, he often became part of it. In December 1929 he was among the fray when police opened fire after striking miners had pelted them with the pavement at Rothbury, and applied his own singlet as a tourniquet to a miner's wound.

The light was so bright in the doorway where he stood, that Hugh's eyes had to re-focus when he looked back inside. He saw an old woman who, with trembling hand held a bunch of flowers and cast it into that sea of colour framed by the sentries. She seemed relieved at that and moved on, with the men of the 14th Battalion standing in line behind her. Some had fared better than others, but all had been etched by time, and many had gone grey, as Bert had done in his last two years. Some came with their children, girls who stood by their fathers carrying posies of violets and roses, and boys who had sat on their fathers' knees listening to stories about Bert in battle.

Over a period of hours more than 6000 people filed past. Warrant Officer Hughes paused later, and showed Hugh a tattered document that he treasured. It was the original nominal roll of the 14th Battalion, from when Hughes had received him at Broadmeadows as a raw recruit. There it was on the page: "Private Albert Jacka, No. 465".

"How would you describe him?" Hugh asked.

"Bert Jacka," he said, "was intelligent, bright, and had every quality of the real man's man. Promotion did not affect him. He remained just as human a fellow as when he was a private." Hugh wrote it down in short hand as his informant spoke.

At 1.30 pm the service began, led by the Padre of the 14th Battalion, the Reverend Francis Rolland, now headmaster of Geelong College. It was transmitted to all the homes in Victoria on the airwaves by radio station 3UZ. The chief mourners who stood near the coffin were Vera and Betty, Bert's parents, Elizabeth and Nathaniel, his sisters, his brothers and their families. The Minister for Defence, Senator Sir George Pearce, who had sparred with Pompey Elliott over the issue of Bert's supersession, represented the Federal Government, while a number of brigadier generals and colonels, including Brigadier-General Brand, and Lieutenant-Colonel "Ferdie" Wright represented the Australian military. Civilian representatives included the state and federal RSSILA presidents, the St Kilda Army and Navy Club, the Lord Mayor, the Mayor of St Kilda, the president of the RACV, a representative of the Hebrew Congregation of St Kilda, and a representative of the Consular corps.

Padre Rolland called on Allan McDonald MLA, one of Captain Jacka's comrades in the 14th Battalion, to deliver an address. Wounded at Bullecourt, he had been a sergeant in Bert's D Company at the Battle of Polygon Wood, where he had shown exemplary courage in taking a difficult group of German pillboxes. Bert was impressed, and had recommended him. In the early 1920s, Bert had supported him when he twice ran unsuccessfully for the seat of Corangamite, but he would be back, just like one of Bert's men, to take it on again, like one of those tough pillboxes at Polygon Wood. He would get it too.

"With heavy hearts we meet today to pay tribute to the greatest fighting soldier the AIF produced, Captain Jacka," he said with his head held high. "We marvelled that such grit, courage and determination could be centred in one person.

"To those who knew him best he was more than a fighting man. He was a friend and an inspiration when fear was about us. He was one of the most gallant men one could conceive – a man who helped make Australian history.

"God knows that in his own greatest troubles Captain Jacka had still time to think of others. A few short months ago our association held a reunion in this building. Never will any of us forget that night and the appeal that he made for the unemployed, and particularly for the unemployed 'Digger'. He is enshrined in our hearts, a dauntless leader, an incomparable soldier, and sincere, loyal, and trusted friend."

Nearer, My God to Thee was then sung by the assembly, followed by *Abide With Me*. For two minutes there was silence, and then the sombre notes of the *Last Post* were played. They brought more tears to Vera's eyes. She could hardly stand on her own, and had to be supported by those who stood around her. Betty was being looked after by Sam and Elizabeth Jacka.

* * *

Outside it was a scorching hot day – almost 109 degrees Fahrenheit – the hottest day in 24 years. A fierce hot wind was blowing down from the north, and there was a general unease brewing in the air, which had a faint burning smell to it. Bushfires raged in the hills around Melbourne and in regional Victoria, creating a strange yellow haze around the edges of the brilliant blue sky. The Otways were ablaze, while in Sydney the leader of the New Guard, Colonel Campbell, was soon to appear in court charged with using insulting language against Premier Jack Lang. It was a matter of free speech Campbell's supporters argued, and thousands of demonstrators would press against the gates in Liverpool Street.

The heat was too much for Bill's daughter, ten-year-old Josephine, whose legs began to give way. Her cousin Frances took her aside into a nearby building and placed her lying down on a cool concrete floor. As she lay there recovering, a battalion of ex-diggers was forming up in Russell Street, south of Collins. They were men not just of the 14th Battalion, but also from the 13th, 15th and 16th battalions. The whole 4th Brigade was to march the final march with Bert.

Bert's long-time business partner, Ernie Edmonds was forming up with the men in Russell Street, where he met with Ted Rule, who came down with the Shepparton contingent led by Ernie Hill. Early in the afternoon of the 17th there had been an abrupt message from Captain Mitchell: "Leave in the morning."

"You know," Ernie said to Ted, "in all the years that we were in business together, we never disagreed on a single thing."

"I know," said Ted, swallowing hard, and fighting back the tears. Bert had recognised his cool head and leadership qualities after only a week at Gallipoli, and had awarded him his first stripes. They were all there forming their four lines in Russell Street: Captain Fred Anderson and Captain Mitchell, tough old Lieutenant Jack Garcia, Private "Sailor" Day, and hundreds of other privates and NCOs. The four deep column of men stretched almost all the way down the hill to Flinders Street.

* * *

Ernie Hill and Bert's friends from the St Kilda Council, the Returned Sailors and Soldiers' League and the Army and Navy Club at St Kilda picked up the coffin and, shoulder to shoulder, arms locked and tightly packed, they slowly step-marched their heavy burden through the doors of "Anzac House" into the searing heat of Collins Street. The men of the Third Division Artillery had drawn their gun carriage, with eight horses chained to it, right under the elms that provided much needed shade.

At 2.50 pm the funeral procession moved off down the street, and then turned into Swanston Street. It was the corner of the Town Hall where he was welcomed with such fanfare in October 1919, and where the two-up school had played defiantly during the police strike. Now its balcony and those of all the surrounding buildings was packed with mourners, hoping to catch a glimpse of the legend as he made his way to his final resting place. The pall bearers who marched beside the carriage were all Victoria Cross winners: R.E. Grieve, A.D. Lowerson, W. Dunstan, J.E. Newland,

W.D. Joynt, R.V. Moon, W. Ruthven, A. Borella and I. Smith. Despite the heat, each man held his hat to his chest while his medals flashed like heliographs in the sun. Mr Arthur Apps of W.G. Apps Pty Ltd, the same undertakers who had arranged the recent funeral of General Monash, marched next to the gun-carriage wearing his tall black top hat.

As the strains of Chopin's *Funeral March* filled the air with melancholy, Donovan Joynt could hardly contain his sorrow. He thought about the day he came across Bert standing outside his store in Elizabeth Street, looking jaded. How hard it had been for him to accept that Bert had been defeated in business. He thought back to the day that he first met Bert at the Australian Officers' club in London, when he was still relatively new to the war. He recalled how overawed he felt to be in the presence of a young man with such a great reputation. "This is the great Jacka that everybody talks about," he thought to himself then – "whose bravery is a by-word amongst diggers." Now, many years later, he marched by his side with the other VCs, having seen what Bert had done to preserve the memory of those who had fallen in the war, and his work to garner the public's financial support for the Shrine. He thought about what he had done for the unemployed in his municipality during the economic war that was still being fought. "What a great Australian we are honouring this day," he thought.

Captain Albert Jacka was leaving the City of Melbourne the same way he had arrived in 1919 – at the head of a long procession that crossed the Prince's Bridge on to the magnificent tree-lined St Kilda Road. Behind the carriage marched over 800 veterans, led by Lieutenant-Colonel Charles Montague Moreland Dare, DSO. How ironic that Bert's old CO, who had tried to block his advancement to officer rank, should now march in the procession behind his coffin. Now Bert led the 14ᵗʰ Battalion, as many thought he should have during the war. They marched in a direct line to the partly built Shrine of Remembrance, still two years away from completion. The line of motorcars in the procession now stretched from the Shrine, all the way back to Anzac House, and the air above the column shimmered from the heat generated by the motors.

As Ernie Hill marched with the coffin bearers, he thought back to the great trials, and in spare moments, the great times he had experienced as one of Bert's subalterns in France. He smiled through sorrow at one of those times. Paris was virtually off limits to them, even though Ernie always reckoned they should have been selling tickets to the place. There was that time a group of 14th Battalion officers had come by some rail travel warrants to Paris. Bert was one of a party of seven hopeful captains and lieutenants who got off at *Gare du Nord* station in Paris. All they had to do now was get past the British MPs at the gate. As they thought about it a British Major-General sent one of his two aides forward with his papers so that he wouldn't have to wait in line. When the aide came back the General's entourage suddenly expanded to ten as they went forward to the gate.

"I say!" said one of the aides, causing the General to turn around to see what the fuss was about. He suddenly found himself staring into Bert Jacka's steely blue eyes, and his gaze drifted down to Bert's tunic, which displayed the maroon VC ribbon. Without saying another word the General did an about face, and proudly led his expanded entourage through the gate. On the other side he was thanked by Bert, given an immaculate salute and bidden farewell by his "temporary staffers". It was so like Bert, Ernie thought.

At the St Kilda Junction 200 unemployed men of St Kilda joined the procession, as well as 500 more diggers. More than 1000 school children from local schools – Windsor, Prahran, South Yarra, Hawksburn, Toorak Central and St Michael's East St Kilda – lined the entry to the cemetery along Dandenong Road. Among the boys from Hawksburn Primary stood eleven-year-old Keith Hooper, who would never forget that day.

* * *

The horses pulling the gun carriage entered the main pathway of the St Kilda Cemetery, and came to a halt right in the centre. Bert would be laid to rest at a spot that looked across the cemetery to Murchison Street, where he had lived with Vera and Betty for the "good parts" before the hard times came. The graveside service was conducted by Rev J. Smiley, who at its conclusion invited Padre Frank Rolland to speak.

"It is difficult to know where to begin when speaking of Captain Jacka's bravery and devotion to duty," said the Padre. "He was much more than a fighter of genius – he was a man of chivalry even towards those against whom he fought. He had no hate for the Turk or the German in his heart. He hated the fact of war.

"Like all strong men he had a vein of the greatest tenderness and gentleness. He thought always of his men before himself, and, above all, he remembered the families of those who fell. Many homes have been comforted by the fine sincerity of his letters.

"His life should be an inspiration of every Australian boy. Now at last he has given up that life for his country. Captain Jacka remembered others, I trust that his country will not forget the family of Captain Jacka."

Brigadier Brand had been thinking about that issue in the last week or so, when it became apparent that Bert was not going to survive. Steps had already been taken to organise a collection that would provide funding for a fitting memorial at the gravesite, and to purchase a home for his widow and child. Two of the major newspapers, *The Herald*, and *The Sun* would spearhead the drive.

"Captain Jacka was a super soldier," Brand began when it was his turn to speak at the graveside, "a born leader with an instinct to do the right thing in a critical situation based on the accepted principles of tactics. A company under his leadership was as good as an additional battalion in a battle. He was an inspiration not only to the 14th Battalion, but to the whole of the 4th Brigade.

"He was conspicuous among numbers of brave men, some VC winners, others holders of the Distinguished Conduct Medal and the Military Medal, others with no decorations at all. The exploit that won him the VC on Gallipoli, the audacious and brilliant counter-attack at Pozieres with a handful of men on the morning of 7 August 1916, and minor enterprises on other occasions were sufficient to place him on a pedestal. But it was at Bullecourt on April 11 1917, that Captain Jacka surpassed even those exploits. For his extraordinary gallantry in that unparalleled infantry adventure a bar to his VC would have been awarded had the operation been a success. It is only on rare occasions that this coveted decoration is awarded when no signal advantage has been obtained. A bar to his MC was the award. Jacka valued this bar more than a DSO."

All that Brigadier Brand said, bar the last sentence, was true. The one decoration that eluded Bert was the DSO, and he wanted it badly. He wanted it for the brilliant counter-attack at Pozieres Ridge, and was promised as much by General Cox, even though he fully deserved a second VC because, as Brigadier Brand had suggested, a "signal advantage" had been achieved. A "signal advantage" had also been achieved at the Battle of Polygon Wood, and no decoration had been awarded to Bert, yet it was at this battle that he showed battalion leadership qualities. As Ted Rule recalled it, at Polygon Wood he led the 14th to victory by the example of his "nonchalant bearing… with not a trace of anxiety or fear".

As he listened to the Old Brig, Ted recalled how pleased he had been with the way Bert had taken charge and led the battalion to victory that day. "Congratulations Jacka. I have recommended you for a DSO," Brand's message read. But instead, Bert had not even received a mention in despatches. Ted was not surprised that there was no mention of Polygon Wood in Brand's speech. No one ever got to the bottom of what went wrong there, but the boys always speculated that the unpleasantness between Bert and Brand at Bullecourt, and in the lead up to Polygon Wood had coloured the latter's judgment. Whether or not Brigadier Brand felt guilty about that, he seemed to have been making amends ever since. How fortunate I was to have known Bert Jacka, thought Ted after Brand's speech.

Mr T. Morgan, the Secretary of the St Kilda Unemployed Organization had had much to do with Bert over the past year and a half. In his mind no man in Australia had done more for the unemployed. He took a keen interest in them, had attended their meetings, talked to them, and got to know each man's difficulties. He had always addressed them with respect as gentlemen when he spoke to them. He had also helped them generously out of his own pocket, even though he himself was in a perilous financial situation at the time.

Newton Wanliss stood stony faced before Bert's final resting place. This was the funeral he could never have for his own son Harold, whose body was not found. To some extent Bert had substituted for his son, and now he had lost him too. Now the biography that Newton had started writing could not be completed, as he wanted Bert's views on key events that had taken place. Newton felt greatly privileged to have shared Bert's friendship, which had given him an insight into his splendid courage, high personal honour, and outstanding manhood. Now, after a heroic struggle in shattered health against impossible odds, he had passed over the great river of death, where so many of his finest comrades had preceded him. In Newton's mind, he was the equal of the greatest heroes of antiquity, and his deeds would stir the blood of Australians for all time, serving as a beacon light to illuminate the future of Australia, that native land that he loved so well and served so nobly.

The firing party and drummers at the graveside were from the 14th Battalion 4th Infantry Brigade. They fired their volleys into the air, and filled it with smoke, echoing the sounds and scenes of the battles he had fought and won. And through it all stood the bronze helmeted spirit of Mars, god of war. Swaying arrogantly with hands held on hips, he laughed, rejoicing at the sight he was now witnessing. He could never defeat Albert Jacka in battle, but now at last, the legend had fallen.

The reporters asked Brigadier-General Brand what it was that most impressed him about Albert Jacka. He replied: "The cheery smile and grand optimism with which he, time and again, went back into the firing line, knowing that he had a wonderful reputation to uphold, and was expected to perform a VC stunt which might cost him his life."

Four months later, at the unveiling of the memorial stone at the St Kilda Cemetery, Brand was again surrounded by representatives of the Press for his comment on Captain Albert Jacka, VC MC and Bar. He told them:

"It is right that such a man's name is handed down in posterity."

EPILOGUE

Vera and Betty Jacka

On 15 May 1932, Vera and Betty stood in front of the memorial to Captain Albert Jacka at the St Kilda Cemetery, as Brigadier-General Brand unveiled it. A few days later *The Herald* reported that Vera was convalescing in a private hospital, and that her sister Molly was looking after Betty. *The Herald* and *The Sun* newspapers led the campaign to raise funds for a cottage, and published photos of the house as well as Vera's letter of gratitude. Vera and Betty lived in the new home during 1932, and the Sands and McDougall telephone directory listed her address as 387 Malvern Road, Glen Iris. Ernest Turnbull and W. Dunstan VC acted as trustees of the property.

On 4 July 1932, Vera loaned Albert Jacka's medals to the St Kilda Army and Navy Club for display. At the ceremony she told members of the club:

I know that several of you assisted him again and again, and by assisting him you naturally assisted me. This club was not a club to him, but a haven, where, amid his wartime friends, he forgot his worries. As I have nothing else of value, I am giving you these medals and decorations for a few years, knowing that you will honour them. On behalf of my daughter Betty and myself, and in deep gratitude,

*I present them to the club. I am giving you also a photograph of my
late husband.*[1]

The photograph of Albert Jacka still hangs in the upstairs bar
at the St Kilda RSL, Acland Street. The medals are now displayed
in the Hall of Valour at the Australian War Memorial in Canberra.

According to Betty, some time after the funeral her mother
was introduced to Frank Duncan, a warehouseman who lived at
6 South Terrace, Clifton Hill. A Catholic widower and father of
seven, Frank Duncan's wife had died in childbirth in 1923. At
fifty-three years of age in 1932, he was twenty years senior to
Vera. They had a brief courtship and were married at St Patrick's
Cathedral on 27 September 1932. By the time of her marriage
to Frank Duncan, Vera had vacated the Malvern Road house that
was provided by public subscription, and was residing at Kingsley
Hall, Cathedral Place, East Melbourne.

Betty describes her mother as having a warm personality, being
a great organiser and accomplished hostess at dinner parties. She
loved to read and go on bush walks, but never went near the water
during their family holidays at Torquay. Betty reports that Vera
always ensured the household was running smoothly, and read to
her every day when she was very young. While Vera had no interest
at all in Australian Rules football, she sometimes accompanied
Frank with a book under her arm, and continued reading it while
all those around her, including her husband (a keen Collingwood
supporter), were jumping with excitement. However, she did
enjoy accompanying her husband to the races, where he was a
member.

On 21 September 1961, Vera died at the age of sixty-three
from an acute respiratory infection, and was buried at Fawkner
Cemetery. There is no doubt that Vera was affected for the rest
of her life by her marriage to Albert Jacka. While in the end she

---

1   (5 July 1932), "Late Capt. Jacka's Medals – Presentation to Club", *The Argus*, p. 7
     (http://nla.gov.au/nla.news-article4461256).

found that she couldn't stay with him for what she felt were good reasons, Betty believes she regretted leaving him. Neither could she ever forget him. To the end, Betty recalls, Vera was moved on Anzac Day when the *Last Post* was played.

Betty completed her education at a Catholic boarding school, and up to the age of sixteen years received a small stipend based on Albert Jacka's war pension. Sometimes she would accompany her mother when she visited her sister, Molly Gleeson, in Sydney. She recalls that the backyard of her Aunt Molly's house at Ryde was home to the most vicious bull ants she ever came across in her youth. She later had a family of her own and maintains her lifelong passionate interest in tennis.

Elizabeth and Nathaniel Jacka

Elizabeth and Nathaniel Jacka continued living in their new house at Bealiba Road, East Caulfield, not far from Bessie and Harold Dowrick. Elizabeth passed away in 1940 at the age of seventy-six, and Nathaniel followed in 1943 aged eighty-two years. They were both buried at the St Kilda Cemetery.

Samuel and Sidney Jacka

Samuel Jacka lived a quiet life as a dairy farmer at Kilsyth. In December 1942, at the age of fifty-six, Sam died of euremia and arteriosclerosis, while his oldest son Leslie was serving in the Second AIF. His sister Fanny (Jacka) Olive's son, William Jacka Olive, also served in the Second AIF.

Sidney Jacka also lived a relatively quiet life compared with the two brothers who went to the war with him. However, in 1950, when the ABC broadcast an Anzac Day program describing Albert Jacka and his brothers as "illiterate yokels" he protested vigorously. *The Canberra Times* recorded that he was demanding an apology from the ABC, and that the script written by Frank Browne and all records of the broadcast be sent to the family so that they could be destroyed. He was quoted as saying:[2]

I had friends at my place to listen to the broadcast. You can imagine how we felt when we heard it.

Like his older brother Albert, Sidney suffered from nephritis, but survived it. However, he also died relatively young of a heart attack.

William Jacka

Bill and Joan Jacka's 160-acre farm south of Berwick has now been surrounded and swallowed up by Melbourne's urban sprawl. The land of their farm was in the vicinity of what are now Soldiers' Road, O'Shea Road and Bridgewater Boulevard, Berwick. After his brother's death, Bill was employed as a journalist at *The Footscray Advertiser*, became more active in politics as a Labor Party counsellor, and in 1940 was elected Mayor of Footscray. As a left-wing idealist of firm convictions, Bill's career as Mayor was punctuated by controversies about matters of politics and principle. He resigned before the expiry of his term.

It appears that Bill came into the 14th Battalion Association in the 1950s. At the time of his death the fundraising campaign of *The Herald* and *The Sun* portrayed Albert Jacka (inaccurately) as a "down and out" digger. This image was further fuelled (unintentionally) by Ted Rule's autobiographical *Jacka's Mob* in 1933. Based on such sources, a 1965 article in *Mufti*, the RSL's Victorian newspaper painted a picture of his brother dying as a penniless hawker of soap. As the senior surviving male of his family, Bill responded with a detailed rebuttal in the next issue:[3]

---

2   (30 May 1950), "Jacka's family condemn broadcast", *The Canberra Times*, p. 3. The matter was also raised in the Federal Parliament by Allan McDonald MHR, who had been a sergeant in Albert Jacka's Company. See (26 May 1950), "Says ABC Cast Slur on VC," *The Age*.

3   Bill Jacka JP (1 November 1965), "Letters: Captain A. Jacka VC, MC and Bar – brother on facts", *Mufti*.

It is a horrible untruth to say he hawked soap through the streets of Melbourne. He did not die penniless. At his death he owned a motor car, had equity in the house he was buying, and had a current life insurance policy... I hope the pages of "Mufti" and the name of this brave soldier and fine citizen, will never again be sullied, by the publication of such a statement.

While Bill was correct in rebutting the image of his brother as a "penniless hawker of soap", records suggest that Albert Jacka was renting at 60 Chaucer Street in the months leading up to his death. On 9 November 1977, Bill Jacka was living in Colchester Road, Kilsyth, and was visited by Jim Poole, President of the Korong Historical Society, who taped a conversation with him about the old days in Wedderburn before the Great War. That year Bill appeared in a documentary film, *Jacka VC* (which is distributed by Sunrise Productions) where he described with heartfelt emotion the sight of his brother's colourless face when he found him unconscious and suffering multiple wounds at a dressing station near Pozieres in 1916. In 1978, Bill died at Box Hill Hospital at the age of eighty-one. His daughter Josephine, who was given the penny by her uncle, Albert Jacka, at the Caulfield Military Repatriation Hospital, still lives in Melbourne and wishes she had kept it.

Newton Wanliss

Apart from writing the *History of the 14ᵗʰ Battalion*, Newton Wanliss maintained a keen historical interest in the American Civil War. He is credited by Douglas S. Freeman, author of *R.E. Lee: A Biography* (1934), with providing a reference for a 1930 article depicting the "friendly fire" mortal wounding of Confederate General "Stonewall" Jackson. In a letter to Australian Great War historian Dr C.E.W. Bean, he compared the 4ᵗʰ Brigade's charge at Bullecourt to General Pickett's charge at Gettysburg.

Since Harold Wanliss's body was never found by the Imperial War Graves Commission, his name was inscribed on the Menin

Gate Memorial at Ypres. Each year while he lived Newton Wanliss continued to place an "In Memoriam" notice in *The Argus* in memory of Harold. In 1943 Newton commenced his Will with the words: "I desire to place on record the pride that I have always felt in the achievements and characters of my two children ... and ... my gratitude for the companionship and devotion they have both invariably extended towards me." As a student of the American Civil War his Will set aside an amount to donate to the Confederate Museum in Charleston, South Carolina. Newton Wanliss died in 1951.

Marion Wanliss

Dr Marion Wanliss continued as a successful medical practitioner, and was often cited in the social pages at prestigious functions. In the late 1930s she was president of the Trinity Women's Association. She never married, and her cousin Tom Wanliss recalls from a visit to her surgery during World War II, that she revealed an admiration for the Soviet model. However, by the 1970s she had swung back to a more conservative standpoint in supporting Malcolm Fraser as the leader of the Liberal Party. She sold Harold's farm at Lorne (including the Wanliss Falls named after her brother) to the State of Victoria to be preserved as natural bushland. The following extract from an article in the *Medical Journal of Australia* written after her death in 1984 gives some idea of her character:[4]

> *In the early 1950s, after presenting a particularly vehement paper at the Lyceum Club, Melbourne, concerning the indiscriminate slaughter of kangaroos, Marion formed the Native Fauna Conservation Society... The Society became large, prestigious and well-endowed. Dr Wanliss conducted the "Marion Wanliss Conservation Camps" for young people which were based at Glen Ewart in the township of Launching Place... Dame Kate Campbell*

---

4   (29 September 1984), *The Medical Journal of Australia*.

recalls that she was castigated by Dr Wanliss for "defiling the bush" when she threw out of the window some hair from her comb, believing that it might assist the birds in their nest building!

In accordance with her wishes, after her death Marion's body was delivered to the Melbourne University Medical School.

Charles Brand

His position as chairman of the committee raising funds for Vera and Betty's house and the monoument to Albert Jacka at the St Kilda Cemetery provided General Brand with considerable public prominence. The following year he retired from the Army with the rank of major general, and a year later in 1934 he was elected as a senator for the United Australia Party. He held his Victorian senate seat until 1947, and used it to further the cause of returned diggers. He died at his Toorak home in 1961, aged eighty-eight.

Charles Dare

Lieutenant-Colonel Charles Dare never forgot 8 August 1915. As a young and newly appointed major, he was thrust into the position of commanding officer of the 14th Battalion in the field after Major Rankine fainted and fell out. At the age of twenty-six he was suddenly the arbiter of life and death for 1000 young men. In an article written some months after Albert Jacka's death, he wrote:[5]

I maintain to this day that we should have held the ridge up which we had advanced, including Hill 60 to the sea, and thus prevented the great waste of life later in trying to regain Hill 60.

While Lieutenant-Colonel Dare was correct in saying the holding of the ground won on 8 August would have saved the waste of life

---

5   C.M.M. Dare (1 August 1932), "No Gains: Many Casualties", *Reveille*, p. 58.

in trying to retake Hill 60, only an unbridled optimist could have thought that those lives would have been spared. It would merely have placed the Australian line closer to the peak of Hill 971, and it is likely that those troops saved from the attempt on Hill 60 would have been expended higher up the slope. The official historian, Charles Bean, blamed Monash for missing an opportunity on the morning of 7 August, when the 4th Brigade did not advance as far as it could have. It was a source of his continuing doubts about Monash as a leader of men in the field.

Apart from leading the 14th Battalion veterans on the day of Albert Jacka's funeral, Lieutenant-Colonel Dare was the keynote speaker at one of the annual observances of his funeral at the St Kilda Cemetery. By 1950 he had moved from Bay Street, Brighton to Smith Street, Lorne, where he spent his retirement. He died at Geelong in 1971, aged eighty-three, and is buried at Lorne.

Ferdinand Henry Wright

Captain Wright wrote a long and affectionate letter to his wife Rosa once he was aboard the hospital ship SS *Dongola*, which carried him to Egypt after his wounding at the base of Quinn's Post.[6] In the hospital at Cairo he met up with Sergeant Reynolds, who had been fitted with a false jaw after it was blown away in the fighting at Gallipoli. Reynolds told him that he had just wanted to report that Captain Hoggart had been killed. Wright had witnessed Captain Hoggart's death himself.

Ferdie Wright continued climbing the corporate ladder of the Australian insurance industry when he returned home from Gallipoli in 1915. In 1933, when he was chairman of the Accident Underwriters Association of Victoria, he won the RACV motor insurance business for the Tariff companies when it was tendered that year. He was president of a number of insurance industry bodies, and belonged to several military and gentlemen's clubs.

---

6   F.H. Wright letter to S. Wright, 3 May, 1915 from SS *Dongola*, Off Gallipoli. Copy provided to author by Steven Marriott.

Wright became the Consul of the Netherlands in Melbourne in 1925, and each year celebrated the anniversary of Queen Wilhelmina's birthday. During World War II he became a senior liaison officer attached to Army Headquarters and carried out a number of secret missions to Malaya, New Guinea and the Netherland Indies. A confidant and friend of the Prime Minister, Sir Robert Menzies, he was awarded an OBE by the Australian Government, and the Dutch made him a Knight Officer of the Royal Order of Oranje-Nassau.

On his ninetieth birthday in 1978 Ferdie insisted on cutting the cake with his sword. He passed away two years later. By that time he might have forgotten about the extraordinary account of the first three days at Gallipoli that he had penned for Newton Wanliss in July 1921, and which greatly influenced the depiction of those days in this book, but he could not have forgotten those days. In Newton's *History of the 14ᵗʰ Battalion* his experiences were compressed into two or three sentences.

Henry Gerald Loughran

Major HG Loughran served with the 14th Battalion at Anzac from the Landing to mid October 1915. He continued to serve with the Egyptian Expeditionary Force from 19 March to June 1916. In the second half of 1916 he returned to Australia to become a medical officer at the Kyneton District Hospital. It was there in 1919 that he battled with the effects of the worldwide influenza epidemic, and for his extraordinary efforts was commended by the Kyneton Hospital Committee.

On 1 August 1933, Dr Loughran's article "Hill 60: 4ᵗʰ Brigade Attacks" was published in the journal *Reveille*, where he wrote:

> ... the actual summit of the hill was never taken — and it did not matter. Its capture would not have effected the issue of the campaign one iota. And yet, for that useless excrescence, brave men's blood was shed like water. In short, Hill 60 might well stand for a symbol of war itself, its ghastliness, and its futility.

Dr. Loughran continued to serve the Kyneton Hospital until his death in 1941, aged in his early sixties. Dr. Loughran's son, John Lewis Loughran was born on 2 August 1914, two days before Britain declared war on Germany, and served as a Medical Officer in the Second AIF.

Ernest Purnell Hill

Ernie Hill remained a councillor of the Shire of Shepparton for many decades, and was its president in 1938, 1953, 1954 and 1964. A keen sportsman, he was the foundation president of both the Shepparton and District Tennis Association and the Shepparton Hard Courts Tennis Association, and a president of the Lemnos Football Club. During World War II he left his wife Doris to look after their orchards and young family. With the rank of lieutenant-colonel, he was occupied on the home front in charge of some training battalions, and oversaw troop movements. He was retired with the rank of colonel, and was still a councillor when he died in 1966, aged seventy-five years.

Frederick Falkiner Knight

Fred Knight continued his active interest in the affairs of the Australian Club, becoming its president. Since he was a keen billiards player and also a member of the Melbourne Club, an F.F. Knight billiards trophy is contested by those clubs each year. Many of the colourful stories of 1920s Melbourne that are presented in this book are drawn from his autobiography, *These Things Happened*. He was also the author of an interesting history of the Australian Club, which is similarly laden with worthy anecdotes of a bygone era. Fred Knight was the host of a well-known Christmas party that provided a perpetual invitation to the invitee. He used to sit on his verandah and mark off the guests on his list as they arrived. Reportedly, if one could not attend, one needed to produce a good excuse.

John Wren

John Wren continued to build his diverse business empire through the 1930s and 1940s, and to court controversy from all quarters. He withdrew support from B.A. Santamaria's Catholic Social Studies Movement in the 1940s, as he thought it would inject sectarianism into the Labor Party. In 1950 the communist Frank Hardy published a best-selling novel titled *Power Without Glory* that portrayed John Wren (John West) and his wife Ellen Wren (Nellie West) in a manner that was considered defamatory. The matter was taken to court by one of Wren's sons, but was lost through the prosecution's unwillingness to admit that Hardy was portraying Wren as West (and therefore Ellie as Nellie). As a Collingwood Football Club devotee all his life Wren and legendary coach Jock McHale jostled their way through the crowd to find a position behind the Collingwood goal posts during the September 1953 grand final clash against Geelong. The Magpies held on to win their first premiership since 1936. McHale died of a heart attack the next day, and thirty-six hours after the game Wren suffered a massive heart attack in his sleepout, dying in hospital a month later. Sport had been his life.

The Cummings Family

In 1933, less than two years after the death of Albert Jacka, Councillor George Cummings died of a heart attack, aged seventy-one, during an operation. His wife Maud died in 1941 at the age of seventy-nine. Her son Edward died of a heart condition less than a year later at the age of forty-seven, and is buried at the St Kilda Cemetery. He never married, possibly due to the effects or stigma of the venereal disease he contracted during the war. His younger brother Cliff died at No. 8A St Leonards Avenue (next door to St Leonards) in 1977 at the age of eighty-two. His only daughter, Kerry, died single in 1972 at the age of forty-one after a drug overdose associated with a heart condition. Miss Alison Cummings was never married, and ended her days in an apartment on Toorak Road West. The last of the Cummings family, she died in 1981 at the age of eighty-four, and was cremated at the Springvale Crematorium.

The fate of the Cummings family is sad considering the grand *café chantant* card and tennis parties that were held at 10 St Leonards Avenue, St Kilda in the late 1920s and early 1930s. Since 1995–1996 the large allotment formerly occupied by the Cummings family is the site of a four-storey apartment building of more than forty apartments designed by prominent architect, Nonda Katsalidis.

Burnett Gray

Burnett Gray lost his seat in the Legislative Assembly in June 1932. Prior to that, at the first St Kilda Council meeting after Albert Jacka's funeral the new Mayor, Councillor Moroney, commented on the heartfelt loss of "a great soldier, a good man and a valued colleague", whom the Almighty had "called from his labours". Several of the councillors spoke, but such was the grief of the normally highly eloquent Burnett Gray, that he had to have his letter of condolence read out for him.

Even in his last few years as a St Kilda councillor Burnett Gray had not forgotten Albert Jacka. On the thirteenth anniversary of his death, at the annual observance at the graveside, Burnett Gray "suggested that a worthy public memorial should be erected, and proposed that with the help of the state government, St Kilda Council and citizens, the 14th Battalion Association could erect a bronze statue on a boulevard named after Captain Jacka near Albert Park Lake".[7] While the bronze statue never eventuated, in 1984 a section of Marine Parade stretching from the Sea Baths past Luna Park was re-named "Jacka Boulevard".

Burnett Gray died in 1968, at the age of eighty-four. Today a childcare centre, the Burnett Gray Centre on Broadway, Elwood,

---

7   (22 January 1945), "Jacka Memorial Proposed", *The Argus*, p. 7 (http://nla.gov.au/nla. news-article1102944).

is named after him, and Burnett Gray Park flanks the Ripponlea Railway Station. A multi-faceted individual, he had written the words to the "Founders' Day Song" of Wesley College while a student there.

Kate, Neil and Violet Elliott and Belle Campbell

The children of Major-General Pompey Elliott who witnessed his traumatic life and tragic demise left no heirs. After abandoning a science degree at Melbourne University Neil Elliott became a patrol officer in New Guinea in 1936. Kate died in 1938, and in July 1939, Violet and Belle were informed that Neil had been killed on active duty. Neil's assistant had rebuked a woman in a village for not keeping it clean. Her father attacked Neil with a knife and was shot dead by him, however, two other villagers speared him to death. Violet became a nurse and saw service during World War II. She was never married and died in 1971.

Mrs "Ma" Futcher

Mrs Susan Patience Futcher, who Vera saw as a mother figure, remained friends with her to the end of her days. She continued living in Mitford Street, Elwood and Betty recalls visiting her there. She died of cardiac failure on 9 May 1959, at the Jessie McPherson Community Hospital in Lonsdale Street. Having lived to the age of ninety-five, Mrs Futcher had sadly outlived seven of her nine children.

Mitsumasa Yonai

Mitsumasa Yonai was captain of the Japanese cruiser *Iwate*, which visited Melbourne in January 1924. His natural charm and Anglophile tendencies may have been one of the reasons that Sir John Monash seemed unconcerned about the rising naval power of Japan. During the 1930s he rose to the rank of admiral and was prime minister of Japan for six months in 1940. He opposed a suicidal war against the United States and the British Empire, and became a target for assassination attempts by the Japanese Imperialist hawks. He therefore remained true to the promise made in 1924 by his vice-admiral, Shichigoro Saito, who said the Japanese would never forget the aid that Australians had provided to the victims of the Tokyo earthquake disaster. Two of the US battleships that visited Australia in 1925, the USS *Pennsylvania* and USS *Oklahoma* were sunk by the Japanese at Pearl Harbor on the "Day of Infamy" in December 1941.

Keith Hooper

Keith Hooper was an eleven-year-old schoolboy at Hawksburn when he watched Albert Jacka's funeral cortege make its way through the gates of the St Kilda cemetery in 1932. When he finished school in 1938 he began as a copy boy at the *Sun News Pictorial*, and also joined the Citizens Military Force. He became a cadet journalist just as World War II broke out, and was called upon to follow in Albert Jacka's footsteps at Bardia, Tobruk, Greece and Crete. As a sergeant in the 2/6th Battalion, he was wounded and taken prisoner by the Germans on the last day of the Battle of Crete. After six attempts, he managed to escape back to the Allied lines and fought with the US 83rd Division at the Battle of Regensburg. At the conclusion of a varied career as a journalist, editor and academic, he retired at the age of eighty-six. At ninety years of age, he now lives in Canberra.

The statue of the Angel of Mercy

The magnificent statue of the Angel of Mercy that once graced the impressive archway of the Equitable Life building (later the Colonial Mutual Life building) in Collins Street was saved from the jackhammers of Whelan the Wrecker, who was commissioned to demolish the building in 1960. When Whelan's men opened up the walls of the building, they found the shirt of the man who had been killed while walking with his daughter in Flinders Lane in the 1890s.

Created in Vienna at the Imperial Art Foundry of the Austro-Hungarian Empire, and having adorned the most impressive office building in Australia, the Angel of Mercy now protects her fatherless family in a forgotten corner opposite the Baillieu Library at the University of Melbourne. However, her half-sized, but otherwise identical twin sister still stands over the archway of the Equitable Life building in George Street, Sydney.

The Colours of the 14th Battalion

The Colours of the 14th Battalion still stand over the entry to the main ballroom at the St Kilda Town Hall, just as Albert Jacka had planned in 1929–1930. In April 1991 a fire destroyed the original ballroom, its lavish organ, and the city's art collection. The Colours survived.

HISTORICAL APPENDIX

An historical appendix was provided at the conclusion of *Hard Jacka* to answer the question: how much of it was fact and how much was fiction? This section provides an answer to that question with respect to the sequel. Like *Hard Jacka*, this book is a novel, which incorporates many fictional scenes, and cannot therefore be regarded as a biography. At the same time, it is essentially a true story based largely on historically documented facts, and provides the reader with greater exposure to the true voice of Albert Jacka than any previous publication, including *Hard Jacka*. This is because the actual words that were spoken or written by Albert Jacka – as they were quoted by newspaper reporters in the days of shorthand, taken down at the Dardanelles Commission, written by him in letters and articles, or jotted down in shorthand by the St Kilda Town Clerk – are fully presented in the text. A straight historical biography cannot provide the reader with this experience.

As in the first novel, the main resources on the 14th Battalion's exploits at Gallipoli have been sourced from C.E.W. Bean's *Official History*, Newton Wanliss's *The History of the Fourteenth Battalion, A.I.F.*, and the memoirs or letters of men who were there, most notably Ferdinand Henry Wright, Frederick Anderson, and Dr Henry Loughran. The Australian War Memorial in Canberra provided access to the source notes used by Newton Wanliss to write his history, as well as other materials on Albert Jacka. As mentioned in the Acknowledgements, the National Library of Australia's digitisation of *The Argus* newspaper provided a very powerful research tool. The articles referred to in footnotes can be accessed very easily on the Internet by typing in the addresses provided.

The two biographies of Albert Jacka have both concentrated on his war record, rather than his life after the war.[8] However, they were helpful starting points for the original research undertaken for this book. The movements of Albert and Vera Jacka and others were derived from Sands & McDougall directories and voting registrations held at the State Library of Victoria, and birth, marriage and death certificates held by the Victorian Department of Justice.

Return of the legend

The Town Hall and the Depot

The account of Albert Jacka's triumphant entry to Melbourne is drawn mainly from the newspaper accounts of the event, in particular the evening edition of *The Herald* on 20 October 1919.[9] Another report appeared a few days later in the *Wedderburn Express*:

> "He refused point blank to be 'interviewed', and would say nothing of himself for publication or other use. For the few moments he was at the depot he was a bundle of nerves, and even declined a cup of tea offered by a willing VAD. As soon as he could he left the depot with his mother who had waited patiently for him, and disappeared from public gaze for the remainder of the day." [10]

Information on the fire that Bert and his two younger brothers ran towards in their youth was obtained from Bill Jacka's recollections

---

8   See Ian Grant (1990), *Jacka VC – Australia's Finest Fighting Soldier*, Sun Books-Macmillan, and Robert Macklin (2006), *Jacka VC – Australian Hero*, Allen & Unwin.

9   (20 October 1919), "Welcome of welcomes for Jacka, V.C. – Melbourne pays spontaneous tribute to Australia's most popular hero", *The Herald*, p. 1. Also see (21 October 1919), "Captain Jacka V.C., Return on S.S. *Euripides* – Great Reception by crowds", *The Argus*, p. 6 (http://nla.gov.au/nla.news-article4668888).

10   (24 October 1919), "Captain Jacka VC", *The Wedderburn Express*.

in 1977, which are held by the Korong Historical Society.[11] The fire at the Korong Flour Mill was discussed in an article in the Society's magazine, *Nuggets or Nothing*.[12]

Meeting with the family at Aunt Margaret's place in North Fitzroy

There is no evidence of what went on at Aunt Margaret's place in North Fitzroy apart from the photograph that was taken there showing that his father Nathaniel was not present. *The Argus* also contained a reference to the song *He was Only a Private, That's All* that had played at the *Majestic Theatre*.[13]

The return to Wedderburn

Albert Jacka's fondness for boxing is well known, and the fact that he attended the fight between Chris Jordan and Tommy Ryan in Melbourne just before his homecoming to Wedderburn was recorded by *The Argus*.[14] The recollections of Albert and Sidney Jacka about their youth (that is, the peach tree and the fire) are based on the reminiscences of Bill Jacka, who recorded them in 1977, well after all his brothers had passed away.[15]

The scenes in the novel where Albert Jacka and his father Nathaniel debate the conscription issue are not historical, and there is no evidence that such a debate ever took place. However the novel's depiction of the issues discussed is based on historical evidence. Nathaniel's reference to his eldest son Sam Jacka riding his bike from St Arnaud to talk to his parents about volunteering for duty was cited in a newspaper report.[16] An article in the *La Trobe Journal* noted that during the 1916 Conscription Debate,

---

11   (1981), "The Korong Flour Mill", *Nuggets or Nothing*, Vol. 9, pp. 9–12; and *Audio interview with William Jacka* (1977), held by Korong Historical Society.
12   (1981) "The Korong Flour Mill," *Nuggets or Nothing*, Vol. 9, pp. 9–12.
13   (29 November 1915), "Majestic Theatre", *The Argus*, p. 9 (http://nla.gov.au/nla.news-article1582283). For music and lyrics see http://nla.gov.au/nla.mus-an4784458.
14   (28 October 1919), "Jordan retains lightweight championship", *The Argus*, p. 8 (http://nla.gov.au/nla.news-article4664673).
15   Audio interview with William Jacka (1977), held by Korong Historical Society.
16   (28 July 1915), "Elder brother's ardour", *The Argus* (http://nla.gov.au/nla.news-article1542058).

Nathaniel had exposed a forged letter written by a non-existent Reg W. Turnbull, who claimed that Albert Jacka had written a pro-conscription letter.[17] In October 1916 Nathaniel had sworn a declaration that this was false.[18] Noting the *Herald* report in 1919 that he was in fact pro-conscription, Powell concluded that Albert Jacka may have changed his mind in the course of the war. However, Powell did not refer to the following letter that appears in the Albert Jacka file held in the National Archives of Australia:

> *Letter from T. Griffiths to "Administrative Headquarters, AIF, London" dated 15 September, 1918.*
>
> *"Jacka is very strongly opposed to returning to Australia just at the present moment for the undermentioned reasons: -*
>
> 1. *He is engaged to a lady in England and has arranged to get married to her within the next two or three months.*
>
> 2. *He is at the present time somewhat estranged from his father who is a strong anti-conscriptionist, Jacka being of course a conscriptionist; and he feels that if he goes out to Australia to help in the conscription campaign it will considerably widen the breach between them — a thing he is particularly anxious to avoid.*
>
> *I gather from other sources that there has been a certain amount of unpleasantness between him and his brigadier."*

The matter of his engagement is a mystery, as there is no other information about it. The contents of this letter were raised in a recent biography of Albert Jacka, which surmised that he would have had mixed feelings about meeting his father after the war.[19] However, no previous publication on Albert Jacka has referred

---

17   Damian Powell (1999), "Albert Jacka VC and the 1916 Conscription Debate", *The La Trobe Journal*, No. 63, Autumn, pp. 31–36.

18   Nathaniel's anti-conscriptionist activities during the 1916 referendum are recorded in the following article: (25 October 1916), "Anti-Conscription – Town Hall Demonstration – Overflow Meetings", *The Argus*, pp. 10–11. (http://nla.gov.au/nla. news-article1607061).

19   Robert Macklin (2006), pp. 214–216.

to his letter favouring conscription and Billy Hughes, which was published as a facsimile by *The Argus* on the morning of the 1917 referendum.[20] In it he wrote:

> *After the way Australian troops have fought to uphold the honour of our little island, Australia, by her vote on conscription, has dragged that same honour in the mud. I only wish I had been back. I would have given them some home truths. I am sure it is out of pure ignorance that people voted "No". They do not realise out there the great issue that is at stake. No words of mine can express my admiration for W.M. Hughes. I only wish we had more statesmen like him.*

The letter was written in Albert Jacka's handwriting, and there is no record of its authenticity being challenged. The fact that his mother had been threatened during the war was recorded by the *Argus*.[21] Nathaniel's references to wartime censorship and his views on Billy Hughes are derived from a letter he wrote to Mr M. Carroll in Ballarat:[22]

> *... reverting to the letter purporting to come from Reg W. Turnbull, in the Argus there is no such man exists, it is a direct fake. When it appeared in the Argus, I was in Melbourne and at once handed to the press a sworn Declaration and the censor pinched it, would not allow it to go into the press, and two different wires that my wife sent to me was censored and I did not get them. The prime minister used my son as a tool to try and put me down. Did we ever think he would stoop so low.*

---

20   (20 December 1917), "Read what Captain Albert Jacka VC Says About the 'No' Vote of 1916", *The Argus*, p. 6. (http://nla.gov.au/nla.news-article1670684). Also see (19 December 1917), "VC Winners – Captain Jacka's Opinion", *The Argus*, p. 8 (http://nla.gov.au/nla.news-article1670604).

21   (6 August 1915), "Hero's mother threatened", *The Argus*, p. 8 (http://nla.gov.au/nla.news-article1545699).

22   Letter from Nathaniel Jacka to M. Carroll, dated 4 November 1916 (copy provided to the author by Mr David Carroll of Adelaide).

Nathaniel Jacka's views on conscription, as spoken by him at an anti-conscription rally at the Melbourne Town Hall in 1916 were reproduced by *The Argus*:[23]

> *Mr N. Jacka, father of Lieutenant Jacka, V.C., said that his three sons had volunteered for the war. They went away from a free country as free men. (Applause) If they had the good fortune to return he wanted it to be to a free country. (Cheers) His sons would scoff at the word "conscription". It was said that the anti-conscriptionists were pro-Germans. Would anyone tell him that that his sons were pro-Germans? (Loud cheers) Although he was opposed to conscription, he said that Australia must do her duty to the Empire. She had done her duty so far, and must go on doing it under the voluntary system. There was no danger of Great Britain falling. She had never been so mighty as today. Australia could not afford 16,500 soldiers a month. We should do our duty in moderation, as we could afford to do. If the vote "Yes" was in the majority we would vote to be put under the iron heel of Prussianism, and under the mailed fist of capitalism. We would vote our wives and children into bondage, and into the workshops to work beside the black, brown and the brindle. (Cheers) His message was: A free Australia for our people, and a free people for Australia (Loud applause).*

Nathaniel's references to "black brown and the brindle" must be read in the context of the times, and its racial intolerance. In their speech, and in the diaries of all AIF men, including Captain Albert Jacka and General "Pompey" Elliott, non-Caucasians were referred to as "niggers".

The "night to remember"

What occurred at the "night to remember" in Wedderburn on 29 October 1919 was recorded in considerable detail by the

---

23   (25 October 1916), "Anti-Conscription: Town Hall Demonstration," *The Argus*, pp. 10–11 (http://nla.gov.au/nla.news-article1607061).

reporter of the *Wedderburn Express*.[24] Other accounts of the evening, and background on the township of Wedderburn, were obtained from a history of the town, and various issues of *Nuggets or Nothing*, published by the Korong Historical Society.[25] It is true that Albert's older brother Sam Jacka responded to the toast to the parents, rather than Nathaniel. It is also the case that Sid Jacka did not attend to receive his medal, but there is no evidence as to why. In the novel it is suggested that he wanted to avoid the confrontation between his brother and father. The appeal by Mrs Dupuy is based on a letter that she wrote to the Australian Army noting she had taken up the issue of her missing son, Jim, with Captain Jacka.[26] However, it is unlikely she did so that evening. The discussion in the novel between Albert Jacka and members of his family that takes place on the way back to the house in Ridge Street is not historical.

Advance Australia!

The Landing

The scenes of the landing at Anzac Cove just before dawn on 25 April 1915 are based on E. Ashmead Bartlett's account of how he landed and came across General Birdwood dictating the "permission to withdraw" letter to General Hamilton on the beach.[27] The scenes in the row-boat containing Major Drake-Brockman and others in his battalion, and his narrow escape on Plugge's Plateau are based on David Cameron's book, which is based on Bean.[28] Other accounts sourced for this section include

---

24 (31 October 1919), "Albert Jacka, VC – His return home – Wonderful enthusiasm shown – A modest hero", *The Wedderburn Express*.

25 J.C. Clements (1973), *A short history of Wedderburn, 1852–1973*; (1977), "Captain Albert Jacka, VC, MC and Bar", *Nuggets or Nothing*, No. 5, pp. 1–8; and, Victoria Gregson, (1989), "The Gregsons of Wedderburn – Some Family Fragments", *Nuggets or Nothing*, Vol. 17, pp. 5–8.

26 See Mrs Dupuy's letter in the Australian National Archives AIF record of Private James Dupuy (Number 568) of Wedderburn, which refers to Captain Albert Jacka.

27 E. Ashmead-Bartlett (1928), *The Uncensored Dardanelles*, Hutchinson & Co., London.

28 David W. Cameron (2007), *25 April 1915: The day the Anzac legend was born*, Allen & Unwin, p. 47.

those of Private Fred Fox and "Anzac".[29] The meeting between General Birdwood and the Official Historian, C.E.W. Bean on the morning of the twenty-sixth is based on Bean's diary.[30]

14th Battalion's Communion Service and arrival off Gaba Tepe

The account of conditions on the *Seang Choon* during the morning of 25 April are derived from diaries, memoirs and letters of Albert Jacka, Fred Anderson, Ferdinand Wright, D.R. Macdermid, and William Howard.[31] Details on Padre Andrew Gillison's reputation as a crack shot at the Melbourne Rifle Club and other descriptions were drawn from the report of a "Special Correspondent" who sailed to Egypt with the 14th Battalion.[32] The depiction of Albert Jacka in these scenes is largely fictional except for his volunteering for medical duty, and his thought that the burning hills of Gallipoli reminded him of a bushfire, as this was noted in his diary.

Landing of the 14th Battalion

The landing of the 14th Battalion draws on Newton Wanliss's *History of the 14th Battalion*, and the source notes, including the diary of William Howard, and the accounts of Captain Wright and Lieutenant Macdermid.[33] Lance-Corporal Fred Anderson's landing later that day with the main body of the 14th Battalion was based on his *Memoirs*. The landing of Sergeant Ernie Hill in the same boat as Colonel Monash is based on the reflections

29   Fred Fox (1938), "Through Death Valley with the ANZACS", and Anzac (1938) "When Our Dead CLOGGED Our TRENCHES – The Turkish Attack on Dead Man's Ridge", *The Great War "I Was There!"* Volume One, Edited by Sir John Hammerton, (London, The Amalgamated Press Ltd).

30   C.E.W. Bean (1983), *Gallipoli Correspondent – The frontline diary of C.E.W. Bean*, Selected and annotated by Kevin Fewster, Allen & Unwin.

31   Fredrick Anderson (1956), *Memoirs* (unpublished) courtesy of Stuart Anderson; Ferdinand Wright to Newton Wanliss, 10 July 1921, AWM 224 MSS 143A; D.R. Macdermid to Newton Wanliss (undated) AWM 224 MSS 143A; *Diary of William Howard* (courtesy of Aileen and Marie Howard).

32   (4 February 1915), "Australia's Second Force – Life on a transport – scene at the rendezvous – some personal notes", *The Argus*, p. 7 (http://nla.gov.au/nla.news-article1494146).

33   AWM 224, MSS 143A.

he passed on to his son, Barrie Hill.[34] The main sources for the defence of Quinn's Post were the recollections of F.H. Wright, and F. Anderson, as well as the writings of C.E.W. Bean and Cameron. Other sources included the account of A.R. Perry of the 10th Battalion.[35]

Percy Black and Harry Murray on Pope's Hill

The activities of the extraordinary duo of Percy Black and Harry Murray on Pope's Hill during the critical first few days at Gallipoli are based mainly on the accounts provided by Hatwell, Franki and Slayter, and Harry Murray's own writing.[36]

Of life and love

Establishing a business

In the two biographies of Albert Jacka it has been assumed that Roxburgh Jacka & Co was the first company formed by Albert Jacka, with John Wren as a silent partner. However, it was the firm of "Messrs. Parker, Roxborough, and Jacka & Co." that placed an advertisement for the summer beverage "Fort-reviver" in *The Argus* of 12 February 1920.[37] On 24 February 1920 the same advertisement re-appeared in *The Argus*, for "Roxburgh, Jacka & Co. Pty. Ltd.", suggesting that the firm had been reconstituted in a short time. The connection with Captain Alexander Parker was severed. In a later article discussing Parker's subsequent insolvency and political career in Prahran, Albert Jacka's name was raised as a former business partner.[38] The meeting at Wren's house is

---

34   Author's correspondence with Barrie Hill.

35   A.R. Perry (1916), "The Landing – by a Man of the Tenth," *The Anzac Book*, pp. 1–4.

36   Jeff Hatwell (2005), *No Ordinary determination: Percy Black and Harry Murray of the First AIF*, Fremantle Arts Centre Press; George Franki and Clyde Slayter, *Mad Harry: Australia's Most Decorated Soldier*, (2003), Kangaroo Press; H. Murray, (1 April 1939), "The first three weeks on Gallipoli", *Reveille*, pp. 10–11, and pp. 60–2.

37   (12 February 1920), "Fort Reviver", *The Argus*, p. 9 (http://nla.gov.au/nla.news-article1677064).

38   (23 July 1921), "Prahran Election – Validity inquired into – Was Mr Parker an Insolvent?", *The Argus*, p. 18. Also see *Re-member* – a database of all Victorian MPs since 1851 "Parker, Alexander Frederick".

not historically sourced, but a similar meeting must have taken place somewhere during this period. Reginald Owen Roxburgh's difficulty with alcohol is referenced from Robert Macklin's biography.[39] However, there is no evidence on why Roxburgh withdrew from the partnership in 1923. The novel suggests that he may have been suspicious of Wren.

14th Battalion and 4th Brigade reunion
The reunion of the 14th Battalion and 4th Brigade Association attended by Captain Jacka and Sergeant Buckley at *Sargent's Café* on 7 November 1919 was covered by *The Argus*, and Albert Jacka's speech at the function was reported in detail.[40] The "taking" of the town of Heberterne by Brigadier-General Brand was reported in an article appearing in *Reveille*.[41] Private conversations at the function are not historical. It is not known whether Newton Wanliss attended the function, but the press records his attendance at later 14th Battalion reunions. A week and a half later Albert Jacka spoke at the Athenaeum Theatre in Collins Street at a fundraiser for the Salvation Army, although this is not referred to in the novel.[42]

The Commercial Travellers' Club and Wren's office
It is very likely that Albert Jacka was a member of the Commercial Travellers' Association (CTA) Club in Flinders street in the early 1920s before the St Kilda Soldiers' and Sailors' Memorial Hall was completed in 1924. While this could not be confirmed by the CTA, a press report dealing with the arrival of the Prince of Wales at the club in 1920 (see below) implies that Jacka was a member.

The private discussion between Wren and his brother Arthur is not historically documented. However, Wren's total trust in Dick Lean (who like Albert Jacka was a Freemason) has been referred to

39   Robert Macklin (2006), p. 234.
40   (8 November 1919), "Victoria Cross Winners – Welcome by Comrades", *The Argus*, p. 21 (http://nla.gov.au/nla.news-article4658549).
41   "Baconstealer" (1 August 1933), "The Old Brig.", *Reveille*, Celebrities of the A.I.F. (No. 36), p. 16.
42   (19 November 1919), "Salvation Army Appeal – The 'Diggers'' Gratitude", *The Argus*, p. 14 (http://nla.gov.au/nla.news-article4652406).

in James Griffin's recent biography of Wren.[43] The scene involving Wren and the dishonest trainer who burst into Wren's office with death threats is drawn from Hugh Buggy's biography of Wren.[44]

St Patrick's Day Procession

In the novel it is assumed that Albert Jacka lived at the Middle Park Hotel from the time he came back to Melbourne from his welcome at Wedderburn. This is the address he gave on his wedding certificate a year later. The newspaper report on the debates preceding the procession, and the events around the march and soon after have been sourced from *The Argus*.[45] The author also viewed the documentary film of the procession that shows Wren greeting the VCs at the station, the procession, the maypole dancing afterwards, and the signing of the VCs' petition to the King at Mannix's mansion, "Raheen".[46] The film is very instructive of Wren's general manner, and charm. In addition to Albert Jacka, Wren was a business partner of Keith Murdoch, Frank Packer, and Edward "Red Ted" Theodore.

Bert and Vera's courtship

The scene in the novel depicting Vera Carey hugging Albert Jacka in the lift of the Olderfleet Building prior to being interviewed for a typist position is based on Ian Grant's biography:[47]

> *Within a few weeks of the company opening its doors, a young lady approached him in the office lift and boldly hugged him.*

---

43   James Griffin (2004), *John Wren — A life reconsidered*, Scribe, Melbourne, p. 32.
44   Hugh Buggy (1977), *The Real John Wren*, Melbourne, pp. 145–146.
45   (24 February 1920), "St Patrick's Procession – Councillor asks questions", *The Argus*, p. 6. (http://nla.gov.au/nla.news-article1678627); (22 March 1920), "St Patrick's Festival – Procession in the city", *The Argus*, p. 8 (http://nla.gov.au/nla.news-article1684731); (30 March 1920), "Victoria Cross Winners – Concert in the Exhibition", *The Argus*, p. 7 (http://nla.gov.au/nla.news-article1687093).
46   See St Patrick's Day Celebrations, Melbourne, 17 March 1920 ("Ireland will be free"), *National Film and Sound Archive*, Title No. 11803.
47   Ian Grant (1990), p. 165.

No reference for this event is provided, so its historicity is not clear, although Vera's daughter has said that she could "well imagine her [mother] doing it".[48] The author knows of no documentary record of the nature of the couple's courtship, so this section of the novel is almost wholly fictional, although the context is based on fact. For example, the couple's date at the *Esplanade Hotel* in St Kilda is not historical, but the discussion about the riot by AIF soldiers who destroyed Anton Weniger's merry-go-round is based on fact.[49]

The presentation of a "golden pass" to Albert Jacka during the interval at the Tivoly Theatre production of *As You Were* in 1920 is historical, and was sourced from an article in *The Argus* covering the event. Similarly, Sergeant Maurice Buckley's impromptu speech for the Irish cause is closely based on the report in the paper.[50] It was also reported that Brigadier Brand then spoke about some humorous events that took place during the war, which amused the audience. There is no documentary evidence that Vera was at the play, as depicted in the novel, so this component is purely fictional.

The reception provided to the Prince of Wales at St Kilda, and his subsequent welcome at the Commercial Travellers' Club in Flinders Street was also sourced from *The Argus*.[51] Hence, the speech made by the Prince, including his reference to Albert Jacka,

---

48   Robert Macklin (2006), p. 241.
49   (17 January 1916), "Riotous Soldiery – disturbance at St Kilda – raid on merry-go-round – several arrests", *The Argus*, pp. 9–10 (http://nla.gov.au/nla.news article2096400).
50   (27 March 1920), "Gala performance at Tivoli", *The Argus*, p. 22 (http://nla.gov.au/nla.news-article1686557); and (23 February, 1920), "Tivoli – 'As You Were,'" *The Argus*, p. 9 (http://nla.gov.au/nla.news-article1678473).
51   (27 May 1920), "Victoria welcomes the Prince – Fog delays landing – Magnificent demonstration – 400,000 people line the streets", *The Argus*, pp. 9–13 (http://nla.gov. au/nla.news-article1706109); (31 May 1920) "Travellers" Club Visit – 'Why should I lose my hat!'", *The Argus*, pp. 7–8 (http://nla.gov.au/nla.news-article1707250); (31 May 1920) "Morning 'off' – Squash ", *The Argus*, pp. 7–8 (http://nla.gov.au/nla.news-article1707250).

are historical. The return of Captain Bill Jacka and his family from England was reported by the Press in July 1920.[52]

The marriage and honeymoon

There is anecdotal evidence that Vera received a frosty reception from Elizabeth and Nathaniel Jacka, and this has been referred to in the two biographies of Albert Jacka. According to Robert Macklin, who based his comment on the testimony of Bill Jacka's surviving daughter, Josephine Eastoe:[53]

> When he brought her to Wedderburn to meet his parents, Nathaniel and Elizabeth warned the rest of the family to stay away. Accordingly, only family legend exists to throw light on the event...

Vera's frosty reception in Wedderburn was presumably because of her Catholic faith in a time of extreme sectarianism, however, Macklin has suggested that it was a product of her "social graces".[54]

Josephine Eastoe is also recorded as doubting whether her parents were even at Albert and Vera's wedding.[55] The fact that Vera's eighteen-year-old brother James Carey signed the marriage certificate as best man suggests that this may be correct. The author is also not aware of any press notices or surviving photographs of the wedding, which appears to have been extremely low key. There is no record of their honeymoon, so the novel's depiction of scenes at Erskine House in Lorne are fictional. However, Albert Jacka's attendance as a pallbearer at Sergeant Buckley's funeral was reported in the Press.[56]

---

52 (28 July 1920) "Soldiers returning", *The Argus*, p. 10 (http://nla.gov.au/nla.news-article4593684).
53 Robert Macklin (2006), p. 242.
54 Robert Macklin (2006), pp. 242–3.
55 Robert Macklin (2006), pp. 243.
56 (28 January 1921), "Sergeant Buckley V.C. – Accident Proves Fatal", *The Argus*, p. 6 (http://nla.gov.au/nla.news-article1734417).

War and police

Dardanelles Commission Hearing dream sequences

Presented as a series of dreams in the novel, the testimony of Captain Albert Jacka under oath at the Dardanelles Commission Hearing is based very closely on the actual transcript.[57] This is Albert Jacka in true conversation, and apart from the transcripts of his discussions as Mayor of St Kilda, letters and direct quotations from press reports, is the most genuine surviving representation of him. Overall, his testimony before the Commission suggests a defensive position with respect to the actions of the British and the Anzacs, and the standard of arrangements (including medical) during the landing. Some of the Commissioners were looking for scapegoats, and Albert Jacka appeared determined not to assist in that process, which at times resulted in some aggressive cross-examination.

Senator Harold "Pompey" Elliott's speeches in the Senate and the Masonic hymn

Senator Harold "Pompey" Elliott's speeches in the Senate in 1921 provide a fascinating insight into the character of this remarkable man, who was like Albert Jacka in some ways, but unlike him in others. The speeches by senators Elliott, Drake-Brockman and others are taken directly from *Hansard* and contemporary newspaper reports.[58] The context of this debate is contained in Ross McMullin's biography of Elliott.[59] Albert Jacka's use of lantern slides in his speech to the Collingwood branch of the Australian Natives' Association was reported in the Press.[60] The lantern slides are held by the AWM. His description in the novel

---

57   Dardanelles Commission Hearings (28 August 1917) *Testimony of Captain Albert Jacka, VC, MC*, pp. 1589–91, AWM 51 103.

58   *Hansard*, (1921), Senate, "Defence Bill"; 28 April, 5 May, 11 May; (29 April 1921), "Battle of Bullecourt – Senator Elliott's charges – 'Captain Jacka Victimised'", *The Argus*, p. 7; and "14th Battalion Command – General Elliott's Criticism", *The Argus*, p. 6 (http://nla.gov.au/nla.news-article1752149 and 1754107).

59   Ross McMullin, *Pompey Elliott*, (Scribe), Chapter 21, pp. 537–564.

60   (23 August 1923), "Reminiscences of Captain Albert Jacka, V.C.", *The Argus*, p. 10 (http://nla.gov.au/nla.news-article2020566).

of the gallant defence of Courtney's Post by Lieutenant Rutland is presented in Jacka's own words, which were published in *The Herald* in 1926.[61]

The scene where Albert Jacka arrives home and is surprised that Vera is able to sing a Masonic hymn is based on the testimony of their daughter Betty, who heard it from her mother. Betty told the author that the only complaint she heard her mother make about her deceased father was that the only wedding anniversary present he had ever given her was a vase on their first anniversary.[62]

Albert Jacka's support for Peter Hansen's campaign at Charlton

The scene at the Victoria Hall in Charlton in August 1921 is based on a newspaper report. Hence, the speech given by the Nationalist Party candidate, Peter Hansen, is historically documented, as is the fact that Albert Jacka was there to support his candidacy.[63] The attendance of Albert Jacka's brothers in law and his brother Sam is not historical.

The Wanliss society wedding

The Wanliss wedding scenes are based on several newspaper reports of the event. A photo of Mrs Mabel Brookes, Mrs Pitt Rivers and other women at the Stonington reception was published in *The Argus*.[64] The Tokyo earthquake disaster occurred just before the wedding, and Lieutenant-Colonel John Peck was in Melbourne to organise the Australian relief effort.[65]

The Police Strike

The personal story of F.F. Knight during the police strike of 1923 is drawn from his autobiographical book, *These Things Happened*.

---

61   Albert Jacka (24 April 1926), "A sheaf of Anzac memories", *The Herald*.
62   Author's correspondence with Albert Jacka's daughter, Betty
63   (29 August 1921), "Korong – Candidate Refutes a Statement", *The Argus*, p. 8 (http://nla.gov.au/nla.news-article4665836).
64   See (17 October 1923), "Social Events: Morrison-Irvine Wedding", *The Argus*, p. 23 (http://nla.gov.au/nla.news-article2000940); and "Reception at Stonnington", p. 17 (http://nla.gov.au/nla.news-article2001010).
65   (10 September 1923), "Japan's need", *The Argus*, p. 11 (http://nla.gov.au/nla.news-article1998519).

Other references drawn upon for this section include the historical work *Days of Violence*, and newspaper reports in *The Argus* and *The Age*.[66] W.D. Joynt's experience, including the report on the meeting of communists at Trades Hall was from his autobiographical *Breaking the Road for the Rest*. The interactions of Sir John Monash, Senator Pompey Elliott and Sir James McCay in the command structure have been sourced from Ross McMullin's biography, *Pompey Elliott*. The author found no evidence that Albert Jacka took any part in the response to the police strike, but there is no doubt that he would have been highly sympathetic to the Special Constables. The fire that destroyed the premises of Jacka Edmonds & Co in December 1923 was reported in the Press.[67]

A country fit for heroes

The Collingwood Town Hall

The ball at the Collingwood Town Hall in July 1924 is based on a newspaper report that described even the dress that Vera was wearing.[68] It is the first reference to Albert Jacka's developing relationship with local government circles. In 1924 Albert Jacka did open the Soldiers' and Sailors' Memorial Hall, which is close to the Collingwood Town Hall on Hoddle Street. The building still stands, but there is no reference to Albert Jacka on it.

With Newton Wanliss at Lissa Thorn

There is no doubt that Albert Jacka met with Newton Wanliss while he was writing the *History of the 14ᵗʰ Battalion*. Newton did own a flat at "Lissa Thorn" in Redan Street, East St Kilda, which would

---

66   Gavin Brown and Robert Haldane, (1998), *Days of Violence: the 1923 Police Strike in Melbourne*, (Hybrid); (2 November 1923), "Police Mutineers – Duty again refused – Ministry's fi m stand – Ringleaders dismissed", *The Argus*, pp. 11–12 (http://nla.gov. au/nla.news-article1994431); (5 November 1923), "Riot By Night", *The Argus*, p. 11 (http://nla.gov.au/nla.news-article1999392); (5 November 1923), "Rioting and Looting in Melbourne", *The Age*.

67   (31 December 1923), "Collins Street Fire", *The Argus*, p. 8 (http://nla.gov.au/nla. news-article1986576).

68   (16 July 1924), "Social Events – Collingwood Mayoral Ball", *The Argus*, p. 22 (http:// nla.gov.au/nla.news-article4272595).

have been convenient for Jacka to visit. Albert Jacka's hand written version of his diary was provided to Newton Wanliss on Roxburgh Jacka & Co letterhead and is currently held in the AWM.[69] On the back of one of the pages is a map of the trench system at Courtney's Post (reproduced in the text), which is marked with a fountain pen, suggesting that Albert Jacka explained his VC action to Newton with the aid of the map.[70] The extract from Padre Francis Rolland's condolence letter for Harold Wanliss was taken from the original, which is held by the AWM.[71] The newspaper article referring to discrimination against Dr Marion Wanliss is from *The Argus*, but there is no record that Newton Wanliss ever discussed this with Albert Jacka.[72]

Address to Honorary Justices and Christmas in Wedderburn

The presentation Albert Jacka made to the Justices of the Peace at the Melbourne Town Hall is sourced from a press report of the event.[73] While drawing on traditions that were widely observed at the time, the scene depicting a Christmas function in Wedderburn is fictional.[74] However, the tensions that were likely to be building between Bert and his brother Bill, are based on an analysis of their divergent political views. At one stage Albert Jacka chaired a meeting of businessmen who were being affected by a strike on the wharves.[75]

Not all diggers who returned from the Great War wanted to remember it, like Albert Jacka and Pompey Elliott did. Many had been so traumatised by what they had witnessed, that all they

---

69   AWM MSS 143 A Parts 4–5.

70   The diary is at AWM224 143A 4 of 14 (Part 4). The map is drawn in the same ink as the diary written by Albert Jacka on Roxburgh Jacka & Co letterhead.

71   AWM 43, A911.

72   (12 December 1923), "Objection to Women Doctors", *The Argus*, p. 8 (http://nla.gov.au/nla.news-article1986760).

73   (23 May 1924), "Honorary Justices – Address by Captain Jacka, V.C.", *The Argus*, p. 5 (http://nla.gov.au/nla.news-article4351065).

74   These traditions are neatly summarised in Ivy V. Arney (1987), *Twenties Child: A Childhood Recollection*, Collins Dove, Melbourne.

75   (30 September 1925), "Interests of Traders – Meeting to be Held Tomorrow", *The Argus*, p. 24 (http://nla.gov.au/nla.news-article2145533).

wanted was to forget it. Albert Jacka's experiences of being in the company of senior AIF officers, and being lauded by the King, the Prince of Wales and other aristocrats are likely to have pushed him to the right. Bill Jacka did not share these experiences, and instead appears to have drifted to the left despite his officer rank. The experience of the Great Depression and the rise of fascism in Europe probably influenced him further in that direction. While it came later, it is worth reproducing the "Foreword" Bill Jacka wrote in 1936 for a publication by the communist front organisation, the League for Peace and Democracy, titled "The Truth about Anzac".[76]

Foreword by Captain W. Jacka (Late 14th Battalion AIF) [77]

Probably at no time in the world's history has such superb courage been shown by a body of men as was shown by the Australian and New Zealand soldiers at Anzac.

Shattered by shells, riddled with bullets, and suffering the pangs of hunger and thirst, many of these men gave their lives believing that in doing so they were making the world safe for democracy, and would end for all time the butchery known as war.

Twenty one years have elapsed since those courageous lives were sacrificed, and today we know only too well that the world has not been saved for democracy and that the last war was not a war to end all wars. It is plain that the sacrifices of the men who gave their lives on the rugged slopes of Gallipoli will have been in vain unless we — the people of Australia — unite in a determined refusal to do the bidding of a small minority that thrives on the business of war.

---

76   David Rose (May 1980), "The Movement Against War and Fascism, 1933–1939", *Labour History*, No. 38, pp. 78–9; and Len Fox (November 1980), "The Movement Against War and Fascism: A View from Inside", *Labour History*, No. 38, pp. 78–82.

77   Len Fox (April 1936), *The Truth About Anzac*, League for Peace and Democracy.

> *To the returned soldiers, the mothers and fathers and the splendid young men and women who have grown up since the last slaughter, I appeal: as one who took part in the Gallipoli campaign to let the rulers of Australia know that you will not tolerate a repetition of what occurred twenty one years ago, that you will not allow your determination and heroism to be prostituted by the masters of the old world, whose only god is profit. Display your courage by refusing to fight in imperialist war under any pretext whatever, and join with those who fight only in the Cause of Peace, and give your hand to the task of building a new world wherein peace and liberty shall flourish, and men and women shall live in harmony with their fellows.*
>
> *April 1936*

These were noble ideals, however in "The Truth about Anzac", the country that "fights only in the Cause of Peace" turns out to be the Soviet Union. The author, Len Fox, was formerly a teacher at Melbourne's elite Scotch College.

The fact that Bill had returned to Australia with his family because he found he couldn't become a "scab" during the Welsh coal strike was recalled by him in his 1977 interview. Similarly, Bill Jacka's discussion about his early days in Wedderburn, and the discovery of the amorous Senior Constable O'Brien is drawn from his 1977 recollections.

Dinner for Frank Boileau at Scott's Hotel

The scene depicting Albert Jacka as chairman of a meeting of businessmen at Scott's Hotel to recognise Frank Boileau for his stand against increased taxation is drawn from a report in *The Argus*. The strong words attributed to Albert Jacka, which provide further evidence of his political orientation, are reproduced from that article:[78]

---

78   (4 April 1925), "Keeping Down Taxation", *The Argus*, p. 35 (http://nla.gov.au/nla. news-article2074397).

Proposing the toast of the guest, the chairman (Captain A. Jacka, V.C.), said that the taxpayers were indebted to Mr Boileau for his opposition to the imposition of an unwarranted increase in State income taxation. The Allan-Peacock Ministry had had the audacity to adopt the Labour party's extravagant proposals, and it was in a great measure due to the alertness of Mr Boileau that the proposals had been rejected. Had the Labour party continued in office taxpayers would have expected to fight against an unscrupulous onslaught upon their savings.

There is no record that Lieutenant Colonel Charles Dare was at this meeting, as suggested in the novel, however the interaction that he had with Newton Wanliss over his war record, particularly his removal from command by Brigadier-General Brand, are based on a letter held at the AWM.[79]

Visit of the US Pacific Naval Squadron and the boxing matches at The Stadium

The visit by the US Pacific Naval Squadron in 1925 has been all but forgotten compared with President Teddy Roosevelt's "Great White Fleet" of 1908. For two weeks Melbourne provided a large range of activities and entertainments to 30,000 US sailors. Admiral Coontz's far-sighted speech at the Commercial Traveller's Association Club is historical, but it is not known whether Albert Jacka and Ernest Edmonds attended, as depicted in the novel.[80]

The scenes at John Wren's Stadium, where US sailors fought Australians in exhibition matches are based on newspaper reports.[81] While the attendance of Albert Jacka's party is not historical, his brother-in-law, Patrick Gleeson (who married Vera's sister Molly)

---

79   Letter from Charles Dare to Newton Wanliss dated 6 July 1923 AWM 224 MSS143A.
80   (25 July 1925), "Travellers' Luncheon", *The Argus*, p. 32 (http://nla.gov.au/nla.news-article2146230); (23 July 1925), "Fleet Arrives To-Day", *The Argus*, p. 11 (http://nla.gov.au/nla.news-article2144895).
81   (30 July 1925), "Boxing: Americans at Stadium", *The Argus*, p. 12 (http://nla.gov.au/nla.news-article2148570).

was the former New South Wales lightweight champion who had
been defeated by Chris Jordan.[82] The stories of the gregarious fist-
fighting graziers, "Dan and Percy", and the "incident" under the
Flinders Street Station clocks are based on the recollections of
F.F. Knight, but their names had to be constructed, as he did not
reveal their true identities.[83]

The attack on Hill 971

Apart from the First Battle of Bullecourt (which is covered in
detail in *Hard Jacka*), the attack on Hill 971 was the most disastrous
battle that the 14th Battalion took part in during the Great War.
The main sources framing the action were C.E.W. Bean's account,
and the chapter devoted to the attack in Newton Wanliss's *History
of the 14th Battalion*. The references to Albert Jacka's notes on
tactics are taken from his notebook, which is held at the AWM.[84]
Similarly, the personal story of Captain Henry Loughran, MO of
the 14th Battalion, is drawn from an extensive letter that he wrote
to Newton Wanliss, which is now held at the AWM.[85]

The crash of '29

Adopting Betty

The references to the tragedies surrounding the construction
of the Equitable Assurance Building are drawn from *A City Lost
& Found*.[86] In a 1934 article, Ted Rule noted that Albert Jacka's
business partner, Ernest Edmonds, had suggested that he and Vera
adopt a child.[87]

---

82   (27 January 1920), "Boxing: Jordan knocks out Gleeson", *The Argus*, p. 6 (http://nla.
      gov.au/nla.news-article1674870).

83   F.F. Knight (1975), *These Things Happened: Unrecorded History 1895–1946*, The Hawthorn
      Press, Melbourne.

84   AWM File: 749/51/26, Record PR 84/333 Lecture notes, autograph book etc of Capt.
      Albert Jacka, 14th BN AIF.

85   AWM 224 MSS 143A.

86   Robyn Annear (2005), *A City Lost & Found – Whelan the Wrecker's Melbourne*, (Black Inc.).

87   E.J. Rule (1 January 1935), "Hero of Epic Fights – Capt. A. Jacka, V.C. M.C. – Death
      Anniversary", *Reveille*, p. 13.

In better days Jacka, at his partner's suggestion, had adopted a child
— he was very fond of children.

This appears to come from his discussion with Edmonds at the opening of the Albert Jacka memorial at the St Kilda cemetery some months after the funeral. However, Betty recalls that Albert Jacka knew her natural father, an ex-digger whose name was Smith, and that the adoption was done privately through a solicitor.[88] Hence, Albert and Vera may not have visited the Children's Welfare Department in Flinders Street as depicted in the novel.

Visit by the Duke and Duchess of York

The visit of the Duke and Duchess of York is based on contemporary newspaper reports.[89] The scene at Government House, when Vera is in the company of the Duchess and asks her permission to use the Princess Elizabeth's name for her adopted daughter is based on the testimony of Betty, who was told this story by her mother some years later. The discussion of the air tragedy over Melbourne is based on a contemporary newspaper report.[90]

The Shrine of Remembrance vs "Anzac Square"

The account of the Anzac Day dinner at Anzac House is based on a combination of Geoffrey Serle's biography,[91] and a press report of the speeches made by Prime Minister Bruce and Sir John Monash.[92] The novel also follows W.D. Joynt's autobiography, where he recalled Monash asking "Say that again Joynt?"[93] It is certain that Albert Jacka sat at the table of 32 VCs with W.D. Joynt, but it is not recorded that they sat together.

---

88   Betty Jacka's correspondence with the author.
89   (22 April 1927), "Landing at St Kilda", *The Argus* (http://nla.gov.au/nla.news-article3850422).
90   (22 April 1927), "Terrible Flying Tragedy", *The Argus*, p. 16 (http://nla.gov.au/nla.news-article3850491).
91   Geoffrey Serle, (1982) *John Monash: A biography*, Melbourne University Press.
92   (25 April 1927), "Spirit of Anzac", *The Argus*, p. 14 (http://nla.gov.au/nla.news-article3850806).
93   W.D. Joynt, VC (1979), *Breaking the Road for the Rest*, Hyland House, Melbourne.

Commemorating 8 August at "Iona"

The commemorative dinners at Sir John Monash's house "Iona" are recorded by his biographer, Geoffrey Serle.[94] The 1927 commemoration depicted in the novel, where Major-General "Pompey" Elliott finds himself seated next to Lieutenant-General Brudenell White did happen, and was recorded by the latter in his diary. Brudenell White noted that it was a "jolly party", but wrote:[95]

> *Had to sit beside Elliott part of the time and we had a reconciliation, but not before I had told him what I thought of him.*

The questions posed by Major-General Johnston to General Thomas Blamey, then the chief of Victoria's police force, are not historical, but the nature of his remarks are based on a letter Johnston wrote to Monash, which was paraphrased by Serle:[96]

> *Major-General George Johnston wrote to Monash to suggest that it would be a great pity to disband the constables, "a wonderfully fine body of men". If made permanent, under Monash's leadership, though non-military and non-political, they could act as strike-breakers, protecting loyalist workers... He told Johnston that the suggestion was in line with a world-wide movement of which the Italian Fascists and the Ku-Klux-Klan were examples... The secret "White Guard" may have derived from Johnston's suggestion but, though he must have known of its activities, Monash was not involved.*

Jacka family gathering at Geelong in 1928

The family gathering at Geelong upon the death of Nathaniel Jacka's mother, Elizabeth, is possibly the time that Thomas Jacka's

---

94   Geoffrey Serle (1982), Chapter 16.
95   R. McMullin (2002), p. 616.
96   G. Serle (1982), Chapter 16.

daughter Irene asked her cousin Albert for an autograph. The autograph book has not survived, but Albert Jacka's response "Only a fool is never afraid", was remembered by Irene's son Malcolm Rowe, who passed it on to the author in correspondence. The fact that Nathaniel's maternal grandfather, Nicholas Tremewan Bottrell, was born during the Napoleonic wars illustrates that these times were not too far removed from the period between the world wars. The fact that Vera's mother Catherine died at the Jacka residence in Murchison Street was referenced from her death certificate.

Fundraising for the Shrine of Remembrance

The novel mentions several instances when Albert Jacka's name was used to attract people to functions raising money for the Shrine of Remembrance, a campaign that was obviously close to his heart. Examples include the *Theatre Royal*, where his speech was paraphrased by a journalist as follows:[97]

> He recalled the details of the first Anzac Day, and then said that everyone would agree that on that day Australia had been lifted from an obscure Dominion to being one of the front-rank nations of the world. Thousands of young Australians were killed then and at later times, and they had set for us traditions that we must live up to. It was for us now to do something to keep evergreen the memory of those fine men who had died. (Applause)

The picnic

The picnic outing depicted in the novel is based on a photograph of Albert Jacka holding his daughter Betty on a bench by the seaside. In the photograph Betty's shoes have been taken off, presumably to

---

97   (18 May 1928), "Shrine of Remembrance – Special Community Singing – Appeal by Captain Jacka", *The Argus*, p. 16 (http://nla.gov.au/nla.news-article3948981). Also see (28 May 1928), "Shrine of Remembrance – Success of Appeal – Gathering at Chelsea", *The Argus*, p. 16 (http://nla.gov.au/nla.news-article3942121); and (23 June 1928), "Shrine of Remembrance – Progress of Work – More than £5000 from Freemasons", *The Argus*, p. 26 (http://nla.gov.au/nla.news-article3929148), which discusses Albert Jacka's visit to the Heathcote Masonic Lodge.

allow her to walk on the sand by the beach. A close look at Albert Jacka's feet shows that they were swollen, as were the fingers on his hands. However, the photograph is from early 1929, when Betty was around two years old.

Albert Jacka as a St Kilda Councillor

The reference to a French father suing a teacher for destroying his son's illusion of Father Christmas was reported in the *Argus*.[98] Vera's bedtime story, and Albert Jacka's tram ride with Betty are not historical. It is not known why Vera didn't attend the dance, which was a historical fact.[99] Several sources were relied on for background information about St Kilda and Elwood.[100]

Armistice Day gathering of VCs at Government House

Captain Albert Jacka VC sat next to Sir Neville Smyth VC for the formal photograph of the gathering of VCs at Government House for Armistice Day in 1928. W.D. Joynt VC stood behind them. There is no record of what they said in private conversation, so the conversations presented in this scene are fictional. Lord Somers' thoughts about Australians are drawn from letters to his sister, now displayed on the Lord Somers Camp website.[101] It is interesting to note that Albert Jacka, coming from a country working-class background, arrived in white tie, while Joynt, who attended the elite Melbourne Grammar School, wore a lounge suit (as did the Governor and Governor-General). Joynt rather unfairly considered himself the "dud" of his classroom "form" (the long bench they sat on), since:[102]

---

98   (30 December 1930), "'Father Christmas' Destroying an illusion – Parent Sues Professor", *The Argus* (http://nla.gov.au/nla.news-article4242403).

99   (21 November 1930), "Charity Ball", *The Argus* (http://nla.gov.au/nla.news-article4225095).

100   John Cooper (1931), *History of St Kilda 1840–1930*, St Kilda Historical Society (www.skhs.org.au/coopers.htm) and Meyer Eidelson (2006), Flood, Fire and Fever – A History of Elwood, (www.skhs.org.au/elwood.htm).

101   Alan Gregory (1987), *Lord Somers: Something of the life and letters of Arthur, 6th Baron Somers* (www.lordsomerscamp. org.au/about/lordsom/titlepage.htn).

102   W.D. Joynt (1979), p. 12.

All except myself were created Knights, one a Lord, two became Lieutenant-Generals, and one, after a fine record with senior rank, became Lord Mayor of Melbourne.

Senator Elliott on compulsory military service

Senator Elliott's exposition on compulsory military service during debate over the Governor-General's speech in the Senate in November 1929 is another example of his blustering style. It also shows a man who continued to be haunted by the lack of recognition he received for his brilliant counter-attack at Villiers-Brettonneux, which he raised yet again.[103]

New St Kilda Baths debate at the Council

Albert Jacka appeared to be opposed to the St Kilda Council taking out a substantial loan in order to build a new Baths on the St Kilda foreshore (the old Baths had burned down).[104] It is possible that Jacka, like Councillor Cummings, thought it was unwise for the council to take on debt in the uncertain times, and instead allow the private sector to take on the risk of construction and operation. It is ironic that Jacka later brought the construction of these baths to fruition when he was Mayor.

The "Big Dipper"

The 14th Battalion Colours and the collapse of Jacka Edmonds & Co. Pty Ltd

The scene in the novel that depicts the presentation of the 14th Battalion Colours at the St Kilda Town Hall is based on an official photograph of the event, and on the program, which is held in the St Kilda Town Hall Archives.

---

103   See *Hansard*, (21 November 1929) Senate, *Governor-General's Speech — Address-in-Reply*, pp. 59–62.

104   (3 December 1929), "In the Suburbs — Foreshore Improvements — St Kilda's Loan Proposals", *The Argus*, p. 11 (http://nla.gov.au/nla.news-article4054172); and, (3 December 1929), "In the suburbs — St Kilda Baths — Loan of £66,700", *The Argus*, p. 15 (http://nla.gov.au/nla.news-article4058348).

Details of the advertising campaign undertaken by Jacka, Edmonds & Co during the first six months of 1930 were taken from the press.[105] The meeting of W.D. Joynt and Albert Jacka outside his Elizabeth Street store was recalled by him in the 1977 documentary film *Jacka VC*.[106]

> *I met Jacka one day outside his electrical store, in which he told me, looking very sad:"I am closing down. I am being closed down.Wren, thinking that he's bought me, wants me to take a course of action politically. But I refused to do so. He said"All right, if you don't I'll close you down.' I prefer to be closed down."And he was.*

While Joynt's comments in 1977 may be as he remembered the 1930 conversation (a distance of forty-seven years), they do not give credit to Wren's years of support and generosity towards Jacka. Details of the meeting of creditors to liquidate Jacka, Edmonds & Co were taken from articles that appeared in *The Argus*.[107] The second article stated that the National Bank of Australasia was fully secured, but did not mention by whom.[108] This created a puzzle that was later resolved by the discovery of a Board Minute of the National Bank of Australasia dated 16 October 1930:[109]

105   See for example, (1 November 1929), "The Silent 'Vortex'", *The Argus*, p. 14 (http://nla.gov.au/nla.news-article4047410).

106   Cooper, R. and N. Beusst (1977), *Jacka VC*, DVD produced by Sunrise Picture Co.

107   (1 October 1930), "Jacka, Edmonds & Co. – In Voluntary Liquidation", *The Argus*, p. 7 (http://nla.gov.au/nla.news-article4201507); (15 October 1930), "Jacka, Edmonds & Co. – In Meeting of Creditors", *The Argus*, p. 4 (http://nla.gov.au/nla.news-article4208864); (17 October 1930), "Jacka, Edmonds & Co.", *The Argus*, p. 6 (http://nla.gov.au/nla.news-article4209481).

108   (17 October 1930), "Jacka, Edmonds & Co.", *The Argus*, p. 6 (http://nla.gov.au/nla.news-article4209481).

109   The author is grateful to Mr Bernard McGrath, Manager, Group Archives, Corporate Office, National Australia Bank, for discovering this Minute, which clarified the mystery surrounding *The Argus* press reports. Geoffrey Blainey (1958), *Gold and Paper – A History of The National Bank of Australasia Limited* (Georgian House, Melbourne) was referred to for context.

Jacka Edmonds & Co Pty Ltd Overdraft limit 11,600 pounds. Security-Guarantee of John Wren — 11,600 pounds. The Chief Manager reported the position in regard to this Propriety, which is in voluntary liquidation, and which has been the subject of notice in the daily Press, the Bank being erroneously listed as an unsecured creditor.

The newspaper report on the scenes of conflict between Nazis and communists in the Reichstag in Berlin appeared in *The Argus* on 15 October 1930.[110]

Albert Jacka as Mayor of St Kilda

Albert Jacka's role as the Mayor of St Kilda was distinguished by his focus on alleviating the conditions faced by families through unemployment.[111] The voice of Albert Jacka at the special public meeting he convened on 13 October 1930, is his, as is the voice of Mr Stenning from the State Relief Committee. These lines come from very detailed minutes taken down in shorthand, probably by the Town Clerk.[112] Background on the family of Councillor Cummings was obtained from AIF enlistment forms and various newspaper articles.

It is likely that Vera was jealous of her husband working closely with other women on committees. From press reports the name of Miss Alison Cummings is the one that is most frequently coupled with Albert Jacka's. Betty recounts that she once asked her mother for a notebook. Presenting her with the book, Vera had said, "That used to belong to your father. I've torn out the ladies' addresses."[113] However, there is no other

---

110   See also (15 October 1930), "Reichstag Scenes – New Fascist Party – Jeers from Communists", *The Argus*, p. 4 (http://nla.gov.au/nla.news-article4208796).

111   Albert Jacka's preference to unemployed returned soldiers was noted in (10 September 1930) *The Argus*, p. 8 (http://nla.gov.au/nla.news-article4189334).

112   See Minutes of meeting convened by the Mayor (Cr. A. Jacka, V.C.) on Monday, 13 October 1930, for the Relief of Unemployment, and Assistance to Hospitals Appeal (held in the St Kilda Town Hall Archives).

113   Author's correspondence with Betty Jacka.

evidence that Albert Jacka played the field, and it would seem totally at odds with his character and circumstances to have ever done so.

The September 1930 fundraising *café chantant* at Councillor George Cummings' boarding house St Leonards is based on actual events.[114] The discussion about gold prospecting is also based on actual events, and in 1931 the St Kilda unemployed were financed by the council to dig for gold.[115] The scene at the Royal Melbourne Yacht Club send off for the Governor-General, Lord Stonehaven, and his speech is based on the newspaper report. While Albert Jacka also spoke at the function, his words were not recorded, and his speech in the novel is fiction based on the author's analysis and opinion on his concerns at the time.[116]

Albert Jacka's response to the criticisms of Mr Harris about a late balance sheet is based on a newspaper report.[117] The fact that I.P. Levoi's office was located across the street from Albert Jacka's firm, and he often visited was noted by Jacka's biographer Ian Grant, who interviewed Levoi's secretary.[118]

"Pompey" Elliott's attempted suicide

The sad story of General Pompey Elliott and his suicide attempts are sourced from Ross McMullin's definitive work, *Pompey Elliott*.[119] While Elliott and Jacka appeared to share traits such as fearlessness in the face of danger and concern for the men under them, the latter did not allow the unfairness of his treatment by the military hierarchy to influence his behaviour in the post-war

---

114   (17 September 1930), "Bridge at St Leonards", *The Argus*, p. 11 (http://nla.gov.au/nla.news-article4194176).
115   (1 July 1931), "Grant for Gold-Seekers", *The Argus*, p. 8 (http://nla.gov.au/nla.news-article4387279).
116   (22 September 1930), "Lord Stonehaven – Farewell by Yachtsmen", *The Argus*, p. 8 (http://nla.gov.au/nla.news-article4196707).
117   (5 May 1931), "St Kilda Carnival – Balance-Sheet Not Delayed", *The Argus*, p. 8 (http://nla.gov.au/nla.news-article4396726).
118   Ian Grant (1990), p. 166.
119   R. McMullin (2002), pp. 652–655.

period. Albert Jacka only agreed to Newton Wanliss writing his biography if the issue of supersession was not raised.[120]

Betty with her parents

The story of "Jitti-jitti the Wagtail" that Vera tells Betty as a bedtime story is fictional, but has been sourced from a 1929 article by Daisy M. Bates that appeared in *The Argus* in a children's section called 'Fun and Fancy'.[121] Albert Jacka's tram ride to the city with Betty is also pure fiction. However, the chocolate Easter egg incident at her fourth birthday was recalled to the author by Betty.

The "White Army" and the "All For Australia" Movement

The "All For Australia" Movement was born out of a concern that Australia was sliding into an economic and social abyss, and was in effect a realignment of conservative forces, including some disaffected Labor Party supporters (like Joseph Llyons). In Volume III of her *History of St Kilda*, Anne Longmire states: "In April 1931 154 of the disaffected asked the Mayor, Councillor Jacka, to convene a meeting of the All For Australia League".[122] Albert Jacka would have needed little prompting. There is no doubt that Albert Jacka and All For Australia League president Ernest Turnbull knew each other (they were photographed together at the foundation stone for the Shrine in 1928), and were like-minded in their support for the League, its criticism of Labor policies, and its principle of building "Australia and the Empire". Turnbull's speech at the St Kilda Town Hall rally in the novel is based on his published speech to delegates at the Melbourne Town Hall on 19 May 1931.[123]

References to the Riverina Movement for secession and rumours about the advance of Bolsheviks from Mildura were taken

---

120   N. Wanliss (5 March 1923), Letter to C.E.W. Bean, AWM43.
121   Daisy M. Bates (12 October 1929), "Jitti-Jitti, the Wagtail", *The Argus*, p. 4 (http://nla. gov.au/nla.news-article4043028).
122   Anne Longmire (1983) *St Kilda: The show goes on – The History of St Kilda Vol. III, 1930 to July 1983*, Hudson, Hawthorn, p. 36; (10 April 1931), "All For Australia – Branch Formed at St Kilda", *The Argus*, p. 8 (http://nla.gov.au/nla.news-article4388736).
123   Ernest Turnbull (1931), *All For Australia League shows the way to Prosperity! AFA Victorian Convention – President's Policy Speech to Delegates.*

from the press at the time.[124] The story of the Wedderburn branch
of the "White Army" who sat in a tree guarding the water works
was told to Michael Cathcart by an "informant" called "Alan" in the
1980s.[125] According to Cathcart, the informant at Donald who told
him of the near catastrophe between Catholics and Protestants,
was ninety-nine year old Arthur Clifford.[126]

The end of Albert Jacka's mayoral role and marriage

Nathaniel Jacka's escape from his burning house in Ridge Street,
Wedderburn, was reported in *The Argus*, indicating the continuing
newsworthiness of anything to do with Albert Jacka's family.[127]
When Albert Jacka's mayoral term expired on 1 September 1931,
Vera's work was honoured by the St Kilda Younger Set:[128]

> *Among those who have appreciated her leadership and support
> has been the St Kilda Younger Set. To say farewell and express their
> good wishes and gratitude before she leaves to make her home in the
> country, the members of the Younger Set entertained Mrs Jacka at a
> very happy party last night, by the courtesy of the management, at
> St Leonards Café, St Kilda Esplanade.*

The reference to Vera leaving to make her home in the country
is curious, and raises the possibility that this was a story devised
to explain her absence from Albert Jacka's side, in order to avoid
the social embarrassment of their separation. There is some
uncertainty about the time that Vera separated from her husband.
The 12 September 1931 opening of the Anglo Dominion Soaps

---

124   (7 March 1931), "Riverina Movement – Rapidly Extending – Great Rally at
        Narrandera", *The Argus*, p. 15 (http://nla.gov.au/nla.news-article4376908).
125   Michael Cathcart (1988), *Defending the National Tuckshop – Australia's secret army intrigue of
        1931*, McPhee Gribble/Penguin Books, pp. 10, 24.
126   Michael Cathcart (1988), *Defending the National Tuckshop*, pp. 9–14.
127   (11 August 1931), "Wedderburn house burnt", *The Argus*, p. 13 (http://nla.gov.au/nla.
        news-article4388736).
128   (2 September 1931), "Social Notes", *The Argus*, p. 11 (http://nla.gov.au/nla.news-
        article4416137).

factory in Footscray, where Albert Jacka obtained employment as a commercial traveller, was covered in the press.[129]

Mars rejoices

The Venetian Court

The scene at the Venetian Court, Hotel Australia, where Vera gained employment, is not historical. There is no historical record of such an attempt by Albert Jacka to convince his estranged wife to come back to him, so this scene is purely fictional. However, on 30 September 1931 there was a parade of new season's lingerie at the Venetian Court at the *Hotel Australia*. It is reasonable to assume that Vera had something to do with it.[130]

In a recent biography Robert Macklin suggested that, having found a job as hostess at the Hotel Australia, Vera "quickly took up with a wealthy businessman, Frank Duncan of Clifton Hill. Jacka was shaken to the core."[131] However, no reference for the "quick take up" was provided by Macklin, and in the absence of any documentary or credible oral evidence, this assumption must be questioned. Her daughter Betty is adamant that as a religiously devout woman, Vera would never have taken up with another man while still married to Albert Jacka.

The fact that Vera and her babysitter, Susan Futcher, continued as vice-presidents of Homoeopathic Hospital Auxiliary even after she had left Albert Jacka was reported in *The Argus*.[132]

Courtney's Post

In the novel Albert Jacka's VC action at Courtney's Post on the morning of 19 May, 1915 is presented as a flashback, while he watches

129   (12 September 1931), "Soap Factory at Footscray", *The Argus*, p. 19 (http://nla.gov.au/nla.news-article4423132).
130   (12 September 1931), "New Season's Lingerie Parade", *The Argus*, p. 3 (http://nla.gov.au/nla.news-article4428374).
131   Robert Macklin (2006), p. 258. However, Frank Duncan's double-storey free standing terrace at 6 South Terrace, Clifton Hill suggests he was "well off" rather than "wealthy". Furthermore, Vera was taking on eight children in the bargain.
132   (17 October 1931), "Homeopathic Hospital Auxiliary", *The Argus*, p. 3 (http://nla.gov.au/nla.news-article4433969).

fireworks exploding over Port Phillip Bay at St Kilda. As explained in *Hard Jacka*, there are several versions of the action, and unexplained questions. It is known with certainty, however, that Albert Jacka entered the trench alone and shot five Turks and bayoneted two more. The version provided here follows that provided by Lieutenant R. Wallace Crabbe with the assistance of Steve DeAraugo on 30 July, 1915 (two months after the event, and three weeks before Crabbe was killed at Hill 60).[133] Some weight has also been given to the version written by Newton Wanliss, as he did discuss it with Albert Jacka (with the aid of the trench map drawn by the latter). As noted by Wanliss, before going on duty Lieutenant Hamilton had remarked that his 21st birthday was coming up, and he hoped he would live to see it.[134] Other accounts consulted were those of C.E.W. Bean,[135] Colonel Courtney,[136] and a correspondent of *The Argus*.[137]

The "Queen of Flowers", social innovation, and the "Illuminated Address"

The description of the "Carnival of Flowers" on Saturday, 24 October 1931 is derived from press reports, and demonstrates that some people still had great fun during the Great Depression.[138] The high level of community spirit that was expressed in the fancy dress and festivities along the St Kilda Esplanade are something to ponder eighty years later. The subsequent debate on social issues relating to late closing, tennis on Sundays and mixed bathing was also covered in detail by *The Argus*.[139]

---

133   AWM 3DRL 606 Item 7 [2].
134   N. Wanliss (1929), p. 45.
135   C.E.W. Bean (10 August 1915), "How V.C. Was Won – Corporal Jacka's Bravery – Story of Incident", *The Argus*, p. 7 (http://nla.gov.au/nla.news-article1546992).
136   (13 October 1915), "Lieut.-Colonel Courtney – Invalided in Ireland – Story of Jacka's V.C.", *The Argus*, p. 8 (http://nla.gov.au/nla.news-article1570224).
137   (3 September 1915), "Anzac Battle-ground – Scene of famous fight – Australia's first V.C.", *The Argus*, p. 5 (http://nla.gov.au/nla.news-article1555984).
138   (26 October 1931), "Carnival of Flowers", *The Argus*, p. 6 (http://nla.gov.au/nla.news-article4426747). For a photograph of the "Queen of Flowers" Miss Mervyn Pitt, see (http://nla.gov.au/nla.news-article4426730).
139   (17 November 1931), "Tennis on Sunday", *The Argus*, p. 7 (http://nla.gov.au/nla.news-article4422686).

Rising political tension in the lead-up to the 1931 Federal election was characterised by some violence. The bombing of Detective H.S. Dunn's house, and that of the Leader of the Opposition were reported in *The Argus*[140] the same day as Prime Minister James Scullin's speech regarding the flawed analysis of communists.[141]

The presentation of the "Illuminated Address" to Albert Jacka at the council meeting of Monday 14 December 1931 is best recorded by the *St Kilda News* that was published the following Friday – the day that he was admitted to hospital. The article noted that:

> *Cr. Moroney desired to couple the name of Mrs Jacka (the ex-Mayoress) with the name of Mrs Jacka (the ex-Mayoress) with all that had been accomplished during Cr. Jacka's term of office. This lady had been a bulwark to Cr. Jacka, and he asked the latter to convey to Mrs Jacka the collective thanks of the councillors and officers for the fine work she had accomplished during the period... Cr. Jacka referred to the great assistance Mrs Jacka had been to him during his period as Mayor, and said that the position was too big a job for even two... Cr. Jacka concluded by thanking the Mayor and councillors for the handsome present, and assured all that both Mrs Jacka and himself would always treasure it.*

This article indicates that Vera was not present at the meeting, and his comments suggest that Albert Jacka had not given up hope that she would return to him. Given that Vera had already left, the speeches of councillors Jacka and Moroney, which give the appearance that all is well, are like coded messages.

---

140   (8 December 1931), "Bomb Outrage", *The Argus*, p. 7 (http://nla.gov.au/nla.news-article4413307).

141   (8 December 1931), "Items of Interest – Mr Scullin and Communism", *The Argus*, p. 3 (http://nla.gov.au/nla.news-article4413210).

The medical examination and the Carnival meeting

The details of medical examinations of Albert Jacka undertaken by Dr Reuben Rosenfield and Dr Montefiore Silberberg at the Caulfield Military Repatriation Hospital on Wednesday 16 December 1931, including his blood pressure and other observations are documented in his *Service Documents*, held by the National Archives.[142] The description of the hospital at the time was based on that provided in the classic novel *My Brother Jack*, postcards and photographs.[143] Given the diagnosis of hypertension and acute nephritis, and the prescription of immediate hospitalisation, it is curious that Albert Jacka was not admitted the next day. It is possible that, as depicted in the novel, he argued for later admission due to his commitment to chair the final meeting of the committee to organise the Saturday Beach Carnival, which was to raise money for the unemployed Christmas dinner.

There is little evidence of what transpired at that last meeting on Friday 18 December 1931, as minutes could not be found. Hence, the discussion depicted in the novel is fictional, even though the facts provided about the St Kilda Football Club Secretary Jack Irvine are true.[144] While there was concern over the state of Albert Jacka's health, there appeared to be no alarm. As noted by Mayor Moroney at the first council meeting after his death:[145]

> He had left a meeting in the Town Hall on the 18ᵗʰ December to go straight to the Caulfield Military Hospital. No one ever dreamed that his complaint was of a mortal nature, but his illness, undoubtedly due to war service, developed rapidly...

---

142   *Service Documents*, Albert Jacka VC, MC and Bar (http://naa12naa.gov.au/scripts/Imagine.asp).

143   George Johnston (1964), *My Brother Jack*, Collins, p. 10.

144   For a photograph of "Little Jack" Irvine at the St Kilda Football Club carnival see: (25 September 1931), "Aiming for Goal", *The Argus*, p. 5 (http://nla.gov.au/nla.news-article4415378).

145   (8 February 1932), *St Kilda Council Minutes*.

Albert Jacka's *Service Documents* note that he was admitted to hospital on 18 December 1931.

The Caulfield Military Repatriation Hospital

Details of Albert Jacka's treatment at the Caulfield Military Repatriation Hospital were obtained from the *Service Documents*. In the 1930s the only treatment available for acute nephritis was to rest in bed, and eat special diets, as there were no drugs available. This approach was confirmed by reference to the *Textbook of Medical Treatment*, first published in 1939.[146]

Bill Jacka's bedside discussion about the excitement caused by Josh Gray's motor buggy in Wedderburn is fictional, since there is very little evidence of what was actually said. However, it is factual in the sense that it was sourced from his 1977 recollections for the Korong Historical Society. Josh Gray was an American from Ohio, who had made his home in Australia after coming for the gold rush.[147]

Councillor Burnett Gray's concerns about the Conservative Opposition were sourced from a number of press reports at the time.[148] Councillor Unsworth's telephone complaint to the hospital administration about Albert Jacka being "held up as an exhibit" for other visitors to Ward 5 is contained in a hospital memorandum in his *Service Documents*.

The scene depicting the telephone call to Ted Rule and Ernie Hill in Shepparton is based on Rule's depiction of it in *Jacka's Mob*, published in 1933.[149] A possible solution to the question of why

---

146   See D.M. Dunlop, L.S.P. Davidson, and J.W. McNee, (1942) *Textbook of Medical Treatment*, Edinburgh, Second Edition, courtesy of Associate Professor Michael Richards.

147   Josh Gray's obituary from the June 1902 issue of the *Wedderburn Express* was published in *Nuggets or Nothing*, in 1981 (Volume 9), pp. 5–7.

148   (19 November 1931), "Mr Burnett Gray", *The Argus*, p. 9 (http://nla.gov.au/nla.news-article4414389); (24 November 1931), "Mr Burnett Gray", *The Argus*, p. 8 (http://nla.gov.au/nla.news-article4434607).

149   E.J. Rule (1933), p. 342. Also see Edgar John Rule (1999), *Jacka's Mob – a narrative of the Great War*, compiled and edited by Carl Johnson and Andrew Barnes, Military Melbourne, Prahran.

Captain Mitchell would have expected to find Ernie Hill rather than Ted Rule at the other end of the line has been suggested by Ernie's son Barrie. He thinks that Mitchell's call may have been transferred through to Hill via Rule's house, by the local telephone exchange operator, Mrs Homewood.

Some comments attributed to Albert Jacka during his stay in hospital have been preserved through press reports, presumably through interviews with Vera. The *Herald* reported:[150]

> *Then, a few days before his death, he said to Mrs Jacka, "This is a rough spin, but we have been through many rough spins together. I'm afraid, Mummy, you'll have to struggle on alone. I feel I'm done."*
>
> *Mrs Jacka did her best to cheer him, and mentioned to him that although they had a long rough spin, it had been good in parts.*
>
> *"Yes, Mummy," he replied. "It was good in parts."*
>
> *Jacka often in the last days expressed to his wife his appreciation of the way she had struggled on gamely with him.*
>
> *A pathetic feature of his illness, however, was that for some time before his death, his sight had failed, and he was unable to see his wife's face or even her hand as she held it before his eyes.*

A long time after Albert Jacka's death, in a "Letter the Editor" of the RSL's *Mufti* journal defending his brother's honour, Bill Jacka attributed the following comment to him:[151]

> *I wish I had gone to Repatriation before this. If I had, perhaps I wouldn't be in this condition today. I know I am not walking out of here.*

---

150   (20 January 1932), "A Cottage For Mrs Jacka – Herald Appeal – VC's Widow Needs Help", *The Herald*, p. 1.
151   W. Jacka (5 September 1964), "Captain A. Jacka VC, MC and Bar – brother on facts", *Mufti*.

Reportedly, Albert Jacka's final words to his father were:[152]

I'm still fighting, Dad.

There is little doubt that Nathaniel Jacka was very proud of his son's record of service on behalf of the unemployed of St Kilda, as depicted in the novel. Albert Jacka's flashback to Gallipoli is of course fictional, but is based on the actual recollections of Bill Howard, who told his daughters Aileen and Marie the story of how Jacka visited him in the dugout at Courtney's Post after the VC action. Howard told his daughters Albert Jacka's response to his question was, "I did my bloody block".[153]

Albert Jacka's *Service Documents* record that Albert Jacka passed away at 11.15 am on 17 January 1932, and that the next of kin present at the time of death was his wife, Vera.[154] It is unlikely that the sad irony of the last morning that Vera and Albert Jacka spent together being their wedding anniversary had escaped her. However, Vera's thoughts, as depicted in the novel, are fictional.

At Anzac House
Ace reporter Hugh Buggy's very well written *Herald* story describing the scenes at Anzac House was the main source for those scenes.[155] Betty told the author she has distinct memories of being looked after by Sam and Elizabeth Jacka at the funeral.

At the St Kilda Cemetery
Keith Hooper, who was among the students of several schools assembled outside the cemetery on Dandenong Road was the

---

152   This was noted by Jacka's first biographer Ian Grant (1989), p. 175, and by Lionel Wigmore and Bruce Harding (1963), *They Dared Mightily*, Australian War Memorial, Canberra, p. 35.
153   Aileen and Marie Howard, correspondence with author.
154   See *Service Documents*, Albert Jacka VC, MC and Bar (http://naa12naa.gov.au/scripts/Imagine.asp) Page 6 of 168, Page 2 of 3.
155   Hugh Buggy, (19 January, 1932), "Diggers Mourn a Man's Man", *The Herald*.

source of information about the schools represented there on that day.[156]

Brigadier-General Brand's comment to journalists at the cemetery was recalled by him in a tribute published by *Reveille*.[157] The final quotation of the novel attributed to Brigadier Brand at the commemoration of the Albert Jacka memorial on 15 May 1932, comes from *The Argus*.[158]

156   Keith Hooper, correspondence with author.
157   Brig.-General C.H. Brand (31 January 1932), "Few Saw Him: All Knew of Him", *Reveille*, p. 3.
158   (16 May 1932), "Albert Jacka's Memorial – Unveiling Ceremony", *The Argus*, p. 8 (http://nla.gov.au/nla.news-article4452106).

ACKNOWLEDGEMENTS

My previous novel *Hard Jacka*, covered the period from when Albert Jacka won his Victoria Cross at Gallipoli on 19 May 1915, up to 15 May 1918, when he was gassed in France and knocked out of the Great War. After reading the manuscript, 14th Battalion Captain Fred Anderson's grandson Stuart told me it made him wonder what came next. *Return of the Gallipoli Legend* provides the answer in a sequel novel based on the sources contained in the Historical Appendix.

Albert Jacka lived an interesting life in Melbourne during the 1920s, and enjoyed civic prominence when Melbourne was Australia's capital city, and St Kilda was the gateway to that city. His story and those of his brother, Captain William Jacka, Brigadier-General "Pompey" Elliott, and other ex-AIF officers and men who had returned from the Great War, reflect some of the triumphs, trials and tribulations of hundreds of thousands of returned diggers in a decade that saw Australia's fortunes rise, and then fall precipitously during the Great Depression. We also see the beginnings of Legacy, the Returned Services League (then known as the RSSILA), and the campaign for the Shrine of Remembrance.

This book depicts the landing of the 14th Battalion AIF at Gallipoli on 25–26 April 1915, and the "black day" it experienced on 8 August 1915. It therefore largely completes the significant military actions of Albert Jacka within the 14th Battalion AIF (omitting Messines). There is a misconception that Albert Jacka's ideas, beliefs and goals were never recorded. They were in fact recorded in his writings, in Minutes held by the St Kilda Council, and in numerous newspaper articles that quoted or paraphrased his speeches. Those thoughts are presented in this novel.

I am grateful to Albert Jacka's biographers, Ian Grant and Robert Macklin, whose research assisted my own research. However, the life of Albert Jacka after the Great War was not examined in detail by these biographies, and his wife, Veronica Frances Carey, was given relatively little attention. My task has been greatly assisted by two important developments. The first is the National Library of Australia's digitisation of *The Argus* newspaper, which was published in Melbourne between 1846 and 1957. It is difficult to overstate what a powerful tool this on-line resource proved to be, not just in reconstructing Albert Jacka's post-war life, but for the broader understanding it provided of the society that Albert Jacka and other ex-AIF diggers lived in after the war.

The second development was my email correspondence with Albert and Vera Jacka's daughter, Betty. I am very grateful to Betty, now a vibrant eighty-three-year old, for engaging in numerous on-line discussions with me about her mother, and for sharing her few remaining memories of her father. She described her early life as something like watching a movie, played over and over again, where she cannot change anything. She provided the stunning photograph of Vera as a young woman, and the enchanting photograph of herself as a two year old standing by her father on a seaside park bench.

Betty and I discussed the photograph of the presentation of the 14th Battalion Colours at the St Kilda Town Hall in April 1930, which I sourced from Cooper's 1931 volume, *History of St Kilda*. It showed a uniformed Captain Albert Jacka standing in front of the portico, with a little girl pressing against his leg. I asked Betty if she was that girl. After several emails, Betty convinced me that she was not. Sometime later I received a scanned copy of the original photograph – Albert Jacka was not in it, proving that the image of Albert Jacka in the *History of St Kilda* had been superimposed.

Campbell Holmes of the Korong Historical Society, twice provided the "Jacka tour" of Wedderburn, and a copy of Bill Jacka's fascinating 1977 taped interview on the early days of Wedderburn, which I passed on to his daughter, Josephine Eastoe (who was present in 1977 when the tape was made). I am grateful to Josephine, who read the manuscript, provided photographs, and the story of the penny that her uncle, Albert Jacka gave her at the Caulfield Military Hospital.

On my second trip to Wedderburn I was accompanied by Jason La Macchia, who is the great grandson of Fanny Jacka (and a great grand nephew of Albert Jacka). Outside the old Mechanics' Institute Hall Campbell told us that people were digging up the main street for gold during the Depression. When Jason retold the story to his mother Val on his return to Brisbane, she told him it was Jason's great grandfather, William Dowsett who was doing the digging, and produced a photograph to prove it. I am grateful to Jason for the great support he has given me, and for providing comments on both books.

William Howard's daughters, Aileen and Marie, provided photographs and their father's Gallipoli diary. In the novel his thoughts at the Communion Service on the morning of the landing were drawn from it. Aileen still remembers her father talking about Albert Jacka's VC action at Courtney's Post as Bill drove her to school in a horse cart when they lived at the Soldier Settlement of Pirlta, near Mildura. Lieutenant Steven De Araugo's son Vin, and grandson Chris, provided photographs. The remarkable thing about these Bendigo families is that they have been friends for more than a century.

As well as providing his grandfather's memoirs and photographs, Stuart Anderson told me he knew a Michael "Ferdie" Wright QC, who turned out to be Captain (later Colonel) "Ferdie" Wright's grandson. Michael put me in touch with his cousin Steven

Marriott, who is the family historian. Having lived close to him, Steven knew him well and supplied a wealth of photographs and historical background on his "larger than life" grandfather. Stuart and Steven had known each other for many years, but were unaware that through their grandfathers, their fates had been intertwined in the 14th Battalion at Gallipoli decades before they were born. Pat Wright also provided information on Ferdie's business career.

Carl Johnson is the editor of Ted Rule's *Jacka's Mob*, which was re-published in 1999 (by Military Melbourne), has an interesting collection of 14th Battalion documents, photographs and memorabilia, and has personally interviewed many Great War veterans. I am grateful for his numerous valuable comments on the manuscript. I also thank Chris Waters, President of the Descendants of the 14th Battalion Association for his comments on the manuscript.

One of the mysteries solved in the course of my research concerned the collapse and voluntary liquidation of Jacka, Edmonds and Co Pty Ltd during the Great Depression. I could never understand how Albert Jacka and his family were able to move back to their house at 23 Murchison Street, East St Kilda on 27 November 1930 and live there while he was Mayor, when his business had been liquidated during October 1930 with tens of thousands of pounds owing. Bernard McGrath, Manager, Group Archives, Corporate Office, National Australia Bank, who found the Minute in a 1930 Board of Directors meeting confirming that the whole of the bank debt owed by Albert Jacka's firm had been secured by John Wren. This had not previously been known.

The Australian War Memorial staff in Canberra assisted my investigations of the detailed source note files left by Newton Wanliss (and donated by Marion after his death), which were used for his *History of the 14th Battalion*. This consisted of various letters — in particular those by Captains Ferdinand Henry Wright and Henry Gerald Loughran, which formed important components of action sequences at Gallipoli. The novel also deals with the aftermath of the death of Captain Harold Wanliss and its effect on his father, Newton, in the post-war period. Harold's cousin, Tom Wanliss, greatly assisted my understanding of his own father Neville Wanliss, his uncle, Newton Wanliss, and his cousin Dr Marion Wanliss. He also provided valuable comments on the manuscript.

I was intrigued by the cryptic reference to a "Hill" in Ted Rule's *Jacka's Mob* (first published in 1933), as he was chosen to be a coffin bearer at Albert Jacka's funeral. I rang the Shepparton RSL, where Kevin Heenan put me in touch with Barrie Hill, who now lives on the Margaret River in Western Australia. Barrie provided a wealth of information about his father, Colonel Ernie Hill, and his father's interactions with Albert Jacka and Sir John Monash. Barrie recalls those nights as a young boy when his father turned off the lights in the lounge at their Soldier Settler house in Lemnos near Shepparton, stoked up the fire, and told him about his days in the 14th Battalion "drover style".

Ross McMullin's definitive biography, *Pompey Elliott*, made a strong impression on me. This extraordinary and powerful character was never far away from Albert Jacka on the battlefields of Gallipoli, France and Belgium, and their paths crossed in dramatic fashion on the floor of the Australian Senate in 1921. Tragically, Pompey's brilliant but tormented mind was finally broken by the Great Depression. Ross McMullin reviewed and provided comments on the parts of the manuscript relating to Pompey. Peter Kelly, who now lives in Pompey's house kindly invited me inside to have a look.

Dalila and Mark Bingham, owned the house at 23 Murchison Street, East St Kilda, where Vera and Albert Jacka spent some of the best years of their life together, and allowed me to visit the house on two occasions. David Dare, the grandson of Lieutenant-Colonel Charles Dare provided details of his career that were handed down in a note written by his grandfather's mother-in-law, Mrs I.H. Moss CBE, JP. Malcolm Rowe, who is a second cousin of Albert Jacka, passed on to me the story of his mother's meeting with him in Geelong in the late 1920s, where she obtained his autograph. The autograph book has been lost, but Albert Jacka's message that "only a fool is never afraid" has remained etched into Malcolm's memory for many years.

I thank Larina Strauch of the Kyneton Historical Society, who researched the background and subsequent life of Captain H.G. Loughran, the 14th Battalion's Medical Officer at Gallipoli. Kay Rowan, Local History Librarian of the Port Phillip Library Service assisted me by searching the Port Philip Council's Archives for materials relating to Albert Jacka's terms as a councillor and Mayor of St Kilda. Staff at the Victorian State Archives provided a number of documents, including the Minutes of the St Kilda Council. Meyer Edelstein, former president of the St Kilda Historical Society, and author of a history of Elwood also provided comments on *Return of the Gallipoli Legend*.

Thanks are also due to the Regional Vice President – Operations of the Rendezvous Hotel group, Geoffrey Johnstone, who allowed me to make copies of the photographs of various rooms of the Commercial Travellers' Association club, which originally occupied the building in Flinders Street. Thanks are also due to Erik Hoos, who assisted with the photographs, and John Coustley and Max Moon of the Commercial Travellers' Association, who showed me photographs and documents relating to its hey-day during the first half of the 1900s.

I would also like to thank the many people associated with historical societies, libraries and RSL clubs around Victoria that have supported me, in particular: Brian Blight, John Cullen, Val England, Christina Fernie, Terry Foran, Pat Grainger, Mary Hay, Gerardine Horgan, Elwyn Hunt, Andrew Kilsby, Jan Lier, Ian Marshall, Tony O'Shea, Keith Richards, Raylee Shultz, Bev Spinks, Larina Strauch and Elizabeth Taylor.

David Carroll of Adelaide provided two letters received by members of his family during the Great War: one a condolence letter from Albert Jacka; and the other from his father Nathaniel, on the conscription issue. One of David's ancestors removed the wounded Peter Lalor from the battlefield at the Eureka Stockade, eleven fought for the country in three wars, and three paid the ultimate price. One who came back from the Great War was David's great grandfather, 4113 Private Christopher Augustus Farrell, who through specific circumstances died alone and destitute. David has approached the Directorate of Honours and Awards for his Service Medals to be declared unissued, so that his descendants might access them.

I am grateful to Associate Professor Mike Richards, of the Royal Melbourne Hospital, who provided advice on Albert Jacka's medical records, and loaned me his father's *Textbook of Medical Treatment*, which was first published in the 1930s. I also thank Associate Professor Andrew McGowan, who is Warden of Trinity College, University of Melbourne, and also an Anglican priest, who commented on my depiction of the Anglican Communion Service on the deck of the *Seeang Choon* on the morning of the Gallipoli landing.

A number of people read and provided helpful comments on the manuscript, including Dr Phillip Ayres, Michael Bird, Dr Ray Challen, Daria Fedewytsch-Dickson, Lieutenant-Colonel Adrian Lombardo, Peter Grogan, Colin Trumble, James van Smeerdijk, Colonel George Wenhlowskyj MC, and Paula Wilton. Some have had particular connections with the story presented here. In 1945 Colin Trumble was a young Australian naval officer who accepted several Japanese swords of surrender in Indonesia and the Philippines. He never met Wren, but was aware of his relationship with the National Australia Bank when he practised as a lawyer in the post-war years. Colin was one of those people on Frederick Falkiner Knight's permanent Christmas party guest list, and remembers Fred sitting on his verandah marking the guests off as they arrived. Colin's son Adam put me in touch with Frederick Falkiner Knight's niece, Judy McKechnie, who supplied me with the photograph of Fred as a young barrister.

I thank my work colleagues at PricewaterhouseCoopers, James van Smeerdijk, Dr Ray Challen, Jeff Balchin, and Dr Martin van Bueren, who provided support and encouragement. I also thank my friends Professor Claudio Veliz, Arlene Tansey, Dr Phillip Ayres and Graham Menzies for their unflinching support. Dr Ayres is a well known biographer who read both manuscripts, and Graham provided insights from his memories of Dame Mabel Brookes, and Sir John Monash's house.

I thank the readers of *Hard Jacka*, whose calls, letters and support inspired the writing of this sequel, including: Lesia Abbinga, Dr David Adams, John Aitken, Stuart Anderson, Doug and Richard Arman, David Asteraki, John Ash, Judy Barry, Paul Bayly, Craig Bellingham, Brian Bottrell, Glen Brown, Chris Browne, Ted Budas, Tony Carroll, Geoff Crapper, George Dimovski, John Downy, Ken Drane, Bruce Ellwood, Zac Fitzgerald, Brother Michael Flaherty, Mark Foxe, Bob Gladstone, Rob Gray, Peter Gray, Robin Hart, Natalie Jacka, Tim Jacka, Bo Kostyszyn, Andrew Lachowicz, Stuart McArthur, Phil Mannell, Steve Murtagh, Geoff Neilson AM, Michael O'Connor AM, Paul O'Connor, Adam Pipe, Lily Semciv, Wes Senjuk, Robert Stock, Alex Sumpter, Mike Tyrrell, Daniel Walmsley, Bernadette Webster, Vince Willcocks, and The Hon. Ken Wright OAM. The latter's 1995 book *A Land Fit for Heroes: The Story of the Soldier Settlement of Red Cliffs after World War I*, provided valuable background material.

I am particularly grateful to Lieutenant General Peter Cosgrove AC, who wrote very memorable forewords to *Hard Jacka* and *Return of the Gallipoli Legend*, and to Dr Peter Binks, Executive Director of the Sir John Monash Foundation (and his predecessor Ken Crompton), which is chaired by General Cosgrove. I also owe a great debt to Professor Geoffrey Blainey AC, who launched *Hard Jacka*, and provided further encouragement during the writing of this sequel. I am also grateful for the support of Cristina Lee and Haylee Kerans, of Harlequin Enterprises, who saw the opportunity for a sequel, and to Jody Lee, who edited the manuscript.

Finally I wish to thank my immediate and broader family for their encouragement and support. For the immediate family this project involved a great sacrifice that has spanned almost a decade.

It should be impossible for one to live in Melbourne without a sense of the rich history of its past, including the people whose lives have been portrayed in this novel. At the Collins Street tram stop on the corner of William Street one stands opposite the Olderfleet building where Albert Jacka first met his future wife, Veronica Carey. Part of this book was written over a coffee in the Negroni cafe that now occupies the former foyer. Around the corner one can see the site of Albert Jacka's later business premises at 50 William Street (formerly the National Mutual/AXA building, and now the Suncorp Bank building). Sir John Monash's State Electricity Commission Headquarters was located a bit further down the street. Just behind the tram stop in William Street stands the Queensland Building, which at one point housed the Brigadier-General Pompey Elliott's law practice.

I hope that readers of this novel will look differently upon the streets of Melbourne and St Kilda when they visit. They may be reminded that at one time those streets were walked by Australia's Gallipoli legends.

Michael Lawriwsky

lawriwsky@smartchat.net.au

INSTITUTIONS AND PLACES MENTIONED IN "GALLIPOLI LEGEND"

Abd-el Rahman Bair, Gallipoli

Accident Underwriters
    Association of Victoria

Achi Baba, Gallipoli

Acland Street, St Kilda

Adelaide, HMAS

Aghyl Dere, Gallipoli

Albert Park Lake, Victoria

Alexandra, Victoria

Alexandria, Egypt

Alfred Children's Hospital

All For Australia League

Anglo Dominion Soaps,
    Footscray

Anzac Cove, Gallipoli

Anzac House, Melbourne

Apps (W.G.) Pty Ltd

Apsley House, No. 1 London

Ararat, Victoria

Arcadia Theatre, St Kilda

Argus, The (newspaper)

Armstrong Street, Middle Park

Arras, Battle of

Art Student's Association,
    St Kilda

Asama, (Japanese Cruiser)

Asma Dere, Gallipoli

Austin Hospital, Heidelberg

Austral Salon

Australian Citizens League

Australian Club, Melbourne

Australian Knitting Mills

Australian Imperial Force
    1st Division
    2nd Division
    3rd Division Artillery
    4th Division
    4th Brigade
    1st Light Horse Brigade
    2nd Field Artillery Brigade
    12th Brigade
    5th Battalion
    7th Battalion
    9th Battalion
    10th Battalion
    11th Battalion
    13th Battalion
    14th Battalion
    15th Battalion
    16th Battalion
    13th Light Horse
    1st Cavalry Division

NAMES OF PEOPLE
MENTIONED IN "GALLIPOLI
LEGEND"

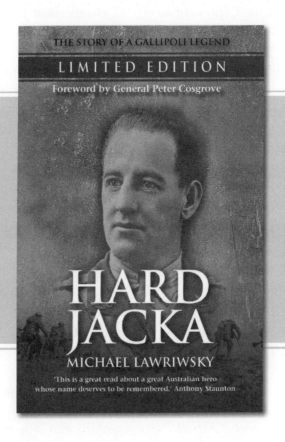

GALLIPOLI:
BIRTH OF A LEGEND

Courtney's Post, Gallipoli, May 19th, 1915

The Turks had launched a massive offensive against the Australians at 3.30 am—determined to break them at any cost. It was around 4.00 am now, and still dark. A deafening roar of gunfire bellowed from the line of Australian trenches, and Acting Lance Corporal Albert Jacka's shoulder ached from the pounding of a hundred kickbacks from his Lee-Enfield .303. It was a man killer the Lee-Enfield, not a rabbit gun, so when you hit someone squarely they would go down—and stay down.

On previous nights the Australians had complained about the bitter cold. It was like that on the Turkish peninsula they called Gallipoli—hot during the day and cold at night—and the boys hadn't been issued with any blankets. Someone higher up obviously had no idea what it was like at *this* coalface. But tonight Jacka (who was always "Bert" to his mates) wasn't complaining. He was on fire, almost literally, as the woodwork of his rifle was becoming too hot to hold.

Ahead of him the velvet-black field bubbled with human form and shadows, both dead and alive, and the live ones were coming for him at speed. Only their eyes and the razor-sharp blades of their bayonets glistened in the faint moonlight. Not much more than a hundred yards of No-Man's Land separated them, and tens of thousands of bullets had been fired to stop them. Yet still they came, the young Turks, running and jumping over the bodies of their fallen brothers.

A strong runner could make the distance in twenty-odd seconds. But you couldn't see him for at least half that time. That left about ten seconds. Not much time to load, aim and shoot at him, and then shoot the one just behind him; and if you missed, or just clipped his wing, his bayonet could be skewering your head like an olive five seconds later.

It focused the mind.

Bang! *Click-click, click-click*. Bang! Jacka squeezed off another clip, shooting at blurred images. Golly, they're brave, he thought. How long can they keep coming like this? It's certain death! He had just turned twenty-two, and the skin on his cheeks was still soft.

If the Turks could smash the Australian line that clung to the ridge at Courtney's Post, everyone knew the consequences. It was only one and a half miles down to the beach. The Turks taking a section of this trench would be like driving a wedge into a block of wood. With a decent blow at that point the block would snap in two, the Turks would be on the beach, and the Aegean Sea behind them would run red with blood. Game over.

Jacka was standing behind a traverse in the trench wall and firing east over the bags on the parapet. To the south of the traverse, in a curved section of trench known as a "bay", were about ten boys from D Company. Beyond them, further to the right, was another bay that contained a machinegun crew. As the boys took aim and fired, the machinegun churned out lead like a meat grinder.

All the guns of D Company were running hot that morning, and still the Turks came. Suddenly a number of grenades plopped into the bay. Too dark to look for them! Too late.

"Bombs!" someone screamed.

"Look out!" The scramble began.

The grenades exploded like a broadside from an old man-o'-war, sending a billowing cloud of dust and smoke up into the sky. Some Aussies were killed instantly; others were either shell-shocked or holding in their guts. A dozen Turks leapt over the parapet and into the trench screaming *"Allah! Allah! Allah! Allah Akba!"*—"God is Great!"

Outnumbered and dazed, the surviving Aussies clambered out of the forward trench and turned down the communication trench towards the reserve trench. The sand-bagged corner of the traverse had protected Jacka against the deadly shrapnel. Lieutenant Boyle put his head around the corner and was shot in the ear. He ran down the communication trench yelling "They've got me! Turks are in the trenches!"

But Jacka didn't run. He moved in, leaned up against the wall of the traverse and began firing down the hollow of the earthen-walled corridor. He couldn't get a clear shot because of the corner in the forward trench, but at least he had them pinned down.

Boyle was checking the boys' ammunition supply when he saw the explosions above the trench line. He was a graduate of the Royal Military College, Duntroon, and only nineteen years old. The Turks were firing over the parados of the trench they'd captured, and hit Boyle in the ear. In shock, and bleeding profusely, he staggered to the rear.

Lieutenant Hamilton, another Duntroon man, rushed up the communication trench past Boyle to meet the Turks. He drew his revolver, and as he ran along traded shots with them over the top of the trenches. A bullet slapped into his head, knocking him to the ground.

There were no officers left.

The crackle of rifle fire continued against the background noise of the machinegun, and every few seconds Jacka would send another round down into the captured trench to remind the Turks that he was there.

Further down in Monash Valley, at the Battalion HQ dugout, Major Rankine, a stout 55-year-old, sat with twenty-one year old Lieutenant Keith Crabbe. Above the chatter of gunfire they heard a desperate call from the ridgeline above. "Officer wanted on the left!"

Rankine ordered Crabbe to get there on the double, and less than half a minute later as he approached along the same communication trench he encountered a number of men, including Private Bill Howard.

"There's a bunch of Turks in the trench, sir!" gasped Howard. "Jacka's holding them off alone." (When he was "in-the-line" he was always "Jacka", even to his mates.)

Crabbe could see Hamilton sitting on the ground up ahead, with his back resting against the wall of the communication trench. Revolver in hand, Crabbe crept ahead of the others. He touched Hamilton's face. It was still warm and sweaty. He picked up Hamilton's limp wrist and felt for a pulse. Nothing. He was sure Hamilton was dead.

Crabbe looked back at the others and shook his head, then continued down the communication trench until he could see Jacka, and vice versa.

"Back out! Turks in here."

Crabbe shuffled back a couple of steps and pointed his revolver at the corner of the forward trench as he spoke.

"Would you charge the Turks if you had some men to back you up?"

Jacka answered "Yes" and then added "I want ten".

Crabbe slipped back into the reserve trench to where a number of men had now gathered, and called for volunteers to back up Jacka.

"I'll do it", said Private Bill Howard.

"You can count on me", nodded Private Frank Poliness.

"Me too", added Private Steve DeAraugo. All three were mates from Bendigo in Victoria. Steve's name was pronounced "Daroosh"—it was Portuguese.

A fourth volunteer, Joseph Bickley, nodded agreement. He was from Hastings in Victoria.

Crabbe looked down the communication trench to its intersection with the traverse where Jacka was standing. He looked back at the men. He tested their resolve.

"Will you charge?" he asked. "It's a tough job. Will you back Jacka up?"

"It's sink or swim", Poliness reaffirmed. He knew that someone had to stop these Turks.